PANDEMOCRACY IN LATIN AMERICA

This book addresses two questions: firstly, how has the fight against COVID-19, especially the individual and collective responses of Latin American nation-states, influenced the relationship between power, people, and statebodies? And secondly, has democracy taken a step back and allowed pandemocracy to replace its long-term legitimising function?

Adopting a Global South perspective, the book explores the constitutional, political and institutional measures that paved the way for several aggressive state policies in various Latin American countries during the COVID-19 pandemic. The contributions provide a detailed review of democratic decay and the 'rule of law' impairment in many countries of the region. The book goes beyond mere observation and explores all the main theoretical elements that can lead to a more comprehensive understanding of the political and normative impact of the pandemic.

In terms of constitutional design and concerning the actual behaviour of political bodies, the fairness and efficacy of Latin American state responses during the COVID-19 pandemic did not rely on civic culture, executive goodwill, or boldness on the part of the judges. The aim of this volume, therefore, is to unravel the most subtle elements of a very puzzling situation.

Multidisciplinary perspectives are deployed to explore how democratic standards and goals have been reshaped by nuanced constructions of certain atavistic normative ideas or even by non-constitutional policies. The book sheds light on the underlying connection between politics and law.

Volume 2 in the Global Pandemocracy series

Global Pandemocracy

The *Global Pandemocracy* series, edited by Konrad Lachmayer and Matthias C Kettemann, dives deeply into the profound implications the COVID-19 pandemic has on democracies and constitutional orders worldwide. As this global crisis unfurled, did democracies and their foundational institutions and principles hold steadfast or did they waver? Across five volumes, each spotlighting a distinct world region, the Global Pandemocracy book series seeks to decode the responses of nation states to this unprecedented challenge – and discuss the recoding of relations and interdependencies between parliamentary powers, executive decision-making and judicial protection.

Consisting of up to 20 compelling contributions per volume, the series probes pressing questions: How did different constitutional structures impact a country's ability to combat COVID-19? Were democratic values sacrificed for a greater good – like public health – leading to a rise in a 'pandemocratic' order? And, most crucially, how did semi-democracies, failing democracies, and illiberal democracies navigate these tumultuous waters?

Guided by individual book editors, these chronicles weave a tale of executive power dynamics, citizen reactions, parliamentary responses and judicial reconfigurations. The *Global Pandemocracy* series bridges the interplay between political science, international relations, and law. It stands not just as a reflective analysis of our past, but as an essential guidepost for future societal lessons from the Corona crisis – for crises to come.

Series Editors: *Matthias Kettemann and Konrad Lachmayer*

Recent titles in the series

Volume 1: Pandemocracy in Europe: Power, Parliaments and People in Times of COVID-19
Edited by Matthias C Kettemann and Konrad Lachmayer

Volume 2: Pandemocracy in Latin America
Edited by Pablo Riberi

Pandemocracy in Latin America

Revisiting the Political and Constitutional Dimension of the Pandemic

Edited by
Pablo Riberi

•HART•
OXFORD • LONDON • NEW YORK • NEW DELHI • SYDNEY

HART PUBLISHING
Bloomsbury Publishing Plc
Kemp House, Chawley Park, Cumnor Hill, Oxford, OX2 9PH, UK
1385 Broadway, New York, NY 10018, USA
Bloomsbury Publishing Ireland Limited, 29 Earlsfort Terrace, Dublin 2, D02 AY28, Ireland

First published in Great Britain 2023
First published in hardback, 2023
Paperback edition, 2025

A catalogue record for this book is available from the British Library.

A catalogue record for this book is available from the Library of Congress.

Library of Congress Control Number: 2023947488

ISBN: PB: 978-1-50996-531-1
ePDF: 978-1-50996-529-8
ePub: 978-1-50996-528-1

Typeset by Compuscript Ltd, Shannon

FOREWORD AND ACKNOWLEDGEMENTS

To what extent has the COVID-19 crisis affected civil relations and democratic trust in Latin America? Should emergency policies carried out during the recent COVID-19 pandemic be decoupled from democratic decision-making standards? Regarding emergency remedies, after grappling with such an overwhelming existential threat, does the democratic principle still remain the most important constitutional source of legitimacy for a civilised political community?

The COVID-19 pandemic calls to mind the staggering number of deaths recorded, hi-tech threatening concerns as well as some other major constitutional puzzlements. The idea of pandemocracy seems to be a highly illuminating concept whose complex nature points to a new and challenging political-constitutional phenomenon. After acknowledging the underlying circumstances of the recent health crisis, observers have been able to resort to this term to make it clear how traditional democratic structures and their constitutional dynamics are definitively drifting away from their original sense.

Many Latin American scholars featured in this volume have relied on the notion of pandemocracy as a novel analytical tool to frame a whole range of constitutional issues under a single newly-coined term. The concept of 'pandemocracy' in this context was conceived to portray the inconsistency of democratic expectations vis à vis polities' awkward emergency reactions. It aims to describe a multifaceted phenomenon that encompasses a range of normative and political issues. As Kettemann and Lachmayer have proposed, it is intended to provide sharper and more finely-tuned linguistic tools. Now, if this concept is evolving in the face of unprecedented emergencies, it is also natural that the underlying constitutional paradigm may be randomly faltering as specific developments take place in different parts of the planet. Indeed, this seems to be the case for Latin American contextual grasps on the matter.

From a constitutional standpoint, the word pandemocracy grapples with two significant epistemic issues. First, the concept alerts us of rights encroachment during the COVID-19 pandemic under the cover of constitutional emergency provisions. Second, it encourages us to come up with a comprehensive constitutional assessment of each affected state's responsiveness, accountability, and representativeness. This analytical turn, then, promises to be useful for gaining a more detailed understanding of the recent COVID-19 health emergency in every regional context.

The goal of this collection of essays, therefore, is to delve into three main concerns: 1) the exploration of the nuts and bolts of the democratic decision-making process during such an extreme emergency; 2) the analysis of the institutional and legal framework through which rulers and representatives carry out their activities; and 3) to provide a normative understanding of the sense of lawlessness and public dismay projected in Latin America.

This volume comprises three main sections plus an introductory and a closing chapter. The first section provides a theoretical framing of the book's core concerns. The second one focuses on national developments during the Latin American COVID-19 pandemic. Finally, the last section portrays a crosscutting analysis of some of the most overwhelming challenges of the Latin American COVID-19 pandemic.

I am delighted to present to you this collection of essays exploring the pandemic's long-lasting effects on Latin American polities. This volume features a comprehensive range of contributions by an outstanding list of global south scholars and others from the global north. We have come together to shed light on some legal, political and institutional concerns and to delve into the underlying causes affecting long-term non-democratic consequences in the region. I am extremely grateful to all the contributing scholars for their generosity and hard work. Many thanks to Sergio Verdugo, Marcelo Figueiredo, Ricardo Ramírez Calvo, Javier Couso, Manuel García Mansilla, José María Serna de la Garza, Trilce Valdivia, Daniela Urosa, José Ignacio Hernández, Delia Ferreira Rubio, Antonio María Hernández, Florencia Saulino, Ignacio Colombo Murúa and David Landau.

I am above all indebted to Konrad Lachmayer whose constant support and steadfast engagement have been indispensable in driving this project forward. I would also like to express my sincere gratitude to Hart Publishing Editor Kate Whetter and Assistant Editor Verity Stuart.

We are currently experiencing tough times in Latin America and beyond. It is my sincere hope that this endeavour may contribute to a more global understanding of the COVID-19 pandemic's consequences and, perhaps, may also help to lead the way for scholars and readers to foresee and prevent non-democratic threats in the future.

Pablo Riberi
Córdoba, May 2023

CONTENTS

PART III
BEYOND STATES

EPILOGUE
A COMPARATIVE OUTLOOK

LIST OF CONTRIBUTORS

Ignacio Colombo Murúa is Professor of Constitutional Law at Universidad Católica de Salta (Argentina), Professor of Political Science at Universidad Nacional de Salta (Argentina) and Director of the Institute of Constitutional Law at Universidad Católica de Salta (Argentina).

Javier Couso is Professor of Law at Universidad Diego Portales (Chile) and Chair in Global Trends in Constitutionalism at Utrecht University (The Netherlands).

Delia M Ferreira Rubio is Doctor Honoris Causa by the Córdoba National University. Chair of Transparency International.

Marcelo Figueiredo is Attorney and Legal Adviser. Associate Professor of Constitutional Law at the Pontifical Catholic University of Sao Paulo. Former Dean of the Faculty of Law. Former Vice President of the International Association of Constitutional Law (IACL-AIDC), President and Founder of the Brazilian Association of Democratic Constitutionalists.

Manuel J García-Mansilla is full-time professor of Constitutional Law and Constitutional Theory at Universidad Austral and Dean of its Law School (Argentina).

Antonio María Hernández is Professor of Constitutional Law and State Constitutional Law and Municipal Law of the National University of Cordoba, Argentina and Postdoctoral Senior Fellow of the State University of New York at Buffalo Law School.

José Ignacio Hernández is Administrative Law Professor, Catholic University and Central University, Venezuela. Invited Professor, PUCMM (Dominican Republic) and Castilla-La Mancha (Spain). Fellow, Harvard Kennedy School.

Konrad Lachmayer is Professor for Public Law, European Law and Foundations of Law in the Faculty of Law and Vice-Dean of the Faculty of Law at Sigmund Freud University (SFU) in Vienna (konrad.lachmayer@jus.sfu.ac.at; www.lachmayer.eu).

David Landau is Mason Ladd Professor and Associated Dean for International Program, Florida State University, College of Law, US.

Ricardo Ramírez-Calvo is Professor of Constitutional Law at Universidad de San Andrés, (Argentina). Member of the Executive Board of the Argentina Association of Constitutional Law (AADC).

Pablo Riberi is Professor of Constitutional Law, School of Law, Universidad Nacional de Córdoba; Professor of Constitutional Theory, School of Political Science, Universidad Católica de Córdoba, Argentina. Member of the Executive Board of the International Association of Constitutional Law (IACL-AIDC).

María Florencia Saulino is Professor of Law at Universidad de San Andres (Argentina) and a Global Clinical Professor of Law at New York University (United States).

José María Serna de la Garza is researcher at the Institute of Legal Research of the National Autonomous University of Mexico and professor of constitutional law at the School of Law of the same university.

Daniela Urosa is Adjunct Faculty and Founding Director of the International Human Rights Practicum at Boston College Law School (United States) and International Ally Professor at Universidad Católica Andrés Bello (Venezuela).

Trilce Valdivia is lecturer in Constitutional Law and Human Rights at Universidad Católica San Pablo, Arequipa, Perú and holds a LL.M. degree in International Human Rights Law from Northwestern University.

Sergio Verdugo is Assistant Professor of Law at the IE University Law School (Spain) and the Secretary General of the International Society of Public Law (ICON-S).

PART I

The Theory

1

Faltering Institutional Responses in Backsliding Democracies

PABLO RIBERI

I. Introduction

No normative system can control human behaviour like the Law.[1] In this context, transboundary law has become a necessary, rational, and sensible feature for civilized life. As Norbert Elias points out, social reality simultaneously yields both civilizational and non-civilizational processes.[2] We live in complex cultural settings where the law permeates and attributes meaning to multiple relationships in civil societies. The law extends to every corner of the world, with vigilant states being overzealous and willing to regulate even the most minor aspects of human life. To put it simply, we live within law-saturated societies.[3]

Since ancient times, constitutional thinking has emphasised that a civilized political community needs stability and legitimacy in its higher institutions.[4] Regardless of the nature of each democratic-republican political system, the authority of those exercising the legitimate monopoly of state power must rely on primary and secondary rules that guarantee two main constitutional aims.[5] First, to avoid violence as a primary tool for conflict resolution, and second, to deploy constitutionally based 'organising/stabilising' practices for civil relations.

As a basic tenet, constitutionalism has taught us that the limitation of power is a core principle that no constitutional order should ever forsake.[6] In both normal

[1] P Riberi, 'When the Center Lies Outside the Figure' in M Jose Serna de la Garza (ed), *COVID-19 and Constitutional Law* (México, IACL-UNAM, 2012) 33–40.

[2] N Elias *El Proceso de la Civilización* (México, Fondo de Cultura Económica, 2012) 20–26.

[3] Stefano Rodotà discusses this concept in his book, *La Vida y las Reglas* (La Vida y las Reglas, Editorial Trotta, Madrid, 2010) 25.

[4] Machiavelli engages with this concern when dealing with 'virtue' and 'fortune' under strain in ch VII of *The Prince*. N Machiavelli, *El Príncipe* (Madrid, A.L, Mateo Editores) 63–71. See also P Bobbitt, *The Garments of Court & the Palace* (London, Atlantic Books, 2015) 74.

[5] HLA Hart, *El Concepto de Derecho* (Abeledo Perrot, Buenos Aires, 1992) 117–125.

[6] My view is that constitutionalism is an ideology rather than a theory. In line with this understanding, as Waldron points out, democratic legitimate practices for non-authoritarian decision-making

and emergency times, a fundamental question in constitutional theory is ever-present: are there actual limits to the law? In other words, does the law encompass everything? On top of that, there are two further questions. Can the rules of law foresee and regulate every extraordinary event? And can the concept of 'pandemocracy' be an epistemic resource that enhances a fair understanding of Latin America's post-pandemic democratic backsliding?[7]

In this context, another major concern for constitutional theory arises, namely the question whether it is sensible to set limits to power during emergencies.[8] In other words, should constitutional rules regulate state emergency powers even in the most extreme situations?[9]

Finally, many whistleblowers have drawn attention toward threatening biopolitical strategies from the government. During the pandemic, as seen in several countries, including some in Latin America, high-tech tools have been employed for the surveillance of people and for monitoring individuals' private activities. With nuanced developments, in Latin America, we are also experiencing challenging times in the face of growing inequalities and untamed technological developments.

A. Framing the Constitutional Issue and Two Basic Insights

Theoretical frame: Every constitutional emergency, such as the COVID-19 pandemic, is embedded in a normative dimension. A fair understanding of an outburst of authoritarianism in the executive branch always requires a prior assessment of the polity's constitutional framework and its limitations. It is also evident that the separation of powers in Latin American constitutional models should never overlook how a democratic basis is needed in all three branches of government.[10] By comprehensively grappling with these concerns, the concept

state bodies need an uncompromised constitutional principle such as 'the separation of powers'. J Waldron, *Political Political Theory* (Harvard, Harvard University Press, 2016) 36–39.

[7] In line with Lachmayer's analysis, the Latin American pandemic highlights the deployment of biopolitical resources by the government. We observed how life and death became a matter of chance, with the population's vulnerable existence depending on the implementation of 'Thanato's law'. K Lachmayer, 'Democracy, Death and Dying: 'The Potential and Limits of Legal Rationalization" in M Kettemann and K Lachmayer (eds), *Pandemocracy in Europe* (Oxford, Hart Publishing 2020) 54.

[8] As Gábor Halmai and Tom Ginsburg point out, it is worth noting that there are constitutions that govern authoritarian regimes as well. G Halmai, 'Does illiberal democracy exist?' in G Amato, B Barbisan and C Pinelli (eds), *Rule of Law v Majoritarian Democracy* (Oxford, Hart Publishing, 2021) 178–179. Additionally, Zachary Elkins, Tom Ginsburg, and James Melton provide a comparative and theoretical analysis of the endurance of national constitutions. Z Elkins, T Ginsburg and J Melton, *The Endurance of National Constitutions* (Cambridge, Cambridge University Press, 2009) 27–28.

[9] Karl Engisch delves into this concept as 'Der Rechtsfreie Raum' (*the non-juridic realm*). K Engisch, *El Ámbito de lo No Jurídico* (Córdoba, Ediciones de la Universidad Nacional de Córdoba, 1960, 63–66.

[10] For a comprehensive understanding of the core concerns of separation of powers, particularly in the context of Latin America, Möllers' insightful contribution deserves utmost attention. See A Möllers, *The Three Branches* (Oxford, Oxford University Press, 2015) 110–126.

of 'pandemocracy' as a conflated normative/descriptive reference can become a rewarding conceptual tool. To elaborate on this, I propose two complementary basic statements.

First insight: The concept of an emergency and all practices, procedures, and rules associated with it, whether regulated in the constitution or not, can never shake off their normativity. Therefore, when facing an extraordinary global event such as the COVID-19 pandemic, the emergency cannot be treated merely as a factual situation. Rather, it needs to be understood in its specific normative meaning. Throughout history, legislators and judges have turned to emergencies as constitutional remedies, granting extreme responses to the executive branch to restore political, economic, social, and environmental normalcy.

Now, it is important to differentiate between an 'emergency' and an 'exception'.[11] While the former can only be understood in constitutional terms, the latter relies on 'extra-constitutional' circumstances where there is no hegemonic ruling power or legitimate norm to authoritatively resolve a terminal political conflict. As Schmitt states, 'sovereign is he who decides on the exception', revealing that the ultimate authority of a disputed political power can only be unveiled or ratified in situations of the most extreme civic unrest.[12] Although I will not delve into this issue, it is worth considering that the concept of pandemocracy may be used to frame the ultimate boundary of constitutional normalcy during the COVID-19 pandemic.

Second Insight: As mentioned, this text aims to explore the nature of non-democratic post-COVID-19 pandemic governance in the region and its detrimental effects on the separation of powers.[13] From a republican-democratic perspective, it is crucial to pay close attention to the performance of the state, particularly the faltering role of many Latin American legislative bodies during this dire situation. And here Möllers' caveat deserves full attention. He rightly stresses that the separation of powers is not only a normative principle but also an operational goal for a constitutional state.[14]

Therefore, a fair constitutional assessment should not rely on abstract utilitarian rationales or unscathed rights rhetoric.[15] Instead, it is important to examine

[11] P Riberi, 'Assessing Republican Wariness in Time of Hazard and Turmoil' in Eberhard, Lachmayer, Ribarov and Tallinger (eds), *Constitutional Limits to Security* (Austria, Nomos-Facultas, 2009). See also, P Riberi, 'La Emergencia como Remedio Constitucional, ¿o Viceversa?' *El Derecho* (Buenos Aires, Jurisprudence and doctrine Law Journal), Año XLIII, Nro. 11349.

[12] Carl Schmitt's *Political Theology* (MIT Press) 5.

[13] To gain insights into the role and internal motivations of Congress within a model of clear separation of powers, Chafetz's analysis is of interest. J Chafetz, *The Congress's Constitution* (New Haven, Yale University Press, 2017) 27–42.

[14] Regarding the methodological and theoretical approach to comparative constitutional analysis of separation of powers, Alexander Möllers' work is highly rewarding. Möllers emphasises the importance of both comparative and normative baselines beyond empirical observations. A Möllers, *The Three Branches* (Oxford, Oxford University Press, 2015) 7, 10.

[15] For a comparative exploration of Latin American constitutional design and the underlying cooperative or non-cooperative grounds, see Negretto's book. GL Negretto, *La Política del Cambio Constitucional en América Latina* (Buenos Aires, Fondo de Cultura Económica, 2015) 66–104.

how institutions, procedures, and rules have deviated from each country's constitutional design template and focus on the actual performance of political bodies. In line with Gargarella, it is more meaningful to delve into the Constitution's 'engine room' rather than aimlessly discuss rights discourse on the shiny deck.[16]

This chapter aims to emphasise how executives have been gaining momentum in Latin America while the dysfunction of the separation of powers has deprived the constitutional system of timely and necessary checks and balances. By doing so, we can achieve a more comprehensive understanding of how all main branches of power have awkwardly interacted during the recent COVID-19 pandemic. We can learn how their uncoordinated performance has accelerated what appears to be the Latin American version of democratic backsliding.

B. The Last Boundaries of Normalcy

Hobbes stressed: '... *[for he that hath the strength enough to protect all, wants not sufficiency to oppress all*'.[17] This statement conveys an enduring caveat in Latin America: fearing Leviathan's rage always seems a sensible feeling. In any case, understanding the pandemocracy must rely on some insights driven by constitutional theory.[18] Here, it is also essential to consider the normative dimension mentioned earlier. To fully comprehend the concept of constitutional emergencies, it is rewarding to trace back their origins and explore how their public meaning has been gaining accuracy over time.

Every constitution establishes a specific power structure, as the Greeks rightly stated, 'laying foundations' (κατάβολη).[19] Moreover, a constitution faithful to the legacy of Enlightenment must also be engaged with human rights protection. In this context, a declared emergency must be seen as a normative concept.[20] The extraordinary powers granted to the Executive during such extraordinary situations must fit within a specific political-legal framework of constitutional reasons. And therefore, interpretative constraints on the scope of these powers should naturally be in place. As Frank Schauer has pointed out, the existence of an interpreter

[16] R Gargarella, *Latin American Constitutionalism 1810–2010* (Oxford, Oxford University Press, 2013) 185–195.

[17] Following this statement, Hobbes further elaborates that 'inconvenience itself arises from the citizens, not from the power of government'. T Hobbes, *On the Citizen* (Cambridge, Cambridge University Press, 2018), ch VI, 84.

[18] Cheryl Saunders highlights how constitutional theory significantly shapes comparative constitutional law analysis. See C Saunders, 'Theoretical Underpinnings of Separation of Powers' in G Jacobsohn and M Schor (eds), *Comparative Constitutional Theory* (Cheltenham, Edward Elgar, 2018) 67.

[19] Modern emergency institutions, such as the 'state of siege' are incorporated into the constitution to prevent the occurrence of civil war, which the Greeks referred to as 'Stasis'.

[20] Hobbes claimed: '(...)Where there is no common power, the law does not exist; where there is no law, there is no justice ...'. T Hobbes, *Leviatán* (Madrid, 1984) Vol I, ch XIII, 138.

holding restricted powers is a consequence arising from the very same idea of rule or a system of rules.[21]

The constitutional equation and balance between freedom and power are often disrupted during unexpected contingencies like constitutional emergencies. However, resorting to such exceptional remedies should never serve as a justification for reckless human rights violations by empowered state authorities. It is crucial to acknowledge that the overall legal-political order is meant to be preserved under the constitutional cloak during emergencies. These should never provide a means to undermine the normative foundations of the rule of law. Consequently, any increase in power and overregulation of rights that may occur must never jeopardise or dismantle the balance set by the constitution.[22]

Accordingly, any alteration that may arise should never be interpreted as a pathway toward an inevitable process of deconstitutionalisation. Constitutional emergencies must never be seen as a legal loophole to exempt state authorities from abiding by constitutional values and principles.

i. Latin American COVID-19 Health Challenges and the Concept of Pandemocracy

The resounding clanging of synchronised blows on frying pans was the spontaneous result of hundreds of thousands of demonstrators flooding the streets of almost every urban center in Argentina on 20 December 2001. This relentless and muffled sound framed the rhythmic increase of popular anger in response to an unprecedented economic and social crisis. Even after almost two decades of democracy, Argentina continues to endure what could be considered one of its most devastating political, economic, and social crises in history. And this is because its lingering effects are still rooted in the population's reluctance to trust those in power.[23]

To fully understand the devastating impact of the pandemic on various Latin American democratic systems, one must not overlook the long-standing history of disproportionate and unconstitutional emergency responses, as well as the enduring institutional design flaws present in many of these constitutional settings. It should be kept in mind that, throughout the region, with a few peculiar exceptions, the constitutional authority has historically experienced repeated processes of

[21] F Schauer, *Las Reglas en Juego* (Marcial Pons, Madrid, 2004) 293.

[22] While Schmitt reintroduces Hobbes' decisionism, it is also evident that the presence of a constitution assumes the normative nature of its provisions. For a better grasp of political obedience grounds, see also P Kahn, *Political Theology* (New York, Columbia University Press, 2012) 17–30.

[23] In any community, it is important to generate public trust. Trust in the Constitution is an essential asset. See P Riberi, 'Disenso, Pesimismo y Desconfianza dentro de los Límites de las Reglas Constitucionales' in C Rosenkrantz and M Bergman (eds), *Confianza y Derecho en América Latina* (Argentina, Fondo de Cultura Económica, 2009) 195–214. See also R Hardin, *Trust & Trustworthiness* (Russell Sage Foundation, 2002) 10–52.

democratic backsliding, including coups d'état, dictatorships, human rights violations, and populist turmoil. However, due to the COVID-19 health emergency, it was not only governance or the checks and balances that were in jeopardy.[24] The chaotic upheaval went beyond that. The extent of popular discontent and disillusionment was such that the frenzied rhythm of the pots and pans still echoes from the 2001 crisis, demanding again that 'they must all go'.

In this context, it is important to understand something rather subtle. The continual cycles of emergency power increases by the executive function are a Sisyphean circuit that, in the long run, eagerly craves more and more expanded emergency powers. This recurrent causal chain has become the main reason for the state's failure, which, understandably, requires the concealment of what may be called a 'self-inflicted emergency process'. Such a circuit looks like an unavoidable nightmare explaining the nuts and bolts of ordinary folks' doomed fate. Indeed, because of such self-inflicted evils, the new emergency policies are usually in direct connection with new increasingly dire outcomes. In other words, neglecting a comprehensive assessment of these ongoing processes over time may perhaps explain why the increasing deployment of new and broader emergency powers by the executive almost always yields worse and worse outcomes.[25] The growing accumulation of fathomless emergency powers also tends to exacerbate people's intolerance toward unaccountable officeholders.[26]

The constitutional significance of the emergency triggered by the pandemic in several countries of the region has reshaped the way constitutional democracy is being construed in several of its fundamental practices. With that being said, the Latin American pandemocracy should be seen as illustrating the same overarching phenomenon, albeit with nuanced variations when compared to previous developments.

In countries like Argentina, during the early stages of the COVID-19 pandemic, several presidents broadcasted extraordinary and aggressive measures against people's freedoms under the guise of opaque necessity, massive propaganda, and mass-media coverage. While most parliaments and courts were shut down to pursue suffocating regulatory goals, presidents instead surrounded themselves with unaccountable boards of scientists and experts. Likewise, as part of a

[24] For a broader understanding of checks and balances from the perspective of political constitutionalism, A Somek, *Cosmopolitan Constitution* (Oxford, Oxford University Press, 2014) 56–58. Also, A Möllers, *The Three Branches* (Oxford, Oxford, Oxford University Press, 2015) 45–46.

[25] According to Adrian Vermeule, relying solely on the written safeguards in the constitution, often referred to as 'parchment' precautions. This author suggests that additional measures are necessary to prevent the unchecked accumulation of power by the executive. A Vermeule, *The Constitution of Risk* (Cambridge, Cambridge University Press, 2014) 54–58.

[26] The Federalist Papers 47 affirms: 'The accumulation of all powers, legislative, executive, and judiciary, in the same hands, whether of one, a few, or many, and whether hereditary, self-appointed, or elective, may justly be pronounced the very definition of tyranny. Were the federal Constitution, therefore, really chargeable with the accumulation of power, or with a mixture of powers, having a dangerous tendency to such an accumulation, no further arguments would be necessary to inspire a universal reprobation of the system'.

biopolitical turn and in the name of social oversight and individual isolation, it could be witnessed how unprecedented high-tech surveillance tools were deployed with stealth in many countries of the region.[27]

As these alleged expert scientific bodies displaced political actors from their constitutional duties, the symbolic legitimacy of a strong executive leadership no longer depended on legislative support or cared for judicial oversight. Regretfully, a backdrop of technocratic rationales, supporting the executive's televised emergency speeches, became an exclusionary reason that shielded presidents from constitutional accountability for their outrageous blunders.

In the face of these circumstances, the concept of pandemocracy allows us to grasp how the democratic perception of a composite of legitimate constitutional goals turned out to be blurred when the COVID-19 health crisis emerged in the region.[28] This implies that exceptional constitutional emergency measures implemented to enhance state authority have finally ended up jeopardizing other fundamental constitutional objectives.

The COVID-19 health pandemic, along with other underlying extreme circumstances, has exacerbated these phenomena. In this context, not only has the political, moral, and emotional relationship between people and public authorities been severely damaged, but it is also evident that the pandemocratic phenomenon has had detrimental effects on different layers of civil, commercial, and family relationships.

In a sense, the notion of 'pandemocracy' is a comprehensive reference point encompassing democratic decay and the aggressive emergency responses that have been undertaken during the COVID-19 pandemic.[29] It also suggests how far-reaching damage has been caused to many public institutions by reckless authoritarian responses from the Executive. In countries like Argentina, for example, both the vertical and horizontal separation of powers have been blatantly undermined during the pandemic. Legislative and judiciary independence have been impaired while subnational autonomies have also been seriously affected by some outrageous Executive decisions.[30]

The Latin American pandemocratic situations emerged within a broader conflict-ridden global context which is characterised by extreme political, legal, and normal instability when coping with overwhelming collective challenges such

[27] For an unsettling portrayal of the current digital threat, see S Zuboff, *The Age of Surveillance Capitalism* (New York, Profile Books, 2019) 3–24.

[28] K Lachmayer, 'Democracy, Death and Dying: 'The Potential and Limits of Legal Rationalization'' in M Kettemann and K Lachmayer (eds), *Pandemocracy in Europe* (Oxford, Hart Publishing, 2020).

[29] In their analysis of the pandemic in Europe, Kettemann and Lachmayer argue that the recent crisis has revealed a shift in power away from the people, resulting in a form of governance where the 'demos' (people) no longer rule. See M Kettemann & K Lachmayer, 'Conclusions: Pandemocracy – Governing for the People, without the People?' in M Kettemann and K Lachmayer (eds), *Pandemocracy in Europe* (Oxford, Hart Publishing, 2020) 338–354.

[30] Some fears, like Tyrannophobia, are justified. Eric Posner and Adrian Vermeule, accordingly, define dictatorship as a system of unchecked rule. See 'Tyrannophobia' in T Ginsburg (ed), *Comparative Constitutional Design* (Cambridge, Cambridge University Press, 2013) 317–322.

as illegal immigration, terrorism, energy supply shortage, and recurrent environmental crises. All these conundrums undoubtedly highlight how democratic and bureaucratic prestige is crumbling while people's trust in well-established public institutions is also fading away.[31]

To put it simply, regarding Latin America, the term pandemocracy conveys a dual aim. First, it highlights the strained relationships that are multiplied within the state.[32] Second, it also draws attention to the long-term institutional effects resulting from the Executive's power increase during the pandemic. In a way, this notion provides a better grasp of the various non-democratic outcomes drawn from the unfettered Executives' pandemic responses.

II. Comparative Emergency Law: General Remarks

Comparative constitutional law provides sound and comprehensive insights when its findings look plausible to the observer's normative sensitivity. The subordination of constitutional reasoning to the logic of necessity, as previously mentioned, is a tautological approach to non-normative constitutional reasoning that distorts the historical meaning of the term 'emergency'.[33] This has been a significant concern in Latin America, where such understanding has led to fallacious reasoning that can be summarised as follows: 'The greater the State's needs, the greater the (Executive's) powers, while greater restrictions on freedom are inevitably enforced'.[34]

Be that as it may, like many other constitutions in the world, most Latin American basic laws contain substantive and procedural provisions that regulate such contingent exceptional situations.[35] However, due to entrenched written provisions as well as nuanced practices, it seems sensible to strike a distinction between regulated and non-regulated emergencies.

[31] Trust facilitates social cooperation and allows individuals to have confidence in their reciprocal expectations. See P Riberi, 'Disenso, Pesimismo y Desconfianza dentro de los Límites de las Reglas Constitucionales' in C Rosenkrantz and M Bergman (eds), *Confianza y Derecho en América Latina* (Fondo de Cultura Económica, 2009) 195–214.

[32] Christoph Möllers highlights the functionalist perspective underlying the concern about the usurpation of power. See C Möllers, 'Separation of Powers' in R Masterman and R Schütze (eds), *Comparative Constitutional Law* (Cambridge, Cambridge, Cambridge University Press, 2019) 239.

[33] O Gross, 'Constitutions and Emergency Regimes' in T Ginsburg and R Dixon (eds), *Comparative Constitutional Law* (Cheltenham, Edward Elgar, 2011) 334–339.

[34] In ch I, Book I of the *Discourses*, Machiavelli affirms that 'men act either out of necessity or by choice'. N Machiavelli, *Discursos sobre la prinera década de Tito Livio* (Editorial Losada, 2003) 53.

[35] It is worth noting David Landau's comparative assessment concerning legal pragmatism. D Landau, 'Legal Pragmatism and Comparative Constitutional Law' in G Jacobsohn and M Schor (eds), *Comparative Constitutional Theory* (Minnesota, Edward Elgar, 2018) 221–228.

Regarding well-established historical constitutional incentives, for example, the Roman Republic created the '*Senatus Consultus Ultimun*', which typically led to the extreme institution of dictatorship. When a Roman citizen was appointed as a dictator, the Republic granted him broad powers without substantive limitations though for a limited window of six months. The goal was to preserve the integrity of the Republic. Broadly speaking, there have been several attempts to incorporate dormant emergency provisions into constitutional documents. For instance, just like the Roman Republic, Machiavelli recognised that, although constrained by appropriate institutional incentives, the allocation or enlargement of new powers should be regulated ex-ante.[36] Likewise, the State of Siege was introduced early on in France on 10 July 1791. Most of the Latin American countries regulate emergencies in their constitutions.[37] Unfortunately, from time to time, this kind of unfettered institutional mechanism has been restored in Latin American countries by military coup d'états and other sorts of authoritarian rule.[38]

A. Non-regulated Models of Emergency

As I stressed earlier, most Latin American constitutions have envisaged provisions that regulate emergencies. However, not every democracy that entrenches human rights and separation of powers has formally regulated emergencies in their texts. For example, countries like Great Britain,[39] Switzerland,[40] Japan or Belgium have no written statements that provide for extraordinary powers or specific liberty restrictions in case of emergencies. Following this trend, we can also note that emergencies have only been briefly addressed in the US Constitution through the 'Habeas Corpus' suspension.

[36] Referring to the unity of action, Machiavelli claims '… [habitual republican responses to emergencies move slowly … and since reaching timely agreements is difficult, medicine looks dangerous when it has to cure something that cannot wait. … Thus, republics must have among their provisions swift and adequate means'. See N Machiavelli, *Discursos sobre la primera década de Tito Livio* (Buenos Aires, Editorial Lozada, 2004) 138–139.

[37] For example, refer to the following sections of the constitutions: section 23 of the Argentine Constitution, section 42 of the Chilean Constitution, section 168 of the Uruguayan Constitution, section 137 of the Peruvian Constitution, sections 212–215 of the Colombian Constitution, and section 29 of the Mexican Constitution.

[38] Once the dictator assumed office with no suspension of other magistracies, they exercised wide-ranging discretionary powers for a fixed period, unless one of the consul's terms expired beforehand. JC Ghirardi, *Derecho Romano* (Buenos Aires, Ediciones Eudecor, 1993) Vol I, 54–55.

[39] The UK's emergency powers, the combination of constitutional rules and principles derived from Parliament's sovereignty, must be construed by a concrete recognition of the government's privileges, all while adhering to Common Law basic principles. EW Böckenforde, *Constitutional and Political Theory – selected writings* (Oxford, Oxford University Press, 2017) 121–123.

[40] Switzerland's declaration of an emergency has always been associated with the 'State of survival'. As noted by comparative constitutional law, it is worth noting that the Swiss chronicle of emergency declarations has also been modeled by a long tradition of specific political practices. See Böckenforde (n 39) 124–125.

B. Regulated Models

Many constitutions, such as those of Germany and Portugal, provide an alternative pattern of increasingly differentiated emergency responses. In the same vein, the Spanish Constitution, for example, regulates three different types of emergencies. Similarly, Brazil distinguishes between the traditional 'State of Siege' and an intermediate 'State of Defence', which can only be declared by the president following the approval of a specific advisory council.

It is also important to bear in mind a key historical experience whose devastating effects followed the enforcement of section 48.2 of the Weimar Constitution. This provision stipulated that, whenever deemed necessary, any declaration of emergency requires nothing further from the President than his mere notification of it to the Bundestag.[41] Before the rise of National Socialism, a series of approximately 250 unratified emergency decisions were enforced by the government. This may explain why the current doctrine of the German Constitutional Court emphasises that emergencies must only be constitutionally implemented with a clear legitimate purpose. And this goal is none other than 'preserving or re-establishing the normalcy and integrity of the constitutional order'.[42]

III. In Case of Emergency, Break the Glass

Latin American presidents have often abused these extreme constitutional provisions for agonistic reasons. As I have already underscored, regardless of their nature, a wide range of events leading to urgent state responses have frequently accelerated what can be referred to as 'self-inflicted emergencies'. What does this mean? Again, it means that the Executive's increased powers during an emergency are, in fact, the result of poor public policies that recklessly worsen the public situation, rather than redressing the government's mistakes. Thus, the cures becomes worse than the disease itself. To quote Ernesto Garzón Valdés, it would be wiser to prevent a catastrophe, such as the previous pandemic, from turning into a *calamity*.[43] Catastrophes represent acts of nature, while calamities are the consequences of human wrongdoing.

Nevertheless, constitutional emergencies must have two specific characteristics. First, under extremely dire circumstances, they should allow certain political

[41] P Riberi, 'Jenseits von Weimar (Más allá de Weimar): El constitucionalismo moderno asediado' in H Seleme (ed), *Instituciones Públicas y Moralidad Política* (Ediciones de la Universidad Nacional de Córdoba, 2015) 158–190.

[42] According to Böckenforde, the basic notes of such a doctrine provide that a. An emergency is a political-constitutional mechanism to preserve or restore constitutional normalcy; b. Its validity cannot replace a Law, not to mention the Constitution, c. During an emergency, special regulations labeled as 'measures' can be enforced; d. Measures are valid for a limited period. Böckenforde (n 39) 117–118.

[43] E Garzón Valdés, *Calamidades* (Barcelona, Gedisa, 2009).

bodies, through well-regulated constitutional procedures, to provide certain political authorities with extraordinary decision-making tools. Second, they should engage all the main branches of the state to implement these provisions in harmony with the entire framework of values, principles, and constitutional rules. This understanding naturally strengthens the normative dimension of the concept of 'emergency', in contrast with the empirical concept of an 'exception'. Therefore, for the sake of a community's future well-being, it seems reasonable that civil liberties may be temporarily weakened and/or subject to new reasonable constraints and regulations.

While the first characteristic is often valued in countries of the region, the second one is rarely respected. To avoid this situation, it would be wise to reframe certain constitutional strategies. As far as I can see, a normative-procedural approach based on a pluralistic decision-making process would enhance the involvement of the three branches of government. Additionally, this approach would not lose sight of those legitimate democratic conditions at stake. In other words, beyond the analysis of substantive law, it is necessary to understand that the constitutional viability of emergencies should be based on well-entrenched democratic safeguards.

So, let me emphasise some final normative remarks:

1. Constitutional regulation of power delegations/increases must never allow the very same power whose competencies are being expanded to unilaterally decide on the timing and extent of such empowerment.
2. While most constitutions authorise the temporary delegation/increase of emergency powers for the Executive, it is essential to anticipate how control mechanisms will prevent unchecked responses when specific contested situations arise.
3. It is important to note that during emergencies, special protections for the Executive and other officeholders would never authorise actions that go beyond the core normative boundaries of the constitution. Both in normal and emergency times, accountability always serves as a necessary constitutional incentive to curb potential abuses of power.[44]

A. Some Basic References to the Argentine COVID-19 Pandemic Crisis

The COVID-19 pandemic has had devastating economic and social consequences. When considering the 'cost of rights' as Holmes did, it is still not easy to determine

[44] Chiebub and Limogi highlight the detrimental impact of executive decree power abuses in Latin America, which have contributed to an imbalance in the functioning of the separation of powers, among other issues. See JA Cheibub and F Limogi, 'Legislative-Executive Relations' in T Ginsburg and R Dixon (eds), *Comparative Constitutional Law* (Cheltenham, Edward Elgar, 2011) 226–229.

how expensive the final bill of the pandemic will be.[45] However, what we already know is that the pandemic placed a heavy burden on the population of many Latin American countries, including Argentina. Furthermore, it exposed numerous institutional deficiencies in a region where economic and social inequalities are overwhelming.

Argentina has a history of political turmoil, including coups d'état with severe human rights violations, as well as cycles of economic crises that have caused chaos and dismay among several sections of the population.[46] Be that as it may, during the twentieth century, emergency legislation passed by Congress undermined many principles such as contractual freedom and the non-retroactive nature of the law. Extraordinary regulatory powers eroded property rights and due process while some court's ludicrous rulings supported measures like mortgage deferments and frozen rental contracts. Additionally, some economic emergency legislation, Executive decrees, and Supreme Court case-law doctrine even endorsed the seizure of private bank deposits as well as the conversion of them into public bonds. This sad case-law record also reveals that foreign currency deposits have been compulsorily exchanged into the local currency, not to mention how, under the cloak of economic emergencies, inflation and foreign debt have brought about interest rates haircuts, or the deferment of maturities.[47]

Concerning COVID-19, extensive executive powers were granted through Act 27.541 enacted before the pandemic. This trend intensified with the issuance of the 'compulsive and preventive social isolation decree – 297/20 (ASPO) –' on 19 March 2020. Subsequently, a cascade of hundreds of executive decrees (DNU) was issued during this period. While the government's early measures looked legitimate and reasonable, over time, the President assumed the role of a kind of '*croupier*' unilaterally awarding benefits and burdens to the population. Naturally, as people's patience wore thin, the government's arbitrary decisions increased, and public disobedience and constitutional challenges multiplied.

The Argentine constitutional order is an example of an imbalanced separation of powers model.[48] For instance, the regulation of the permanent bi-chamber

[45] S Holmes and C Sunstein, *The Cost of Rights* (Norton & Company, 1999).

[46] The Argentine Constitution extensively regulates the state of emergency. In addition to provisions regarding the declaration of war – Art 75, subsection 25 – the key provision dealing with emergencies is the *state of siege* – Art 23; 75 subsection 29; 99 subsections 16 and 61. As regards the Executive legislative competencies during emergency times, the Constitution has exceptionally allowed the President to issue executive orders labeled as 'necessary and urgent decrees' – DNU: Art 99, subsection 3 – and it also authorises him to issue delegated decrees when Congress has specifically granted such a delegation in the field of administration or as a result of a declared emergency (DD: Art 76).

[47] Some examples of case law include '*Ercolano v Lantieri*' (Fallos: 136:131), '*Horta v Harguindeguy*' (Fallos: 137:47, 1922), '*Cine Callao*' (Fallos: 247:121, 1960), '*Mango v Traba*' (Fallos: 144:219, 1925), '*Avico v De la Pesa*' (Fallos: 172:21), '*Prattico Carmelo v Basso y Cía*' (Fallos: 246:345), and '*Peralta, Luis v Estado Nacional*' (LL., 1991-C, 140).

[48] For further discussions on democratic dialogue and emergencies in Latin America, you may refer to the work by Gargarella and Roa-Roa titled 'Diálogo Democrático y Emergencia en América Latina' (MPIL Research Paper No 2020-21).

committee in the Argentine Congress, which should prevent the Executive's abuse of legislative decrees and delegated legislation, is highly deficient. Given the prevailing hyper-presidentialism in the country, even under normal circumstances, the Executive's powers appear excessive and prone to encroach on other branches' competences.[49] The rhetoric of the emergency, through 'force majeure', and/or 'fait accompli', has justified how factual needs outweigh all normative constraints. Naturally, such platitudes have also been key in the process of removing republican reluctance against the Executive's expansionism.

Unfortunately, during the COVID-19 pandemic, there was little chance of either the political authorities or their health advisors being confronted or put to rights by the legislative and judicial branches. The poor performance of the whole democratic political system has persistently hindered reasonable and comprehensive debates on such matters.[50] Nonetheless, there is a silver lining. Many COVID-19 executive decrees, whose vague claims of 'necessity' and 'urgency' did not meet the constitutional threshold stated in section 99, inc. 3 CA, have been subjected to judicial review by the Argentine Supreme Court. Although somehow belated, with significant case law doctrine rendered through numerous 'amparos', the Argentine Supreme Court is resuming its constitutional role.[51]

IV. Separation of Powers and Republican Democratic Goals

A liberal-republican constitution comprises two fundamental elements: power and liberty.[52] Regarding the former, among other goals, the constitution provides the institutional democratic framework for appointing representatives, government officials, and magistrates. It also informs us about the legitimate source power of their authorities while acknowledging their limits by creating a balanced constitutional setting.[53] As for liberty, the constitution prevents the overlapping of vertical

[49] For instance, many Executive Decrees (DNU) have been issued ever since Argentina's democratic restoration (1983). Eg, Alfonsín 10; Menem 545; De la Rúa 89; Duhalde 158; Néstor Kirchner 270 and Cristina Fernández de Kirchner 81; Macri 69. Alberto Fernández has issued more than 117 to date.

[50] It is perhaps worthwhile here to refer to Pasquino, who provides a compelling comparative analysis, categorising democratic achievements into full and flawed democracies, hybrid regimes, and authoritarian regimes. This analysis explores the complexities of democratic governance. See G Pasquino 'Is democracy still the worst form of government except all others?' in G Amato, B Barbisan and C Pinelli (eds), *Rule of Law v Majoritarian Democracy* (Oxford, Hart Publishing, 2021) 227–230.

[51] See A Hernandez 'Las Emergencias por COVID-19 en Argentina' in N Gonzalez and D Valadés (eds) *Emergencia Sanitaria por COVID-19 – Derecho Comparado* (Universidad Nacional Autónoma de México, 2020) 23–39.

[52] P Riberi, 'La Forma Constitucional – especulaciones sobre la apariencia de un ente sin contornos' in P Riberi and PS Ugarte (eds), *Decisión Democrática y Forma Constitucional* (Instituto de Investigaciones Jurídicas de la UNAM, 2022) 38.

[53] The principles of horizontal and vertical separation of powers, along with checks and balances, are fundamental constitutional principles that contribute to the democratic legitimacy of political systems.

and horizontal competencies while enshrining a core set of rights that should be enjoyed by all individuals.

Now, under more stringent democratic standards of legitimacy, the comparative constitutional analysis leads us to acknowledge at least three crosscutting basic goals in every liberal-democratic constitutional polity. What are these essential objectives? Well, under the above-mentioned perspective, the main aims are the following: 1. To produce a representation, which requires constitutionalising the state's legitimacy by fleshing out the people's democratic connection with their representative institutions; 2. To promote governance and responsiveness, which means fostering the state's effective/efficient decision-making process; 3. To lay down proper controls, which implies embedding political, administrative, and judiciary mechanisms, practices, and proceedings of accountability.

Now, let us explore how state power works in the region. To deal with this concern, it is essential to delve into three fundamental approaches.[54] Which are they?

The first one aims to achieve a sound understanding of the ontology of power and political legitimacy.[55] The question here is what is a regime? And regardless of the authorities' external traits, this abstract quest allows us to establish the authentic source of legitimacy.[56] The second approach examines power dynamics in space, exploring the interactions among subnational political entities within a given territory, namely unitary or federal forms of states.[57] Finally, the third approach focuses on the diachronic processes through which the interplay of different state branches serves to conceive and implement a wide range of norms and political decisions.[58]

Hence, after figuring out how political power manifests in space and over time, any observer can unravel the form of state and the form of government. Naturally, he can also make out the kind of regime under consideration. Depending on how syncopated or isolated decision-making processes are operating within rather independent and/or more entwined state branches, diverse forms of government are deemed to fulfill a complex composite of institutional aims in a unique timeframe. Indeed, as Maurice Duverger accurately underlines, the model of 'separation of powers' vis à vis that of 'collaboration of powers' is a watershed sorting out two

Jeremy Waldron provides a detailed scheme for understanding the content of these principles in his book. J Waldron, *Political Political Theory* (Cambridge, MA, Harvard University Press, 2016) 49.

[54] While exploring the concept of constitutional form, I take advantage of this triple perspective. See P Riberi, *Decisión Democrática y Forma Constitucional* (IIJ, UNAM, México, 2022) 25–30.

[55] Riberi (n 52) 25–30.

[56] Concerning this issue, I share Tamas Gyorfy's insight that western societies' political institutions have historically been aiming toward the democratisation of government. See T Gyorfi, *Against the New Constitutionalism* (Cheltenham, Edward Elgar, 2016) 43.

[57] AM Hernández, *Estudios de Federalismo Comparado* (Rubinzal-Culzoni, 2018) 9–27.

[58] Chiebub and Limogi have conducted a comprehensive structural analysis of Legislative-Executive relations, particularly in presidential democracies. See Cheibub and Limogi (n 44) 214–216.

basic competing power-organising principles for variants of presidentialism and parliamentarism.[59]

In Latin America, there are nuanced governmental structures and institutional forms that might provide new features to supplement Duverger's table. For example, we are currently coming across plenty of variants of semi-presidentialism or semi-parliamentarism whose subtle features make them 'hybrid' conflated exceptions to the above-mentioned original constitutional models. We can also note some 'distorted models' that, in their state's imbalanced performance, are destined to fail in most of their original design goals.[60] Hyper presidentialism or the so-called imperial presidentialism may showcase this institutionally frustrating Latin American trend.[61]

A. 'Departmentalism' and People's Democratic Expectations

No republican constitutional order can survive unless it inspires strong popular support. Republican history tells us that a robust set of collective liberties and values thrives when political institutions reflect democratic participation, public deliberation, and civic engagement. Unlike what has been happening in Latin America, both in normal times and during emergencies, three republican pillars, namely 'popular sovereignty', 'the rule of law', and the principle of 'non-domination', are meant to harmoniously play together.[62] And incidentally, the proportionate alignment of these columns is crucial for ensuring the smooth interplay of three state branches.

Latin American emergency responses during the pandemic were grossly inadequate, uncoordinated, and inconsistent with the principle of checks and balances.[63] The possibility of legitimate constitutional remedies in the face of an

[59] See M Duverger, *Institutions Politiques Et Droit Constitutionnel* (Thémis, Presses Universitaires de France, 1970) 162–201.

[60] As Somek underlines, it is a significant theoretical given that the 'Madisonian' separation of powers assumption takes for granted that 'the interest of a person holding office will coincide with the interest of the department of government to which the office is linked' …. And further the author says: 'personal ambition is supposed to drive people to assert the institution's position within a system of separation of powers'. See Somek (n 24) 4.

[61] Simón Bolivar's preference for a consular model is indicative of this tradition. As Günter Frankenberg highlights, this type of democratic Caesarism was deeply ingrained in early Latin American constitutional experiments. G Frankenberg, *Comparative Constitutional Studies – Between Magic and Deceit* (Cheltenham, Edward Elgar, 2019) 100–101.

[62] From the viewpoint of political constitutionalism, the commitment to a republican constitution is based upon a combination of practices and key normative elements. See P Riberi, 'La «Querelle» entre política y derecho' in C Parmigiani, M Miranda and M Barbará (eds), *Derecho y política en la encrucijada: problemas y perspectivas* (Córdoba, Editorial Ciencia, Derecho y Sociedad de la Facultad de Derecho de la Universidad Nacional de Córdoba, 2019) 24–32.

[63] Concerning the prevention of tyranny, Josh Chafetz, provides interesting insights. See Chafetz (n 13) 303–305.

overwhelmingly extreme sanitary situation encompasses a broad set of democratic practices. To better understand how the in-game between *constitutional ethos* and *constitutional design* has awkwardly unfolded in the region, it is necessary to examine how agonistic institutional practices have deviated from their original constitutional goals.[64] Furthermore, it is worth noting that a long record of military interventions has not only lowered popular expectations concerning deliberative outcomes but also undermined civic opposition to the violent enforcement of non-democratic decisions.

In my opinion, the inbalanced performance of the constitution's power structure has not received sufficient attention in Latin America. Moreover, neither the *Schmitt v Kelsen* theoretical debate nor any form of legal realist construction has successfully provided a comprehensive understanding of why the complex amalgamation of constitutional values, principles, and rules has seldom succeeded in the region.[65] Accordingly, more blatantly, as regards the pandemic in Latin America, it is not easy to understand the reasons why several constitutions' inner controlling structures have been either upholding or tolerating unconstitutional emergency laws and authoritarian policies.[66]

Given the distorted assimilation of the US's separation of powers model in the region, my view is that the COVID-19 health emergency not only sped up an arbitrary process of individuals' rights abridgments but also triggered a dangerous process of democratic disarray. Hyperpresidentialism, as historical records recall us, has been significantly detrimental to the rule of law.[67] Alas, its long-lasting presence in Latin America has brought about a corrosive impact on the whole constitutional culture of the region.[68]

With regards to the role of the courts during emergencies, it seems sensible to reject two uncompromised trends, namely blind self-restraint and untamed activism. Bearing in mind what happened in countries like Argentina, where people were forcibly isolated and abusively deprived of many of their rights, it would be wiser to rely on a foreseeable pattern of engagement of the courts. And here, my insight is that the US's Supreme Court Justice Jackson's concurring opinion in *Youngstown Sheet v Sawyer* provides a sound standard for making out courts' deferment toward executive emergency decision-making.[69] Depending on how unconstitutional and

[64] Concerning Machiavelli's Philosophy of State, Bobbitt points out. 'The habits and ethos of a society will determine its fate. For a state, this is a matter of its constitutional forms and practices. The interplay between strategic and legal innovation – the outer and the inner membranes of the state – as these confront the vagaries of Fortune shapes the state and brings successes or failure'. Philip Bobbitt explores similar themes in his book, *The Garments of Court & the Palace* (Atlantic Books, London, 2015) 70.

[65] Here it is interesting to recall Alexander Bickels' caveat in the *Harvard Law Review*: 'No good society can be unprincipled, and no viable society can be principle-ridden.'

[66] Riberi (n 1) 39–40.

[67] J Linz, & A Valenzuela, *Crisis presidencialismo 1. Perspectivas comparativas* (Madrid, Alianza Editorial, 1994) 176–178.

[68] B Ackerman, 'The New Separation of Powers' (2000) 113 *Harvard Law Review* 633–725.

[69] *Youngstown Sheet & Co v Sawyer*, 343 U.S. 579 (1952).

non-democratic emergency regulations seem to be, Justice Jackson promotes a diverse increasing range of strictness in courts' scrutiny. Interestingly, the circumstances surrounding this conflict might bear some resemblance to the situation in Argentina during the pandemic, where administrative regulations following the Executive's Emergency Decree 260/2020 placed heavy burdens on some private companies whose medical high-tech production was seized and subjected to stringent oversight on the part of the Federal Health Ministry.[70]

In contrast to what often occurs in other constitutional democracies, many Latin American polities consented to increased and unrestrained executive powers. Comparative constitutional law, however, provides interesting institutional examples of enhanced state-branch dynamics.[71] Although meant for a parliamentary system, section 37(2) of the South African Constitution, for instance, enables the interplay of political branches when a long-lasting emergency calls for permanent oversight. Bruce Ackerman highly values this emergency provision as it provides for what he labels an *escalating cascade of supermajorities*.[72] Under this provision, the granting, endurance, and increase of the executive's emergency powers are not subject to material restrictions. Such empowerment has a deadline and is destined to be terminated unless an increasingly demanding number of legislative supports allow it to last longer.[73]

V. Conclusion

Charles Tilly emphasises that the building of Republican states has always been centered around controlling violence. Even in the face of such a global pandemic or threats to national security, constitutional limitations and fundamental controlling institutions should never be forsaken. A republican approach, therefore, duly relies on public responsiveness and governmental accountability within a robust normative framework of legitimate constitutional rules and decent political practices. Whether in normal or emergency times, constitutional remedies must never be employed to undermine individuals' rights or the very foundations of democracy.

[70] Indeed, during the COVID-19 pandemic, the Minister of Health unilaterally intervened in the production, marketing, and distribution of ventilators manufactured by Leisitung and Tecme in the Province of Cordoba.

[71] The normative debate regarding the constitutionality of statutes and other decisions should not be limited to the judicial sphere alone. According to Adrian Vermeule, the deliberative capacities of Congress are crucial elements in a democratic context. A Vermeule, *Mechanism of Democracy* (Oxford, Oxford University Press, 2007) 217–218.

[72] See B Ackerman, 'The Emergency Constitution' (2004) 113 *Yale Law Journal* 1029.

[73] David Dyzenhaus provides bold criticism of Ackerman's approach. He openly rejects Ackerman's stance. D Dyzenhaus, *Schmitt v Dicey: Are states of emergency inside or outside the legal order?* in AM Hernández (ed), *Constitucionalismo en Tiempos de Emergencia* (IACL-AIDC, AADC, Advocatus, 2007) 95–135.

Acknowledging the difference between 'emergency' and 'exception' is a key analytical tool.[74] As highlighted, many of these aggressive regulations have brought about what can be described as 'self-inflicted' emergencies. What does this mean within the COVID-19 context? It means that the executive's increase of powers in response to the emergency has resulted in subsequent uncontrolled policy-making mistakes, which in turn have triggered major new emergencies, leading the Executive to seek even greater powers for dealing with its past errors. In other words, in Latin America, unchecked emergency cures tend to be worse than the disease.[75]

Therefore, an emergency must never be declared to wipe out the very same constitution which enables the Executive's exceptional powers. For any civilized community, accordingly, preventing catastrophes such as the pandemic could become a calamity if such remedies jeopardize the matrix of the enabling foundational norm: the Constitution. As stressed before, we should be clear that catastrophes are due to forces of nature, whereas calamities are the direct result of poor human agency.

Hence, by attempting to replicate the US's separation of powers model, many Latin American democracies have found themselves trapped in a dreadful dilemma: either they endure governmental frustration in achieving checks and balances or descend into authoritarian chaos when an unfettered Executive unleashes itself from constitutional limitations.[76] Furthermore, during times of political, economic, or social turmoil, ordinary people should never be governed or treated as outsiders or mere spectators of an unfamiliar constitutional drama. It is evident that during emergencies, civil liberties can be subject to further regulations while expanded power boundaries are set for the sake of people's future well-being. Notwithstanding this, it is crystal clear in light of the concept of pandemocracy that opaque decision-making can open the gates for democratic decay and authoritarian rule.

In short, a constitutional assessment of the COVID-19 emergency responses in Latin America should never lose sight of the most fundamental issue at stake. In my view, this common unfortunate blunder stems from a fundamental theoretical misunderstanding. Latin American constitutional settings undergo a basic practical incapacity that has been undermining their political stability and, on top

[74] P Gragl, 'Lawless Extravagance: The Primacy Claim of Politics and the State of Exception in Times of COVID-19' in M Kettemann and K Lachmayer (eds), *Pandemocracy in Europe* (Oxford, Hart Publishing, 2020) 17–24 .

[75] Here, it is convenient to rely on Wallace's caveat. Particularly, it is important to make a clear-cut distinction between political leaders making up some tough policies during emergency times vis à vis other individuals' decisions rendered under strict duress or necessity. Everyone in the latter case is compelled to do what they did or had no choice whereas in the former, there are always alternatives. This reasoning counts in the face of 'self-inflicted' emergencies. R Jay Wallace, *Responsibility and the Moral Sentiments* (Cambridge, MA, Harvard University Press, 1998) 146.

[76] For a more detailed description of how the separation of powers functions in the original template of the US constitutional model, see N Devins and L Fisher, *The Democratic Constitution* (Oxford, Oxford University Press, 2004) 77–101.

of that, has also brought about a less vibrant constitutional engagement. I believe that beyond any moral or legal wrongdoing and beyond any possible institutional design shortcoming, the basic situation is that many political communities of the region are unaware of an essential practical principle.

As I have already pointed out, the overriding concern is that both *power-holders and power recipients have failed to understand or to make a difference between the practical meaning of constitutional politics and ordinary politics.*[77] Such ignorance had and still has a negative impact on people's reluctance to abide by their most peaceful and significant covenant of conviviality. This misunderstanding, by the way, produces a clear detrimental effect on long-term cooperative goals. When during a pandemocratic context, 'ordinary politics' and 'constitutional politics' get mixed up, the unintended degradation of the latter is likely to cause ruthless non-democratic policies and more aggressive human rights abuses.

[77] P Riberi, 'Populist and non-democratic reading of the Constitution – Sad lessons from Latin America' in F Gardós-Orosz, and Z Szente (ed), *Populist Challenges to Constitutional Interpretation in Europe and Beyond* (Abingdon, Routledge) 310.

2

How the Pandemic Changed Democratic Regimes

SERGIO VERDUGO

I. Introduction

Almost everywhere in the world, the measures taken to deal with the COVID-19 pandemic empowered the executive branch at the expense of legislators and judges. Many leaders with authoritarian or populist inclinations seized the opportunity to maximise their power while eroding critical democratic principles. Even leaders without those inclinations increased their political power, partly because they needed to push through swift and technically well-grounded solutions. Even though the results of the policies introduced during this time are mixed – scientists will discuss the results for years, and many governments made decisions the scientific community deemed to be incompetent, ill-informed, or taken in bad faith – a common trend could be seen across the globe: the primary responsibility for carrying out the measures to face the health and economic challenges of the pandemic mostly remained in the hands of executive branch officers, and legislators often had limited powers or influence.

This fact is not wholly unexpected. After all, legal systems typically assign emergency powers to the executive branch in times of crisis. Crises will likely be more effectively handled by those with access to information, authority, and control over healthcare and security infrastructures. This may occur even at the cost of introducing tension into the traditional separation of powers model. Besides this, recent quantitative data shows a significant divergence in how legislatures have been limited or shut down during the Pandemic.[1] Even states with well-functioning democratic institutions, such as Australia, seemed to be affected by a sort of 'technocratic autocracy' that marginalised the role of legislators.[2]

[1] See I Waismel-Manor et al., 'Should I Stay (Open) or Should I Close? World Legislatures during the First Wave of COVID-19' (2022) *Political Studies* www.ssrn.com/abstract=4055128 (accessed 20 December 2022).

[2] EL Windholz, 'Governing in a Pandemic: From Parliamentary Sovereignty to Autocratic Technocracy' (2020) 8 *The Theory and Practice of Legislation* 93.

Finding outlier cases to these trends can be beneficial to understand the global and comparative dynamics briefly mentioned in the paragraphs above. Chile is a useful outlier example. In a global context where the executive branch has grown in power, and despite the strong formal powers of the former Chilean President (see section III), President Sebastián Piñera – a right-wing politician elected a year before the pandemic started – failed to completely control the mechanisms to deal with the pandemic from both an economic and health-related perspective. Instead, a shift in the balance of power can be observed during this period that benefited Congress, which connects to the massive protests that took place in October 2019 – before the pandemic hit Chile in March 2020.

Unlike the global trend, the Chilean Congress became a relevant political player during the pandemic. It never interrupted its operations and quickly enacted the norms that allowed it to function remotely while becoming particularly productive in enacting new policies to deal with the pandemic.[3] Contrasting with other countries facing threats to their democratic institutions, the main risk for Chilean democracy was not executive branch aggrandizement – which could arguably still exist from a legal perspective – but the existence of populist narratives coming from individual legislators seeking re-election. The implications of what happened in Chile should not suggest that Congress aggrandizement is necessarily better than executive aggrandizement, as we are still yet to understand how serious the political risks associated with congressional aggrandizement are. Nevertheless, this chapter provides a cautionary note to those that seek to constrain the rise of an overpowered executive branch by emphasising the powers of legislators.

I argue that, even though there are good reasons to protect or strengthen legislators during extraordinary situations – so they can ensure that the governments are accountable for their abusive actions during periods of emergency – shifting the power balance in favour of a collective legislative body while diminishing the relevance of the head of the executive branch may generate political collective action and accountability problems. For example, legislators may engage in vote trading to approve short-term policies that elevate spending at the expense of undermining the sustainability of long-term agendas, without providing solutions to long-term problems and without making clear who is responsible for the associated risks and costs. Though understandable, scholars working on how the pandemic impacted democratic regimes have generally overlooked these types of collective action problems. This chapter aims to initiate a conversation to fill this gap.

The following section will identify the democratic risks associated with the COVID-19 pandemic from a comparative perspective. Section III will situate the

[3] See D Lovera and C Valdés, 'Emergencia y Proceso Legislativo. 'Con Un Poco de Ayuda de Mis Amigas'' in PC Vásquez (ed), *La Ley de la Emergencia. Ensayos sobre el derecho, la excepción y la pandemia* (Santiago, Ediciones DER, 2021).

Chilean case in the context of the 2019 social unrest and the constitution-making process, and briefly refer to the powers of the President. Section IV will explain how the President lost power during the Pandemic. Section V will focus on one of Chile's most critical legislative struggles during the Pandemic. Section VI will conclude the paper by briefly presenting some preliminary lessons.

II. The Pandemic-Related Risks Threatening Constitutional Democracies

The COVID-19 pandemic pushed many governments to take extraordinary measures to contain infection rates. They typically established the prohibition of gatherings, social distancing, the temporary closure of businesses, travel restrictions, and lockdowns. These measures harmed several rights[4] but were often supported by groups of experts recruited by the executive branch. These actions also included policies to mitigate the pandemic's harsh economic consequences. Many people needed to pay their rent but were not allowed to work; employers were supposed to keep paying salaries, but they could not take an adequate income due to the lockdowns, and so on.

Some legal systems required the executive branch to use emergency powers to justify these restrictions on rights, the reallocation of budgets, and the extraordinary use of military support. Most, if not all, governments operated within an emergency regime in practice.[5] Decisions were supposed to prioritise the population's health over individual rights. Typically, the literature on emergency powers has claimed that a Schmittian and post-Madisonian approach to using emergency powers implies the emergence of an unbounded executive branch that can hardly be constrained.[6] The measures of 'de-juridification', which are supposed to be temporary,[7] can become permanent without justification,[8] despite sunset

[4] See, eg, A Spadaro, 'COVID-19: Testing the Limits of Human Rights' (2020) 11 *European Journal of Risk Regulation* 317. More generally on how states of exception are at odds with individual rights, see D Dyzenhaus, *The Constitution of Law: Legality in a Time of Emergency* (Cambridge, Cambridge University Press, 2006).

[5] Some political leaders, notably in Latin America, had only declared states of emergency but operated as if they had the powers that the state of siege (a more extreme regime involving more powers for the executive branch) would bestow. See R Gargarella, 'Democracy and Emergency in Latin America' in MP Maduro and PW Kahn (eds), *Democracy in Times of Pandemic. Different Futures Imagined* (Cambridge, Cambridge University Press, 2020) 68–69.

[6] See T Ginsburg and M Versteeg, 'The Bound Executive: Emergency Powers during the Pandemic' (2021) 19 *International Journal of Constitutional Law* 1498.

[7] A Kouroutakis and S Ranchordás, 'Snoozing Democracy: Sunset Clauses, De-Juridification, and Emergencies' (2016) 25 *Minnesota Journal of International Law* 29.

[8] See, eg, JE Finn, 'Sunset Clauses and Democratic Deliberation: Assessing the Significance of Sunset Provisions in Antiterrorism Legislation' (2010) 48 *Columbia Journal of Transnational Law* 442.

clauses supposed to minimise the risk of abuse of authority[9] and explicit constitutional regulations restricting the period during which emergency powers can be used.[10]

Even though constraining the executive branch is possible – and common,[11] as the Brazilian Parliament and judges facing President Bolsonaro's policies illustrate[12] – nobody seems to challenge the idea that the executive branch tends to become stronger in these kinds of emergencies, often at the expense of the other branches of government. Parliaments generally lack the necessary speed and technical capacity to make quick and well-planned decisions. Citizens and legislators typically look to the executive branch officers and ask them to provide solutions. In this context, legislatures could – and perhaps should – become less relevant than in normal times. Regarding the pandemic, the legislature's role was partly relegated to the crucial task of maintaining some oversight of the executive branch's actions.

Abusive behaviours, including political self-entrenchment, are a natural threat to democratic regimes when a crisis calls for the use of emergency powers.[13] The legality of the measures taken in times of crisis is a question that frequently remains open.[14] Executive officers could be tempted to use their emergency powers to placate protests, restrict the freedom of speech of their opponents, seize the opportunity to give themselves more power, control the media – as in Greece[15] – pass political reforms that could infringe judicial independence, or reduce the power of sitting legislators – as arguably happened in Israel[16] – and so on. An important example was Hungarian Prime Minister Viktor Orbán's 'Enabling Act', which

[9] A Kouroutakis, 'The Virtues of Sunset Clauses in Relation to Constitutional Authority' (2020) 41 *Statute Law Review* 16.

[10] See different types of regulations in J Ferejohn and P Pasquino, 'The Law of the Exception: A Typology of Emergency Powers' (2004) 2 *International Journal of Constitutional Law* 210.

[11] Ginsburg and Versteeg (n 6).

[12] See EPN Meyer and T Bustamante, 'COVID-19 in Brazil: A Sick Constitutional Democracy' [2021] *VerfBlog* verfassungsblog.de/covid-19-in-brazil-a-sick-constitutional-democracy/ (accessed 17 January 2023). See also, EPN Meyer, ULSilvério dos Reis and B Braga de Castro, 'Courts and COVID-19: An Assessment of Countries Dealing with Democratic Erosion' [2023] *Jus Cogens* link.springer.com/10.1007/s42439-023-00072-1 (accessed 17 January 2023).

[13] Also, see how populist and illiberal theories can be used to justify autocratic measures in the context of the Pandemic. G Halmai, 'The Pandemic and Illiberal Constitutional Theories' in MC Kettermann and K Lachmayer (eds), *Pandemocracy in Europe. Power, Parliaments and People in Times of COVID-19* (Oxford, Hart Publishing, 2021).

[14] See, eg, R Valutyté, D Jociené and R Azubalyté, 'Legality of Human Rights Restrictions During the COVID-19 Pandemic Under the European Convention on Human Rights' (2021) 26 *Tilburg Law Review* 1.

[15] A Kouroutakis, 'Abuse of Power and Self-Entrenchment as a State Response to the COVID-19 Outbreak: The Role of Parliaments, Courts and the People' in MC Kettermann and K Lachmayer (eds), *Pandemocracy in Europe. Power, Parliaments and People in Times of COVID-19* (Oxford, Hart Publishing, 2021) 39.

[16] See N Mordechay and Y Roznai, 'Constitutional Crisis in Israel: Coronavirus, Interbranch Conflict, and Dynamic Judicial Review' [2020] *VerfBlog* verfassungsblog.de/constitutional-crisis-in-israel-coronavirus-interbranch-conflict-and-dynamic-judicial-review/ (accessed 17 January 2023).

gave him unlimited regulatory powers.[17] He could renew his decrees, prohibiting Parliament from revising the powers it had just delegated to Orbán, except by a two-third vote after the 'state of danger' ended. Before the Enabling Act was enacted, Orbán used the pandemic crisis to appoint military officers in charge of strategic companies and to control information, and passed a modification to the criminal code allowing the prosecution of anyone disseminating 'untrue fact or any misrepresented true fact' about the pandemic, among other examples.[18] Legislators are required to demand the preservation of core constitutional principles that could prevent the country from diminishing its democratic institutions but, as in Hungary, those legislators may not have the necessary majorities to act.

In those cases where presidents did not do enough or even opposed taking measures recommended by the scientific community, they were to blame for the rapid spread of the pandemic and the opportunistic use of the means they had at their disposal. This happened, for example, when President Trump used the medical supplies' reserve to benefit states with Republican governors and gave less help to states run by Democratic governors[19] or when he ordered his name to be printed on the memos of checks issued to help millions of Americans, in order to receive the credit for the Congress statute regulating the COVID-19 relief package.[20]

Commentators distinguish between the types of executive branch engagement with the pandemic as 'executive overreach' and 'executive underreach'.[21] The former fits with governments aggrandizing their power positions. The latter consists of leaders refusing to pursue a plan to mitigate the threat when they possess all the required information and have the authority to do something about it. Either way, the political responsibility is usually allocated to the executive branch officers, who could use the crises triggered by the pandemic as an excuse to implement opportunistic decisions at the expense of legislatures and the opposition and could also fail to deal with the pandemic's consequences successfully.[22]

Even though the oversight role of parliaments was not an easy task to achieve, it was crucial. It could prevent or denounce abuses of power,[23] and arguably help

[17] See, eg, JHH Weiler, 'COVID, Europe, and the Self-Asphyxiation of Democracy' in MP Maduro and PW Kahn (eds), *Democracy in Times of Pandemic. Different Futures Imagined* (Cambridge, Cambridge University Press, 2020) 141–144.

[18] See KL Scheppele and D Pozen, 'Executive Overreach and Underreach in the Pandemic' in MP Maduro and PW Kahn (eds), *Democracy in Times of Pandemic. Different Futures Imagined* (Cambridge, Cambridge University Press, 2020) 40–43.

[19] ibid 44.

[20] Kouroutakis (n 15) 37.

[21] Scheppele and Pozen (n 18).

[22] As Neil Walker has argued, the crisis of democratic leadership feeds into and feeds off the crisis of the COVID-19 Pandemic. See N Walker, 'The Crisis of Democratic Leadership in Times of Pandemic' in MP Maduro and PW Kahn (eds), *Democracy in Times of Pandemic. Different Futures Imagined* (Cambridge, Cambridge University Press, 2020).

[23] For a map of the types of oversight that parliaments have developed during the pandemic in the context of executive branch dominance, see E Griglio, 'Parliamentary Oversight under the COVID-19 Emergency: Striving against Executive Dominance' (2020) 8 *The Theory and Practice of Legislation* 49.

legitimise the reasonable measures taken to deal with the consequences of the pandemic.[24] Paralysing parliaments – and judicial scrutiny – should never be justified, even in an emergency.[25] But parliaments faced many challenges:[26] First, they needed to continue operating under unfavourable conditions. Adopting digital alternatives that could allow them to adapt to the new working conditions was not always an obvious solution: sometimes, there are rules requiring a physical presence, mandatory quorum requirements, and political practices that are hard to change. Second, the centralisation of authority in the executive branch could encourage the evasion of parliamentary scrutiny and the circumvention of the powers of legislators, reducing the ability of parliaments to check the exercise of power by administrative agencies and other officers of the executive branch. Third, legislatures sometimes lacked the information to perform their checking function correctly. Fourth, the executive branch can control the legislature and discourage legislators from exercising their checking powers effectively.[27]

Examples abound. In Italy, the Parliament was marginalised, and the checking mechanisms against executive actions were reduced significantly, including lowering standards for accountability and transparency.[28] In the US, most measures came from executive officers with 'sketchy authorization in existing statutes, and with little control in issuance'.[29] In France, all relevant measures were decided by the President in a centralised way while dislocating the ordinary decision-making processes and weakening democratic bodies,[30] and the main check turned out to be criminal law investigations.[31]

[24] J Petrov, 'The COVID-19 Emergency in the Age of Executive Aggrandizement: What Role for Legislative and Judicial Checks?' (2020) 8 *The Theory and Practice of Legislation* 71. For a similar argument looking at the case of Switzerland, it could be argued that parliaments can – or should – become more relevant when the measures adopted to deal with the emergency last for too long. The longer they last, the more involvement parliaments should have. See F Uhlmann and E Scheifele, 'Legislative Response to Coronavirus (Switzerland)' (2020) 8 *The Theory and Practice of Legislation* 115; O Ammann and F Uhlmann, 'Switzerland: The (Missing) Role of Parliament in Times of Crisis' in MC Kettermann and K Lachmayer (eds), *Pandemocracy in Europe. Power, Parliaments and People in Times of COVID-19* (Oxford, Hart Publishing, 2021).

[25] See an argument in K Lachmayer, 'Democracy, Death and Dying: The Potential and Limits of Legal Rationalisation' in MC Kettermann and K Lachmayer (eds), *Pandemocracy in Europe. Power, Parliaments and People in Times of COVID-19* (Oxford, Hart Publishing, 2021).

[26] At some point, parliaments were shut down or their operations substantially limited for more than 2 billion people around the world. See C Provost, N Acher and L Namubiru, 'Alarm as 2 Billion People Have Parliaments Shut or Limited by COVID-19' www.opendemocracy.net/en/5050/alarm-two-billion-people-have-parliaments-suspended-or-limited-covid-19/ (accessed 17 January 2023).

[27] Also, I Bar-Siman-Tov, 'COVID-19 Meets Politics: The Novel Coronavirus as a Novel Challenge for Legislatures' (2020) 8 *The Theory and Practice of Legislation* 11.

[28] A Vedaschi, 'The Marginalization of Parliament in Facing the Coronavirus Emergency: What about Democracy in Italy?' in MC Kettermann and K Lachmayer (eds), *Pandemocracy in Europe. Power, Parliaments and People in Times of COVID-19* (Oxford, Hart Publishing, 2021).

[29] JR Maxeiner, 'America's COVID-19 Preexisting Vulnerability: A Government of Men, Not Laws' (2020) 8 *The Theory and Practice of Legislation* 213.

[30] S Brunet and F Gárdos-Orosz, 'The Hyper-Executive State of Emergency in France' in MC Kettermann and K Lachmayer (eds), *Pandemocracy in Europe. Power, Parliaments and People in Times of COVID-19* (Oxford, Hart Publishing, 2022).

[31] O Beaud, 'From Political Accountability to Criminal Liability: The Strange Case of French Penal Populism' in MP Maduro and PW Kahn (eds), *Democracy in Times of Pandemic. Different Futures Imagined* (Cambridge, Cambridge University Press, 2020).

Given the facts described above, it should come as no surprise that parliaments became less politically salient during the pandemic, and that the main risk of democratic erosion came from the likely aggrandizement of the executive branch's power. However, Chile was different. The next sections will explain how Congress became the main protagonist of politics while the President lost political power. Even though the reasons are mainly associated with context-dependent factors, there are lessons to learn from the Chilean case, as I will briefly explain in the final section.

III. Chile's 2019 Social Outburst and the Pandemic as an Opportunity for President Piñera

In October 2019, before the pandemic hit Chile, massive demonstrations took over the streets, with protesters calling for the protection of a heterogenous set of social demands. The demonstrations started with a group of students protesting against the rise in the price of the Santiago metro ticket. Other groups quickly joined, and more demands were made: protests against the social security system, the healthcare system, and the problems of housing and education were joined by hundreds of thousands of Chileans and took over the streets, arguably fuelling the demand for a constitutional replacement that could recognise social rights.[32] Episodes of unjustified violence took place, and the Piñera administration's response was both severe and flawed. The President quickly used his emergency powers[33] and ordered the armed forces to help control the violence. But the situation got out of control. Human rights abuses were committed, and the protestors were not placated. Many people demanded the President's resignation, and violent groups threatened to break into government buildings and the President's private residence.

Even though the President offered a package deal to improve a range of social rights areas, and gave a symbolic gesture of unity by inviting the presidents of all branches to give a joint statement, it was too late for him to control the situation. After a meeting in his private residence, one of the secretaries of state announced that the government would support a constitution-making process and called political parties to initiate negotiations in Congress. It was implied that the President would endorse a multi-party agreement and that he would not lead the process. It was a way of saving Piñera's administration. It was also an implied recognition of political defeat for Piñera's supporting coalition, as they had previously opposed a constitutional replacement.[34]

[32] On how the social demands could join into a shared demand for constitutional replacement, see J Suarez-Cao, 'Reconstructing Legitimacy After Crisis: The Chilean Path to a New Constitution' (2021) 13 *Hague Journal on the Rule of Law*.

[33] Decree 472, Ministry of Interior, October 2019.

[34] See the reasons why the right-wing parties endorsed the agreement for a new constitution in MC Escudero, 'Making a Constituent Assembly in Chile: The Shifting Costs of Opposing Change' [2021] *Bulletin of Latin American Research*.

In November 2019, most political parties agreed to open a constitution-making process, and soon thereafter;[35] in December, Congress passed a constitutional amendment to ensure that the process could happen legally.[36] Even though it is possible that President Piñera tried to influence the design of the rules for the constitution-making procedure, he could only have done so from behind the scenes. He faced enormous pressure not to intervene. It was time for Congress to act and for the President to step back.

Even though it was unlikely that replacing the Constitution would solve many of the problems denounced by the protests in the short term,[37] it was still a popular demand that had long ranked high in the polls.[38] The existing Constitution was still connected to the Pinochet dictatorship, some argued that it did not protect enough social rights Chileans care about, and others claimed that it prevented majority rule from actually deciding relevant policies.[39] Previous attempts at replacing the 1980 Constitution had failed symbolically (2005)[40] or politically (2017),[41] so the question of whether Chile should change its Constitution – and how – remained open. The political system evidenced high levels of legislative gridlock and not enough incentives to build the necessary majorities to pass relevant social reforms.[42]

In this context, along with the declining approval ratings of President Piñera[43] and his inability to set the agenda of the constitution-making process, Congress became the primary actor in Chilean politics, perhaps only behind the social movements that were leading the protests in the streets.

When COVID-19 hit the country in March 2020, President Piñera had a unique opportunity to show strong leadership and recover his influence. He certainly had

[35] See a helpful summary in J Couso, 'Chile's 'Procedurally Regulated' Constitution-Making Process' (2021) 13 *Hague Journal on the Rule of Law* 235.

[36] On the rules of the constitution-making process, see M Prieto and S Verdugo, 'How Political Narratives Affect the Self-Enforcing Nature of Interim Constitutions' (2021) 13 *Hague Journal on the Rule of Law* 265.

[37] I have discussed this elsewhere. See R Dixon and S Verdugo, 'Los derechos sociales y la reforma constitucional en Chile: hacia una implementación híbrida, legislativa y judicial' (2021) 162 *Estudios Públicos* 31.

[38] PNUD, *Opinión Ciudadana y Cambio Constitucional. Análisis Desde La Opinión Pública* (Programa de Naciones Unidas Para el Desarrollo 2015).

[39] See, eg, F Atria, *La Constitución Tramposa* (LOM, 2013); F Atria et al., *El Otro Modelo* (Debate, 2013); C Huneeus, *La Democracia Semisoberana. Chile Después de Pinochet* (Taurus, 2014).

[40] See some explanations on why the 2005 reform was passed in F Uggla, "For a Few Senators More'? Negotiating Constitutional Changes During Chile's Transition To Democracy' (2005) 47 *Latin American Politics and Society* 51; C Fuentes, 'Shifting the Status Quo: Constitutional Reforms in Chile' (2015) 57 *Latin American Politics and Society* 99.

[41] See S Verdugo and J Contesse, 'Auge y Caída de un Proceso Constituyente: Lecciones del Experimento Chileno y del Fracaso del Proyecto de Bachelet' (2018) 4 *Derecho y Crítica Social* 139; F Muñoz, 'Crítica del Imaginario Histórico del Proceso Constituyente de Bachelet' (2018) 4 *Derecho y Crítica Social* 149.

[42] See S Verdugo, 'On the Protests and Riots in Chile: Why Chile Should Modify Its Presidential System' [2019] *International Journal of Constitutional Law Blog* www.iconnectblog.com/2019/10/on-the-protests-and-riots-in-chile-why-chile-should-modify-its-presidential-system/ (accessed 17 January 2023).

[43] cadem.cl/plaza-publica/.

a range of legal tools at his disposal. Compared to US presidents, Chilean presidents have a large set of powers to influence legislation with mechanisms such as exclusive legislative initiative in matters requiring public spending,[44] and the ability to accelerate legislative debates and force legislators to vote on specific Bills.[45] The Constitution also gives the President explicit emergency powers[46] and broad sub-statutory regulatory authority.[47] The Health Code gives wide-ranging legal authority to the President, who can take extraordinary measures that do not require congressional consent. As a result, for many matters, the President did not need to use his emergency powers – often subject to congressional control – because it was legally sufficient to invoke the infra-constitutional regulations.[48]

Moreover, courts were generally deferential to the powers of the President;[49] many rules enacted by the executive branch were not subject to administrative review;[50] and the Comptroller General – an independent agency that oversees the legality of executive orders and other norms enacted by executive branch officers – protected the President's powers by limiting the local governments' regulatory capacity to engage with the pandemic.[51] In this context, we might have expected the President to use the situation to placate the protests, seize the opportunity to regain control over the country's political agenda, and show the public that his government was capable of protecting the citizens in challenging times while improving the President's approval ratings.[52] The opportunity to get his government back on track was certainly there, and the attempt was evident. But he failed.

When Piñera's Secretary of Health announced that the Pandemic was pushing the government to postpone the *entry plebiscite* – the referendum that was going to decide whether Chile would change its Constitution – legislators made it clear that any political decision on the issue would first be discussed

[44] See the Chilean Constitution, Art 65.

[45] ibid, Art 74.

[46] ibid, Arts 39–45.

[47] See an explanation of the regulatory framework to engage with the crisis in G Jiménez, PG Hidalgo and P Marshall, 'Chile: Legal Response to COVID-19' in J King and O Ferraz (eds), *The Oxford Compendium of National Legal Responses to COVID-19* (Oxford, Oxford University Press, 2021).

[48] See, in particular, Art 36 of the Health Code.

[49] See, eg, J Contesse, 'Exceptional Regulations for an Exceptional Moment: The Law and Politics of COVID-19 in Chile' (2021) 73 *Administrative Law Review* 121, 127–130.

[50] Exempted resolutions are not reviewed by the Comptroller General, and the government released more than 100 in 2020. See Jiménez, Grez Hidalgo and Marshall (n 47) 21.

[51] General Comptroller, Dictamen N° E8935: www.contraloria.cl/pdfbuscador/dictamenes/0E8935N20/html (accessed 17 January 2023).

[52] It could be argued that the President's emergency powers and the infra-constitutional regulations empowering the executive branch were hardly compatible with the Constitution. See, eg FS Barrientos, DE Cáceres and FR Wittwer, 'El Tratamiento de Los Desastres Socio-Naturales: Antecedentes y Desafíos Ante El Debate Constituyente En Chile' (2022) 20 *Estudios Constitucionales* 81. Still, those concerns did not play a role in explaining why the President lost influence in engaging with the pandemic. From a purely legal perspective, it is safe to say that the President was the most important legislator. But only legally.

by Congress.[53] The major political defeat suffered during the social outburst could never be overcome.

IV. Towards a 'De Facto' Parliamentary Regime?

After the political crisis started, President Piñera was in a weak political position. He lacked majority support in Congress, and the President of the Medical Association, Izkia Siches – who would then become President Boric's Minister of Interior – became a key opponent of the government. Like other rising political and social leaders, Siches used her influence and media presence to force the government to enact radically restrictive measures involving lockdowns, travel restrictions, and business limitations. The government had created a 'social roundtable' to collect advice on how to deal with the pandemic, and that roundtable also incorporated opponents of the government, including Siches – who typically published the minutes of each session.[54] Piñera's Minister of Health, who had initially opposed the strong measures suggested by the scientific community and was in a permanent struggle with Siches, was impeached by the lower chamber of Congress and eventually resigned.

Impeachment occurred frequently in Chilean politics during the pandemic. As the approval ratings of the President and his government fell,[55] so too did the political costs of calling for impeachment.[56] The opposition even attempted to impeach President Piñera twice. One of those impeachments occurred after a political scandal involving Piñera's family and a personal friend in a business decision related to a mining project that was contingent on the approval of permits.[57] The opposition also made nine impeachment bids against executive branch senior officers.[58] Even though most of these impeachments did not end up in the subjects being removed from office, they achieved the purpose of putting pressure on the government, prevented the government from controlling the public agenda, and frequently ended with a resignation of a crucial government official. Perhaps the most critical impeachment bid was that against Piñera's Minister of the Interior,

[53] It is therefore surprising that some scholars have used this episode to claim that it is an example of how President Piñera used the COVID-19 pandemic as an excuse to postpone the referendum when the new date, decided by Congress, only harmed the electoral possibilities of Piñera's supporting coalition. Contrary to this position, see Gargarella (n 5) 74.

[54] Jiménez, Grez Hidalgo and Marshall (n 47) 46.

[55] The approval rating of President Piñera was 14% in October 2019 and 9% in April 2021 (Cadem.cl. Encuesta Cadem.).

[56] See an explanation in CA Martínez and AL Olivares, 'Chile 2021: Entre un Intenso Calendario Electoral y la Acusación Constitucional en Contra de Sebastián Piñera' (2022) 42 *Revista de ciencia política* (Santiago) 225.

[57] ibid 245–246.

[58] Compared to previous administrations, nine is a particularly high number: previous administrations received two (2014–2018), four (2010–2014) and one impeachment challenge (2006–2010). See observatoriocongreso.cl/acusaciones-constitucionales/ (accessed 17 January 2023).

the most important officer of the executive branch after the President. The Senate approved that impeachment, and Congress succeeded in removing the minister in question. Impeachment was not the opposition's only mechanism to destabilize the Piñera administration. For example, in the short time between May 2020 and October 2020, the lower chamber of Congress established five commissions to investigate irregularities.[59]

The government's low popularity ratings did not help Piñera's supporting coalition from an electoral point of view, as the pandemic years were a bad time for the coalition's electoral performance. The alliance was defeated during the entry plebiscite of 2020; it suffered significant defeats during the 2020 regional elections; it was heavily defeated during the election of the Convention members in 2021 – losing its veto power in the Convention – and it did not win the first round of the Presidential elections in 2021. Piñera was unable to secure the election of an ally as his successor.[60] As the mainstream parties of the right weakened, new competing parties appealing to right-wing voters started to grow – that is, the *Partido Republicano* and the *Partido de la Gente*. President Piñera's supporting coalition also began to lose discipline. Several mayors openly criticised Piñera and enacted illegal rules to deal with the pandemic,[61] while many legislators from the right supported proposals from the left aimed at using pension savings to deal with the economic hardships of the pandemic – I will come back to this issue in the next section.

Unlike other right-wing governments that tried to be soft on the measures taken to protect their pro-business narratives, the Piñera administration became particularly harsh. The measures adopted by the government during the pandemic seemed to be primarily driven by the pressure put on the government by the opposition. If the government received criticism, it was because its measures were not strong enough. In the end, the main body checking the government and discussing the most critical measures to deal with the relief packages of the economic crisis was Congress, even if, at least from a purely legal perspective, Congress did not have many powers and only the President could initiate legislative Bills authorising public spending.

Legislators routinely demanded that the executive branch increase the relief packages, and the government typically tried to meet Congress in the middle. The government's emergency family income proposal (*Ingreso Familiar de Emergencia*) was a crucial example. The opposition parties partially rejected the emergency income proposal on the grounds that the proposed funding was insufficient, forcing President Piñera to use his veto power,[62] and later expand the financing of the emergency income. Additional funding was even later made available as

[59] Jiménez, Grez Hidalgo and Marshall (n 47) 31.
[60] See the electoral results in www.servel.cl (accessed 17 January 2023).
[61] Contesse (n 49) 126.
[62] Lovera and Valdés (n 3) 46.

part of an agreement between Piñera's secretary of finance and Congress's finance committee.[63] Another example involves a deal that the government made with electricity companies. The government was trying to prevent any suspension of services due to outstanding payments by private individuals so that Chileans could continue using electricity, and the companies had agreed to the postponement of payments.[64] However, legislators had presented other Bills on the matter, rejected Piñera's proposal, and passed a law after overriding the President's veto.[65]

Legislators started to initiate Bills in subjects where they were not supposed to act. According to the Chilean Constitution, a crucial aspect of the Chilean hyper-presidential regime is that a number of matters – including spending, creating new public organs, social security, labour law regulations, and taxes – can only be regulated by laws initiated by the President and not legislators.[66] Had legislators initiated these matters in the past, they should have had the sponsorship of the President, or otherwise their Bills would have been considered unconstitutional.[67] Moreover, omnibus legislation is highly discouraged by the Chilean Constitution, as legislators do not have – in theory – the formal authority to make or influence proposals on these subject matters.[68] They are only supposed to approve or reject what the President presents to them.[69] These rules aim to strengthen the President's power and face the problems of logrolling and omnibus Bills while allocating political accountability to the executive branch and discouraging legislators' rent-seeking behaviour.[70] The Constitutional Court has explicit powers to review legislative proposals that could violate the Constitution.[71] The President, or a legislative minority, has the authority to petition a declaration of unconstitutionality to the Constitutional Court.[72]

Parliamentary practices questioned all these sets of institutional arrangements, as politicians from the opposition had openly violated these rules, often claiming that it was more important to respond to social demands than to respect the

[63] Jiménez, Grez Hidalgo and Marshall (n 47) 91.

[64] ibid 99–100.

[65] See Law 21, 249.

[66] Chilean Constitution, Art 65.

[67] See a description of Congressional decision-making procedures and the authority of the President in SS Velasco, *Congreso Nacional y Proceso Legislativo* (Thomson Reuters – P Universidad Católica de Chile, 2015).

[68] Chilean Constitution, Art 69.

[69] On the origin of these rules, see A Fermandois and J García, 'Origen Del Presidencialismo Chileno: Reforma Constitucional de 1970. Ideas Matrices e Iniciativa Legislativa Exclusiva' (2009) 36 *Revista Chilena de Derecho* 281.

[70] See CA Geywitz, *Elementos de Derecho Constitucional Chileno* (Santiago, Editorial Jurídica de Chile, 1971); JAT Valdés, *La Técnica Legislativa* (Santiago, Editorial Jurídica de Chile, 1960); G Piedrabuena, *La Reforma Constitucional* (Ediciones Encina 1970).

[71] Chilean Constitution, Art 93.

[72] In the past, the Constitutional Court has been a reliable protector of the legislative powers of the President. See J García and S Verdugo, 'El Respeto Por Las Ideas Matrices de Los Proyectos de Ley. Estudio de La Jurisprudencia Del Tribunal Constitucional' in *Congreso Nacional. Libro en Homenaje al Profesor Alejandro Silva Bascuñán* (Editorial Jurídica de Chile – Asociación Chilena de Derecho Constitucional, 2013).

Constitution, and the government rarely brought a case to the Constitutional Court – I will show an example in the next section. A statement by Adriana Muñoz, then the President of the Senate, claimed that she preferred to 'commit a sacrilege against the constitution and be removed from her position rather than to ignore an urgent social demand'.[73] The government voiced its concern against the unconstitutional parliamentary practices by suggesting the creation of a committee to examine whether Bills presented by legislators fulfilled the constitutional requirements,[74] but that initiative failed.

Legislators breaking the constitutional rules attempted to control the social agenda related to the pandemic and also to the social demands that had come to the fore during the 2019 demonstrations. For example, they discussed proposals to establish a universal minimum income,[75] expand the mining permits (a royalty tax),[76] suspend gasoline and petrol taxes,[77] establish free transportation during electoral periods,[78] and create a wealth tax against the rich.[79] These types of legislative proposals violated the President's legislative powers as specified in the Constitution, while shifting the agenda-setting power from the executive branch to Congress. Some of these proposals were indeed rejected on the grounds that they were unconstitutional,[80] but the reality is that they triggered political debates that the President could not win. One important Bill that was questioned because of who initiated it but was nevertheless approved – among others by votes from the parties of Piñera's supporting coalition – was the expansion of maternity leave benefits.[81] In the end, as some observers commented, at 'times, the executive has lost control of the legislative process – it has suffered landslide government defeats over social and employment protection measures, and key private members' bills on this subject matter have gained precedence over governmental bills'.[82]

In addition to all the rules enacted to regulate the constitution-making process and all the necessary reforms to adapt the process to the social demands – which included the enactment of additional reforms to help adjust the new constitution-making process to the pandemic, pass a gender-parity rule for the electoral process

[73] Latercera.com, La polémica alocución de la presidenta del Senado en debate por postnatal: Prefiero cometer un sacrilegio con la Constitución y ser destituida que pasar por sobre una demanda urgente de las madres, 03 de junio de 2020.

[74] Lovera and Valdés (n 3) 49.

[75] 'Procedencia de una renta básica universal de emergencia' (Boletín N°14.2228-07).

[76] 'Compensación a favor del Estado por la explotación de la minería del cobre y litio (Royalty Minero)' (Boletín N°12.093-08).

[77] 'Suspensión del impuesto específico de gasolinas de automotrices y petróleo diesel' (Boletín N°14.210-07).

[78] 'Postergación de las elecciones en consideración a la pandemia, donde el problema estuvo en una indicación parlamentaria cuyo objetivo era establecer la gratuidad del transporte pública durante esos días' (Boletín N°14.138-07).

[79] 'Impuesto al patrimonio' (Boletín N°13.555-07).

[80] Lovera and Valdés (n 3) 45–46.

[81] ibid 46.

[82] Jiménez, Grez Hidalgo and Marshall (n 47) 81.

of the Convention and allow for reserved seats for indigenous peoples, among others[83] – Congress became the primary institution discussing the economic measures taken to deal with the pandemic. This was an unprecedented change in Chile's political history, since the executive branch typically becomes the centre of dealing with deep crises, as had happened, for example, during the 2010 earthquake, when Congress merely supported all measures and emergency powers ('estado de catástrofe') invoked by the President.

How Congress handled the legislative agenda at the expense of the President's powers triggered a debate about how the balance of power was changing. Some started to speak about the existence of a 'de facto parliamentary regime'. Senator Jaime Quintana, for example, declared that the government had failed to face a series of challenges and that 'even though I do not like unconstitutional legislative bills and I am no promoter of a de facto parliamentary regime, I am merely recognizing it'.[84] To be sure, Chile retained a presidential regime – no prime minister was appointed, presidential elections were held separately, etc – but the existence of the debate on the political regime is a helpful illustration of how the balance of political power was perceived at that time. Though it is probably too hasty to claim that a de facto parliamentary regime has replaced the presidential regime, it is clear that the most powerful institutional actor in dealing with the pandemic was not the President. The following section shows how this problem occurred in the most important political struggle in dealing with the pandemic: whether Chileans should be allowed to withdraw their retirement pension savings to alleviate the economic difficulties triggered by the pandemic.

V. Congressional Aggrandizement and the Battle Over Retirement Pension Savings

Arguably the most important example of how the balance of power shifted after October 2019 was the way institutions handled the issue of whether the withdrawal of retirement saving funds should be used to ease the financial hardship of those in need. Before explaining the conflict, some context information is required. Under Chilean law, everyone must save part of their income to build an individual pension fund that can then be used to pay for retirement pensions after the person retires. The funds were managed by private entities that took a commission for administration. People could not use these funds before retiring. This system reproduced the labour market problems and ended up triggering highly unequal

[83] See S Issacharoff and S Verdugo, 'The Uncertain Future of Constitutional Democracy in the Era of Populism: Chile and Beyond' papers.ssrn.com/sol3/papers.cfm?abstract_id=4323864 (accessed 17 January 2023).

[84] Emol.com, Senador Quintana (PPD) dice que 'parlamentarismo de facto' se da debido a la 'ausencia' del Gobierno, 18 de noviembre de 2020.

pensions.[85] Large protests against the Chilean social security system took place before the 2019 social outburst,[86] even though the outburst helped to highlight those protests and the system became widely unpopular.[87]

The discussion on whether it made sense to use retirement savings to help deal with the economic crisis associated with the pandemic, was critical not only because of what it meant for Chileans seeking economic relief but also because of three additional reasons: first, as matters of social security can only be regulated by laws initiated by the President, the discussion could have involved a challenge against President Piñera's formal legislative powers in a way that resembled the debates explained in the previous section.[88] Second, the discussion also affected the politically salient debate on the possible reforms of the unpopular social security system, as it threatened its financial sustainability. As the main foundations of the social security system are arguably recognised in the Constitution,[89] withdrawing the funds also involved highlighting substantive criticisms against the Constitution. Endorsing the protesters complaining against the system was attractive for politicians trying to appear to be responsive to the social demands that fuelled the protests of 2019. Third, one of the associated strategies to allow the withdrawal of those funds consisted of including a transitory clause to the Constitution. As proponents of that amendment had argued that they only needed the approval of three-fifths of legislators – instead of the more difficult two-thirds majority that the Constitution requires for amending specific chapters – setting a political precedent on how low the legislative majorities could be for approving transitory constitutional clauses could pave the way for enabling more reforms to the regulations of the constitution-making process.

Legislators succeeded in allowing people to withdraw 10 per cent of their pension savings three times.[90] The first case involved the existence of two Bills introduced to Congress. One of these proposed amending the Constitution to authorise the withdrawal with a temporary norm, and the other proposed a

[85] Public spending in Chile is equivalent to 2.9% of the gross domestic product, compared to an average among OECD countries of 8%. OECD, 'Pensions at a Glance 2019: Country Profiles – Chile' (2019): www.oecd.org/els/public-pensions/PAG2019-country-pro!le-Chile.pdf (accessed 17 January 2023). Also, see I Madero-Cabib et al., 'Private Pension Systems Built on Precarious Foundations: A Cohort Study of Labor-Force Trajectories in Chile' (2019) 41 *Research on Aging* 961.

[86] On the demands for removing those privately-run companies, see JR Bugueño and A Maillet, 'Entre Marchas, Plebiscitos e Iniciativas de Ley: Innovación En El Repertorio de Estrategias Del Movimiento No Más AFP En Chile (2014–2018)' (2019) 48 *Izquierdas* scielo.conicyt.cl/scielo.php?script=sci_arttext&pid=S0718-50492019000400001 (accessed 17 January 2023).

[87] In December 2019, 94% of Chileans wanted to reform the privately-run companies that manage the savings. (Cnnchile.com, Cadem: 94% de los chilenos cree necesario una reforma a las AFP y Piñera sigue con 80% de desaprobación, 30 de diciembre de 2019).

[88] I have explained this at greater length elsewhere. See M Poehls and S Verdugo, 'Auge y Caída de las Reformas Constitucionales Inconstitucionales en Chile. Comentario a las Sentencias del Tribunal Constitucional roles 9797-2020 y 10.774-2021' [2022] *Anuario de Derecho Público UDP* 263.

[89] See one argument, eg, in RM Pessoa, 'La Vulneración al Mínimo Vital En El Sistema de Seguridad Social Chileno' (2019) 29 *Revista Latinoamericana de Derecho Social* 219.

[90] See, boletines N°13.950-07, 14.054-07, 14.095-07 y 14.210-07, and Laws 21,330, 21,248, 21,306.

regular legislative Bill. As only the President could legally initiate Bills involving modifications to the social security system, the Bills presented by legislators were unconstitutional, and President Piñera did not even need – in theory – to veto them. The Constitutional Court could theoretically stop legislators from enacting an unconstitutional statute. Many thought that these popular proposals, even if harmful to the long-term pension savings of Chilean employees,[91] could be used to spur the reforming of the social security system.

President Piñera opposed the withdrawal of the retirement savings but acted pragmatically. It was not only against the policies that typically right-wing politicians had advocated in Chile – by defending the privately-run companies that manage the retirement savings – but it was also a policy that was going to harm those retiring in the future and possibly set a political precedent that could reduce the President's control over norms regulating the constitution-making process. It was a policy most notably promoted by Pamela Jiles, a populist and radical anti-party celebrity who had been elected as a member of the Chamber of Deputies.

Still, whether supportive of Jiles or not, most legislators – even from the right-wing coalition – could not resist championing a popular policy against an unpopular system. Even when economists from all sides of the political spectrum opposed it on economic grounds – for example, it was going to create inflation, weaken the pension funds in the future, etc.[92] – Jiles and her allies got the votes to approve an amendment adding a temporary norm to the Constitution, to allow the withdrawal and to approve the regular norm.

The President probably did not want to oppose the policy explicitly. Instead of using his veto power, he bargained with legislators. His strategy was to get the Constitutional Court to declare the unconstitutionality of the amendment while simultaneously supporting the legislative proposal after legislators had modified it to reduce its wider consequences.[93] He also advocated adding taxation and limits to the withdrawal. That way, at least, he could fight for a more targeted policy without allowing the political precedent of using constitutional amendments against his will.[94] The Constitutional Court declared that the proposed constitutional amendment was unconstitutional in a controversial and divided decision that introduced the unconstitutional constitutional amendment doctrine in Chile.[95] Even though the President won the case in the Court, the controversy came at great political cost for President Piñera and his coalition. It is what partly explained the poor electoral performance

[91] Even the current President, Gabriel Boric, who at that time was part of the Chamber of Deputies and opposed President Piñera, has changed his mind and currently disagrees with the policy. He also appointed a secretary of finance who had, in the past, openly disagreed with it.

[92] See, eg, www.bbc.com/mundo/noticias-america-latina-55433497 (accessed 17 January 2023).

[93] See Law 21,306.

[94] See Law 21,295.

[95] Tribunal Constitucional, 9797-2020, 30-12-2020. On the limited way the Court had considered this theory in the past, see S Verdugo, 'The Role of the Chilean Constitutional Court in Times of Change' in R Albert, C Bernal and JZ Benvindo (eds), *Constitutional Change and Transformation in Latin America* (Oxford, Hart Publishing, 2019).

of the right-wing coalition during the electoral process of the Constitutional Convention. The President also became irrelevant during the Convention's process, which was largely unbalanced in favour of different leftist groups.[96]

President Piñera's strategy could also be seen as a desperate short-term solution to contain a defeat that was impossible to avoid. The Constitutional Court eventually changed its doctrine – perhaps some judges felt that President Piñera had used them and still violated the Constitution, so their decision became meaningless[97] – and stopped defending the President's legislative powers when a new case arose regarding a new attempt at withdrawing the pension funds by declaring that it lacked jurisdiction.[98] A constitutional amendment was able to be approved after all.[99]

A later case arose when private insurance companies alleged that the permission to withdraw retirement savings passed by the later constitutional amendment – which also involved the possibility of getting back the money paid to insurance companies when purchasing retirement plans called 'rentas vitalicias' – but the arguments used in the decisions of the Court could not affect the validity of the laws approved. They declined to accept arguments related to the legislative procedure and, instead, focused on substantive fundamental rights arguments that had little – if any – implications for the powers of the President.[100]

As a result, the President's veto power became irrelevant, the possibility of using the Constitutional Court to protect his legislative powers dissipated, and the fact that legislators had opened the door for legislative and constitutional initiatives in these subject matters shifted the balance of power. As the power of exclusive initiative was aimed at giving the President control of budgetary items and allocating financial responsibility and power into the hands of the executive branch, the change implied a constitutional reallocation of political power and accountability, making the political process more vulnerable to accepting populist and illegal policies promoted by legislators, and increasing a significant collective action problem in Chilean politics.

VI. The Problems of Congressional Aggrandizement

In a recent article, Neil Walker claimed that the pandemic could potentially exacerbate a crisis of democratic leadership.[101] However, unlike the global trend of

[96] On the Constitutional Convention's composition, see C Le Foulon and V Palanza, 'Elecciones a La Convención Constituyente: Innovación y Renovación' (2021) 580 *Puntos de Referencia – Centro de Estudios Públicos*.

[97] See Poehls and Verdugo (n 88) 266–267. Also, see the statement that Justice Aróstica made to the press in radio.uchile.cl/2021/04/27/ivan-arostica-y-tercer-retiro-el-punto-central-no-es-quien-hace-las-leyes-sino-que-hacer-para-solucionar-los-problemas-de-la-gente/ (accessed 17 January 2023).

[98] Constitutional Court, judicial decisions No 10.774-2021, 29 April 2021.

[99] See Law 21,330.

[100] See CS Gesell, 'Los Casos de 'Rentas Vitalicias' y La Consolidación de La Acción de Inaplicabilidad Como Amparo de Derechos Contra Actos Del Legislador' (2022) 46 *Actualidad Jurídica*.

[101] Walker (n 22).

executive branch aggrandizement, the Chilean experience illustrates how an opposite dynamic can be triggered: congressional empowerment. Today, we have little understanding of the consequences when legislative aggrandizement happens in the context of emergencies – most scholars focus on executive power. The analysis of the Chilean case is an attempt to start a conversation that can help fill this gap.

As the Chilean case shows, important collective action problems that invite populist narratives to thrive can occur. Unlike other countries that faced undemocratic threats to their political systems, Chile's main risk was not incumbent self-entrenchment. Instead, the main threats came from the narratives that dominated legislative debates in Congress. This issue connects to the collective action problem that legislators often have. While they are not responsible for public spending – and they surely do not need to solve the long-term problem of using retirement pension savings – they can be inclined to promote short-term solutions that can help them maximise their chances of getting re-elected. This problem can grow exponentially in times of crisis that are fertile for populist rhetoric to grow, even if that means infringing explicit constitutional restraints. This populist threat raises a question that needs more academic discussion: how to prevent inappropriate congressional aggrandizement without undermining relevant democratic principles? Or rather, how to avoid collective action problems that can compromise the integrity of the political structures that sustain the democratic process in the long term?

Even though more research is needed to understand fully the lessons the Chilean case can teach us, some preliminary implications are worth identifying. Parliamentary aggrandizement has its own risks, which are not sufficiently theorised in literature. An initial assessment can identify the existence of populist narratives becoming hegemonic, rule-of-law costs, gridlock, and collective action problems that can compromise the political structures in the long term. And these are by no means minor problems in any democratic country.

PART II

The Practice

3

Pandemocracy in Argentina

MANUEL J GARCÍA-MANSILLA AND RICARDO RAMÍREZ-CALVO

I. Introduction

The COVID-19 pandemic caused numerous restrictions on public liberties. From forced lockdowns to mandatory vaccination, government intervention across the globe imposed unprecedented limitations on individual rights. Fear caused by the pandemic increased calls to suppress individual rights for the sake of an undefined 'common good'. Such a reaction seems to translate into action the words of Louis de Saint-Just: 'The legislator holds sway over the future. It is up to him to want what is good. It is up to him to make men what he wants them to be.'[1]

The pandemic has been used to justify multiple constitutional anomalies as if the end always justifies the means. It is commonplace to quote a statement by Cicero in *De Legibus* to support the adoption of extra-constitutional measures in case of emergency: *Salus populi suprema lex est*, which can be translated as 'the safety of the people is the supreme law'. However, Cicero's statement has been misquoted and the mistake is carelessly repeated. The correct statement is *Salus populi suprema lex esto*, which means 'the safety of the people ought to be the highest law'.

The famous British jurist John Selden explained that:

> 'There is not any thing in the World more abused than this Sentence, *Salus populi suprema lex esto*, for we apply it, as if we ought to forsake the known Law, when it may be most for the advantage of the People, when it means no such thing. For first, 'tis not *Salus populi suprema Lex est*, but *esto* [...] That is, in all the Laws you make, have a special Eye to the good of the People'.[2]

What may seem a mere linguistic technicality has important consequences for the correct interpretation of Cicero's utterance. Far from being the enunciation of a

[1] Quoted by F Bastiat, *The Collected Works of Frédéric Bastiat. Vol. 2: The Law, The State, and Other Political Writings, 1843–1850* (Indianapolis, Liberty Fund, 2012) 134.

[2] J Selden, *The Table Talk* (London, John Russell Smith, 1860) 211, caption *People*. This book was originally published in 1689.

principle that authorises governments to ignore the laws during emergencies, it is a recommendation for them to properly discharge their duties.

In addition, it should not be overlooked that Cicero was talking about the duties of a military commander on the battlefield. McIlwain accurately maintains that the extension of powers during emergencies has been justified

> by misquotation of Cicero's *Salus populi suprema lex esto*, turning his *esto* into an *est*, and perverting the mere exhortation addressed to the commander of an army in the field into a general maxim of arbitrary government. The argument for emergency powers is not an unsound one – far from it; but it becomes a grave menace to individual liberty when 'the sole judge, both of the danger, and when and how the same is to be prevented, and avoided,' is a king; and may be such even when the sole judge is a representative assembly; the more so if only a partisan, a corrupt, or an 'unreformed' one.[3]

But even accepting the extension of Cicero's statement beyond military command, it does not contain any justification for absolute power during emergencies. Straumann rightly expounds: 'I believe Selden to be quite correct in assuming that the phrase in question put forward a supreme principle for the conduct of consuls in office, rather than placing the consuls above the law.'[4] He adds: 'When ordinary legislation does not seem to suffice, and extralegal measures are said to be needed, these are both defended and argued against in the name of rules that have a higher degree of validity than mere laws.'[5]

The opposite view asserts that governments cannot remain unarmed in cases of serious public emergency. That objection was properly summed up by Thomas Jefferson:

> A strict observance of written laws is doubtless one of the high duties of a good citizen, but it is not the highest. The laws of necessity, of self-preservation, of saving our country when in danger, are of higher obligation. To lose our country by a scrupulous adherence to written law, would be to lose the law itself, with life, liberty, property and all those who are enjoying them with us; thus absurdly sacrificing the end to the means.[6]

Pursuant to this interpretation, laws are regarded as necessary and minor casualties in the battle for survival. The essential aim must always be *salus populi*. This idea was summarised in Justice Robert Jackson's words, later reproduced by Justice Arthur Goldberg, that the Constitution is not a suicide pact. Justice Jackson ended his dissent in *Terminiello v Chicago* by saying: 'The choice is not between order and liberty. It is between liberty with order and anarchy without either. There is danger that, if the Court does not temper its doctrinaire logic with a little practical

[3] CH McIlwain, *Constitutionalism: Ancient and Modern* (Indianapolis, Liberty Fund, 2007) 4, note 6.

[4] B Straumann, *Crisis and Constitutionalism* (Oxford, Oxford University Press, 2016) 35–36.

[5] ibid 63.

[6] Letter from Jefferson to JB Colvin, 20 September 1810, in *The Life and Selected Writings of Thomas Jefferson. Including the Autobiography, the Declaration of Independence and his public and private letters* (New York, The Modern Library, 2004) 556.

wisdom, it will convert the constitutional Bill of Rights into a suicide pact.'[7] Justice Goldberg, in turn, maintained in *Kennedy v Mendoza-Martinez* that 'while the Constitution protects against invasions of individual rights, it is not a suicide pact'.[8]

Neither Justice Jackson nor Justice Goldberg explains what is the limit for governmental action during emergencies. Are all means allowed or are there still some limits that cannot be trespassed? Do all constitutional rights perish on the altar of necessity? This is particularly troublesome since the world seems to be in a constant state of crisis, real or fake. Both democratic and authoritarian leaders invoke the common good to justify measures purportedly aimed at coping with crisis. However, as explained by Paul Diehl,

> [t]he common good, that incomprehensible and vague term, is the most universal slogan and, therefore, also the most meaningless with which the people have been seduced. It allows any interpretation and, therefore, it becomes a comfortable pretext in the hands of power hungry dictators.[9]

The purpose of this chapter is to analyse the response provided by the Argentine Government during the COVID-19 pandemic in the context of the constitutional framework and the constitutional mechanisms provided for in the Argentine Constitution to deal with emergency situations.

II. Emergencies: Within or Outside the Legal Framework?

The authors outlined in the previous section reflect the dilemma faced by the study and the regulation of emergencies. Some maintain that the state of emergency cannot be legally regulated, because it is precisely the negation of the law. Others, on the other hand, affirm that the law, especially the Constitution, must provide for the state of emergency and indicate its limits.

One of the main modern defenders of the first of these positions was Carl Schmitt. In his *Political Theology*, Schmitt asserts that the exception cannot be factually limited and, at best, the legal system must content itself with characterising it as a case of extreme danger, a danger to the existence of the state, or the like.[10] For Schmitt, the state of emergency cannot be contained within the legal system, it exceeds it and, therefore, is outside it. Its consequences, such as the extension of powers of the government in such cases, must be unlimited.[11] The true emergency

[7] 337 U.S. 1 (1949), at 37.
[8] 372 U.S. 144 (1963), at 160.
[9] P Diehl, *Deutschland ist tot … es lebe Deutschland* (Heidelberg, Freiheit-Verlag, 1947).
[10] C Schmitt, *Politische Theologie. Vier Kapitel zur Lehre von der Souveränität*, 9th edn (Berlin, Duncker & Humblot, 2009) 14. The book was originally published in 1922.
[11] ibid.

requires an unlimited exercise of powers, that is, the suspension of the entire legal order.[12]

According to this interpretation, an emergency situation proves that the state predates the legal order. In an emergency,

> the State remains, while the legal order withdraws. Although the state of exception is an order in the legal sense, since it is different from anarchy or chaos, it is not a legal order. The existence of the State has here superiority over the validity of the legal norm. The decision is freed from all normative ties and becomes truly absolute.[13]

Schmitt insists on this concept and maintains that in an emergency 'the State suspends the legal system based on its right to self-preservation. [...] in the case of an exception the norm is annihilated'.[14]

In another of his writings dedicated specifically to the analysis of dictatorship, Schmitt had already partially advanced these ideas. Thus, he maintains that there are legal norms and norms that implement the law. In a dictatorship such as one justified by the emergency, which he calls a commissary dictatorship, the application of the latter (the rules that implement the law) is suspended to protect the validity of the former (the true legal rules). The principle would be: 'when the body of the constitution is under threat, it must be safeguarded through a temporary suspension of the constitution. Dictatorship protects a specific constitution against an attack that threatens to abolish this constitution'.[15]

Schmitt's starting point is that a legal system presupposes that a normal condition applies. In an emergency, such a normal condition disappears and it must be restored in order for the law to be applied. For Schmitt, 'dictatorship is like the act of self-defence: never just action, but also reaction'.[16] The actions of a dictator are aimed at recovering that state of normality endangered by the emergency.[17] The commissary dictatorship, as opposed to the sovereign dictatorship, does not imply the destruction of the constitution. That is why Schmitt states that 'the constitution can be suspended without ceasing to be valid because the suspension only represents a concrete exception'.[18]

It is difficult to differentiate between what Schmitt believes is a breach of the constitution and what he calls a suspension of the constitution, since his explanations are both concise and obscure. In his *Theory of the Constitution* he refers to violations of the constitution as 'violations of constitutional norms in one or more specific cases, but as an exception, that is, under the condition that the violated provisions remain in force without the rest of them being modified, that is, they are

[12] Schmitt (n 10) 18.
[13] ibid.
[14] Schmitt (n 10) 19.
[15] C Schmitt, *Dictatorship* (Cambridge, Polity Press, 2014) 118.
[16] ibid.
[17] ibid.
[18] ibid.

not permanently rescinded or temporarily out of effect (suspended)'.[19] However, this concept is not easily distinguishable from the suspension of the constitution, which Schmitt defines as 'the temporary interruption of the validity of one or more constitutional provisions'.[20] It is difficult to understand if in an emergency a violation or a suspension of the constitution exists. It seems that, for Schmitt, a suspension of the constitution differs from a violation not in its content, but in its justification. In other words, a suspension of the constitution is a violation of it, but one justified by the emergency situation.

Schmitt is not an innovator in terms of the scope or consequences of the state of emergency, but rather in linking it to the concept of sovereignty. Other modern authors had already held similar views, insofar as the state of emergency authorises setting aside the legal order, even within a constitutional state. Barthélemy maintained in 1915 that

> [t]his principle of legality is the fundamental guarantee of modern law; highlighting its importance is never exaggerated. However, it should not be taken to the absurd. The law is made by the State, not the State by the law. If the circumstances are such that they force a choice between the two, it is the law that must be sacrificed for the sake of the State: Salus populi suprema lex esto.[21]

These theories start, as indicated above, from a conception of the state as prior to the legal order, which is its creation. The law, being a creation of the state, cannot logically limit the action tending to the protection of its creator. It is a logical derivation from that starting point: without a state, the legal order is meaningless. Few authors today would admit to following Schmitt's ideas, due to their strong negative associations, but they apply them without naming him. When it is stated that the emergency caused by the pandemic was not foreseen by the constitution and, thus, the law cannot limit the actions of the state when it comes to protecting public health, the argument is in fact that the state of emergency is outside the legal order and, as a consequence, it allows governments to ignore most constitutional limitations for the sake of coping with the exception. Constitutional rights are sacrificed on the altar of efficacy or necessity. Schmitt's theories are repeated.

In a somewhat cryptical fashion, Agamben explains it as follows:

> [I]f exceptional measures are the result of periods of political crisis and, as such, must be understood on political and not juridico-constitutional grounds (De Martino 1973, 320), then they find themselves in the paradoxical position of being juridical measures that cannot be understood in legal terms, and the state of exception appears as the legal form of what cannot have legal form.[22]

[19] C Schmitt, *Verfassungslehre*, 10th edn (Berlin, Duncker & Humblot 2010) 99 and 100. The book was originally published in 1928.

[20] ibid 100.

[21] J Barthélemy, 'Du Renforcement du Pouvoir Exécutif en Temps de Guerre' in G Jèze (ed), *Problèmes de Politiques et Finances de Guerre* (Paris, Alcan, 1915) 121 and 122.

[22] G Agamben, *State of Exception* (Chicago and London, The University of Chicago Press, 2005) 1.

During the COVID-19 pandemic, it was common for public officers to assert that when public health is at stake, constitutional freedoms cannot be invoked. This is the concrete application of Schmitt's postulates on the state of exception, thus turning the Executive into the sovereign, who decides not only on the existence of the emergency but also on the scope of the measures to face it.

However, these theories are difficult to reconcile with the fact that most modern constitutions expressly provide for the consequences of the declaration of a state of emergency and limit the powers of governments during the exception. It is frequently overlooked that a state of emergency does not suspend the legal order altogether, but only limits parts of it. This is certainly the case with the Argentine Constitution, which contains an express provision to deal with a state of emergency and limits its consequences.

As stated above, theories that maintain that the state of emergency is outside the legal order must necessarily start from the idea that the state predates the legal order. However, this proposition is far from being generally accepted. In fact, it is hardly reconcilable with liberal democracy, in which the constitution creates the state. Liberal democracy is based on the notion that society grants nothing to the individual, but it is the individual that grants society the right to regulate certain areas of life but retains for itself all other rights not otherwise surrendered to society. In a liberal order, the state is the creation of the legal order and, should the legal order be suspended, the state itself would lose its foundations, and it would suspend itself. As stated by Thomas Paine, '[a] constitution is a thing antecedent to a government, and a government is only the creature of a constitution. The constitution of a country is not the act of its government, but of the people constituting a government'.[23]

The same conclusions can be drawn from a theory compatible with the rule of law, without resorting to contractual theories. Kelsen criticised the dual concept of law and state, which is at the basis of the idea that in case of emergency the law must be suspended to protect the state:

> If traditional theory of law and state opposes the state to the law as an entity different from the law, and at the same time asserts that the state is a legal being, they accomplish this by comprehending the state as a subject of obligations and rights, that is, as a legal person, and at the same time attributing to it an existence independent of the legal order. […] the public law theory assumes that the state as a collective unit and subject of willing and acting, exists independent of, and even preceding, the law.[24]

Kelsen specifically addressed the consequences of such dualistic theory with regard to emergency situations:

> According to this ideology law in the strict sense of the word does not prevail in so-called public law – as it prevails in private law – but rather the interest of the state, the public

[23] T Paine, *Rights of Man* (New York, Barnes & Noble Books, 2004) 39. The book was originally published in 1791.

[24] H Kelsen, *Pure Theory of Law* (New Jersey, The Lawbook Exchange, 2006) 284 and 285. The book was originally published in 1934.

> welfare which under all circumstances must be realized; consequently the relationship between general norm and executive organ in public law is different from that in private law: not (as in private law) strict application of statutes to concrete cases, but the unfettered realization of the state's purposes merely within the framework of the law and, in an emergency (in case of what is called in German political theory *Staatsnotrecht*) even against the law.[25]

The dualist view is untenable in a liberal democratic order. The state is not above the law but is a creation of the law. A constitution is a law that governs those who govern the people and not a law that is governed by those who govern the people.[26] Its application is not at the discretion of those who govern, subject to their will. There is no middle ground: either the emergency is governed by law or it is the negation of law, a kind of 'no-laws-land'. This is but a direct repudiation of the idea of 'a government of laws and not of men' which is the foundation of the idea of the Rule of Law.

The consequence of the dualist theory is to reject law altogether as a limit to the state. A law that can simply be ignored by the sovereign is no law in a proper sense. This is precisely what the dualist theory contends:

> The laws, according to the dualist, are general commands of the sovereign representative of the state. The sovereign will, for the most part, govern on the basis of general commands. But he can (and sometimes ought) to [sic] choose to work around or to disregard his own commands and exercise legitimate political authority in other ways than through mechanisms of legality. Any state, the dualist claims, possesses the power to act in legally unauthorized ways, regardless of the restrictions positive law may purport to put on the exercise of public power.[27]

III. The Dualist Theory Applied to the Interpretation of the Constitution

Another application of the dualist theory appears in the interpretation of constitutions. Some authors suggest that the emergency authorises a different reading of the constitution. According to this view, in times of normality, the constitution is interpreted in a way in which the powers of government are limited and this is strictly construed. However, in case of emergency, constitutional interpretation must necessarily mutate and allow governments to take certain actions which would be otherwise prohibited in normal times. William Rehnquist, former

[25] ibid 282.

[26] As Barnett explains, 'The Republican Constitution, then, provides the law that governs those who govern us and it is put in writing so it can be enforced against the servants of the people, each of which must swear to obey 'this Constitution'' (R Barnett, *Our Republican Constitution. Securing the Liberty and Sovereignty of We The People* (New York, Broadside Books, 2016) 23 and 24).

[27] L Vinx, *Hans Kelsen's pure theory of law* (Oxford, Oxford University Press, 2007) 16.

Chief Justice of the US Supreme Court, put it in the following words: 'the laws will not be mute in times of war, but they will speak with a somewhat different voice'.[28]

Ferejohn and Pasquino describe that dualists believe that in times of normality government is characterised by the observation and protection of individual rights and the distribution of power among different actors, while during emergencies government is identified with dictatorship, the temporary suspension of individual rights and the concentration of power in a single centre superior to those rights.[29]

Dualism assumes that there are exceptional circumstances that cannot be governed by normal means. Necessity has no law, which is the translation into facts of the Roman maxim *necessitas non habet legem* coined by Publilius Syrus at the time of the final collapse of the Roman Republic.[30] For the dualist, the existence of an imperious necessity authorises us to set aside the constitution and the laws. In other words, if necessity cannot be made to conform to law, law must conform to necessity.[31] The first legal consecration of this legal principle would have been in canon law.[32]

More recently, Donoso Cortés described this theory in his *Discourse on Dictatorship*:

> I, gentlemen, who believe that laws have been made for societies, and not societies for laws, say: society, everything for society, everything by society; society always, society in all circumstances, society on all occasions. When legality is enough to save society, legality; when it is not enough, dictatorship.[33]

Donoso adds that

> social life, like human life, is composed of action and reaction, of the ebb and flow of certain invading forces and certain resistant forces. […] When the invading forces are poured out, the resistant forces are poured out too; they are poured out by the government, by the authorities, by the courts; in a word, by the whole social body; but when the invading forces are concentrated in political associations, then necessarily, without anyone being able to prevent it, without anyone having the right to prevent it, the resistant forces themselves are concentrated in one hand. This is the clear, luminous, indestructible theory of dictatorship.[34]

For the Spanish authoritarian thinker, laws (including the constitution) are designed to be applied in moments of normality. In times of danger, they must

[28] W Rehnquist, *All the Laws but One: Civil Liberties in Wartime* (New York, Vintage Books, 2000) 225.

[29] J Ferejohn and P Pasquino, 'The law of the Exception: A Typology of Emergency Powers' (2004) 2(2) *International Journal of Constitutional Law* 224.

[30] Q Skinner, *The Foundations of Modern Political Thought*, 13th edn (Cambridge, Cambridge University Press, 2005) Vol I, 254.

[31] ibid.

[32] J Kohler, *Not kennt kein Gebot* (Berlin and Leipzig, Walther Rothschild 1915) 2.

[33] JDonoso Cortés, 'Discurso sobre la dictadura' in *Discursos Políticos* (Madrid, Tecnos, 2002) 5 and 6.

[34] ibid 7.

be set aside for the sake of the common good. In particular, any distribution of power, however minimal, yields to the need to oppose the forces of revolutionary chaos.[35] It is not an opposition between dictatorship and freedom, but between two dictatorships: the dictatorship of insurrection, which comes from below, and the dictatorship of order, which comes from above. Donoso chooses the latter.[36] For him, the threat of destruction justifies the existence of dictatorship:

> I say, gentlemen, that dictatorship in certain circumstances, in given circumstances, in circumstances such as the present,[37] is a legitimate government; it is a good government, it is a profitable government, like any other government; it is a rational government, which can be defended in theory, as it can be defended in practice.[38]

These same ideas were translated into the German maxim *Not hat kein Gebot*, the meaning of which is exactly the same as the above-quoted Latin phrase of Publilius Syrus. Imperial Chancellor Theobald von Bethmann-Hollweg used it in the *Reichstag* to justify the invasion of Belgium at the outbreak of World War I: 'My lords, this violates the precepts of international law. But we are in a situation of necessity. And necessity has no law.'[39]

In order to justify extra-constitutional measures, it has been argued that 'the State is an organization whose existence must be maintained at any cost […]. That is why the State can impose the highest demands on the individual.'[40] This notion is completely alien to liberal constitutions. The state is not the true reality of the individual, as Mussolini claimed. To the contrary, in a liberal democracy, the individual is considered as a value in itself and not as one piece of the social body of which it is a part.

Those who maintain the theory of the dualist interpretation of the constitution, are in fact applying the principles of the dual state, to use Ernst Fraenkel's expression. In a dual state, a normative state exists in normal times, 'an administrative body endowed with elaborate powers for safeguarding the legal order as expressed in statutes, decisions of the courts and activities of the administrative agencies',[41] but it coexists with a state of prerogative in cases of emergency, 'a governmental system which exercises unlimited arbitrariness and violence unchecked by any legal guarantees'.[42] The state of prerogative is the prelude to totalitarianism and, in light of human history, to suppose that it is merely transitory is a dangerous naivety.

[35] Donoso does not believe in separation of powers even in normal times.

[36] Donoso Cortés (n 33) 29.

[37] Donoso refers to the revolutionary events of 1848.

[38] Donoso Cortés (n 33) 7.

[39] Speech held before the *Reichstag* on 4 August 1914, T Bethmann-Hollweg, *Sechs Kriegsreden des Reichskanzlers* (Berlin, Reimer Hobbing, 1916) 10.

[40] Kohler (n 32) 32.

[41] E Fraenkel, *The Dual State. A Contribution to the Theory of Dictatorship* (New Jersey, The Lawbook Exchange, 2006) xiii. The book was originally published in 1941 in English and describes the functioning of the Nazi regime.

[42] ibid.

IV. Emergencies and Regulation of Constitutional Rights

Whatever the situation in other countries may be, in Argentina the state is not above the law, but was created by it and is subject to the Constitution and all the laws of the land. Nothing is further from what the Argentine Constitution provides than to assert that the government is entitled to obviate the law to deal with a state of emergency. The Constitution in Argentina not only expressly provides rules to cope with states of emergency and determines the limits of the powers of the government in those circumstances, but also unequivocally prohibits the granting of unlimited powers under any circumstance.

Section 23 of the Constitution provides:

> In the event of domestic disorder or foreign attack endangering the full enforcement of this Constitution and of the authorities hereby established, the province or territory which is in turmoil shall be declared in a state of siege and the constitutional guarantees shall be suspended therein. But during such a suspension the President of the Republic shall not issue judgments or apply penalties on his own. In such case, his power shall be limited, with respect to persons, to their arrest or transfer from one place of the Nation to another, should they not prefer to leave the Argentine territory.

This provision shows that the Constitution is a document intended to govern both in times of normality and in emergency situations. This implies that it must be applied fully and perhaps with greater intensity in times of crisis. Its main purpose is to protect individual rights and secure liberty for all. The individual is the centrepiece of our constitutional system. As admitted by an authoritarian author, this is 'the determining thought of the chapter of the Declarations, Rights and Guarantees of the Argentine Constitution, in the part that imports a definition of the essential relations of man with the State'.[43]

Nothing in the Constitution authorises us to make a different interpretation in cases of emergency and, as a consequence, to suspend rights without a declaration of the state of siege. The constitutional text is very clear and foresees exactly what measures are allowed in cases of necessity. The framers of the Argentine Constitution were perfectly aware that the country would face emergencies and states of necessity. They had suffered tyrannies, persecutions, exile, civil war and emergencies of all kinds, including an infectious disease like the yellow fever. To face them, they included a provision regulating the state of siege, the grounds for which are described in section 23 of the Constitution in such a broad manner to allow it to be applied to all kinds of extraordinary situations.

The framers were wise enough to anticipate that necessity would be used as an excuse to violate individual rights and the separation of powers, as had been the

[43] AE Sampay, *La filosofía del iluminismo y la Constitución argentina de 1853* (Buenos Aires, Depalma, 1944) 22.

norm in the years prior to the enactment of the Constitution. To avoid this, they included a provision that prevents the alteration of the principles, guarantees, and rights recognised in the constitutional text through the implementing laws:

> Section 28: 'The principles, guarantees and rights recognized in the preceding sections shall not be altered by the laws that regulate their enforcement'.

In addition, they expressly prohibited the granting of extraordinary powers to the executive. Section 29, which is rather unique among world constitutions, provides that:

> Congress may not vest in the National Executive Power – nor may the provincial legislatures vest in the provincial governors – extraordinary powers or the entire public authority; it may not grant acts of submission or supremacy whereby the life, honour, or fortune of the Argentine people be at the mercy of governments or of any person whatsoever. Acts of this nature shall be null and void, and shall render those who propose them, consent to them, or sign them, liable and subject to the penalties for the infamous traitors to the fatherland.

It is no coincidence that this provision has been placed exactly after the rule prohibiting the alteration of rights by regulatory means. The two provisions constitute two sides of the same coin. Sections 28 and 29 impose a strict observance of the Constitution, both in times of normality and in times of necessity. To invoke emergencies for the purpose of suspending the validity of the Constitution is grossly unconstitutional, even if those suspensions are disguised under the garb of a most intense regulation of rights or a dual reading of the Constitution. The Argentine constitutional text expressly provides for the measures authorised to face emergencies and the only one that allows the suspension of rights is the state of siege and then only to the extent that any suspension of rights is required to control the specific emergency.

No emergency authorises the suspension of the Constitution or of the application of laws. The suspension of individual rights, except through the application of the state of siege, is not allowed by the Constitution. This is the only constitutional mechanism that allows the suspension of specific constitutional rights and this may only be done with the limitations indicated in section 23 of the Constitution.

The function of section 23 of the Constitution is to allow the adoption of extraordinary measures to deal with equally extraordinary situations. In these exceptional cases, constitutional guarantees yield to the imperative need to avert a very serious danger that threatens the full validity of the Constitution. These threats are not only due to political factors. It is true that, as Jackson stated, the Constitution is not a suicide pact. Those framing our Constitution were so aware of this that they foresaw a mechanism to deal with states of danger and emergency within the Constitution.

However, the state of siege, as provided in the Argentine Constitution, is far from allowing the establishment of a constitutional dictatorship, like that of ancient Rome. Nor does it suspend the validity of the Constitution, as was the case in France with the Constitution of the Year VIII and in Chile with the Constitution of 1833. The Argentine Supreme Court recognised this fact when it declared that '[t]he state of siege, far from suspending the rule of the Constitution, is declared to defend it'.[44] Public authorities continue to function in a normal way and the specific measures adopted by the President of the Nation are subject to judicial control. Article 43 of the Constitution expressly provides that habeas corpus is not suspended during the state of siege.

The abuse of the state of siege in the past by military dictatorships causes immediate objections to be raised at any mere reference to it. However, this unconstitutional practice should not prevent the application of an institutional remedy when it is indispensable. It should be recalled that Article 29 of the Constitution prohibits the granting of extraordinary powers or the addition of public power. This rule establishes an insurmountable limit for the exercise of the powers of the Executive Branch, which also applies during a state of siege. The measures adopted must be strictly aimed at avoiding the danger for which the state of siege was declared. As with any exceptional power, its interpretation must be restrictive. Despite any precautions these may raise, the memories of past abuses cannot lead us to discard this mechanism and remain inactive when facing real emergency situations. It is precisely through constitutional mechanisms that any restrictions of constitutional rights that may be necessary to control a crisis are best implemented and ordered.

Notwithstanding the clear provisions of the Constitution, the government did not declare the state of siege during the COVID-19 pandemic. It imposed broad suspensions of numerous constitutional rights and not even through laws approved by Congress, but by emergency decrees issued solely by the President. The justification for it was, once again, that necessity has no law. The majority leader in Congress even declared that during a pandemic no constitutional rights exist. In a similar fashion, the director of the office of the legal counsel of the presidency said that the Constitution was not drafted to cope with a pandemic. In accordance with such absurd interpretations, the President is allowed to implement any measure he deems adequate to deal with the emergency.

Rights are not absolute and the Constitution itself provides that they are subject to regulation by law. However, this legislative power to regulate rights does not authorise their suspension or nullification. As stated in section 28, quoted above, rights cannot be altered under the pretext of their regulation. The power to regulate a right is, in essence, of a permanent nature, for situations of normality. An emergency does not authorise the imposition of more strict regulations than in normal times.

The restrictions imposed by the Executive in Argentina during the pandemic were not the exercise of the power to regulate rights. They implied in many cases the outright suspension of the enjoyment of those rights. No regulatory power

[44] 'Alem', Fallos:54:432, 456 (1893).

authorises such a suspension. Hence, they could only be imposed as merely transitory restrictions, which could last until the emergency disappears. The only constitutional provision that allows for such restrictions is the declaration of the state of siege. This may seem to be a mere formal objection, but it touches the very foundation of constitutional government. It is not through the regulation of rights that the necessary measures to control an emergency can be imposed.

The need to adopt extreme restrictions to the exercise of constitutional rights, even assuming hypothetically that they were indispensable, cannot make us lose sight of the fact that such a regulation violates section 28 of the Constitution. The state of necessity, even in the case of health emergencies, does not grant public authorities powers not provided for in the Constitution. This is where the idea of the state of siege comes in, which, being strictly transitory, authorises the adoption of these extreme measures and the control of their eventual excesses. The COVID-19 pandemic is one of those emergencies for which section 23 was included in the constitutional text. At first glance, one might think that the state of siege is only intended for cases of violence or insurrection. However, the Constitution is clear when it speaks of internal commotion that endangers its exercise.

As stated above, the majority of the restrictions were created by emergency decrees issued solely by the President. It has been erroneously asserted that such decrees are the appropriate mechanism for the restriction of rights due to the pandemic. It is overlooked that emergency decrees are an exception to the express prohibition for the President to issue legislative provisions. Although the Constitution allows the President in section 99.3 to issue emergency decrees, it strictly limits such power to the cases in which it is impossible to follow the normal procedure for the enactment of laws by Congress.[45] Emergency decrees may not be used as a tool to circumvent or bypass Congress.

Only in those very limited cases can the Executive Power exercise powers that belong to the Legislative Power. Congress was in session throughout the pandemic. Thus, the requisite exceptional situation required by the Constitution to allow the issuance of emergency decrees was not met. In addition, Congress also lacks the power to suspend constitutional rights recognised unless a state of siege is declared. This conclusion stems from the above-quoted section 28 of the Constitution, which prohibits the alteration of rights through regulation. Suspending a right implies its alteration, from the moment it prevents its enjoyment.

The restrictions imposed during the pandemic did not establish conditions for the exercise of constitutional rights, which would have been considered a

[45] Section 99.3, paras 2 and 3 of the Constitution provides that: 'The Executive Power may not issue dispositions of a legislative nature in any case whatsoever, under penalty of their absolute and incurable nullity. Only when exceptional circumstances make it impossible to follow the regular procedures provided by this Constitution for the passing of laws, and the situation does not involve rules that regulate criminal, tax, or electoral matters or the regime governing political parties, may [the President] dictate decrees by reason of necessity and urgency, which are to be decided at a general meeting of Ministers, who must endorse them, together with the Chief of the Cabinet of Ministers.'

regulation, but rather prohibited the exercise of those rights. This rules out from the outset that emergency decrees constitute the constitutional means to suspend the exercise of constitutionally recognised rights. The emergency regulations issued by the President of the Nation due to the COVID-19 pandemic were not a more intense regulation of those rights, but an unconstitutional prohibition of the enjoyment of them.

V. Conclusion

It has been commonplace in history to appeal to the state of necessity and the need to protect the people to justify extraordinary measures and suspend the constitution and the laws, not only in Argentina but throughout the world. The justification is always the same: the need to avert a grave danger. Behind this reason is usually hidden a latent authoritarianism, always eager to limit individual liberties.

Since Spinoza, several authors have drawn parallels between the limitations that laws impose on rulers (in modern times, constitutions) and the story of Ulysses, the goddess Circe and the song of the Sirens.[46] As is well known, after paying homage to Ulysses and his men, the goddess Circe warned them that the return to Ithaca would be full of dangers:

> Next you will come to the Sirens who beguile all men that approach them. Whoever encounters them unawares and listens to their voices will never joy at reaching home, his wife and children to greet him. Instead the Sirens' tempt him with their limpid song, as they sit there in the meadow with a vast heap of mouldering corpses, bones on which hangs the shrivelled skin. Plug your comrades' ears with softened beeswax lest they listen, and row swiftly past. And if you must hear, then let them first tie you hand and foot and stand you upright in the mast housing, and fasten the rope ends round the mast itself, so you can delight in hearing the Sirens' voices. And should you beg your crew to free you, let them only bind you more tightly.[47]

The Sirens represent the temptation to suspend the laws every time it seems expedient and the ropes tying Ulysses to the mast are the limitations included in the constitutions against those temptations. Spinoza puts it as follows:

> We can explain it clearly with the example of Ulysses. Ulysses' companions complied with his command, when they refused to untie him, while he was tied to the mast of the ship and enraptured by the song of the sirens, despite the fact that he commanded them to do so in the midst of multiple threats. And it is attributed to his prudence that, afterward, he thanked his companions for having complied with his first intention. Following this example of Ulysses, kings also often admonish judges to do justice without regard to anyone, not even to the king himself, if in some special case he should

[46] Among many others, J Elster, *Ulysses Unbound* (Cambridge, Cambridge University Press, 2000); JE Finn, *Constitutions in Crisis* (Oxford and New York, Oxford University Press, 1991).

[47] Homer, *The Odyssey*, Book XII.

> order them to do something which they know to be against the established law. Kings, indeed, are not gods, but men, who often allow themselves to be deceived by the song of sirens. Hence, if everything depended on one's fickle will, there would be nothing fixed.[48]

Constitutional provisions that deal with emergencies, such as the state of siege in the Argentine Constitution, function in a similar way. Knowing that, like Ulysses tempted by the song of the Sirens, we will not be rational in times of grave danger, we decide to tie ourselves to the mast of constitutions and laws and order judges to plug their ears to avoid heeding our pleas. Unfortunately, in Argentina, as in many other countries around the world, judges have not done their part and have allowed themselves to be influenced by the orders of those who circumstantially wield power, demanding that they be freed from the bonds and constraints imposed by the constitution and the laws. The result has been that Argentina has been shipwrecked on the rocks, not once, but many times. The response to the COVID-19 pandemic was no exception.

The Argentine Constitution does not allow a Schmittian reading of the emergency. Section 23 does not consecrate a presidential dictatorship. Section 29 creates an insurmountable and categorical limit that cannot be forgotten. Such a provision leaves no doubt that the Executive Branch may never be granted extraordinary powers or the sum of public power. In other words, the President cannot be elevated to the category of a dictator.

Since the Argentine Constitution contains an express provision to deal with emergencies, nothing allows the application of other remedies not provided for therein. The suspension of constitutional guarantees is strictly linked to the causes that motivate the state of siege. Although not required by the Constitution, it would be good institutional practice for Congress, the only body authorised to declare a state of siege in cases of internal commotion, to set the limits of it by law. Section 75, paragraph 32, grants this authority to Congress when it provides that it has the power to make all laws and regulations that may be convenient for the exercise of its constitutional duties and all others granted by the Constitution to the federal government. This power gives Congress the authority to establish the precise limits of the powers that the President may exercise during the state of siege.

Even in the absence of a congressional regulation establishing the limits of the state of siege, the power of the President in such cases is not unlimited. In addition to the express limit contained in section 29, the state of siege is an exceptional remedy and, as such, must be construed restrictively. Both Congress and the Judiciary continue to perform their duties during a state of siege. Also, as already mentioned, Section 43 of the Constitution provides that the writ of habeas corpus is not suspended during the state of siege. This is another indication that the powers

[48] B Spinoza, *Tratado Político* (Madrid, Alianza Editorial, 1986) 141. This book was originally published as *Tractatus Theologico-Politicus* in 1670.

that the President may exercise during a state of emergency are not unlimited, not even the express power to arrest people granted by section 23 of the Constitution.

The framers did not follow the example of other constitutions of their time which provided that the state of siege suspended the constitution.[49] No governmental power is unlimited. Such an idea contradicts the very notion of a constitution. If the purpose of the state of siege is to allow the government to adopt the necessary measures to control an emergency, it is a necessary and inescapable consequence that the only extraordinary measures that may be adopted are those directed to achieve this target. Thus, not all constitutional rights are suspended during the state of siege, only those whose exercise is related to the emergency that caused the declaration of the state of siege. Otherwise, the constitution would cease to be in force and the President could assume dictatorial powers.

This is not a merely formal or theoretical contention. Liberal constitutional democracy requires that procedures should be strictly adhered to. The end does not always justify the means. If a constitution provides for a specific mechanism to cope with an emergency, nothing allows us to proceed differently. If public authorities are forbidden to suspend rights except in the case of a state of siege, it is inadmissible to assume that this only applies in normal situations and that in cases of emergency the constitution should be kept locked in a secluded cabinet. Liberal democracy plainly rejects Rossiter's proposed interpretation that 'no sacrifice is too great for our democracy, not even the temporary sacrifice of democracy itself'.[50]

There are numerous examples in the world that illustrate the nefarious consequences of granting unlimited powers to rulers on the grounds of emergency. The infamous Article 48 of the Weimar Constitution and the extensive use of it during the later days of the Weimar Republic should be a powerful warning against allowing the concentration of powers in the executive. Even Rossiter, who advocated in favour of granting broad exceptional powers to the President in cases of emergency, is forced to admit that the 'techniques of constitutional dictatorship designed and put into practice for the defence of the [Weimar] Republic were in the end to play a considerable role in its destruction'.[51]

Constitutions must be applied both in normal and abnormal situations. To put constitutions on pause during emergencies until normal times return means to 'wait for the patient to heal before applying the treatment'.[52] Strict observance of the constitution is the only effective remedy for any emergency.

[49] This is specially true in connection with the draft constitution proposed by Juan Bautista Alberdi in 1852 and the 1833 Chilean Constitution.

[50] C Rossiter, *Constitutional Dictatorship* (New Brunswick, Transaction Publishers. 2004) 314.

[51] ibid 31.

[52] These words were said by Salustiano Zavalía, delegate to the Constitutional Convention of 1853, to counter the proposal to delay the enactment of the Constitution until normal times returned (E Ravignani, *Asambleas Constituyentes Argentinas*, (Buenos Aires, Peuser, 1937) Vol IV, 480).

4

Pandemocracy in Brazil

MARCELO FIGUEIREDO

I. Introduction

This chapter aims to address empirical and normative considerations regarding the emergence of COVID-19 in Latin America in general and in Brazil in particular.

We are interested in answering the following questions: how have nation-states responded to the challenge of COVID-19? How are these responses compatible with the traditional constitutional design and conditions of legitimacy found in the constitutional democracies of nation-states?

Is it possible to claim that a pandemocracy is in place, which has had the effect of dismantling the relevant features that allow democratic politics and the division of powers to be recognised?

Who effectively took normative and legislative action in response to the challenges of the pandemic? How has hyper-presidentialism in Latin America been strengthened by it? Finally, what new dangers were brought about by the pandemic?

II. Contextualising the Theme in Latin America – Initial Considerations

We believe that Lilia Moritz Schwarcz[1] accurately synthesises the environment in which Brazil was forged and which explains, even today, many of the characteristics present in the Brazilian people and in Latin America:

> Brazil has a very peculiar history, at least when compared to that of its Latin American neighbors. Almost half of all enslaved Africans were brought to Brazil, leaving their homelands by force and violence; after independence, and surrounded by republics, we formed a very popular monarchy for more than sixty years, and which enabled us to keep intact the borders of a giant, continent-sized country. To top it off, as we were a Portuguese colony, we speak a language that is different from our neighbors'.

[1] LM Schwarcz, *On Brazilian Authoritarianism* (São Paulo, Companhia das Letras, 2019) 11.

In fact, the deep roots of authoritarianism, especially in Brazil, are still a reality. In truth, there are eight facts that, according to Lilia Moritz Schwarcz, greatly influence political thought and bureaucratic and authoritarian practices, as better clarified in the following sections.

A. Slavery and Racism

In Brazil, the slave system became such a deep-rooted model that it became a language, with serious consequences. From the sixteenth to the seventeenth century, this scandalous injustice, supported by the trick of legality, became embedded here.

Slavery was much more than an economic system: it shaped behaviours, defined social inequalities, made race and colour markers of fundamental differences, ordained labels of command and obedience, and created a society conditioned by paternalism and a very narrow hierarchy.

B. *Mandonismo*[2]

Friar Vicente do Salvador, Brazil's first historian, concluded: 'No man on this earth is a *republicist*,[3] nor does he care for or protect the common good, but each one for his private good.' Five centuries later, our Republic remains inconclusive; each one thinking first of his private interests and only afterwards of public interests which concern our *res* ('affair') *publica*.

The beginning of this long history can be traced back to the sixteenth century, when the Portuguese metropolis, unable to populate such a vast territory, chose to govern its American domain by delegating powers to a series of colonists, who became lords of extensive domains. This was the spirit and basis of colonisation in Brazil; large estates, generally monocultures, concentrated in the hands of a few men.

C. Patrimonialism

From the beginning of this brief history of five centuries, Brazil's difficulty in building a structure designed for the common good became evident. In place of this, various forms of cronyism – the exchange of favours, friends at court, the famous

[2] *Mandonismo* is a Brazilian Portuguese word used in the political science context to describe one of the characteristics of the exercise of power by oligarchic and personalised structures, throughout the history of Brazil.

[3] Term used in Portuguese that means a person without notion of the republican ideals.

habit of cutting in line, or the use of intermediaries – took root in this land, leading to the abusive use of the state for private ends.

What is certain is that a serious republican deficit will persist in Brazil as long as such practices continue to reign within the political system and at the heart of the country's public institutions.

D. Corruption

If patrimonialism is the first enemy of the Republic, the second principal adversary goes by the name of corruption. It is a practice that degrades the trust placed in others and disaggregates the public space, diverting resources and citizens' rights. Not coincidentally, it is often associated with the mishandling of public funds and the lack of control of government policies.

Regardless of the form assumed, what is certain is that corruption leads to the distortion of customs, making them immoral and unethical. Its consequences affect not only the private sphere, they also end up directly affecting the well-being of citizens. Spending on private enrichment reduces public resources and investment in health, education, security, housing, transportation, or social and infrastructure programs.

E. Social Inequality

A crucial problem in our republican agenda is the ongoing and shameful social inequality, inherited from the past, but produced and reproduced in the present. According to a report produced by Oxfam Brazil in 2018, Brazil is the 10th in the global ranking of income inequality.

The phenomenon of inequality is deeply rooted in Brazil and is manifested in economic and income inequality, inequality of opportunities, racial inequality, regional inequality, gender inequality, generational inequality and social inequality, resulting in the differing levels of access to health, education, housing, transportation and leisure.

F. Violence

The daily number of homicides in Brazil is equivalent to the number of people killed in the crash of a fully loaded Boeing 737–800.[4]

[4] As per Atlas of Violence 2018, produced by the Institute for Applied Economic Research (Ipea) and the Brazilian Public Security Forum (FBSP).

Brazil has become the main corridor for the transit of drugs to North America and Central Europe, according to the United Nations Office on Drugs and Crime (UNODC). Internally, consumption is also high: the country is the second largest consumer of cocaine in the world.

Violence in the countryside is another reality. The dispute for land ownership in the countryside is one of the greatest causes of death in Brazil and victims are largely from the indigenous populations, whose constitutional rights, allowing them to own land that belonged to their ancestors, are constantly disrespected.

G. Race and Gender

Every society shapes its own markers of difference. That is, it transforms physical differences into social stereotypes, generally of inferiority, and thus produces prejudice, discrimination, and violence.

In the list of social markers with an impact on the reality in which we live are included categories such as race, generation, place of origin, gender and sex orientation, and other elements that can produce various forms of hierarchy and subordination. In our society, the perverse use of these categories has generated all kinds of situations that involve racism, lead to feminicide, produce misogyny and homophobia, and are used to justify a widespread 'rape culture', with rape figures at alarming levels, even if the offences are mostly silenced in the country.

Inequality is perceived throughout the existence of these people and through various socioeconomic indicators, in a merciless combination of social vulnerability and racism that accompanies them throughout their lives.

Therefore, Brazil's inequality is strongly addressed at the black and young population, a component associated with a series of socioeconomic inequalities clustered around race, gender, generation, and region, and is the first step towards the development of focused public policies and affirmative actions capable of resolving specific inequities.

III. The Brazilian Constitutional Structure

There is a myth that Brazil is a nation averse to conflict, peaceful in nature and democratic with regards to the coexistence of genders, races, and ethnicities, and this may lead to the perception of a kind of paradise of tolerance in the midst of an inclement world.

These generalising definitions, however, do not survive a confrontation in the countryside, a police raid in the cities, an argument between politicians, an armed robbery, a traffic dispute, or an ethnic census that reveals the country's persistent structural inequality.

Father Antônio Vieira (1608–97), dedicated his life to the task of catechising the gentiles of the new land: a Portuguese America. There is an especially significant passage which he dedicates to describing the dissimilarities between the marble statues and the myrtle statues and, from these, establishes parallels between the coexistence and the clash of two diverse cultures: the colonists and the natives.

Evangelising the pagans in Europe was an arduous, painful, and costly task; however, the result remained forever, hard and tough as white marble. To catechise the 'Brazils' was a very different task. It meant taming a myrtle, a shrub with malleable branches, which accepted pruning and immediately took the shape one wanted, but, at the first careless move, returned to its original design.

Politically, intolerance reveals itself as a conduct that seeks to erase or simply does not accept points of view different from the individual's own. This behaviour often uses prejudice and the dissemination of stereotypes as a means to assert itself. Racism, sexism, misogyny, anti-Semitism, homophobia, religious or political pragmatism and hatred of foreigners are all known forms of social intolerance.

Intolerance weakens our democratic rule of law, which calls for respect for different ideas, experiences, practices, options, and customs. Democracies work best, according to Steven Levistky and Daniel Ziblatt, and survive longest when constitutions are reinforced by democratic, unwritten norms.[5]

All these sociopolitical characteristics are present to a greater or lesser extent in Brazil, and in Latin America in general.

In his analysis, the late Professor Jorge Carpizo,[6] researcher emeritus of the Universidad Autónoma de México, proposes four points when studying democracies in Latin America. One is of a formal nature and consists of holding free, objective, fair and periodic elections. Three others are of a material nature, namely: a) respect for and protection of human rights, primarily civil and political rights; b) the importance of the opposition; c) the de-concentration of power and the balance between its organs.

He states that electoral democracies in our region, in general terms, have not been able to successfully carry out the fight against the great plagues: poverty and social inequality; the discrediting of political parties and the political class; and corruption and impunity in several countries at the end of the twentieth century and beginning of the twenty-first century, where there is a strong tendency towards hyper-presidentialism.

[5] LM Schwarcz, *On Brazilian Authoritarianism* (São Paulo, Companhia das Letras 2019) 27, 41, 64, 88, 126, 152, 161, 174, 177, 207, 208, 214, 220.

[6] J Carpizo, 'Tendencias actuales del constitucionalismo latinoamericano' in M Carbonell, J Carpizo and D Zovatto (eds), *Tendencias del Constitucionalismo en IberoAmérica* (México, Universidad Autónoma de México, International Institute for Democracy and Electoral Assistance, Spanish Agency for International Development Cooperation and the Ibero-American Institute of Constitutional Law, 2009) 1–31.

There is contempt for the rule of law and the law. Democracy in most Latin American countries is an unfinished and unconsolidated task. There is constant concern about political and electoral setbacks.

Today, the purpose of democracy in Latin America must be to achieve higher levels of social welfare for the majority population, but it also implies, among other aspects: respect for social movements, economic and democratic demands of industrial and agrarian workers and their unions, the production and distribution of popular consumer goods, public higher education with academic excellence, and the fight against impunity and corruption.

In Brazil, the 1988 Constitution is currently in force, the first Constitution after the long dictatorial period experienced by our region – approximately between the 1960s and 1980s.

At the time of its promulgation, the Constitution had 245 Articles, distributed in its nine main titles, as well as 70 Articles in its transitional provisions. Since then, the constitutional text has been changed more than 128 times by virtue of various amendments and a specific revision process that took place in 1993–94 until 2022–23.

Despite the numerous amendments to date, the structural principles of the Constitution have hardly changed. In the titles and chapters on federalism, separation of powers, and fundamental rights, only secondary provisions were amended. The parts most affected were undoubtedly those relating to public administration, the economic order, and the social order.

As fundamental aspects of the 1988 Constitution, we quote the following points,[7] mentioned by Virgílio Afonso da Silva:[8]

A. Republic

Provided for in Article 1 of the Constitution, Brazil is a federative republic, an institutional choice made in 1889, after the Brazilian and Portuguese empire had reigned here.

B. Federation

The Brazilian federation is formed by the indissoluble union of states and municipalities and the federal district. It does not admit secession. Brazilian federalism underwent countless and profound variations throughout the twentieth century: dual in its beginnings, only nominal during the most authoritarian periods, potentially cooperative in other periods, sometimes decentralised, but most of the time with a clear tendency toward centralisation.

[7] V Afonso da Silva, *Direito constitucional brasileiro* (São Paulo, Edusp, 2021) 84–93.

[8] The concepts below are mostly taken from the work of Virgílio Afonso da Silva, with whom we agree. Afonso da Silva, ibid.

Although the enactment of the 1988 Constitution marked an attempt to establish robust federalism, after an extremely centralising period under the previous Constitution of 1969, numerous factors have undermined the achievement of this task, such as extreme regional inequality and the centralising judicial precedents of the Brazilian Supreme Federal (STF).

As a result, although the 1988 Constitution provides for several competing powers, to be exercised by all units of the federation – which could foster cooperation among them – the fact is that, in numerous areas, the Union (federation) clearly has, at least with respect to legislative powers, a dominant role, leaving very little to the other state-members.

Another factor that worries and shakes cooperation in the Brazilian federation is not only a federal centralism, but also a judicial interpretation of competences that until today, with rare exceptions, has privileged federal competences to the detriment of state and municipal ones. The federation is also a fundamental principle that cannot be abolished by constitutional amendment.

C. Democratic Rule of Law

The Constitution states that Brazil constitutes a *Democratic State of Law*. As we know, the Rule of Law should be understood, above all, as the guarantee of the exercise of state power based on law, not on arbitrary or personal will. But it is more than that. By Democratic State of Law, it should be understood that the 1988 Constitution protects or tries to protect democracy, which is supported by popular power (Article 1 of CF/1988), also through representative democracy.

D. Separation of Powers

Article 2 of the Brazilian Federal Constitution provides that the Legislative, the Executive and the Judiciary are powers of the Union, which remain 'independent and harmonious among themselves'. Moreover, Article 60, section 4, III, includes the separation of powers in the list of fundamental principles, which in fact are much more theoretical than practical. On a day-to-day basis, there are numerous frictions and tensions between the powers, despite the formal separation of their functions, regarding the organisation of each of them.

E. Presidentialism

Brazil is a country that has operated a presidential system since the promulgation of the Republic in 1889. The relationship between the President of the Republic and the National Congress – the core of a governing system – has varied considerably over these numerous years. The history of the Brazilian system of government in the twentieth century has witnessed a series of institutional instabilities, confrontations, mutual blockages, coups and even a short-lived parliamentary experiment between 1961 and 1963 (which was also the product of one of these many crises).

Still, the central features of the presidential system – a directly elected, fixed-term president not dependent on a vote of confidence by the legislature, and a National Congress also directly elected for a fixed term, which cannot be dissolved by the president – have been present in all Brazilian Constitutions since 1891.

Since 1988, Brazil's presidential system has coexisted with a highly fragmented party system. As of May 2019, 29 parties had at least one representative in the National Congress.

At the outset of the Coronavirus pandemic (COVID-19), we had a President-elect (Jair Bolsonaro) who created a deep divide between Congress and from most of Brazilian society. His capacity to generate conflicts was immense. He fomented radical groups in the press, propagated false or unproven news, and has discriminated against regional groups who are supposedly against him.

Besides having a very rudimentary and crude form of discourse, he did not have the slightest ability to govern, in addition to encouraging hate speech, and despising political and cultural minorities. In this tense climate, it is no surprise that various political conflicts arose and that these, in most cases, flowed into the Judiciary, in general, and into the Supreme Court, in particular.

The latter Court, given the existence of an analytical and generous Constitution in terms of fundamental and human rights, opens up and accepts a series of demands that, in principle, could be resolved in the public arena (Congress), especially through the very extensive control of constitutionality (*judicial review)* that exists in Brazil.

As we will see below, to exemplify this scenario, disputes over federative jurisdiction became common after the advance of the pandemic, involving disagreements about which authority is the most legitimate or appropriate to decide on the authorisation for businesses to operate in the capitals of the country, as in the Municipality of Rio de Janeiro, the capital of the State of Rio de Janeiro.[9]

F. Directive Constitutionalism

The 1988 Constitution has a broader and more ambitious objective beyond protecting freedoms and defining the basic rules of state organisation. It is a clear example

[9] Whether it would be the President of the Republic, the State Governor, or the Municipal Mayor. At the time, the President of the Republic gave an interview to the press against the Executive Orders issued by the government of the State of Rio de Janeiro that established isolation measures and the closure of businesses activities. The Mayor of Rio allowed them to reopen, but soon after, the Governor intervened and revoked it. Legal chaos ensued and the population, until a later judicial decision, did not know what to do. The same occurred in relation to the closing of airports and roads throughout the country. Many state governors tried to isolate their respective territories and prevent the circulation of people coming from places with a high infection levels. Other governors went to the Judiciary to erect a sanitary barrier to travellers coming from other regions of Brazil's immense territory.

of a constitution that intends to change the status quo by defining objectives to be pursued and establishing public policies in various sectors. It is, therefore, a constitution that aims to be *directive.*

Directive constitutions face peculiar challenges that do not affect other constitutions. Their directive character is expressed mainly through *programmatic norms*, which, as their name suggests, establish programs to be put into practice. These programs, generally quite ambitious, are difficult to carry out, however. While it is true that state actions cannot deviate from them, the interpretation of what it means to fail to comply with them is complex and subject to deeper disagreements than those that arise from the interpretation of other types of norms.

Article 3 of the 1988 Constitution contains the main programmatic norms of the Constitution, those that should guide the interpretation of all the others. According to this article, the fundamental objectives of the Federative Republic of Brazil are:

> (i) build a free, just and solidary society; (ii) ensure national development; (iii) eradicate poverty and marginalization and reduce social and regional inequalities; (iv) promote the good of all, without prejudice of origin, race, sex, color, age and any other forms of discrimination.

Article 170, which establishes the objectives and principles of the economic order, is also an example of a programmatic norm.

G. International Relations

Article 4 of the 1988 Constitution establishes:

> The Federative Republic of Brazil shall be governed in its international relations by the following principles: I – national independence; II – prevalence of human rights; III – self-determination of peoples; IV – non-intervention; V – equality among states; VI – defense of peace; VII – peaceful settlement of conflicts; VIII – repudiation of terrorism; IX – cooperation among peoples for the progress of mankind; X – granting of political asylum.

In international relations, it is not enough for Brazil to respect other states, and it must also engage in forms of international cooperation. The clearest expression of this duty is the sole paragraph of Article 4, according to which Brazil shall seek 'the economic, political, social and cultural integration of the peoples of Latin America, aiming at the formation of a Latin American community of nations'.

H. Fundamental Rights

One of the highlights of the 1988 Constitution is its generous declaration of fundamental, political, and social rights. These are addressed in Title II (Article 5) and from Article 6 onwards. Guaranteeing and ensuring performance of a long list of rights in a country as unequal as Brazil is a challenge of enormous proportions.

Perhaps the greatest challenge is to ensure the right to equality and other rights closely associated with this, such as social rights in general. In this context, the debate on the efficacy and effectiveness of constitutional rules is particularly relevant, especially because the mere positivisation of ideals is not enough to bring about social change, and robust public policies are required to achieve this end. The role of jurists and non-legal experts, as well as that of the Judiciary and political powers in this area, has been the subject of countless debates in recent years.

I. Secularism

With the end of the monarchy in Brazil and the Proclamation of the Republic in 1889 came the federative form and presidentialism. As a consequence of this historical moment, the Constitution of 1891 broke the alliance between the state (monarchical regime) and the Church.

The 1988 Constitution maintained break (Aticle 150, VI, 'b'), but does not prohibit alliances with churches for the purpose of collaborating with the public interest, especially in the area of health and education. It is also interesting to note that the preamble of the 1988 Constitution alludes to the 'protection of God', a circumstance that has no bearing on the separation between the Church/churches and state.

IV. Constitutional Considerations Regarding COVID-19

As we know, every crisis reveals the intimacies of power. The COVID-19 pandemic was no exception. All of us citizens of the world have seen during this period the mistakes made by governments in the management of this global crisis that will have many more effects in the near future.

To a large extent, in our region, presidential systems concentrate great power without much internal or congressional control. For this reason, it may not be possible to tame violence, eradicate corruption, mitigate inequality or ease social injustices.

In analysing the situation in his country, Mexico, Diego Valadés[10] highlights personalism in the exercise of power, including in the management of the pandemic. He states that personalism is accentuated when national and state leaders have charismatic magnetism and use it to the limit of their possibilities.

[10] D Valadés, *Constitucionalismo crítico – ideas para la transición constitucional en la era post COVID-19* (Spain, Siglo Veintiuno, 2021) 10–21.

Because of this, the axes of the constitutional system are broken. Hypertrophy affects the presidency of the Republic and local governments, as well as political representation and the administrative structure at all levels of government, causing progressive atrophy.

The eminent professor states:

> In Mexico, as in almost all countries, opinion about the handling of the health crisis was divided. This is not relevant. What does count is that the political representation bodies, federal and local, had a minor presence. There was no deliberation about the health measures and, therefore, they ended up being decisions dictated vertically, not seconded by the political forces, unlike what happened in the reformed presidential and parliamentary systems. The Congress of the Union also did not intervene in the approval of economic measures to preserve jobs. At a time of maximum visibility of the performance of power, the Mexican representative system was blurred.
>
> [...]
>
> During this difficult stage, the absence of the opposition became evident. After the rescue of some political figures, the parties have shown their irrelevance. This is also part of the institutional deficit, as parties are the basis of all representative democracy. Their weakness is not due to electoral results or the capabilities of their leaders, but to the institutional design of the system. In Mexico, political minorities have very few rights. The electoral system is neat and efficient, but it is not enough in itself to ensure institutional democracy. While in a well-constructed democracy the majority governs and the minority controls, the Mexican Constitution still does not incorporate efficient political controls that allow minorities to fulfill their functions.

Apparently, the situation in Mexico is set in a general context, more similar to what happened in Argentina. In Brazil, however, the crisis unfolded differently, as we shall see below.

A. COVID-19 and the Brazilian State Response

Initially, we recall that in the terms of the Federal Constitution, *health*, so considered as a social right (Article 6), is the right of all and the duty of the state, guaranteed through social and economic policies that aim to reduce the risk of disease and other illnesses and to provide universal and equal access to actions and services for its promotion, protection, and recovery (Article 196).

It has been constitutionally established that public health measures and services are integrated in a regionalised and hierarchical network and constitute a single system (Article 198). In addition to its other legal duties, the Unified Health System (SUS) is responsible for undertaking sanitary and epidemiological surveillance measures (Article 200, II).

The federal Union, the states, the federal district, and the municipalities have common jurisdiction for the care of *health* and public assistance, and for the protection and guarantee of persons with disabilities (Article 23, II). The federal Union, the states and the federal district are responsible for legislating concurrently on the protection and defence of *health* (Article 24, XII). The municipalities are responsible for legislating on matters of local interest (Article 30, I) and for providing, with the technical and financial cooperation of the Union and the state, *health* care services for the population (Article 30, VII).

These constitutional provisions are sufficient to demonstrate the statutorily enshrined status of the sanitary public interest as a specific type of public interest in the Brazilian legal system. Nothing is more congruent with a democratic state based on the Rule of Law, founded on human dignity (Article 1, III), which has among its objectives to promote the welfare of all without prejudice of origin, race, sex, colour, age, and any other forms of discrimination (Article 3, IV).

The sanitary public interest (of public health), constitutionally enshrined, is also protected at the infra-constitutional level by Law No 8080/1990 (SUS Law), which provides for the conditions for the promotion, protection and recovery of health, and for the organisation and operation of the corresponding services.

The SUS, inspired by the English model, covers the actions intended for sanitary and epidemiological surveillance. According to José Roberto Pimenta Oliveira and Dinorá Adelaide Musetti Grotti:[11]

> Another immense challenge arising from the spread of COVID-19 is the urgent need to improve inter-federal relations, aiming at the adoption of harmonious anti-COVID-19 measures by all state entities (Federal Union, States, Municipalities and Federal District). The public health interest requires the debate on the distribution of administrative powers in public health matters.

In addition to Law No 6259/1975, which alludes to the obligatory notification of diseases, and Law No 6437/1977, which deals with violations of federal health legislation and its sanctions, the most direct response to the pandemic was given through Federal Law No 13.979/2020, which provided for measures to address the public health emergency of international importance resulting from the coronavirus.[12]

These are public health measures provided for in Article 3 of Law 13979/2020, which may be adopted by the competent authorities:

> (i) isolation; (ii) quarantine; (III) determination of compulsory medical examinations, laboratory tests, collection of clinical samples, vaccination and other prophylactic measures, or specific medical treatment; (iv) epidemiological study or investigation; (v) exhumation, necropsy, cremation and handling of cadaver; (vi) exceptional and

[11] JRP Oliveira and DAM Grotti, 'Public Interest and the Challenges of Providing Assistance to Public Health: The Administrative-legal Framework and Jurisdiction of State Entities in Fighting the COVID-19 Pandemic' in AN Dal Pozzo and M Cammarosano (eds), *The Implications of COVID 19 in Administrative Law* (São Paulo, RT, 2020) 83.

[12] It should also be recalled that the National Congress approved Legislative Decree No 395, of 9 July 2009, the International Health Regulations that had been approved at the 58th General Assembly of the World Health Organization (WHO) on 15 June 2005. The Presidency of the Republic, in turn, issued, on 30 January 2020, Decree No 10,122, formalising that decision. Then, Law No 13979 was approved by the National Congress, on 6 February 2020, providing 'for actions for facing the public health emergency of international importance resulting from the coronavirus responsible for the outbreak of 2019'.

> temporary restriction, as per technical and grounded recommendation of the National Health Surveillance Agency (ANVISA), on highways, ports or airports of entry to and exit from the Country, and interstate and intercity locomotion; (vii) dispossession of goods and services from natural or legal persons, with payment of fair compensation a *posteriori;* and (viii) exceptional and temporary authorization for the import of products subject to sanitary surveillance without registration with ANVISA, provided that duly registered by a foreign sanitary authority, and provided for in an act of the Minister of Health.

People shall be subject to the compliance of the measures under Article 3, and their non-compliance will result in legal liability (Article 3, section 4).

We note that the measures to address the pandemic are unilateral administrative acts, endowed with presumption of legitimacy, imperativeness, enforceability, and self-performance, as the case may be. They are extremely incisive measures in the legal sphere of individual rights. Law No 13979/2020 was regulated by Decree Nos 10292/2020 and 10212/2020. Subsequently, the Ministry of Health, through Ordinance No 188/2020, declared a Public Health Emergency of National Importance (ESPIN), due to human infection by the new coronavirus (2019-nCoV). In turn, the Inter-ministerial Ordinance No 5 of the Ministry of Justice and Public Security and Health, of 17 March 2020, defined the compulsory nature of the measures to address the public health emergency, provided for in Law No 13,979. Ordinance No 356/2020[13] of the Ministry of Health established the regulation and operation of the provisions of Law No 13979/2020, because it is an exclusively technical issue and of a specific area, which can be regulated by such means, without an Executive order (decree), which is a constitutional requirement (Article 84, IV, of CF/1988).

In the case of the federal government, the President of the Republic requested the National Congress to recognise the occurrence of the state of public calamity, justifying that, due to the pandemic, the compliance with the fiscal target would generate risks of paralysing the public order, effective until 31 December 2020. On 20 March 2020, the National Congress enacted Legislative Decree No 6/2020, by means of which 'it recognizes, exclusively for the purposes of Article 65 of Federal Law no. 101/2000, the emergence of a state of public calamity'.

As pointed out by José Roberto Pimenta Oliveira and Dinorá Adelaide Musetti Grotti:[14]

> The 1988 Constitution – although it has contributed to the consolidation of the process of democratization of the country, from the point of view of the distribution of powers, could not satisfactorily find the balance in federative relations, because an excessive imbalance of powers persists, leaning towards the Union.
>
> […]

[13] Which ordered isolation, a measure aimed at separating symptomatic or asymptomatic people, infected or under investigation for their contamination by the new coronavirus, in order to prevent the spread of infection and local transmission.

[14] JRP Oliveira and DAM Grotti, 'Interesse público e desafios de tutela da saúde pública: regime jurídico-administrativo e competência dos entes federados no enfrentamento da pandemia da COVID-19'

But, as such actions are embedded in the national public calamity scenario, the Union's jurisdiction prevails, under the specialty criterion, and the measures of the States, Municipalities and Federal District must adapt to the central regulations, under penalty of invalidity. This does not prevent the State, Municipal and District public authorities from contributing to the solution of health problems that are spreading in their territories, and thus directly affect their orbit of administrative performance on behalf of health, taking into account that the national solution requires planned, combined, permanent, efficient and impersonal action of all members of the Federation.

V. The Coronavirus Pandemic and the Crisis Scenario in Brazil

Although the whole world has been affected by the woes of the same pandemic, each country has reacted according to its specific governmental guidelines to face the critical situation.

According to Beatriz Lameira Carrico Nimer:[15]

> It is evident the intensification of the strong political and ideological crisis that the country has been facing in recent years, marked by the election of 'myths' considered intangible and irreproachable by part of the population. Add to this the proliferation of false news on social networks of the Internet, which spread reckless conspiracy theories against the media and the scientific community.
>
> The polarization between *left* and *right* – which are concepts completely unknown to the majority of the population, but repeatedly stated in alienating methods of virtual sharing, creators of the idea of 'us against them' – now reveals a new facet: the division between those in favor and those against the quarantine.
>
> The perception that has arisen is that those who prioritize the fight against coronavirus by restricting the movement of people would be careless in relation to the negative economic impacts of such measures; and, in the opposite direction, the idea would be that those who prioritize the economy would not have sensitivity and commitment to the preservation of human lives threatened by the pandemic. Society is, then, at the mercy of political-ideological clashes, without direction towards centralization and uniformity.
>
> When a power institution stands out – such as the Executive, nowadays – it is imperative that it becomes subject to greater surveillance and oversight by society and by the bodies intended for this purpose. In this context, the Judiciary plays an important role in controlling legality and constitutionality, and should steer its actions toward the guarantees of the Rule of Law, to keep the social order.

in AN Dal Pozzo and M Cammarosano (eds), *As implicações da COVID 19 no direito administrativo* (São Paulo, RT, 2020) 103, 108, 109.

[15] BLC Nimer, 'Limites da atividade jurisdicional de controle das ações e omissões administrativas no combate à pandemia da COVID 19' in AN Dal Pozzo and M Cammarosano (eds), *As implicações da COVID 19 no direito administrativo* (São Paulo, RT, 2020) 599.

A. Jurisdictional Action in the Control of Public Policies to Face the Pandemic

In January 2020, the WHO declared the outbreak of the disease caused by the new coronavirus (COVID-19) a Public Health Emergency of International Concern. In March, the situation was classified as a pandemic.

Given the gravity of the case, the Brazilian Government, at the federal, state and municipal levels, took steps to combat the crisis caused by the disease. However, the disagreements between the federal entities and the entities representing civil society brought to the Judiciary conflicts that put to the test the basic principles of Brazilian federalism.

Law No 13.979/2020, of national character, was enacted to provide for the measures to face what it called a 'public health emergency of international importance due to the coronavirus that led to the 2019 outbreak'. Subsequently, regulatory acts came both from the federal government and from state and municipal governments.

Among the measures adopted, the enforcement of 'quarantines' became controversial, with the suspension of face-to-face services for the public in commercial establishments and service providers, with the exception of activities considered *essential*, which usually cover the areas of health (such as hospitals, clinics, drugstores and cleaning services), food (supermarkets, home delivery services by restaurants), supply (gas stations and motor vehicle garages) and security.

The normative framework for the subject was not uniform, varying according to local governments. Some adopted more restrictive measures on the movement of citizens, even imposing sanctions for noncompliance, while others opted to relax the quarantine rules in favour of getting the economy moving.

In light of this, several issues have been brought to judicial review, both to check the actions of the government and to check omissions.

In March 2020, the Democratic Labor Party (PDT) filed a Direct Action for the Declaration of Unconstitutionality (ADI 6341) against the rules added to Law No 13.979 by Provisional Presidential Decree (MP) No 926/2020, seeking a declaration of partial incompatibility of the MP with the Federal Constitution with respect to the amendments made by Article 3, I, II and VI and paragraphs 8, 9, 10 and 11 of Federal Law No 13979/2020.

In a precautionary measure issued on March 24 in connection with ADI 6341, Justice Marco Aurélio found that MP No 926/2020 did not violate the Federal Constitution. Subsequently, by majority vote, the Plenary of the Brazilian Supreme Court endorsed the precautionary measure granted by Justice Marco Aurélio (Reporting Justice), deeming Law No 13.979/2020 constitutional.

As we pointed out, the list of activities considered essential was made by local governments.

With the adoption of Provisional Presidential Decree (MP) No 926/2020 came the fear that the President of the Republic would consider a wide range of economic activities as essential, thus allowing greater movement of people and agglomerations – with the consequent exposure of the population to the serious risk of contagion from COVID-19.

When adjudicating the Precautionary Measure in the aforementioned ADI, the Brazilian Supreme Court, by majority vote, gave an interpretation in conformity with the Constitution and explained that, although the President of the Republic may provide, by decree (executive order), for essential activities, the other spheres of government *may also do so, in a concurrent and decentralised manner, thus guiding their public health actions and services, regionally, under the terms of Articles 23, II and 198, I, of the Brazilian Constitution.*

Likewise, and in general, in several other cases adjudicated by the Brazilian Supreme Court, the application of the constitutional provision was confirmed, with respect to the division of powers, in the face of the exceptional pandemic caused by the new coronavirus, authorising the taking of actions by all public entities, in that the strict compliance with the maintaining of the federative system is mandatory.

The Chief Justice of the Court decided to suspend these decisions on the grounds that the ruling of the matter is reserved for the exercise of discretionary authority of the Public Administration, that is, the Judiciary could not focus on the analysis of criteria of convenience and opportunity. In addition, one determined that the state government would be adopting effective measures in fighting the pandemic, so that the issuance of sparse judicial commands could generate instability and disorder in the plan of action of the state government.[16]

Another important case concerns the forced entry into public and private properties by a public agent, properly designated and identified, in case of abandonment, absence or refusal of a person to allow access, when this is deemed to be essential for disease containment.

The situation, provided in Article 1, section 2, of Law No. 13.301/2016, relativises the fundamental right to inviolability of the home in favour of the need to ensure public health through the action of health surveillance, even without a court order, in view of the emergency situation.

Very different, clearly unconstitutional and illegal situations are those in several countries that limited the movement of people to prevent the spread of COVID-19. In some cases, the police themselves were authorised to arrest individuals who did not obey their orders.

Diego Valadés[17] is certainly correct when he says:

> Even assuming that this measure (detention) was legal, the confinement of people, even for a few hours, ended up exposing them to contracting the disease from which they wanted to be protected. Clearly it was an unreasonable act and, therefore, arbitrary. Another case of irrationality consisted of penalizing those who travel in their private

[16] Nimer ibid 602.
[17] Valadés (n 10) 35.

> cars, obliging them to take public transport, thereby increasing the risk of infection. Even though they had the legal power to impose these kinds of restrictions, their lack of rationality turned them into arbitrary measures.

Other legal rules establish the possibility of involuntary interdiction of persons, with the restriction of personal liberty in favour of health protection. For example, Law No 10216/2001, which provides for the involuntary hospitalisation of people with mental disorders. Another is Law No 11343/2006, modified by Law No 13.840/2019, which admits, in its Article 23-A, section 3°, II and 5°, the involuntary hospitalisation of drug addicts.

In these cases, as Rafael Carvalho Rezende Oliveira warns:[18]

> The weighting performed by the legislator relativized the fundamental right to freedom in favor of the fundamental right to health. Due to the radical nature of the measure, the implementation of involuntary hospitalization should be considered exceptional, requiring adequate justification, supported by a detailed and individualized medical report. It is possible to realize, therefore, the feasibility of restricting fundamental rights, notably freedom and property, in order to meet the right to health, provided that these restrictions are proportional and justified. Due to the crisis in public health, arising from the pandemic of COVID-19, restrictive and temporary measures are, in many cases, necessary to face the problems.

B. Judicial Review of Decrees that Define Essential Activities

It also seems interesting to recall the control of administrative regulation of essential activities permitted in the midst of the COVID-19 pandemic.

Once restrictions were imposed on all levels of government, the President of the Republic intended to bring to himself the power to define the activities that could (indeed should) continue to function.

Thus, through Provisional Presidential Decree No 926/2020, powers were then included to provide for regional and municipal restrictive measures, covering essential services and activities, specified by decree, in this case, Federal Decree No 10.292. This, then, included several activities as essential, such as lottery agencies that provide payment services, and religious activities, so that places of worship could continue to operate.

This obligation to continue operating, however, could have the opposite effect in combating the spread of the virus, by encouraging crowds.

Another problem is that essential activities were already regulated in Article 10 of Law No 7783/1989, which regulated the right to strike in private activities, and does not include religious activities in its list.

[18] RCR Oliveira, 'Estado de necessidade administrativa: novo coronavírus e os remédi [State of administrative necessity: new coronavirus and the remedies of the right] in M Carvalhosa and F Kuyven (eds), *Impactos jurídicos e econômicos da COVID-19* (São Paulo, RT, 2020) 455–59.

Thus, understanding that the decree went beyond the regulatory power, as it unconstitutionally innovated in the legal system in force, the Federal Prosecution Office filed a lawsuit seeking judicial review of the administrative act in order to recognise its illegality.

Although the preliminary injunction had been granted at first instance (in the trial court), the Chief Justice of the Federal Regional Court of the 2nd Region unfortunately found that the Executive could indeed regulate the essential activities and suspended the injunction, declaring the decree valid and effective until adjudication of the merits of the action.

Based on this decision, several municipalities prohibited the operation of places of worship in their localities, in clear conflict with the federal decree.[19]

Subsequently, in April 2021, the Brazilian Supreme Court, by a nine to two vote, guaranteed the constitutionality of the ban on in-person religious celebrations at the most dramatic moment of the COVID-19 pandemic emergency.

The majority of the judges of the Court held that the freedom to profess religion in worship services is not an absolute right and may be temporarily restricted to ensure guarantees to life and health. The State Decree was therefore considered constitutional (ADPF No 811).

Finally, we mention the filing of an Action against the Violation of a Constitutional Fundamental Right (ADPF No 672-DF), analysed on 8 April 2020, under the court reporting of Justice Alexandre de Moraes.

In the complaint, he argued:

> the government has not always made adequate use of its prerogatives to address the public health emergency, constantly acting in an insufficient and precarious manner, and has committed irresponsible actions that are contrary to the health protocols approved by the scientific community and applied by Heads of State around the world.

He also stated that the President of the Republic had become an 'aggravating agent of the crisis'; that the actions of the federal government in the economic area would be insufficient to guarantee the maintenance of production, employment, and income in various sectors of the economy, particularly for informal workers and the low-income population.

It also points out, as fundamental precepts that have been violated: the right to health (Article 6, CF/1988) and the right to life (Article 5, CF/1988); the federative principle (Article 1, CF/1988), to the extent that the President of the Republic acts to undermine and discredit policies adopted by other federal entities based on their respective constitutional powers (Articles 23, II, and 24, II, of CF/1988); and the independence and harmony between the branches of government (Article 2, CF/1988).

[19] M de Lima Porta, MPR Coelho and TN Bonametti, 'Reflexos da pandemia na COVID-19 na Justiça' [Reflexes of the COVID-19 pandemic in the Judiciary] in AN Dal Pozzo and M Cammarosano (eds), *As implicações da COVID 19 no direito administrativo* (São Paulo, RT, 2020) 683.

The Supreme Court, in deciding the case, concluded:

> It is a well-known fact the serious divergence of positions among authorities of different federal levels and even among federal authorities of the same level of government causes insecurity, uneasiness and justifies fear within the whole society.

It noted the need to respect the principle of separation of powers and federalism – fundamental clauses of the Brazilian Constitution and limiting the possible arbitrary exercise of power – an essential element in the interpretation of Law No 13979/2020, Legislative Decree No 6/1020, and Presidential Decrees Nos 10.282/2020 and 10292/2020.

And it further highlighted the points stated below.

That the severity of the emergency caused by the coronavirus pandemic required the Brazilian authorities, at all levels of government, to adopt the concrete implementation of public health protection, with the use of all possible and technically sustainable measures to support and maintain the activities of the SUS.

That in the exercise of his attributions, the President of the Republic was guaranteed the judgment of convenience and opportunity, being able, among the legal and morally admissible hypotheses, to choose those he understood to be the best for the public interest in the scope of health, assistance, and economy.

That it was not appropriate to grant a precautionary measure in order for the Judiciary to substitute the discretionary judgment of the Executive Branch and determine the President of the Republic to carry out specific administrative measures, but that the measures taken, and any omissions could be brought to judicial review if unconstitutional or abusive.

That the Federal Council of the Brazilian Bar Association (applicant) was right, with respect to federalism and its constitutional rules of distribution of powers enshrined in the text of the Constitution, as well as with respect to the request that the powers of governors and mayors be respected with regard to the operation of economic activities and the rules of agglomeration.

That the constitutional adoption of the federal state gravitates around the principle of autonomy of the federative entities, presupposing the division of powers in the legislative, administrative and tax areas.

And in relation to health and public assistance, including with respect to the organisation of food supply, the Brazilian Constitution enshrines, in its Article 23, II and IX, the existence of common administrative jurisdiction between the Union, states, federal district and municipalities. And, in Article 243, XII, of the same text, it provides the concurrent jurisdiction between the federal Union, states and federal district to legislate on the protection and defence of health, enabling the municipalities to supplement the federal and state legislation as appropriate.

Finally, the Supreme Court considered:

> present the unequivocal plausibility of a possible federal conflict and the evident social and public health risks with danger of irreparable harm, the precautionary measure was partially granted to recognize and ensure the exercise of the concurrent jurisdiction of state and district governments and supplementary jurisdiction of municipal

> governments, each one in the exercise of its attributions and within its respective territories, for the adoption or maintenance of restrictive measures legally permitted during the pandemic, such as the imposition of distance and social isolation, quarantine, suspension of educational activities, restrictions on trade, cultural activities and the movement of persons, among others, regardless of supervening federal act to the contrary, without prejudice to the Union's general jurisdiction to establish restrictive measures throughout the national territory, if it deems necessary.

In view of all the information collected, let us move on to the conclusions.

VI. Conclusions

Since the colonisation period, both Spanish and Portuguese America have been governed in a deeply authoritarian manner, which has significantly conditioned political thought and bureaucratic practice and which is still seen today. Patrimonialism, corruption, social inequality, violence, prejudice, and intolerance are realities that pose challenges for our region.

Despite redemocratisation, with free and periodic elections, electoral democracy has not been able to successfully carry out the fight against the great plagues: poverty, inequality, the discrediting of political parties and the political class, corruption, and impunity.

The 1988 Constitution was a great advance compared with the past. However, Brazil lacks cooperation among federal, state, and municipal political persons. In general, there is a federal centralism that affects the entire federation. An excessive imbalance of powers persists in favour of the federal Union.

Latin American and Brazilian presidentialism are characterised as strong models in a fragmented party system. The parties, with very few exceptions, are unable to approach society and its most basic needs.

With the weakening of Congress and the strengthening of the Executive Branch, many of the national problems are directed to the Judiciary, which is not always the ideal interlocutor to solve society's sensitive conflicts.

With the pandemic, the perception is that those who prioritise the fight against the coronavirus by restricting the movement of people would be careless about the negative economic impacts of this measure; they would lack sensitivity and commitment to the preservation of human lives threatened by the virus.

Given the severity of the pandemic, the Brazilian Government, at the federal, state, and municipal levels, adopted means to combat the crisis caused by the disease. However, disagreements between the federal entities and entities representing civil society brought conflicts before the Judiciary that put to the test the basic principles of Brazilian federalism.

In several judgments, the Brazilian Supreme Court has confirmed the application of federal, state, and municipal jurisdictions by authorising all to take action against the pandemic, maintaining the federative pact and avoiding insurmountable conflicts.

It was possible to perceive restrictions of fundamental rights, notably freedom and property, in order to meet the right to health, but these were deemed to be proportional and justified restrictions – even occasionally reviewed by the Judiciary.

In Brazil, the advance of the pandemic gave rise to a dispute of federative jurisdiction focused on which authority is the most legitimate to solve the problems brought by it.

5

Pandemocracy in Chile

JAVIER COUSO

I. Introduction

Over the last couple of years much has been written on the impact of the COVID-19 pandemic in democratic countries. This once-in a lifetime event led to unprecedented restrictions on important rights imposed on citizens by their own governments, in order to prevent the expansion of a rapidly spreading and, at the beginning, very dangerous virus. While the reaction by governments differed in terms of the scope and extension of the social distancing policies that most of them introduced, the curtailment of fundamental rights, in particular the rights to free movement and of assembly, was a common feature.

As in previous pandemics, the most common first response to the health crisis triggered by COVID-19 was to impose lockdowns and other restrictions to the right of free movement of the people. While ubiquitous, the severity of the confinements varied hugely within different countries, ranging from being ordered to stay at home for months on end (with permission to leave home for only a few hours a week), to be free to walk at will at any time around a rather ample radius from home. Aside from the restriction on the freedom of movement imposed on millions of people as a way to deal with the pandemic, some governments saw in the health crisis triggered by the COVID-19 pandemic an opportunity to advance partisan political objectives (for example, some authoritarian-leaning leaders displayed the extraordinary powers granted to them to fight the pandemic to forbid public demonstrations by opposition groups). This abuse of the emergency powers was, of course, common in some countries, but absent in others. Thus, while COVID-19 represented a common threat in every country in the world – and triggered similar responses to it – the abuse of the exceptional powers granted to governments was not universal, but, I submit, a function of the previous state of democracy and the rule of law in different countries. This explains why in some nations the pandemic became an excuse for authoritarian-leaning authorities to abuse emergency powers in order to engage in so-called 'self-entrenchment strategies'[1] while, in others, the executive branch used those powers with prudence, allowing the democratic process to function reasonably well.

One clear indicator to distinguish between a country where democracy in times of pandemic led to an authoritarian abuse of the extraordinary powers granted to the government or, for the contrary, to a reasonable exercise of the latter, is whether or not the democratic system continued to operate in a way that allowed for the alternation of power. Of course, the latter does not mean that only in those countries that experienced a shift in government during the pandemic there was no abusive use of the extraordinary powers granted to the executive branch (that would be a very silly way to ascertain the latter). Having said this, if a shift in the control of government happened during the pandemic in a democratic country, we can be fairly confident that even severe public health measures adopted to fight the spread of COVID-19 were not put at the service of self-entrenching objectives by incumbent governments.

At this point, the reader might reasonably object that the above-mentioned aspect of the problem represents a rather poor consolation for the millions of citizens of countries where the encroachment on civil liberties went too far during the worst of the pandemic (even in the absence of authoritarian-leaning governments attempting to take the opportunity provided by it so that they could perpetuate their hold on power). Indeed, the sheer costs in terms of rights-curtailment imposed on the people due to an overreach by democratically-conscious governments could have been so severe as to generate unacceptable outcomes, even if perpetrated by governments animated by the noble aim of saving the lives of those most likely to lose it due to COVID-19. In other words, the understandable focus that some analysts have placed on the abuse of extraordinary powers granted to executives branches in countries where the latter engaged in self-entrenchment strategies, should not makes us oblivious to the possibility that even leaders with impeccable democratic backgrounds and purposes might have gone too far in their zeal to protect the population of their countries from the virus, so much so that the constraints in the fundamental rights of the people they ruled was unacceptably high from a liberal-democratic standpoint.

II. The Social and Political Context of Chile at the Arrival of the COVID-19 Pandemic

After introducing what I take to be two critical aspects of the relationship between the COVID-19 pandemic and the rights-endangering impact of the extraordinary measures taken by governments of democratic regimes (that is, first, the excuse

[1] See A Kouroutakis, 'Abuse of Power and Self-entrenchment as a State Response to the COVID-19 Outbreak: The Role of Parliaments, Courts and the People' in MC Kettemann and K Lachmayer (eds), *Pandemocracy in Europe. Power, Parliaments and People in Times of COVID-19* (Oxford, Hart Publishing, 2021).

that the pandemic offered authoritarian-leaning leaders to abuse extraordinary powers in the midst of that health crisis for partisan purposes, and, second, the excessive restrictions of liberties and freedoms taken by administrations with no authoritarian purposes), I now turn to the way this problem played out in Chile.

One of the peculiar features of pandemocracy in Chile is that COVID-19 arrived in this country when it was confronting the most disruptive (and violent) social and political crisis in a generation. Indeed, just a few months before the virus arrived (in March 2020), Chile had experienced social uprising that mobilised millions of people who took to the streets their demands for social and economic change. This – largely unexpected – movement had started on 18 October 2019, when hundreds of public services and private companies were put on fire and looted, a crisis that led the government to impose a constitutional state of exception (labelled 'State of Emergency') to try to control the situation. After an extremely violent start (some 20 subway stations were destroyed by the fire during the first two days of rioting), a week later over a million people peacefully demonstrated in several cities demanding social and economic change (as well as other demands), a development that lent the mobilisation process a degree of legitimacy that it would have lacked if it had it been circumscribed to rioting and looting.

Considering that the State of Emergency allowed the executive branch to ask the armed forces to engage in law and order functions (for which the military is not trained), it should come as little surprise that some demonstrators were killed by the latter in the two weeks that the constitutional state of exception was in force. Furthermore, the intensity of the rioting led to an overreaction of the regular police that left over 100 demonstrators with eye injuries. The national – and international – scandal triggered by these human rights violations escalated the political crisis so much so that President Piñera was forced to reshuffle his cabinet, and, eventually, call all the political parties to agree on a constituent process. While the change of cabinet and – more critically – the start of a process of constitutional change appeased the social and political crisis, by March 2020 the campaign for an 'entry' referendum (aimed at asking citizens whether or not they wanted a new constitution) scheduled for early April, was already polarising the country again. At precisely that moment, the utterly unexpected happened, as the COVID-19 pandemic made its entrance in the Chilean scene.

It is hard to convey how strange the irruption of the pandemic felt, when Chile was in the middle of such intense social and political struggles. While the decision to try to institutionally channel the social uprising with a constituent process helped manage what at some points seemed like an explosive situation, many analysts were expecting a resurge of violence as the 26 April entry referendum was approaching. But then a pandemic that most Chileans saw as something remote and alien (happening thousands of miles away, in China and Europe), became eerily close to home. As if recovering from an unexpected punch, slowly but surely, even the most agitated demonstrators had to confront the fact that something fundamentally out of their control (and of a truly global scale) had aborted the social uprising. The sudden shift in the preoccupations of Chileans triggered by the arrival of the COVID-19 pandemic explains that – in just two weeks – the cities of the country went from being full of angry demonstrators to places where millions of citizens remained obediently at home glued to their television sets trying to make sense of what would happen next with what seemed to most of them as an unprecedented challenge.

As in the case of war, nothing can help a shaky government more than the threat of a feared pandemic. With images of massive deaths in developed countries being televised on a daily basis, the Chilean Government saw an opportunity to take the initiative, after months of being on the defensive, and call all the political parties to confront this health crisis united. Sensing that the bulk of the population had shifted from disbelief that COVID-19 would reach the country, to the sheer fear that it could bring huge loss of life, the government announced that it was forced to imposed a – very different – constitutional state of exception than the one it had resorted to a few months before. This was the so-called 'State of Catastrophe' (which had been typically used in previous decades to deal with the natural disasters such as earthquakes, floods and avalanches). Thus, in a matter of days, a country that was about to enter the final weeks of a crucial electoral event (the 'entry referendum' of the constituent process), shifted from being massively politised to obediently following the health authorities as they introduced, first, the use of facial masks and, then, imposed a severe lockdown on most of the national territory.

As it can be appreciated, for the extremely discredited and fragile Piñera administration, the pandemic came as an unexpected blessing. Of course, the government was preoccupied with the health and economic challenges that COVID-19 presented, but this was the kind of task that the President knew could help him get the initiative and – hopefully – overcome a social and political crisis that almost threw him out of office a couple of months earlier.[2]

III. The Constitutional and Legal Framework for the Management of the Pandemic in Chile

The first governmental reaction to the COVID-19 pandemic in Chile happened on 5 February 2020, when the Ministry of Health issue a so-called 'health alert',[3] for the entire national territory. The measure, adopted through Executive Decree

[2] Piñera had been impeached in December 2019 by almost all opposition parties for the human rights violations that took place in the first weeks of the social uprising. Thanks to a handful of votes the impeachment was not approved by the lower house of Congress. For more information on this proceeding, see communication issued by the official website of the Chamber of Deputies of Chile, in: www.camara.cl/prensa/sala_de_prensa_detalle.aspx?prmid=138911.

[3] See: www.bcn.cl/leychile/navegar?idNorma=1142163&idParte=&idVersion=.

No 4 of the Ministry of Health, was justified as a tool 'to address the public health threat posed by the global spread of the "New Coronavirus 2019 (2019-nCoV)"'. This initial state response to the pandemic included a wide range of extraordinary powers granted to the Ministry of Health,[4] which were of an administrative nature, with the exception of the faculty 'to order the mandatory use of masks and other related medical devices in means of transportation, classrooms, workplaces and, in general, in any other place of public access or where there is an agglomeration of people' (a measure that was not immediately adopted). The mostly administrative and logistical nature of Executive Decree No 4, combined with and the fact that the power to order the massive use of masks was not initially exercised, meant that for the bulk of the Chilean population this first governmental response to the pandemic went largely unnoticed.

The circumscribed measures taken in early February changed dramatically when, on 11 March 2020, the World Health Organization officially declared COVID-19 to be a pandemic and, especially, when the first case of the virus was detected in Chile (on 3 March). Due to these developments, on 18 March, President Piñera declared the already mentioned – 'State of Catastrophe' in of the entirety of Chile's territory for a period of 90 days, in view of the 'public calamity' generated by the COVID-19 pandemic.[5]

At this point, it is pertinent to briefly report how the Chilean constitutional order regulates the constitutional states of exception and, in particular, the one that concerns us in this case (the 'State of Catastrophe'). As it is well known, the most consequential feature of a state of exception is that they typically allow the suspension or restriction of some fundamental rights (although, in some cases, they can go as far as to authorise the full 'suspension' of the Constitution on a temporary fashion). In Chile, constitutional states of exception have a long tradition, going back to the very outset of the nation as an independent state, in the early nineteenth century. Ever since then, constitutional charters have given the executive branch extraordinary powers to deal with different kinds of emergencies. While – for the first century and a half – the emergencies allowing for the declaration of

[4] This administrative action gave the Ministry of Health extraordinary powers, including the authorisation to hire extra personnel to face the pandemic; carry out the direct acquisitions of goods, services and equipment; coordinate the distribution of pharmaceuticals and medical supplies required to meet the demand of the population; disseminate health measures in the mass media; deliver, free of charge or onerously, medicines, medical devices or other sanitising elements to target groups previously defined by this sanitary authority; establish the maximum price to be paid by the general population for certain pharmaceutical products, medical devices, sanitary elements and supplies, as well as health benefits and sanitary services, as well as all the goods and services necessary to meet health needs; directly import medicines, supplies and medical devices that are necessary for the fulfillment of the powers granted to the health sector by this decree. Finally, this regulation stated, the Ministry of Health could, in the case of imported products, be exempted from one or more obligations contained in Law No 19.886.

[5] The adoption of this state of exception was done through Executive Decree No 104, of the Ministry of Interior, in pursuant of Law No 18.415, which regulates the constitutional states of exception. See: drive.google.com/file/d/1kQij4Gxjfl6P811yGAS83SytGySF8oeJ/view.

a constitutional state of exception were an external war, a civil war and serious political unrest, the Constitution of 1980 added a new state of exception, the 'State of Catastrophe', aimed at granting the President extraordinary powers to deal with emergency situations of a natural character (such as earthquakes, fires, floods, and the like).

One particular feature of Chile's regulation of the states of exception is that the Constitution of 1980 includes a section solely devoted to deal with the former.[6] Thus, Articles 39 to 45 provide a rather detailed regulation of the different factual contexts that authorise the executive branch to declare each of the four different constitutional states of exception contemplated by the fundamental charter: a) external war (allowing for the declaration of a 'State of Assembly'); b) internal war, or grave commotion (authorising the declaration of a 'State of Siege'); c) grave alteration of the public order, or grave threat to the country's national security (allowing for the declaration of a 'State of Emergency'), and, finally; d) public calamity (authorizing the declaration of a 'State of Catastrophe').

As opposed to the emergencies allowing for the declaration of the traditional states of exception (war, civil war, and political unrest), in the case of a 'public calamity' (the factual precondition that authorises the government to declare a State of Catastrophe), the Constitution of 1980 prescribes that that President is not required to ask congressional permission after declaring it in order for it to continue.[7] Instead, Chile's charter only requires the executive branch to *inform* Congress of the specific measures adopted by virtue of this state of exception. Furthermore, Congress can only override a declaration of a State of Catastrophe when at least six months have passed since it was declared by the government, and only if the motives triggering it 'have absolutely ceased'.[8] Having said this, the Constitution prescribes that, if the President wants to extend a State of Catastrophe beyond one year, it necessarily requires congressional approval.

[6] The general regulation of the four different states of constitutional exception authorised by the 1980 Charter starts with Art 39, which begins with the following statement: 'The exercise of the rights and guarantees that the Constitution assures to all persons may only be affected under the following states of exception: external or internal war, internal commotion, emergency and public calamity, when they seriously affect the normal development of the institutions of the State.' See: www.bcn.cl/leychile/navegar?idNorma=242302.

[7] See Art 41 of the Constitution of 1980: 'The state of catastrophe, in case of public calamity, shall be declared by the President of the Republic, determining the area affected by the same. The President of the Republic shall be obliged to inform the National Congress of the measures adopted by virtue of the state of catastrophe. The National Congress may annul the declaration after one hundred and eighty days have elapsed if the reasons for the declaration have absolutely ceased. However, the President of the Republic may only declare a state of disaster for a period exceeding one year with the consent of the National Congress. Said agreement shall be processed in the manner set forth in the second paragraph of Article 40. Once the state of catastrophe has been declared, the respective zones shall be under the immediate dependence of the Chief of National Defense appointed by the President of the Republic. He shall assume the direction and supervision of his jurisdiction with the powers and duties indicated by law'. See: www.bcn.cl/leychile/navegar?idNorma=242302.

[8] See Art 41 of the Constitution of 1980: www.bcn.cl/leychile/navegar?idNorma=242302.

Regarding the measures that, during a State of Catastrophe, the President is authorised to adopt, the Constitution prescribes the following:

> By declaring a state of catastrophe, the President of the Republic may restrict the freedom of movement and the right of assembly. He may also order requisitions of property, establish limitations on the exercise of the right to property and adopt all extraordinary measures of an administrative nature necessary for the prompt restoration of normality in the affected area.[9]

As it can be appreciated, the most important rights and liberties that can be restricted by a declaration of a State of Catastrophe are the freedom of movement; the right of assembly; and private property (although, as we shall see below, in cases of requisitions, they always give a right to a full compensation to the affected owners, once the emergency is over). Having said this, note that the expression used by the Constitution with regard to this measures is 'restrict' which, in the Chilean constitutional tradition, is opposed to the expression 'suspend' (a more drastic curtailment of a right or freedom, since while a 'restriction' cannot absolutely end the enjoyment of at least part of the fundamental right affected by a state of exception, a 'suspension' is considered to allow for the absolute deprivation of a given right, albeit temporarily).

In addition to the power to restrict the fundamental rights and freedoms mentioned above, during a State of Catastrophe the executive branch is authorised to 'to adopt all the extraordinary measures of an administrative nature that are necessary for the prompt reestablishment of normality in the affected area',[10] a prerogative understood to give the President a wide range of administrative powers that do not involve the curtailment of fundamental rights. Finally, it is worth pointing out that the Constitution ends its regulation of the State of Catastrophe be prescribing that, upon the declaration of the latter: 'the respective zones (declared to be in this 'state') shall be under the immediate dependence of the Chief of National Defense appointed by the President of the Republic. The latter will assume the direction and supervision of its jurisdiction with the powers and duties indicated by law'.[11]

After declaring the restrictions that can be imposed on some fundamental rights by a declaration of a State of Catastrophe (as well as other extraordinary powers granted to the government to deal with public calamities), the Constitution goes on to establish some safeguards aimed at preventing the abuse of this extraordinary power. The first such safeguard is the constitutional mandate that a so-called 'organic law'[12] would further regulate the states of exception, legislation that the

[9] See Art 43 of the Constitution of 1980: www.bcn.cl/leychile/navegar?idNorma=242302.

[10] See Art 43 of the Constitution of 1980: www.bcn.cl/leychile/navegar?idNorma=242302.

[11] See Art 41 of the Constitution of 1980: www.bcn.cl/leychile/navegar?idNorma=242302.

[12] Under Chile's current constitutional charter (dating from 1980), an 'organic law' is a particularly relevant piece of legislation which the Constitution requires has to be approved, modified or derogated by a qualified majority (it used to be 4/7 of the existing members of both chambers of Congress until 2022, but it was recently reduced to an absolute majority of existing members of Congress).

Constitution mandates should 'contemplate what is strictly necessary for the prompt reestablishment of constitutional normality and may not affect the competencies and functioning of the constitutional bodies or the rights and immunities of their respective holders'.[13] More importantly, the 1980 charter ends its regulation of the states of exception (including the State of Catastrophe) by giving individuals whose constitutional rights are affected by any particular measure adopted in virtue of the former, 'the guarantee of recourse to the judicial authorities through the corresponding appeals'.[14] Thus, even though the courts cannot second-guess the executive branch's assessment of the factual circumstances justifying the declaration of a particular state of exception, it provides ample judicial supervision of the constitutionality of the measures adopted by the government in virtue of those states. A key consequence of this provision is that, if the President restricts rights and freedoms that she is not allowed to curtail or, if the restriction imposed goes beyond what is reasonably necessary to confront the emergency at hand, the courts can step-in, and protect individuals from an improper restriction of their fundamental rights.[15]

As it can be appreciated from this account of the constitutional provisions dealing with the states of exception in the 1980 charter, there is a rather detailed regulation of this matter, including the one used to confront the COVID-19 pandemic (the State of Catastrophe). What is more important, the analysis of the above-mentioned constitutional clauses reveals that, while the executive branch have ample prerogatives under a state of exception, including ones that can significantly affect important constitutional rights, there is nothing like a 'suspension' of the constitution, since the courts can always review the constitutionality of the governmental measures that impact on the people's rights. This represents a crucial feature of Chile's regime of constitutional exception, since it ensures that the rule of law is guaranteed even in the presence of extraordinary powers granted to the executive branch.

As for the organic law that further regulates the different states of exception (Law No 18. 415), in the case of the State of Catastrophe it provides even more measures that the authorities can adopt. Since, as it is obvious, the organic law cannot transgress the constitutional regulations analysed before in this section, there is some overlap in the measures authorised, but also more specific descriptions of the extraordinary powers that the executive is granted by a State of Catastrophe. Thus, for example, the law prescribes that once the latter is adopted, 'the powers vested in the President of the Republic may be delegated, in whole or

The constitutional mandate that a specific matter ought to be regulated by an 'organic law' expresses the high relevance that the Constitution gives to that matter.

[13] See Art 44 of the Constitution of 1980: www.bcn.cl/leychile/navegar?idNorma=242302.

[14] See Art 45 of the Constitution of 1980: www.bcn.cl/leychile/navegar?idNorma=242302.

[15] In the case of restrictions on private property rights, the Constitution of 1980 declares that: 'The requisitions carried out shall give rise to compensation in accordance with the law. The limitations imposed on the right to property will also be subject to compensation when they entail the deprivation of any of its essential attributes or faculties and thereby cause damage to the property.'

in part, to the heads of the National Defense that he may designate'.[16] This delegation of extraordinary powers to members of the military – while somewhat shocking at first sight – has, nonetheless, been a feature of the State of Catastrophe that has triggered little public controversy, since the Chilean Armed Forces (even before the military regime) have traditionally had an important role in rescue operations in the recurrent natural catastrophes that the country has always endured (especially in the case of earthquakes, in what is one the most seismic countries in the world). Following this tradition, the law allows the President to delegate in military officers the power to

> assume command of the Armed Forces and the Forces of Order and Public Security that are in the area declared to be in a state of emergency, for the purposes of ensuring public order and repairing or preventing the damage or danger to national security that has given rise to said state, having to observe the administrative powers of the institutional authorities placed under his jurisdiction.[17]

Other extraordinary powers granted to the executive by the legislation regulating the states of exception that it is worth noting, is the authority of those in command of a specific territory under the constitutional state of catastrophe to

> 'control the entrance and exit of the zone declared to be in a state of emergency and the transit in it'; 'to dictate measures for the protection of works of art and public utility services, mining, industrial and other centers'; 'to order the collection, storage or formation of reserves of food, articles and merchandise required for the care and subsistence of the population in the area and to control the entry and exit of such goods'; 'to determine the distribution of the free or onerous use of the aforementioned goods for the maintenance and subsistence of the population of the affected zone'; 'to establish conditions for the holding of meetings in places of public use'; 'to directly issue instructions to all the officials of the State, of its companies or of the municipalities that are in the area, with the exclusive purpose of remedying the effects of the public calamity'; 'to disseminate through the means of social communication the necessary information to give tranquility to the population'; 'to dictate the necessary guidelines and instructions for the maintenance of order in the zone';

and, finally, 'to exercise any other powers granted by law in its capacity as such'.[18]

As it can be appreciated, the measures listed above are consistent with what most public authorities need to do when facing a natural disaster (or another public calamity) impacting a large territory, such as those aimed at maintaining the public order and coordinating the work of authorities in order to act in a more effective and expedient way to address the calamity at hand. There are, finally, provisions for disseminating critical information to the population. In terms of the rights affected by these measures, they all relate to restrictions on the freedom of movement; the right to assembly; and property rights.

[16] See Art 6 of the Law No 18.415: www.bcn.cl/leychile/navegar?idNorma=29824.
[17] See Art 5 of the Law No 18.415: www.bcn.cl/leychile/navegar?idNorma=29824.
[18] All the extraordinary measures mentioned are granted by Art 7 of the Law No 18.415: www.bcn.cl/leychile/navegar?idNorma=29824.

I have described in some detail the constitutional and legal framework dealing with states of exceptions in general, and with the State of Catastrophe in particular, because, within the Latin American scene, Chile is rather exceptional in that the gap between the constitutional/legal regulation of states of exception and what actually happens on the ground is smaller than in other countries of the region. In other words, what the Constitution and relevant legislation prescribes in this domain, matters more than what it is the case in other countries of the region.[19]

With the juridical background of Chile's State of Catastrophe in mind, it is worth highlighting that, the fight against the COVID-19 pandemic represented the first time that this particular state of exception was declared in all the country's territory, in contrast with the experience of previous decades, when the public calamities at hand were circumscribed to the specific regions where earthquakes, floods, fires, and other natural disasters happened.

IV. The Measures Adopted by the Executive Branch under the State of Catastrophe

As Cervantes et al. report (citing Cofre),[20] soon after the declaration of the State of Catastrophe, a series of measures were taken by the health authorities, including 'a "selective and dynamic" confinement, border closure and control, sanctions for COVID-19 infected persons who failed to comply with mandatory quarantine, a permanent curfew, and a generalized identity check by the Ministry of Health'.[21] Except for the identity check, all the above mentioned measures represented restrictions (some severe, others mild) to the freedom of movement of Chileans, measures which, in contrast with other countries, were generally complied with by the population.

Of all the measures actually adopted in virtue of the extraordinary powers granted to the executive branch, the most severe and rights-diminishing one was clearly the series of lockdowns that were imposed in most cities of the country. Indeed, as it was described earlier in this chapter, the lockdowns in Chile were among the most stringent in the world, since they involved forcing the population to stay at home for months on end with the right to exit only a couple of hours per

[19] See G O'Donnell, *Polyarchies and the (un) Rule of Law in Latin America* (Instituto Juan March de estudios e investigaciones, 1998) Vol 254, 1–28.

[20] See Cofre, cited by Cervantes et al., 'Los estados de excepción en tiempos de pandemia. Un estudio comparado en América Latina' (2020) 20 *Revista 'Cuadernos Manuel Giménez Abad'* 179–206.

[21] Cervantes et al. add that: 'As a first measure, total isolation was ordered in certain localities and, in the less affected ones, a dynamic isolation by time slots in the less affected localities. In all cases, the movement of people over 80 years of age was prohibited. These measures were tightened as the virus spread in the different localities.' ibid 192.

week. Having said this, the 'selective' nature of the lockdowns meant that in some areas (particularly remote rural areas) the confinement was in place for only short periods of time.

In view of the presidential faculty to delegate in the heads of the National Defence its extraordinary powers in the different regions of the country, supervision of the population's compliance with the measures taken by the government was given to both the police and to the Armed Forces. What is interesting is that, perhaps due to the historical tradition of calling on the latter to help in cases of large earthquakes (and other natural disasters), there was no loss of life due to the presence of the military in the streets (in contrast with what had happened during the worst moments of the social uprising of October–November of 2019).

In terms of the actions taken by the government to compensate for the imposition of lockdowns that prevented large segments of the population from going to work, something that was particularly damaging to the domestic economy of millions of Chileans during the first 'wave' of the pandemic (in the period April–July 2020, when working from home was still rare), it is worth noting that the government plan to help struggling business and confined workers was considered to be extremely modest, which translated into the increase in the indebtedness of a large percentage of the Chilean households.[22] At the beginning of the pandemic, criticism of the lack of sufficient financial help to those experiencing confinement was rather small (in fact, the opposition complained that the aid was too little, too late, but it still approved the legislation needed to materialise the latter).[23] This, however, would change towards the middle of the year 2020, when opposition members of Parliament started advocating for legislation allowing Chileans to retire part of their pension funds to pay for the cost of being unable to work

[22] Claudia H Bendersky argues that: 'The reluctance of the state to intervene has been evident with respect to economic measures to combat the pandemic. While Chile, with a public debt of less than 30% of GDP, proposes solutions that represent about 5% of GDP, other countries in the region, with less debt capacity, are making much more substantial efforts. The State of Catastrophe seems to have been invoked more for repression than for effective public action. Intervention in key markets has been timid.' See CH Bendersky, 'Chile: entre el estallido social y la pandemia' (2020) 18 *Análisis Carolina* 1, 2.

[23] Rossana Castiglioni summarises well the first economic measures introduced by the government: '(…) on March 19, the Minister of Finance, Ignacio Briones, announced the adoption of an Emergency Economic Plan to contain the effect of the health crisis. Thus, the government undertook to prepare a bill to protect the income of those who had to stay at home and could not work by means of teleworking, the delivery of a bonus for people without formal jobs and the postponement of tax, social security and debt payments to alleviate the burden on companies and avoid job losses. Subsequently, on April 8, the government announced the second part of its plan, aimed at protecting economic activity by guaranteeing greater liquidity for companies. This would be done through the use of financing lines guaranteed by the State to offer credit to companies that required it. The creation of a fund to safeguard the income of informal workers was also announced. Some of these measures were progressively expanded and refined. Thus, on April 12, Piñera announced that a fund to protect the income of informal workers would be created.' See R Castiglioni, 'La política chilena en tiempos de pandemia' (2020) 287 *Nueva Sociedad* 68–79, 71.

(as a result of the long-term lockdowns they were force to endure).[24] Eventually, this piece of legislation – which was strongly objected to by the government – was approved, and millions of Chileans retired large amounts of money to deal with basic needs. This first retirement opened the door to a second, and eventually a third retirement of pension funds, actions that in time had a devastating impact on both the pension system and the monetary system (which in time led to historic levels of inflation for Chile).

There is, of course, no space in this chapter to analyse the details of the – initially – flawed economic aid packages and the negative impact that they had on the lives of Chileans and the health of the economy in the long run, but, the facts described above are just one example of the devastating impact that the severe lockdowns had on the life of the population of the country. Not to mention the impact that these measures had on the mental health and educational life of millions of children.

V. The Population's Reaction to Pandemocracy in Chile

In the previous sections we have provided a – necessarily brief – summary of, first, the social and political context of Chile when the COVID-19 pandemic reached the country, in order to then give an account of what was the constitutional and legal background of the response by the government to this unprecedented pandemic. Then, we have mentioned the most severe measures taken by the government (the long and strict lockdowns) and some of the impact that this had on the daily lives of Chileans. In this section, we shall quickly review the reaction exhibited by the Chilean population – and its legal and political elites – to the imposition of a state of constitutional exception such as the State of Catastrophe.

When one takes stock of how intensively mobilised the Chilean people had been in the immediate preamble of the arrival of the COVID-19 pandemic, it is just astonishing how quickly that shifted to a law-abiding population facing one of the world's most severe and extended lockdowns and other restricting measures. While the sheer fear of sudden death and serious illness of course played a role in

[24] A recent study reports that: 'On July 30, 2020, Law No. 21.248 was published in Chile, allowing the first withdrawal of 10% of pension funds. This measure, catalogued at the time as 'exceptional', allowed through a constitutional modification the voluntary withdrawal of 10% of the accumulated individual capitalization funds, establishing maximum withdrawal values and subject to the payment of taxes. According to the Superintendency of Pensions, as of July 31, 2021, more than 11 million workers had requested it, withdrawing an average of 1 million 417 thousand pesos (approx. US$ 2000). Of the total number of workers who requested their withdrawal, 21.7% withdrew the total of their pension funds. In relation to the uses that households made of the first 10%, a study released by the Santiago Chamber of Commerce, indicated that 51% of the beneficiaries used it to buy food and basic necessities; 28% to pay debts and 29% to pay for basic services (electricity, water and gas)'. See L Pérez-Roa, 'Los retiros de los fondos provisionales y las finanzas: nuevas rutas de extracción financiera' (2022) 20 *Revista Nuestra América* 2.

this dramatic shift in the state of mind of millions of Chileans, the fact that – once a vaccine was announced, and something resembling a normal life slowly started to come back – the previous degree of agitation did not return as strongly as some had feared, suggests that the pandemic did, indeed, change the social environment that the country had experienced between October 2019 and March 2020.

While, during the very first period of the pandemic (during the first 'wave' of contagions, in March–July 2020), compliance with strict measures ordered by the health authorities might be explained by the sobering effect that the pandemic had even within the most radical groups (who saw their elders fall ill and die due to a then little known virus), the relative moderation that they exhibited once that first wave was over (and, more fundamentally, when a vaccine was announced) seemed to be a function of the fact that the constituent process became a tangible reality when, on 25 October 2020, a large majority of the voters approve of the option of having a new Constitution in an 'entry referendum'. This important step towards institutionally 'channelling' what had been a strong call for social transformation, seemed to have appeased groups that saw in that process a way to, finally, get a degree of social equality that was lacking. Thus, in the following months the control of the pandemic walk hand in hand with, first, the campaign to elect members of the Constitutional Convention (in May 2021), and then the actual deliberations of the later. The fact that that same year a presidential campaign was under way, explain why even the most radical groups shifted from demonstrating in the streets to participating in a constituent process and on a presidential campaign where the most radical left since the return to democracy would end up winning the election.

In the midst of a 2021 full of electoral events, the successful policy displayed by Piñera's government in terms of both getting enough COVID-19 vaccines and then getting the bulk of the population immunised speedily, transformed the social meaning of the pandemic for Chileans, from a horrible unknown threat, to an eminently manageable public health issue.

VI. Conclusion

In the introduction of an important report on the global impact of the COVID-19 pandemic, the international NGO, Freedom House, summarises in this way the challenges that the former posed:

> The coronavirus outbreak presents a range of new challenges to democracy and human rights. Repressive regimes have responded to the pandemic in ways that serve their political interest, often at the expense of public health and basic freedoms. Even open societies face pressure to accept restrictions that may outlive the crisis and have a lasting effect on liberty.[25]

[25] See Freedom House's Report 'Democracy During Pandemic': freedomhouse.org/issues/democracy-during-pandemic.

This account of the threats involved in the way both authoritarian and democratic governments dealt with the COVID-19 pandemic summarises well some of the most crucial issues to look at when approaching the way different countries behave in the face of this life-changing experience.

Writing when the pandemic seemed to be evolving into a regular/recurrent virus, one can look back and judge with more hindsight how the different states behaved in the face of it. Once this exercise is performed, a variety of governmental attitudes become apparent. In the most authoritarian regimes, the fate of the health of the people was critically dependent on the whim of the heads of government. If the latter thought that the pandemic was 'just a flu', or in other ways minimised the risks and discarded what the scientific evidence suggested as the most sensible way to protect the population form the coronavirus, the consequence was a terrible excess of serious illness and death. If, on the contrary, the leaders were persuaded of the gravity of the threat posed by the COVID-19 pandemic, hundreds of thousands of lives were spared. In democratic settings, the balance of powers between the executive, legislative and judicial branches – and the existence of a free media that could give voice to physicians and health scientists – was able to moderate the impact of heads of government who were in denial concerning the severity of the threat posed by the pandemic (and their consequent inaction against it).

While the above speaks to the human rights to life and health care, the pandemic also posed threats to other crucial rights of the people, such as freedom of movement, the right to assembly, freedom of religion, and so on. As importantly, the pandemic offered the opportunity to authoritarian-leaning leaders to use the extraordinary powers granted to them to fight the pandemic in ways that benefited them politically (what has been labelled 'self-entrenchment strategies'),[26] endangering the health of democracy.

As it was suggested in the introduction to this chapter, one expedient way to know if a head of government in a democracy in times of pandemic (a 'pandemocracy') abused the extraordinary powers given to them to deal with the coronavirus (or not), is to check if during that period a shift in government happened. If that was the case, one might be inclined to think that no abuse of power by the executive branch took place. The problem with this 'test' is, of course, that only a small group of democracies had scheduled general (or presidential) elections during the pandemic. And even where those elections did take place it could well have been the case that a non-abusive leader manage to prevail elections without abusing their powers (as it was the case in countries where perfectly reasonable democrats won precisely because of how well they managed the pandemic). Notwithstanding the flaw of the 'test' under scrutiny, it might come handily when assessing the impact of a pandemocracy where a general (or presidential) election was scheduled to take place during the pandemic, and the opposition did prevail. If that is

[26] See n 1 above.

the case, the hypothesis that in such a country no 'self-entrenchment strategies' took place seemed to have the upper hand.

As it happens, that is exactly the situation experienced by Chile, a country where the Constitution gave the President extraordinary powers to deal with the COVID-19 pandemic, but where the former did not abuse them, so much so, that during the pandemic no less than four national elections (an entry referendum; the election of members of a constituent body; local and parliamentary elections; and last, but not least, a presidential election) were conducted in a perfectly free and fair fashion, and where the government coalition lost all of them. Aside from what these lasts facts suggest, qualitative assessments (such as Freedom House's 'Democracy during pandemic' report),[27] found that Chile's democracy remained 'about the same' during the pandemic (as opposed to the 80 countries where democracy became 'weaker' in that period).[28] A finding consistent with the 'test' suggested above. Furthermore, the fact that the head of the executive branch of Chile did not abuse of his (constitutionally-granted) extraordinary powers seems to be a function of the fact – in spite of intense social and political crisis the country had experienced just months before the pandemic – it had a consolidated rule of law in place.

Having discarded that in Chile the extraordinary powers granted to the executive branch were abused by it with self-entrenching purposes, the question of whether or not the measures adopted by the government went too far in their zeal to fight COVID-19 (unnecessarily restricting important rights), remains a critical one. When this issue is analysed in the case of Chile, the assessment is very different from the one just done with regard to the state of democracy. As we have seen earlier in this chapter, the confinements to which most of the Chilean population endured were unnecessarily severe and prolonged (while the economic aid provided by the government during the first wave of the pandemic, extremely poor). The damaging consequences of lockdowns that prevented millions of people from even taking a walk around their homes for months on end, while preventing most of them from earning a living, are hard to ascertain with precision, but they were substantial, and are the responsibility of a government that acted as if controlling the coronavirus was the only value at play. When one adds to the equation the unusually high levels of domestic violence experienced by women and children in the midst of the seemingly unending lockdowns, the conclusion that there must have been a more sensible way to establish quarantines seems unavoidable. In sum, Chile's pandemocracy represents a peculiar case of a country where a government with good intentions (and with an impeccable democratic behaviour during the pandemic), nonetheless imposed measures that gravely transgressed important rights of millions of people. This suggest that, evaluating the rights performance of democratic regimes in times of pandemic demands a variety of perspectives.

[27] See n 16 above.
[28] See freedomhouse.org/report/special-report/2020/democracy-under-lockdown.

6

Pandemocracy in Mexico

JOSÉ MARÍA SERNA DE LA GARZA

I. Introduction*

The purpose of this chapter is to review the way in which constitutional institutions interacted in Mexico during the COVID-19 pandemic.[1] As we will see, the Congress of the Union, dominated by the party of the federal Executive and its allies, did not play a counterweight role throughout the pandemic. It was not a forum for deliberation, for dialogue to consider alternatives or for monitoring the measures adopted by the federal government to address the health crisis.

For its part, the judiciary, specifically the federal courts, did play a counterbalancing role in various situations, either limiting the federal government because it considered that its measures violated constitutional principles and rights, or forcing the government to act in a certain way to provide adequate health protection for vulnerable groups. As for the subnational governments, it can also be said that they were a balancing factor in an environment marked by the confrontation between the federal government and a large section of the opposition governors, as well as by the lack of effective vertical coordination. Perhaps this explains why, by the beginning of 2022, Mexico was one of the worst-hit countries in the world

* This chapter reflects some of the ideas that I have published in two previous works. One of them, published in Spanish, is JSerna de la Garza, 'Resistencia y debilidades del Estado democrático de Derecho en México frente a la pandemia de COVID19' in A von Bogdandy, A Malamud and MM Antoniazzi (eds), *La Democracia ante la pandemia. Transformaciones Interamericanas* (Heidelberg, Max Planck Institute for Comparative Public Law and International Law, 2022). The other one, electronically published, is JSerna de la Garza, 'Covid-19 and Constitutional Law: the case of Mexico' in J Serna de la Garza (ed), *Covid-19 and Constitutional Law* (Mexico, UNAM, 2020).

[1] My reflections follow the guidelines found in works like C Ayala Corao, *Retos de la Pandemia del Covid-19 para el Estado de Derecho, la Democracia y los Derechos Humanos* (MPIL Research paper Series, No. 2020-17, Germany, Max Planck Institute for Comparative Public Law and International Law, 2020); and A von Bogdandy, JM Casal and MM Antoniazzi, *La Resistencia del Estado Democrático de Derecho en América Latina frente a la pandemia de COVID-19* (Caracas, Centro para la Intergración y el Derecho Público y Max-Planck-Institut für ausländisches öffentliches Recht und Völkerrecht 2021).

in terms of COVID-19 fatalities, with more than 300,000 deaths attributed to the disease, according to officially recognised data.

The chapter is organised in the following way: first, I will refer to the constitutional norms that grant powers to certain federal state bodies during health emergencies (section II); second, I will review how the federal Congress responded to the crisis and the way it interacted with the federal government (section III); third, I will examine the role played by federal courts in solving cases brought to them through the writ of *Amparo* by plaintiffs that sought protection of their constitutional rights to life, to health and freedom of movement (section IV); fourth, I will review the role played by subnational governments during the health emergency, and the way they interacted among themselves and with the federal government (section V); fifth, I will address some issues related to democracy and electoral processes during the pandemic (section VI); and sixth, the chapter ends with a final reflection on the impact that the pandemic had on some fundamental constitutional principles such as democracy, separation of powers and federalism.

II. Constitution and Allocation of Powers During a Health Emergency

The policy area that in Mexico is known as 'general health'[2] is subject to a regime of 'concurrent powers'. By this term, we understand the possibility of sharing responsibilities among the different levels of government in the design and implementation of public policies on the same subject matter, according to a distribution of competences defined by the federal Legislature. In this way, 'general health' is a subject matter on which the federal Congress can pass a statute law which distributes competences and responsibilities between the federal and state levels of government.

Thus, in the General Law on Health, passed by the federal Congress, there is a chapter on 'Distribution of competences' between the federal and state governments. Within this Chapter, Article 13.A establishes the powers of the federation concerning general health; Article 13.B. determines the powers of the states in connection with the same matter.

Mexico's federal Constitution establishes two different schemes to deal with emergency situations. One of them is the one provided for in Article 29, which indicates (without going into all the details) the hypotheses in which rights can be restricted or suspended ('In cases of invasion, serious disturbance of public peace, or any other situation that puts society in grave danger or conflict') and

[2] For an examination of Mexico's health system, see generally MG Block et al., 'Mexico, Health System Review' *Health Systems in Transition* (World Health Organization, 2020) Vol. 22, No 2.

the state bodies that can restrict or suspend rights ('only the President of the United Mexican States, with the approval of the Congress of the Union or the Permanent Committee[3] when the latter is not in session'). This article also provides for the possibility that Congress grants 'authorizations that it deems necessary for the Executive to deal with the situation'.[4] It should be noted, from the outset, that this constitutional mechanism was not used in Mexico to deal with the health crisis caused by COVID-19.

The second scheme is the one provided for in the three bases of section XVI of Article 73 of the Constitution, as follows:

> 1st. The Council of General Health will report directly to the President of the Republic, without the intervention of any Secretary of State, and its general provisions will be mandatory in the country.
>
> 2nd. In case of epidemics of a serious nature or danger of invasion of exotic diseases in the country, the Secretary of Health will have the obligation to immediately dictate the essential preventive measures, subject to being subsequently sanctioned by the President of the Republic.
>
> 3rd. The health authority will be executive and its provisions will be obeyed by the administrative authorities of the country.

These provisions are the product of the debates that took place within the Constituent Congress of 1917. They were proposed by the medical doctor and constituent deputy José María Rodríguez, who justified them based on three reasons: a) the need to create public agencies capable of reacting in a fast and effective way in the face of the different problems that could arise in the country in the field of health; b) said bodies should have the necessary material and human resources to carry out their actions; and c) they should also have the power to issue mandatory provisions for the entire territory without the intervention of other administrative authorities.[5] Moreover, and regarding the third base, in the debate of the constituent congress it was estimated that it was essential that the provisions issued by the health department should have a general character, in order to avoid 'enormous losses of lives and capital'.[6]

Based on these constitutional provisions, and also based on the existing federal legislation on health (the General Law on Health, hereinafter GLH), as of

[3] The Permanent Committee of the federal Congress responds to the need to guarantee the institutional presence of the federal legislative power in the country's political affairs, during Congress's recess. It is formed of 37 legislators (19 deputies and 18 senators). They are designated by the respective house on the eve of Congress's recess. Notably, and in spite of the fact that no rule states that the Permanent Committee should have a plural composition, the body includes legislators of all parties represented in Congress.

[4] These 'authorizations' imply granting the federal Executive the power to legislate.

[5] For a review of the proposals of the constituent deputy José María Rodríguez, see JRC Díaz and DJS Mejía, 'El Consejo de Salubridad General en la Constitución Mexicana de 1917' in FG Domínguez (ed), *Secretaría de Salud: La Salud en la Constitución mexicana* (México, Secretaría de Cultura, INEHRM, Secretaría de Salud, 2017) 79.

[6] ibid.

23 March 2020, the two federal instances with powers in the field of public health and in particular in relation to the fight against pandemics, that is, the Council of General Health (CGH) and the Secretary of Health (SH), began to adopt various measures on a national level to face the health crisis.

The first of these measures was the 'Decree by which the General Health Council recognizes the epidemic of disease caused by the SARS-CoV2 virus (COVID-19) in Mexico, as a serious disease of priority attention, establishing the activities of preparation and response to said epidemic' (23 March 2020); followed by the 'Decree establishing the preventive measures that must be implemented to mitigate and control the health risks involved in the disease caused by the SARS-CoV2 virus (COVID-19)' (issued by the SH on 24 March 2020).[7]

Subsequently, on 30 March 2020, the CGH issued the 'Decree declaring the epidemic of disease caused by the SARS-CoV2 virus (COVID) as a health emergency due to *force majeure*'; and the following day (31 March 2020), the SH issued another decree to implement various 'extraordinary measures', of which the following stand out: a) the immediate suspension, from 30 March to 30 April, of non-essential activities in the public, private and social sectors, in order to mitigate the spread and transmission of the virus in the community; b) only a limited set of activities, considered essential, could continue in operation, including those related to public security and civil protection,[8] to the defence of national integrity and sovereignty, and to the administration of justice and activities of both federal and state legislatures; c) voluntary home confinement of the population not participating in essential work activities, as well as those who are in the highest risk groups; d) it was established that, once the suspension of non-essential activities and home confinement were concluded, the SH would issue the guidelines for a staggered return to normal activities.

Various criticisms have been levelled at the CGH and its actions in the context of the pandemic. First, this council was criticised because of its late response to the pandemic, since evidence that the crisis was coming began to appear in March of 2020, and it was not until the end of that month that the CGH declared an emergency. A second criticism was that despite the collegiate structure of the council, which, without entering into great detail, brings together high-level public servants (at the federal and state levels) and leaders from academic institutions (experts), in practice, decisions were made by the SH. And third, it has been pointed out that the Internal Regulations of the CGH do not include a procedure to regulate the expedition of a declaration of a health emergency, which implies that the way to do it is at the discretion of the SH, who is a subordinate of the President of the Republic.

[7] This decree established measures of social distancing in public spaces and temporarily suspended activities involving physical concentration, transit or displacement of people, until 19 April 2020.

[8] In Mexico the expression 'civil protection' (in Spanish '*protección civil*'), refers to the powers and responsibilities of public and private actors, allocated to face situations in which the population might be in danger, such as earthquakes and hurricanes.

To conclude this section, it is possible to say that during the health emergency due to COVID-19, Mexico's federal Executive acted with constitutional and legal authorisation, considering that the regulatory framework gives it a great margin of decision and action, in what some have identified as a health 'dictatorship'.[9] It is a constitutional and legal scheme that operates through instances dependent on the federal Executive, without authorisation from Congress, and without the limitations and controls of the mechanism of suspension or restriction of rights of Article 29 of the federal Constitution.[10]

III. The Role of the Federal Congress During the Health Emergency

The involvement of the Congress of the Union in the response to the health crisis was minimal. Congress did not participate in the declaration of the health emergency, since, as already stated, the mechanism of Article 73.XVI of the Mexican Constitution was resorted to (a mechanism that does not give Congress any power in health emergencies). In addition, Congress did not participate in defining the timing of the state of health emergency. The timing and rhythms (both of the lockdown and of reopening) were defined by the federal Executive (in a conflictive relationship with the Executives of the states, as will be seen later).

To a large extent, the passive role of the federal Congress during the health emergency was due to the fact that the party of the President of the Republic (MORENA) has control of the majority of seats in both chambers of the federal legislative body, as will be explained in what follows.

The Mexican Congress of the Union is made up of two chambers: the Chamber of Deputies and the Senate. The first is made up of 500 deputies (300 of relative majority and 200 proportional representation). In this chamber, the percentage of seats per party since March 2020 when the health crisis began and until the 6 June 2021 general election was the following: National Regeneration Movement (MORENA), 50.4 per cent; National Action Party

[9] See EA Córdoba, 'Educación, propaganda o 'dictadura sanitaria'. Estrategias discursivas de higiene y salubridad públicas en el México posrevolucionario, 1917–1945' (2007) 33 *Estudios de historia moderna y contemporánea de México* 57–88.

[10] Eg, Art 29 of the Mexican Constitution states that when the restriction or suspension of the constitutional rights and guarantees ends, because the deadline was met or the Congress so ordered, all legal and administrative measures taken during the restriction or suspension will be void immediately, ordering also that the President of the Republic cannot make comments to the decree through which the Congress revokes the restriction or suspension of the constitutional rights and guarantees. Moreover, this Article states that the decrees enacted by the President of the Republic, during the restriction or suspension of the constitutional rights and guarantees, shall be immediately reviewed by the Supreme Court of Justice of the Nation, which shall rule on their constitutionality and validity as soon as possible.

(PAN), 15.4 per cent; Institutional Revolutionary Party (PRI), 9.6 per cent; Labor Party (PT), 9.2 per cent; Citizen Movement (MC), 5.4 per cent; Social Encounter Party (PES), 4.8 per cent, Democratic Revolution Party (PRD), 2.4 per cent; Green Ecologist Party of Mexico (PVEM), 2.2 per cent; moreover, there were also three deputies with no party affiliation.

For its part, the Senate has a total of 128 seats. Sixty-four are elected according to the traditional system (FPTP system, two per state); 32 seats are elected in each state, and are allotted to the party that gets the second place in the corresponding senatorial election (the first minority), while the remaining 32 are elected by PR, on the basis of closed and ranked lists nominated by political parties, which are assigned in proportion to each party's share of the national vote. The percentage of seats by party in the Senate in March 2020 and up to the 6 June 2021 election was as follows: MORENA, 42.6; PAN, 19.5; PRI, 10.1; PT, 4.6; CM, 6.2; PES, 3.1; PRD, 2.3 and PVEM, 5.4 per cent; in addition, there was one senator with no party affiliation. With these data, it is possible to see that MORENA and its allies in Congress (PT, PES and PVEM) had the absolute majority of the votes in both chambers (66.6 per cent in the Chamber of Deputies and 55.7 per cent in the Senate). In turn, this means that the governing bodies and all of the committees of both chambers of Congress were under the control of the ruling party and its allies. This was the case of the health committees of the Chamber of Deputies and of the Senate, to which we turn our attention in what follows.

A. The Health Committee of the Chamber of Deputies

During the health crisis, this committee was made up of 38 members, of which 28 were from MORENA and its allies, which represents 73.6 per cent of the total (Morena 20; PT five; PES two; and PVEM one). In spite of this composition, one would suppose that this commission would have had an active and leading participation in monitoring the way in which the Executive responded to the health crisis. However, this was not the case.

On the website of the Health Committee of the Chamber of Deputies there is information on approved minutes, initiatives and proposals. The minutes are Bills that were approved in the Senate and have been turned over to the Chamber of Deputies for examination, discussion and voting; initiatives are Bills or legal reforms that are presented within the Chamber of Deputies itself for discussion and voting, while proposals refer to the so-called 'points of agreement' (in Spanish '*puntos de acuerdo*'), which are expressions of political positioning of the Chamber, generally directed to the federal Executive, encouraging or demanding the government to act in a certain way.

However, according to the information published on the aforementioned website, of the two minutes approved between 2020 and 2021, none refers to the issue of the pandemic. Likewise, of the 51 initiatives approved between 1 October

2019 and 3 March 2021, only one refers to the issue of the pandemic.[11] Lastly, of the 12 proposals reported as approved by the Health Commission of the Chamber of Deputies between 1 October 2019 and 15 December 2020, none refers to the COVID-19 health crisis.

The Health Committee of the Chamber of Deputies, widely dominated by the MORENA and its allies, spoke out from the beginning to support the federal government's strategy and actions to deal with the COVID-19 health crisis. In contrast, opposition parties within the Chamber of Deputies did criticise the federal government's policies for dealing with the COVID-19 pandemic. For example, the group of deputies from the PRD demanded that the federal government listen to and take into account the proposals of a group of scientists, specialists, and former health sector officials who considered that the government had not taken the best measures to effectively combat the pandemic.[12] Likewise, deputies from opposition parties such as PAN, PRI, MC and PRD called for a national dialogue to establish an 'Agenda Propositiva', proposing measures that were different from the ones that were being implemented by the federal government, to safeguard the lives of Mexicans and guarantee that no family was left without money because of the global economic crisis due to the pandemic.[13]

B. The Health Committee of the Senate

Let us now look at the performance of the Senate's Health Committee, which was formed with 18 members, of which during the health emergency 10 belonged to MORENA and its ally the PT, that is, 55.5 per cent of the total. Regarding this commission, in the first place it is pertinent to note that in its Activities Report, dated September 2020, the only mention of something related to the pandemic is the following:

> This year 2020 has been a difficult year for our country and for the Powers of the Union due to the global pandemic of the Covid-19 virus, as a result of which the Health Commission participated in the adaptation of secondary legislation in connection with the T-MEC.[14]

[11] This initiative intended to make an addition to Art 76 Bis of the GLH and was proposed by the deputy Alejandro Videma Velázquez (from MORENA). The aim of this initiative was to establish guidelines for the provision of mental health services to the population with the objective of reducing the levels of stress, anxiety or depression originating from the confinement measures issued to face the health crisis due to COVID-19. The initiative was published in the parliamentary Gazette of the Chamber of Deputies on 21 April 2020.

[12] Chamber of Deputies, Note No 4694, 28 March 2020.

[13] Chamber of Deputies, Note No 4921, 21 April 2020.

[14] The T-MEC (Mexico-United States-Canada Treaty) was created to replace the North American Free Trade Agreement (TLCAN).

On the other hand, according to information that can be found on its website, of 55 opinions discussed by the Senate Health Commission between 19 March 2020 and 29 April 2021, only four referred to the COVID-19 pandemic.

From the above, it can be concluded that the Congress of the Union did not exercise true check and balance functions with respect to the Executive throughout the health crisis. On the contrary, it is possible to say that the pandemic contributed to the centralisation of power around the federal executive branch, in a system that even before the health crisis was already significantly centred on the President of the Republic. The President's party has a majority in both chambers of Congress, which stopped meeting from the end of March 2020. This has meant that health measures – as well as measures related to the mitigation of the economic impacts of the pandemic – have been adopted by the President of the Republic and the SH in a vertical manner, almost without deliberation.

IV. The Role of Courts During the Health Emergency

Federal courts continued working during the health emergency, albeit in a limited fashion,[15] hearing cases brought to them through the writ of *Amparo*, which is the main procedural instrument that people who live in Mexico can resort to in order to secure their constitutional rights. *Amparo* cases can be brought to challenge both actions and omissions of federal and state authorities that imply a violation of human rights, as enshrined in the Constitution and in international treaties on human rights.

Additionally, within the writ of *Amparo* proceeding, there is an injunction (or *precautionary measure*) that is called a *suspension*, which has the effect of ordering a public authority to stop the actions or omissions that potentially represent violations of human rights until the case is decided on its merits. Moreover, a suspension also allows federal district judges[16] to order the responsible authority to act in a particular way.

The writ of *Amparo* proceedings for constitutional protection can last for months, but a suspension can be decreed the moment that a plaintiff brings their action to a federal court. In the context of the COVID-19 pandemic, many federal district judges ordered suspensions in order to protect the right to life and the right to health of numerous plaintiffs, as will be described in what follows.[17]

[15] From the end of March 2020, federal and state courts stopped functioning in a regular manner. Those that had the technological possibility and the capacity to continue functioning virtually did so in a limited manner, which was the case of federal courts. But most courts at the state level were shut for months. Some lawyers even presented legal cases against the closure of the courts and in favour of gradual reopening, with whatever health measures were required to do so safely.

[16] Federal district judges are the first instance court in *Amparo* proceedings.

[17] For a general reflection on the role of courts during the pandemic, see generally T Ginsburg and M Versteeg, 'The Bound Executive: Emergency Powers During the Pandemic' (26 July 2020) *Virginia Public Law and Legal Theory Research Paper No. 2020-52* (University of Chicago, Public Law Working

A. Medical Staff

There were cases of doctors and nurses who sought and obtained protection via federal justice through the writ of *Amparo*, in order to force the authorities in the health institutions where they were employed to provide them with the equipment they needed in order to work safely and minimise the risk of infection, in addition to providing them with the training to use said equipment in a safe manner. Additionally, there were cases of medical personnel who obtained legal protection through a suspension, allowing them not to work in a hospital where there were patients infected with COVID-19 until the relevant authorities provided them with the protective equipment they required to work safely. Still others obtained protection so as not to have to work in a hospital, because they had a chronic illness (asthma, high blood pressure, diabetes) which made them particularly susceptible to fatal consequences were they to become infected with COVID-19.

B. Indigenous Peoples

It is also worth mentioning the protection sought by indigenous Tsotsil, Tzeltal, Zoque and Chol peoples, to demand that information regarding health measures and actions resulting from the COVID-19 pandemic be made available in their languages. In this case, the relevant district judge ordered the authorities to provide the information in these languages; moreover, he ordered that this information should be disseminated in the media (audiovisual, oral and graphic) 'respecting the cultural specificities of each people'.

Another case that was widely discussed in the media was the collective protection case brought by members of the Maya Ch'ol nation (based in the municipalities of Palenque, Ocosingo and Salto del Agua, state of Chiapas), against the continuation of the mega-project known as the 'Tren Maya'.[18] In this case, the district judge who heard the case determined that the federal government should abstain from continuing the construction of said project in the aforementioned municipalities during the pandemic, as continuing construction could put at risk the health and lives of the population there.

C. Persons with Some Disability

Constitutional protection through the writ of *Amparo* was also sought by a group of deaf people who lacked accessible information about the current situation with

Paper No 747) available at: ssrn.com/abstract=3608974 or at dx.doi.org/10.2139/ssrn.3608974 (accessed 24 May 2022).

[18] A huge train route that is being built in the Yuctán peninsula.

the pandemic and the measures that should be taken. In this case, the district judge ordered the federal health authorities to use the Mexican Sign Language (MSL) in all official communications, as well as establishing support services for communication in health centres, via certified sign language interpreters.

D. Persons Deprived of Liberty

Various writ of *Amparo* cases were brought in connection with persons who were imprisoned in jails. For example, in one case, the district judge in the city of Tuxtla Gutiérrez (State of Chiapas) ordered state authorities to define the preventative measures and actions necessary to contain and avoid the spread of the virus in a prison established in that state, and to guarantee the right to health and life of prisoners. In Mexico City, another district judge ordered local authorities to follow health and prevention protocols inside prisons; to institute effective general health measures; to carry out actions to detect cases of COVID-19 in prisons; and to guarantee that prisoners could have communication with the outside world (specifically with their families).

E. Migrants

Other *Amparo* cases related to migrants. For example, there was a case in which the first district judge specialising in administrative matters (with jurisdiction in Mexico City) ordered federal migration authorities to free all the migrants who were detained in stations or shelters of the National Institute of Migration, so as to avoid outbreaks of COVID-19. Moreover, this district judge ordered the federal government to design and implement the protocols and measures that were required to guarantee the life, safety and health of migrants expelled from the US to Mexico during the COVID-19 health crisis.[19]

F. Freedom of Movement

Article 11 of the Mexican Constitution recognises the freedom of movement, but it also establishes the possibility that statutes on emigration, immigration and general health can establish limitations on this right.

Having said that, federal policies during the COVID-19 pandemic were not based on implementing mandatory confinement. Rather, federal health authorities

[19] Fundación para la Justicia y el Estado Democrático de Derecho, *Informe sobre los efectos de la pandemia de Covid-19 en las personas migrantes y refugiadas. Violaciones a Derechos Humanos documentadas por organizaciones defensoras y albergues en México* (México, 2020).

asked the population to voluntarily 'stay at home'. In contrast, some state governors took more restrictive measures and thus decreed mandatory confinement, which led to charges of unconstitutionality. For example, on 20 April 2020, the governor of the State of Michoacán issued a decree which declared mandatory confinement, establishing harsh restrictions on the movement of persons, along with penalties for those who infringed those restrictions.

That decree was challenged by a group of professors from the Law School of the Nicolaíta University of Michoacán. In this case, the district judge (the seventh district judge based in the State of Michoacán), granted a suspension of the decree. However, the state governor appealed this suspension, which was reviewed and eventually revoked by the second collegiate circuit court specialising in labour and administrative matters, based on the argument that according to the Law on *Amparo*, a suspension cannot be granted if the social interest would be negatively affected by said injunction, which would have happened in this case, as it would have impeded the carrying out of measures to effectively fight the spread of the disease.

On the other hand, there have been cases of municipal authorities who, in an unconstitutional and illegal manner and without the powers to do so, imposed severe restrictions on people's free movement. For example, there is the case of a couple, María Elena LS and José Luis SV, who left their community in order to work, but when they tried to return to their home they found that the municipal authorities had decided not to allow anyone into the community so as to avoid the spread of the coronavirus.

Given this situation, the couple sought constitutional protection through an *Amparo* action, which was denied by the tenth district judge in Oaxaca, who argued that the municipal authorities had acted to protect the social interest of residents. However, the couple appealed the decision and eventually the collegiate circuit court specialising in civil and administrative matters of the 13th circuit reversed the district judge's decision and granted the suspension of the municipal authorities' restrictions on the freedom of movement of people in their community, since they were not allowed, according to the Constitution, to suspend or restrict human rights. As the circuit court pointed out, this was particularly true when the restriction of the freedom of movement affected other rights, like those of the couple's youngest son not to be separated from his parents (in connection with the principle of protecting the best interests of the child, established in paragraph nine of Article 4 of the Mexican Constitution).[20]

The cases that I have mentioned were more or less successful, since plaintiffs were able to protect their rights, particularly through the precautionary measure of suspension. However, it cannot be said that this was a general pattern, since many barriers preventing effective access to federal justice were present throughout the

[20] These events occurred in the community of Concepción Las Mesas, Mesones Hidalgo, Putla de Guerrero, Oaxaca State.

pandemic, as documented by two civil society organisations: *Fundación para la Justicia y el Estado Democrático de Derecho, A.C.* and *Derechos Humanos y Litigio Estratégico Mexicano, A.C.*[21]

V. The Performance of Subnational Governments During the Health Emergency

In relation to the actions of subnational governments during the COVID-19 health emergency, this section will examine: a) whether they had independent powers to determine and implement their own responses to the pandemic; b) if they were involved in designing or implementing the national response; and c) if they resisted in any way the measures dictated by the federal government.[22]

First of all, it is notable that there was a lack of communication between the federal SH and state governments during the health emergency. As stated above, the issue of 'general health' is concurrent between the federal and state governments. In the case of pandemics like COVID-19, the federal SH can adopt 'extraordinary actions' with regards to health, and state governments are obliged to follow federal guidelines. However, what we saw during the entire health crisis was a series of conflicts, disagreements and failed encounters between federal and state authorities in connection with the moment to declare the health emergency, the different kinds of health security measures to be adopted, the moment to declare the lockdown, its intensity, and the timing and strategy of reopening. This is due in large part to the non-existence of an institutionalised agency that ensures communication and the harmonisation of public policy between the President of the Republic and state governors.

Let us start by remembering that the distribution of the 32 governorships in March 2020, when the health crisis began, and until the election on 6 June 2021, was as follows: Institutional Revolutionary Party (PRI), 12; National Action Party (PAN), 9; National Regeneration Movement (MORENA), 7; Party of the Democratic Revolution (PRD), 1; Citizen Movement (MC), 1; besides, there was one governor who had no party affiliation.

The first measures in response to the pandemic were taken by some state governments, and even by some municipal governments. For example, while the federal government was still refusing to accept the danger and dimension of the pandemic, the governments of Jalisco and Nuevo León ordered the closure of

[21] Fundación para la Justicia y el Estado Democrático de Derecho, *El Acceso a la Justicia en México durante la Pandemia de Covid-19. Análisis sobre la actuación del Poder Judicial de la Federación*, (Mexico City 2021).

[22] For a reflection on how federal and non-federal states responded to the pandemic, see generally D Cameron, *The Relative Performance of Federal and Non-federal Countries During the Pandemic* (Canada, Forum of Federations, 2021).

activities in movie theatres, casinos, and other social gathering places from mid-March 2020. At the same time, the municipal government of San Pedro Garza García, in the State of Nuevo León, after confirming the infection of 12 people, ordered the closure of bars and gyms (and made it clear that it was ready to use the police to implement these measures). Simultaneously, the state governments of Tabasco, Yucatán, Tamaulipas and Sonora restricted tourist access to the beaches. Likewise, the governments of Jalisco and Chihuahua determined that people over 60 years of age and pregnant women should stay at home and avoid going to their workplaces. Finally, also in mid-March, the government of Mexico City began to take steps to sanitise public transportation and cancel mass events.

State governors responded to the health crisis along partisan lines. In other words, those who belonged to the same political party as the President of the Republic followed federal policies and guidelines without much criticism (with a couple of exceptions). For their part, the governors of opposition parties created different groups to form a common front to resist some of the policies of the federal government or to propose alternative policies to face the health emergency.

The most visible grouping was the so-called 'Federalist Alliance': this group was formed of governors from the left, centre and right of the political spectrum and included the governors of Aguascalientes (PAN), Coahuila (PRI), Guanajuato (PAN), Jalisco (MC), Colima (PRI), Michoacán (PRD) and Nuevo León (no party affiliation). Their main claim during the health emergency was the need to review the centralised character of Mexico's fiscal federalism.[23]

Three other groups of governors were formed: 'Northeast-Pacific Alliance', with seven opposition governors from Nuevo León (no party affiliation), Coahuila (PRI), Durango (PRI), Tamaulipas (PAN), Jalisco (MC), Colima (PRI) and Michoacán (PRD); the 'Central-Bajío-Occidente Alliance', formed with the governors of Aguascalientes (PAN), Guanajuato (PAN), Jalisco (MC), Querétaro (PAN) and San Luis Potosí (PRI)); and the 'Association of Governors of National Action' (GOAN), made up of nine PAN governors.

On the other hand, the absence of effective coordination between the federal government and state governments during the health crisis was notable. Some of these governments were already taking measures from mid-March 2020, while the CGH (federal) only met on 19 March 2020 to assess the situation.

An example of disagreements between federal and state authorities occurred in mid-April 2020, due to the receipt of federal aid in the form of different protection materials to counter the pandemic: the governors of Michoacán, Aguascalientes and Quintana Roo denounced these materials as being of poor quality, and decided to return them to the federal government, considering them useless.

[23] For an analysis of Mexico's fiscal federalism, see generally: EC Mendoza, 'Fiscal Federalism in Mexico: Distortions and Structural Traps' [2013] *Urban Public Economics Review* 18.

Relations between the Jalisco government and the federal government were particularly rough. For example, on 13 March 2020, after the World Health Organization declared a global health emergency, the governor of Jalisco announced the first restrictive measures of his government to prevent infections (ie, cancellation of mass events, suspension of classes in schools). But these measures were criticised by the federal SH as unnecessary. Subsequently, and contrary to federal policy, the governor of Jalisco announced a testing program to detect people infected with COVID-19. Later (on 16 April 2020), the federal SH accused the municipal government of Guadalajara (capital of the State of Jalisco) of not complying with the suspension of non-essential activities ordered by federal authorities. Finally, the governor of Jalisco rejected the possibility of returning to in-person classes due to the pandemic, contradicting the federal Secretary of Education who had announced the return to classes as of June or July 2020.

In addition, several examples of horizontal cooperation among state governments can be mentioned. For example, the governors of Nuevo León, Tamaulipas, Coahuila, Durango and Michoacán agreed to make an account of the expenses their governments had to incur in order to face the health crisis and to claim reimbursement from the federal government of those expenses. They argued that they had faced the crisis with their own ordinary resources, but since the health emergency was an extraordinary situation, they were entitled to receive extraordinary financial support from the federation.

For their part, the governors of Jalisco, Aguascalientes, Querétaro and San Luis Potosí agreed on a series of measures to deal with the pandemic in a coordinated manner, such as defining a strategy to support the electrical and automobile industry. The governors of these states also formed the 'Alianza Centro-Bajío-Occidente' (a regional alliance), whose purpose was to support each other in obtaining medical supplies for their hospitals.

Despite the centralised character of Mexico's federal system,[24] subnational governments showed that they had a certain margin of autonomy in managing the health crisis caused by COVID-19. As we have seen above, opposition governors were able to resist various policies and guidelines of the federal government and to propose alternative policies and measures to deal with the pandemic.[25] They also managed to organise strategies of horizontal cooperation. However, an

[24] See generally: J Serna de la Garza, *El Sistema Federal Mexicano. Un Análisis Jurídico* (Mexico, Porrúa/UNAM, 2010).

[25] For comparative purposes, it is interesting to point out that in other Latin American countries that are not federal but have a certain type of political-administrative decentralisation, there were also tensions in intergovernmental relations related to the fight against the pandemic. Such is the case of Colombia, where the increase and intensity of intergovernmental tensions seem to have depended on factors such as the level of institutional capacity of subnational governments, political identification with the President of the Republic, and the prospective political agenda of the mayors of the largest cities. See RA Bello-Gómez and P Sanabria-Pulido, 'The Costs and Benefits of Duality: Colombia's Decentralization and the Response to the COVID-19 Pandemic' (2021) 55 *Revista de Administração Pública* 1, 165–179.

efficient mechanism of vertical cooperation was visibly lacking.[26] Notably, there were no regular meetings between the federal and state Executives to agree on policies against the pandemic, in spite of the fact that from March 2020 many state governors requested a meeting with the President of the Republic, with this not taking place until 19 August 2020.[27]

VI. Democracy and Elections

There were legislative and municipal elections scheduled in the States of Coahuila and Hidalgo on 7 June 2020. However, the state of the health emergency made it clear that the basic conditions for carrying out the corresponding electoral processes could not be fulfilled. Carrying out the elections would have put the health and lives of millions of citizens and the electoral workers involved at risk. Given these circumstances, the question was: what was the constitutional means to satisfactorily solve this extraordinary situation?

The constitutional solution was found in Article 41, section V, second paragraph, subhead c) of the Mexican Constitution, which allows the General Council of the National Electoral Institute (INE) to 'Bring to its knowledge any matter within the competence of the local electoral organs when its transcendence or importance requires so or when the matter shall be used to establish an interpretation criterion.' It is worth clarifying that this power of the INE was the product of a political-electoral constitutional reform on 10 February 2014, which established a system of concurrence with regards to the organisation of state elections. Under this system, the INE and the electoral Local Public Agencies (OPLES) share powers and responsibilities in the organisation of electoral processes in the states, and the possibility was left open, through the rule quoted above, for the INE to exercise the 'power of attraction' and absorb the functions of the OPLES.

This rule found in Article 41 of the Mexican Constitution, together with the decree declaring a health emergency caused by a force majeure with regards to the SARS-CoV2 (COVID-19) epidemic and the 'Declaration of a Health Emergency' by the CGH, published in the Official Gazette of the Federation on 30 March 2020, was the constitutional and legal basis for the decision by the

[26] For a review of Mexico's intergovernmental relations from a comparative perspective, see generally JW Hopkins, 'Intergovernmental Relations in Mexico and the United States: a comparative perspective' (1990) 56 *International Review of Administrative Sciences*.

[27] Another example not only of lack of coordination but also of open conflict between the federal and state governments occurred in Brazil. See E Massard da Fonseca, N Nattrass, LB Arantes and FI Bastos, 'Presidential Denialism and the Subnational Government's Response' in SL Greer, EJ King, E Massard da Fonseca and A Peralta-Santos (eds), *Coronavirus Politics: The Comparative Politics and Policy of COVID-19* (Ann Arbor, Michigan, University of Michigan Press, 2021) 494.

General Council of the INE to postpone the elections in Coahuila and Hidalgo until health conditions allowed them to proceed.

In essence, what the INE did was to postpone the steps and the activities that were to come (including the election day), so as to reschedule them when the health conditions to carry them out were in place, with the full guarantees of political rights, but also keeping in mind the right to the protection of health as described in Article 4 of the Mexican Constitution and in various international treaties which the Mexican government has ratified.[28]

The constitutional solution that the General Council of the INE devised was the best available under the circumstances. However, constitutional and legal norms regarding the issue of elections do not actually contain rules or guidelines directly applicable to the extraordinary circumstances that we experienced during the COVID-19 health emergency, which led to something that had never occurred in the country's democratic lifetime: the postponement of electoral processes.

Finally, we can also see how the pandemic impacted the integration of a state agency that is particularly important in Mexico: the INE, which is in charge of organising elections at the national and state levels. This institution is headed by a General Council composed of 11 people, the terms of four of whom ended in March of 2020. The designation of new council members is done by the Chamber of Deputies, but the chamber decided to suspend the proceedings for choosing the four new councillors 'until the necessary conditions are met', and so the General Council of the INE worked with only seven members, until the new councillors were finally designated by the end of July 2020.

VII. Final Reflection

The political history of Mexico is marked by hyper-presidentialism and by the concentration of power around the President of the Republic. During the more than 30 years of the dictatorship of General Porfirio Díaz (1877–1910), and 70 years of a hegemonic party system (1929–2000), democracy, the principle of separation of powers and a federal system formed with 'free and sovereign' states were more an ideal to be achieved than a reality.

After a long period in which the erosion of the hegemonic party system took place, thanks to intense struggles to democratise the country and decades of political-electoral reforms, in the year 2000, the Presidency of the Republic shifted to an opposition party (PAN), when Vicente Fox came to power (he was President of Mexico between 2000 and 2006). That year marked the beginning of the era of the so-called 'divided governments', lasting until 2018, in which the presidents did

[28] Resolution INE/CG83/2020 of the General Council of the INE, through which the exercise of the power of attraction is approved, leading to the temporary suspension of local electoral processes in Coahuila and Hidalgo because of the COVID-19 pandemic, caused by SARS-COV2. 1 April 2020.

not have an absolute majority in any of the chambers of the Congress of the Union. This meant, among other things, that in order to approve legislation, budgets and constitutional reforms, the head of the Executive and the political parties with representation in the federal Congress had to engage in dialogue and to negotiate in order to reach agreements.[29]

Nevertheless, things have changed since 2018. Using an 'anti-system', 'anti-elite', 'anti-traditional political parties' narrative, and with all the political force derived from the electoral results of that year, President Andrés Manuel López Obrador, founder of MORENA, has managed to concentrate power in a way that has not been seen since the time of the hegemonic party system (1929–2000). Controlling the absolute majority in both houses of the Congress of the Union, MORENA and its allies have been able to approve laws and budgets with very little consultation with the opposition or with other social groups. They have also been able to control or weaken the autonomous constitutional agencies, by promoting the appointment of people loyal to the President of the Republic to lead them, by significantly limiting their resources, or by delaying the appointment of public servants who should be involved in the management and decision-making of said agencies.

This was the scenario when the COVID-19 pandemic arrived in Mexico in March 2020, a scenario characterised by the concentration of presidential power, and a breakdown or weakening of balances and counterweights. The pandemic has contributed to speeding up this process.

[29] For a more detailed review of this political and constitutional evolution, see generally J Serna de la Garza, *The Constitution of Mexico, a Contextual Analysis* (Oxford, Hart Publishing, 2013).

7

Peru: Executive v Legislative Wars Amidst a Global Pandemic

TRILCE VALDIVIA

I. Introduction

Peru was one of the countries worst hit by the COVID-19 pandemic. It not only had the highest mortality rate in the world, but also faced a major political crisis at the peak of the pandemic, with legislative acts coming from an amateur and populist legislative power and the vacancy of former President Vizcarra. In Peru, the state of emergency lasted 955 days. During this period, the Executive Power had the leading role in the management of the pandemic. By contrast, Congress had a marginalised role in the implementation of measures against the pandemic, but a starring political role, passing a series of constitutional reforms and exercising political control over the Executive authorities by taking advantage of blurred constitutional provisions.

In this chapter, we will attempt to show how the lack of clarity in the constitutional design of the checks and balances between the Legislative and Executive powers played an essential (and negative) role in managing the pandemic. Instead of facing the emergency, politicians from both the Executive and Legislative appeared to be paying more attention to their political and legislative wars than to dealing with the pandemic and guaranteeing constitutional rights.

Section II will present the situation of Peruvian democracy just before the pandemic, in order to show how weak it was before the arrival of COVID-19. Section III describes the main characteristics of the Peruvian form of government and the regulation of emergency regimes in the Constitution of 1993. Finally, in section IV, we will examine the most controversial measures adopted by the Executive and Legislative branches, which range from quarantines and mandatory vaccination measures to vacancy motions and declarations of unconstitutionality of congressional acts.

II. The State of Peruvian Democracy before the Pandemic

2018 was a rather peculiar year for Peruvian politics. President Kuczinski resigned due to his links with the Odebrecht scandal, after two attempts by Congress to make vacant the office of the Presidency. Next in line for the office of President was Vice President Martin Vizcarra, who was sworn in as President in March 2018. Vizcarra's government was characterised by constant confrontation with the majority party in Congress, led by Keiko Fujimori (the candidate who had lost to Kuczynski in the second round of the 2016 presidential election).

In July 2018, during his address to the nation, Vizcarra announced that his government had evaluated a series of constitutional amendment proposals concerning: a) the composition and election of the members of the National Council of the Magistracy; b) the prohibition of parliamentary re-election; c) the reinstating of a bicameral legislative branch; and d) the regulation of the private funding of political parties. The proposals were intended to be the governmental response to a series of corruption scandals that had erupted during 2017 (involving members of the Judicial System) as well as to the infamous *Odebrecht affaire*, which evidenced the shady deals between private mega corporations and political parties. All the constitutional amendment Bills obtained more than 66 approval votes in Congress, as required by Article 206 of the Peruvian Constitution. Three Bills were ratified by referendum, the reinstating of a bicameral legislative branch was rejected.

After the referendum, tensions between the Executive and the Legislative only continued to grow. In March 2019, the Executive introduced a political reform package, composed of 12 Bills, four of which were constitutional amendments. Congress delayed the debating of these Bills and even rejected the elimination of parliamentary immunity. In response to this, on 4 June 2019, the Prime Minister raised a motion of confidence involving six Bills of the political reform package, among them two constitutional reform Bills, one insisting on the elimination of parliamentary immunity and the other proscribing convicted people from running for public office. If the motion was not approved, the President could opt to dissolve Congress according to Article 134 of the Constitution.[1] The entire Bill package was approved on 26 July 2019, two days before President Vizcarra's address to the nation.

In his speech, the President announced that it was the Executive's intention to call for early general elections. A Bill to this effect was sent to Congress on 31 July 2019. Congress considered that instead of the proposed Bill, the President and Vice President shall resign according to Article 115 of the Constitution,

[1] Congress had already rejected a motion of confidence proposed by the first Cabinet of President Kuczinsky.

leaving the government under the administration of the Head of the Legislative branch, whose duty it was to call immediately for presidential elections. As expected, the Executive disagreed, since its purpose was to end the mandate of the majority party in Congress. Thus, it decided to introduce a constitutional amendment Bill to call for early General Elections. Pedro Olaechea, then Head of the Legislative branch, requested the opinion of the Venice Commission, expressing his preoccupation with 'the possibility of the Executive branch using, once again, a question of confidence to force a vote in favour of this constitutional amendment'.[2] The amendment Bill was filed by the Constitution Committee leaving the Executive's hands tied.

After this victory, the majority party in Congress accelerated the election of new Magistrates for the Constitutional Tribunal.[3] It chose to 'invite' certain candidates, instead of convening a public contest.[4] On the same day scheduled for the election procedure, the Executive Power decided to make use of a question of confidence once again. The Prime Minister at the time, Salvador del Solar, requested the floor and presented an oral motion of confidence regarding; a) a Bill to reform the election process of the magistrates of the Constitutional Tribunal; and b) stopping the ongoing election procedure. The Congress' plenary left aside the vote for the approval or denial of the motion and continued with the election procedure, with one of the candidates being chosen. Immediately, two members of Congress raised objections to the election procedure. Later that day, the Congress plenary voted in favour of the motion of confidence presented by the Prime Minister and agreed to discuss a Bill to modify the election procedure for the Tribunal's members. However, it was too late. While Congress was voting on the motion of confidence, the President, in a live address to the Nation, was announcing his decision to dissolve Congress in accordance with Article 134 of the Constitution and calling for general congressional elections. His decision was justified by the assumption that the motion of confidence had been denied de facto when Congress continued with the election procedure.

The President of the dissolved Congress, Pedro Olaechea, who then became President of the Congressional Permanent Assembly, initiated a dispute of powers claim ('*conflicto competencial*') against the Executive Branch before the Constitutional Tribunal. This alleged that the Executive Branch had interfered with Congressional powers for having issued a motion of confidence on an exclusive congressional faculty, such as the election of the Constitutional Tribunal magistrates. There was a majority decision (four votes to three) in favour of the constitutionality of the dissolution of Congress. The Congressional elections were

[2] Venice Commission, 'Opinion on linking constitutional amendments to the question of confidence' (Venice Commission 2019) No 964/2019: www.venice.coe.int/webforms/documents/?pdf=CDL-AD(2019)022-spa (accessed 10 October 2022) 14.

[3] Six out of seven members of the Constitutional Tribunal had expired mandates.

[4] Both procedures were contemplated in Art 8 of the Organic Law of the Peruvian Constitutional Tribunal.

held in January 2020. During this time, the so-called parliamentary interregnum, the Executive Branch legislated through Urgency Decrees. The new Congress was installed on 17 March 2020, just two days after the issuance of the Supreme Decree that declared a state of emergency in the whole country due to the COVID-19 pandemic.

III. Relevant Peruvian Legal Framework

A. Peru's Semi-presidential Regime

The Peruvian government system is a hybrid regime, which has a presidential office at its core, but also incorporates several institutions from parliamentary models. According to the Constitutional Tribunal, the form of government is presidential since a president elected by the people acts both as the head of state and head of government and is neither elected nor removed from office by Congress. Nevertheless, strictly speaking, the Peruvian form of government is not purely presidential, since it has incorporated aspects such as the Cabinet or the Chief of Cabinet, along with censure and confidence motions voted on by Parliament.[5] Eguiguren considers that in the history of Peruvian constitutionalism the definitive turn towards a strengthening of the Executive Branch occurred with the enactment of the Constitution of 1979. Between 1933 and 1979, no popular elected government could finish its term due to the constant conflicts with the Legislative Body. These constant crises led to military coups d'état.

For this reason, the Constitution of 1979 strengthened the powers of the Executive Branch but kept its main hybrid features by giving Congress a series of control mechanisms over the Executive. In the same vein, the Constitution of 1993 continued the approach of increasing the powers of the Executive Branch.[6] It allowed immediate presidential re-election up to two terms, it authorized the President to dissolve Congress if it censored or refused the vote of confidence of three successive Cabinets, it adopted a unicameral Congress of 120 members and it suppressed the Congressional powers of ratification of high military officers, Supreme Court justices, and ambassadors. But, above all, it established a very strong presidential immunity since the President is not politically liable to sanction by Congress in the same way as other high-ranking public officers. According to Article 117 of the Peruvian Constitution:

> During his term of office, the President of the Republic may only be charged with: committing high treason; preventing presidential, congressional, regional or

[5] *Caso sobre la disolución del Congreso de la República* [2020] Peruvian Constitutional Tribunal Exp. N°006-2019-CC/TC.

[6] The original text of the Constitution of 1993 would have regulated what Nino and Gargarella have named 'hyperpresidentialism'. See CS Nino, 'The Debate Over Constitutional Reform in Latin America' (1992) 16 *Fordham International Law Journal* 635.

> municipal elections; dissolving Congress, except in cases as set forth in Article 134 of the Constitution; and preventing the meeting or operation of Congress, the National Election Board, or other bodies of the election system.

In Eguiguren's opinion, those drafting the Constitution of 1993 opted for this to preserve the continuity of the presidential function and to avoid the President becoming the victim of political revenge.[7] This regulation has been the subject of discussion by some authors, who have proposed a Constitutional Amendment of Article 117 to widen the range of cases that can trigger presidential liability and give Congress the chance to start an impeachment procedure. Eguiguren proposes new grounds for presidential impeachment, such as the committing of very serious offences, felonies, or serious infractions against the Constitution.[8]

It is known that presidentialist regimes have two crucial defects.[9] The first one, referred to as the problem of legitimacy, presupposes that 'no democratic principle exists to resolve disputes between the executive and the legislature about which of the two actually represents the will of the people'.[10] The second one is their lack of flexibility, since the President must remain in office for a fixed term.[11] Nevertheless, presidential regimes, particularly in Peru, are currently more likely to be flexible. Even if, according to Article 117, the President may only be charged for four crimes, the 2000 Congress managed to remove Fujimori from power by applying Article 113 of the Peruvian Constitution, which regulates the scenarios for a presidential vacancy. According to Article 113:

> The President of the Republic may vacate his office for the following reasons:
> 1. Death of the President of the Republic.
> 2. His permanent physical or moral incapacity declared by Congress.
> 3. Acceptance of his resignation by Congress.
> 4. His departure from the national territory without permission from Congress or his failure to return within the agreed time.
> 5. His removal from office after having been penalized for any of the violations mentioned in Article 117 of the Constitution.

The second clause of Article 113, permanent moral incapacity, can more easily provide the basis for a procedure to indirectly impeach the President, due to its vagueness and scope for different interpretations. In line with Article 89-A of the Rules of Congress, 87 votes (two thirds of Congress members) are required to pass a vacancy motion. According to García Chávarri, the term 'moral incapacity' has

[7] F Eguiguren, *Las relaciones entre el Gobierno y el Congreso en el régimen político peruano* (Lima, Palestra, 2021).

[8] ibid.

[9] M Alegre and N Maisley, 'Presidentialism and Hyper-Presidentialism in Latin America' in CH Mendes, R Gargarella and S Guidi (eds), *The Oxford Handbook of Constitutional Law in Latin America* (Oxford, Oxford University Press, 2022).

[10] JJ Linz, 'The Perils of Presidentialism' (1990) 1 *Journal of Democracy* 51, 63.

[11] L Marsteintredet and E Berntzen, 'Reducing the Perils of Presidentialism in Latin America through Presidential Interruptions' (2008) 41 *Comparative Politics* 83, 85.

historically been interpreted as mental incapacity. Nevertheless, from an analysis of the latest attempts to vacate a president based on permanent moral incapacity, we can conclude that it encompasses the improper performance of presidential duties, ethical misbehaviour and misdeeds against the dignity of the office.[12]

For authors such as Hakansson, the form of government imposed by the Peruvian Constitution of 1993 is far from being a purely presidential model. It is closer to a model that scholars have called *neopresidencialismo*. This is characterised by a strong Executive in which, comparatively, the President of the Republic holds more powers than Congress to the extent that he can neutralise Congress' counterweights in moments of extreme tension, especially when the government has a parliamentary minority,[13] as is the case with congressional dissolution after the denial of two successive motions of confidence.

B. Emergency Powers under the Constitution

The rules of the emergency or exceptional Constitution are found in Article 137. Nevertheless, as Siles has argued, emergency rules have found their way into many laws.[14] The Peruvian Constitution envisages two emergency scenarios: first, the state of emergency, a regime that is applied in the case of neutral emergencies (such as natural disasters) as well as in the case of internal political emergencies that seriously affect the life of the nation; and second, the state of siege, which can be applied in the case of war whether external or internal. According to Article 137 of the Constitution, the President, with the consent of the Council of Ministers, shall issue a Supreme Decree declaring the state of emergency or the state of siege for a determined period (a maximum of 60 days in the case of a state of emergency and 45 days in the case of a state of siege) in all or part of the national territory. The exercise of the following rights can be suspended: the right to personal freedom and security, the inviolability of the home, freedom of assembly and freedom of movement within the national territory. The President shall inform Congress or its Permanent Assembly of the issuance of this Decree. However, Congress does not carry any special powers to control the issuance of these Decrees. During an exceptional regime, Congress is authorised by the Constitution to meet. The extension of a state of emergency requires the issuance of a new decree but not congressional approval, on the contrary, the extension of a state of siege requires congressional approval. It is worth mentioning that, given that Peru's recent history is marked by the state's struggle against terrorist

[12] A García, 'La incapacidad moral como causal de vacancia presidencial en el sistema constitucional peruano' (2013) 18 *Pensamiento Constitucional* 383.

[13] C Hakansson, *El neopresidencialismo. La forma de gobierno de la Constitución peruana* (Lima, Yachay Legal, 2022).

[14] A Siles, *La implacable erosión institucional: el estado de emergencia en la constitución peruana ante amenazas de naturaleza política a inicios del siglo XXI* (Pontificia Universidad Católica del Perú, 2021) 422.

movements, current regulations of the state of emergency have a clear military approach. Article 137 mandates that 'armed forces may assume control over domestic order if the President of the Republic so decides'.

Hence, the government has opted to design a particular state of sanitary emergency, regulated by Legislative Decree 1156.[15] Under Article 7 of this law, a state of sanitary emergency will be declared on the National Health Authority's own initiative or at the request of the regional or local governments in the event of a high risk of damage to the health or life of their populations stemming from two of the following causes: a) the existence of epidemic outbreaks; b) the occurrence of infectious diseases with great epidemic potential; c) the occurrence of cases of eradicated diseases; d) the occurrence of rapidly spreading epidemics that affect more than one region; e) the occurrence of pandemics declared by the WHO; and f) the existence of events that affect the continuity of the health services that generates a sudden decrease in operational capacity and other situations that seriously endanger the health and life of the population as determined by the Health Ministry. The state of sanitary emergency shall be declared by the Executive Branch via a Supreme Decree. This decree shall contain the list of entities that will perform duties to alleviate the health emergency and a list of the goods and services required to overcome the emergency. These goods and services will be acquired without a prior public tender. The disposition of Legislative Decree 1156 shall be complemented by the mandates of the General Law on Health, Law 26842, which in Articles 76 to 87 grants the Ministry of Health the competence to carry out all the actions needed to combat communicable diseases. Also, it allows the national health authorities to proportionally limit rights such as the right to property, the right to work, the right to freedom of conscience and economic liberties.

C. Peru as a Unitary and Decentralised State

Article 43 of the Peruvian Constitution establishes that the Peruvian form of government is 'unitary, representative, and decentralized'. Originally, in the version enacted in 1993, the Constitution regulated the decentralisation process under Articles 188 to 199. It created 24 departmental units, as well as the existence of municipal governments. Although the Constitution arranged that regional elections should have been held by 1995 at the latest, it was not until 1998 that Congress enacted the Law on the Framework for Decentralisation. However, this law did not offer an agenda to strengthen the decentralisation process; on the contrary, it created the Transitional Regional Administration Councils, entities that were highly dependent on the central government. In 2002, a full reform of this chapter of the Constitution was carried out. It was accompanied by the enactment of the Basic Law on Decentralisation and the Organic Law of Regional

[15] Legislative decrees are norms enacted by the Executive Branch under congressional delegation.

Governments. With regard to the regulation of the competences of the different levels of government, the Constitutional Tribunal has specified that, given the fact that the Peruvian government is unitary and decentralised, this means first that, while there are exclusive powers granted to the national government and other powers accorded to the lower levels of government, there are also shared competences, which require coordination and reciprocal respect from the different levels of government.[16] The national government's role is strengthened by the residuality principle, under which a competence that has not been explicitly attributed to a lower level of government should be attributed to the national level of government. Also, the national government exercises a 'leading' or 'steering' role when defining sectoral policies as well as their implementation.[17] In the view of many experts, the reform was mainly a political decision.[18] It proposed a regional level of government with political, economic, and administrative autonomy. With the passing of time, larger amounts of the national budget were being destined to regional governments to attend the most pressing needs in their territories. Unfortunately, these regional authorities still lacked the capacity and personnel to properly handle these matters. And, although regional governments do not have exclusive competences in many areas, as is the case with health,[19] they have been incapable of adequately executing the assigned budget and spending it to solve their region's structural problems.

The state of sanitary emergency was declared in Peru by Supreme Decree 008-2020-SA published on 11 March 2020. The measures adopted under this decree were complemented by the declaration of a state of emergency in the whole country by Supreme Decree 044-2020-PCM published on 15 March 2020. This Supreme Decree suspended the exercise of the rights to freedom of movement, freedom of assembly, inviolability of the home, freedom of arbitrary arrest and a series of economic liberties in certain industries. Under Urgency Decree 026-2020, the Executive adopted a series of extraordinary measures to fight the pandemic, for instance modifying a series of budgetary lines and regulating teleworking. By Ministerial Resolution 155-2020-MINSA, COVID Commands were created, public institutions under the supervision of the Ministry of Health that oversaw the implementation, execution, control, and evaluation of care processes for COVID-19 cases in the whole territory.

Regional and municipal governments did not play a major role in the fight against the pandemic. The most important measures were adopted at the national

[16] *Presidente de la República v Gobiernos Regionales de Cusco y Huánuco* [2005] Peruvian Constitutional Tribunal 0020-2005-AI/TC and 0021-2005-AI/TC.

[17] ibid.

[18] C Casas, 'Avances y Perspectivas Del Proceso de Descentralización En El Perú' (CIES. 2004) cies.org.pe/investigacion/avances-y-perspectivas-del-proceso-de-descentralizacion-en-el-peru/ (accessed 28 November 2022).

[19] The Constitution prescribes shared competences between the national government and the regional government. However, in the case of epidemics, Art 82 of the General Law on Health allows the National Health Authority (Minister of Health) to arrange the use of all the existing medical care resources in public and private health institutions of the affected areas.

level. Regional governments were instructed by the national government to ensure that all hospitals in their regions were operating at full capacity, and they received funds to hire new personnel and to give special payments to health workers. They were also asked to cooperate with the national police to ensure the implementation of the measures adopted by the national government, and to cooperate with the national government in the progressive resumption of the economy. Municipalities were asked to coordinate with national authorities to cooperate in the oversight and inspection of events that involved people congregating in both indoor and outdoor spaces. They were also invited to ask for funding from the Ministry of Social Inclusion to implement special programs for the support of vulnerable sections of the population.[20]

Congress did not play a starring role either. By issuing Law 31011, it delegated a great number of legislative powers to the Executive Branch in matters such as health, taxation, investment, public order, labour, education, protection of vulnerable population sections, industry, and tourism. The idea was that, at the beginning, the Executive and Legislative branches of power were collaborating to fight the pandemic.[21] However, this proved not to be the case. Unfortunately, Peru was the country worst-hit by COVID-19 and had the world's highest COVID death rate, with the disease causing the death of 6,000 people for every million inhabitants.[22] Most Peruvian hospitals outside the urban area (and even in the urban area) were ill-equipped and lacked not only ICU beds, but also, and most importantly, oxygen supplies. An underfunded public healthcare system, along with a huge informal economy and overcrowded living conditions, contributed to this horrendous situation.

IV. Controversial Legal Responses During the Pandemic

A. The Threat to Fundamental Rights

Peruvians faced a state of emergency of astonishing length. As was stated before, the state of emergency was declared by Supreme Decree 044-2020,[23] initially for

[20] Viceministerio de Gobernanza Territorial, 'Guía Breve Para Organizar La Respuesta Regional Ante El COVID-19' (Presidencia del Consejo de Ministros, 2020).

[21] Ley que delega en el Poder Ejecutivo la facultad de legislar en diversas materias para la atención de la emergencia sanitaria producida por el COVID-19 of 27 March 2020 (Law No 31011).

[22] J Beaubien, 'Peru Has the World's Highest COVID Death Rate. Here's Why' (27 November 2021) *NPR* www.npr.org/sections/goatsandsoda/2021/11/27/1057387896/peru-has-the-worlds-highest-covid-death-rate-heres-why (accessed 28 November 2022).

[23] Decreto Supremo que declara Estado de Emergencia Nacional por las graves circunstancias que afectan la vida de la Nación a consecuencia del brote del COVID-19 of 15 March 2020 (D.S. No 044-2020-PCM).

only 15 days starting on 16 March 2020. It was renewed 10 times and lasted until 30 November 2020. A new declaration was issued by Supreme Decree 184-2020,[24] initially meant to last 31 days, starting on 30 December 2020, and this was renewed 13 times until 27 February 2022. Again, a new declaration was issued by Supreme Decree 016-2022,[25] which was renewed three times, before Supreme Decree 130-2022[26] on 26 October 2022 finally put an end to the state of emergency in Peru. This means that Peruvians spent a total of 30 months under a state of emergency. Such frequent renewal of states of emergency may look odd to the readers of this chapter, but it is not a rare phenomenon in Peruvian constitutionalism. As Siles argues, on several occasions, states of emergency have been renewed without further justification, and furthermore, some regions of the country live in a permanent state of emergency, as is the case of the VRAEM region.[27]

It is relevant to acknowledge that, over the course of such a prolonged state of emergency, the measures limiting fundamental rights varied with time. During the first stage of the pandemic, rights such as freedom of movement, inviolability of the home, freedom of assembly and personal freedom were limited. People were only authorised to frequent public roads when they needed to obtain essential services and goods. Many businesses were not permitted to operate, thus limiting economic freedoms as well. Military forces were told to maintain public order. Urban public transportation was granted permission to operate but reduced to 50 per cent of its capacity. All public highways were closed, as were airports and other transport terminals. Interprovincial and regional transportation was forbidden. By Supreme Decree 057-2020,[28] the mandatory use of face masks in public and closed spaces was imposed. Under Supreme Decree 080-2020,[29] the government authorised a progressive resumption of economic activities, as well as lesser limitations to fundamental rights. It was a four-phase plan. The first phase authorised the operation of those economic activities related to mining and industries

[24] Decreto Supremo que declara Estado de Emergencia Nacional por las graves circunstancias que afectan la vida de las personas a consecuencia de la COVID-19 y establece las medidas que debe seguir la ciudadanía en la nueva convivencia social of 29 November 2020 (D.S. No 184-2020-PCM).

[25] Decreto Supremo que declara Estado de Emergencia Nacional por las circunstancias que afectan la vida y salud de las personas como consecuencia de la COVID-19 y establece nuevas medidas para el restablecimiento de la convivencia social of 25 February 2022 (D.S. No 016-2022-PCM).

[26] Decreto Supremo que deroga el Decreto Supremo 016-2022-PCM, sus prórrogas y modificaciones of 26 October 2022 (D.S. No 130-2022-PCM).

[27] A Siles, 'Problemática Constitucional del Estado de emergencia en Perú: Algunas cuestiones fundamentales' (2017) 15 *Estudios Constitucionales* www.estudiosconstitucionales.cl/index.php/econstitucionales/article/view/386 (accessed 10 November 2022).

[28] Decreto Supremo que modifica el Artículo 3 del Decreto Supremo No 051-2020-PCM, que prorroga el Estado de Emergencia Nacional declarado mediante Decreto Supremo No 044-2020-PCM, por las graves circunstancias que afectan la vida de la Nación a consecuencia del COVID-19 of 2 April 2020 (D.S. No 057-2020-PCM).

[29] Decreto Supremo que aprueba la reanudación de actividades económicas en forma gradual y progresiva dentro del marco de la declaratoria de Emergencia Sanitaria Nacional por las graves circunstancias que afectan la vida de la Nación a consecuencia del COVID-19 of 3 May 2020 (D.S. No 080-2020-PCM).

such as fishing, forestry, paper, glass, textiles, construction or restaurants (only for delivery). It started in May 2020. Phase II permitted malls and stores to open; it started in June 2020. Phase III authorised restaurants to open, but not bars, and also allowed the operation of regional and national transportation services (land, river, rail, and air). Finally, in Phase IV, bars, restaurants, cultural centres, movie theatres, gyms and bars were permitted to operate with limited capacity. The resumption of economic activities was not unified across the whole country's territory due to different levels of COVID infections. Phase IV started in December 2020. It was not until September 2022 that Peruvians were authorised to take off their masks in open public spaces.[30] The use of face masks in closed spaces has been optional since 1 October 2022.[31]

Although obvious, it is important to highlight that the worst affected right was the right to access to health. Peruvians did not have the chance to access quality health services. Hospitals were overcrowded and there was a lack of oxygen across the country's territory. Many people died waiting for an ICU bed. The most affected citizens were certainly those in a condition of poverty, who lacked savings and consequently were more prone to contagion, since they often had informal jobs and needed to obtain a daily income. Despite the Ministry of Health signed an agreement with 12 private healthcare providers to derive patients from public hospitals that lacked ICU beds capacity, most families, desperate for saving a relative, hired the services of private clinics on their own, getting into large unpayable debts.

Fundamental rights such as the right to education and the right to freedom of religion also suffered unreasonable restrictions. By Supreme Decree 094-2020, the government established several measures towards a 'new social coexistence'.[32] Among other things, it ordered that educational services should be provided remotely. Unfortunately, this mandate was extended until March 2022. According to the World Bank, this has caused a setback of ten years in Peruvian education levels. Regarding the right to religious freedom, it was not until 2 November 2020 that churches and temples were reopened.[33] At first, the government only

[30] Decreto Supremo que prorroga el Estado de Emergencia Nacional declarado por el Decreto Supremo No 016-2022-PCM y modifica el Decreto Supremo No 016-2022-PCM of 27 August 2022 (D.S. No 108-2022-PCM).

[31] Decreto Supremo que prorroga el Estado de Emergencia Nacional declarado por el Decreto Supremo No 016-2022-PCM, que declara Estado de Emergencia Nacional por las circunstancias que afectan la vida y salud de las personas como consecuencia de la COVID-19 y establece nuevas medidas para el restablecimiento de la convivencia social of 29 September 2022 (D.S. No 118-2022-PCM).

[32] Decreto Supremo que establece las medidas que debe observar la ciudadanía en la Nueva Convivencia Social y prorroga el Estado de Emergencia Nacional por las graves circunstancias que afectan la vida de la Nación a consecuencia del COVID-19 of 23 May 2020 (D.S. No 094-2020-PCM).

[33] Decreto Supremo que modifica el Decreto Supremo No 116-2020-PCM, que establece las medidas que debe seguir la ciudadanía en la nueva convivencia social y prorroga el Estado de Emergencia Nacional por las graves circunstancias que afectan la vida de la Nación a consecuencia del COVID-19, modificado por los Decretos Supremos No 129-2020-PCM, No 135-2020-PCM, No 139-2020-PCM, No 146-2020-PCM, No 151-2020-PCM, No 156-2020-PCM, No 162-2020-PCM y No 165-2020-PCM of 22 October 2020 (D.S. No 170-2020-PCM).

authorised the celebration of extraordinary religious services, but at the suggestion of religious authorities, the government approved the celebration of all religious services with a capacity of 30 per cent. Furthermore, the Peruvian Government introduced mandatory vaccination, by which it required everyone over the age of 18 to carry a certificate proving that they had completed, in Peru or abroad, a vaccination course against COVID-19. Without this certificate, people would not be able to enter closed spaces where economic and religious activities are held, such as casinos, cinemas, theatres, banks, gyms, shopping centres, means of transportation, and others. Workers were also required to share with their employers their complete vaccination status if they provided face-to-face services. Otherwise, they needed the employer's approval to perform their duties remotely.[34]

It is worth mentioning that a group of citizens filed a writ of *amparo* against the Presidency of the Council of Ministers for violating their constitutional rights by imposing the mandatory use of face masks in the context of the state of emergency declared due to the COVID-19 pandemic. The writ of *amparo* reached the Constitutional Tribunal, which denied the petition. The Tribunal deemed the declaration of the state of emergency as a legitimate and proportional measure.[35]

The Peruvian response to the pandemic revealed the key role the head of the Executive has during a state of emergency and how this regime marginalises Parliament, as well as the Constitutional Tribunal. The Legislative Branch does not have any role in controlling the prolongation of a state of emergency, which is at the sole discretion of the Executive Branch. Moreover, the decrees under which states of emergency are declared are administrative dispositions and hold a lower rank than laws; accordingly, they cannot be reviewed by the Constitutional Tribunal, and only by lower instances of the Judicial Power if a 'popular action' writ is filed against them. Perhaps the only role members of congress can have in a state of emergency is very similar to the one of ordinary citizens, by filing habeas corpus actions against the emergency decrees issued by the government.

B. Political Wars

As if the pandemic's deaths were not enough, Peru was also embroiled in a severe political crisis. The newly-elected Congress began its activities one day after the declaration of the state of emergency on 16 March 2020. On 19 March 2020, Congress elected its new Chair, Manuel Merino, from the Acción Popular political party. He had some previous political experience as congressman.

[34] Decreto Supremo que modifica el Decreto Supremo No 184-2020-PCM que declara Estado de Emergencia Nacional por las graves circunstancias que afectan la vida de las personas a consecuencia de la COVID-19 y establece las medidas que debe seguir la ciudadanía en la nueva convivencia social of 9 December 2021 (D.S. No 179-2021-PCM).

[35] *Santiago Araujo Alvarez Quesada y otra v Tercera Sala Constitucional de la Corte Superior de Justicia de Lima* [2022] Peruvian Constitutional Tribunal 00233-2022-AA/TC.

The President of the Republic called for a general election on 8 July 2020.[36] Nevertheless, it was not long until tensions first arose between Congress and the Executive, particularly regarding certain Bills that Congress approved as laws and that were of dubious constitutionality, this being questioned by the Executive Branch before the Constitutional Tribunal. These tensions increased, though the straw that broke the camel's back was surprisingly a showbiz rumour, known as the 'Richard Swing scandal'. Richard Cisneros was a not-very-popular Peruvian singer who had been hired by the Ministry of Culture on several occasions, at a cost amounting to US$50,000. What was the role of the President in this scandal? Apparently, Cisneros was a close friend and sort of political adviser to Vizcarra and received public contracts in return. A first motion of vacancy for permanent moral incapacity was filed against Vizcarra on 11 September 2020. The motion went to a vote on 18 September 2020, but it did not obtain the 87 votes needed. Nevertheless, Congress persisted, and a new motion was filed on 2 November 2020. On this occasion, the motion was based on a series of criminal charges for corruption during Vizcarra's mandate as Regional Governor of Moquegua. On 9 November 2020 the motion was voted on and approved by Congress with 105 votes.[37]

Article 115 of the Constitution stipulates that, in the event of the declaration of temporary or permanent moral incapacity of the President of the Republic, the first vice president shall assume the corresponding duties; in their absence, the second vice president shall do so, and in the event of the incapacity of both, the duty falls to the President of Congress. Vizcarra did not have any successor remaining on the Executive's list, since the Second Vice President, Mercedes Araoz, resigned supporting Congress after its dissolution in 2019. That is why Manuel Merino De Lama, the President of Congress at the time, assumed the Presidency of the Republic. When he was ousted, Vizcarra was hugely popular, and after the declaration of vacancy, several social protests occurred. The uniform demand of the protesters was 'Dump Merino'. The government responded with a severe use of force, and sadly, two young protesters died. Manuel Merino's Presidency lasted from 10 November 2020 to 15 November 2020, the day when he finally resigned.[38] The entire Congress Presiding Board also resigned, generating a power vacuum. Later that day, Congress met to elect a new Presiding Board composed of members of congress who had not voted in favour of the presidential vacancy motion. A consensus was not reached until 17 November 2020, when Francisco Sagasti

[36] Decreto Supremo por el que convocan a elecciones generales el 11 de abril de 2021, para la elección de Presidente de la República, Vicepresidentes, Congresistas y Representantes ante el Parlamento Andino of 8 July 2020 (D.S. No 122-2020-PCM).

[37] Resolución del Congreso que declara la permanente incapacidad moral del Presidente de la República y la vacancia de la Presidencia de la República of 9 November 2020 (R.L. No 001-2020-2021-CR).

[38] Resolución Legislativa del Congreso por la que se acepta la renuncia del ciudadano Manuel Arturo Merino de Lama al cargo de Presidente de la República y se declara la vacancia de la Presidencia de la República of 15 November 2020 (R.L. No 007-2020-2021-CR).

was elected as President of Congress, consequently, President of the Republic and Mirtha Vasquez as First Vice-President, in consequence, President of Congress. The main achievement of Sagasti's government was the procurement of COVID vaccines, for which purchase and transport contracts were concluded during his tenure. The first batch of vaccines arrived in Peru on 7 February 2021.

The events of November 2020 were deemed to be a coup d'état by a significant proportion of the Peruvian public. Those who held this view alleged that the interpretation of a 'permanent moral incapacity' had been manipulated by Congress and that there was not enough evidence to link Vizcarra with the alleged acts of corruption. It is important to mention that only days after the first vacancy motion against Vizcarra was introduced, the Executive Branch public defender sued the Legislative Power for intending to erode the Executive Branch's constitutional competences, and demanded precautionary measures. The Constitutional Tribunal rejected this demand and, in its final decision issued on 19 November 2020, it declared the action as inadmissible.[39]

However, it was not long before another political scandal caused renewed turmoil in Peruvian politics. In February 2021, it was discovered that President Vizcarra and his wife, along with the Minister of Health Pilar Mazzetti, the Minister of Foreign Affairs Elizabeth Astete, and many other high-ranking public officers, had been secretly vaccinated while Chinese company Sinopharm was performing its vaccine trial in Peru. All the individuals involved were sanctioned by Congress for 'violation of the Constitution' with the punishment being disqualification from performing public functions according to Article 100 of the Constitution. In the case of Vizcarra, the sanction was very severe since it amounted to ten years. Before the scandal had come to light, Vizcarra had decided to take advantage of his political capital and run in the congressional elections. Despite the 'vacunagate' scandal, he was elected. However, due to the sanction imposed on him, he was unable to take up his congressional post.[40]

Instead of bringing a period of stability, the new general elections merely caused the political situation to deteriorate still further. A series of legislative amendments were passed by Congress to suspend some of the constraints imposed by Electoral Laws for the registration of certain candidatures. According to Article 111 of the Constitution, the President of the Republic is elected by direct suffrage. In case no candidate obtains an absolute majority, a run-off is held between the two candidates with the highest two relative majorities. In the 2021 elections, Pedro Castillo and Keiko Fujimori obtained the two highest relative majorities, 19.099 per cent and 12.368 per cent respectively. The results of the ballotage granted victory to Pedro Castillo from Peru Libre, a left-wing party, by

[39] *Poder Ejecutivo v Congreso de la República* [2020] Peruvian Constitutional Tribunal 002-2020-CC/TC.

[40] Resolución Legislativa del Congreso que inhabilita por diez años para el ejercicio de la función pública al expresidente de la República Martín Alberto Vizcarra Cornejo of 16 April 2021 (R.L. No 020-2020-CR).

a margin of less than 45,000 votes. Fujimori claimed that fraud had taken place and only accepted Castillo's victory nine days before he was due to take the oath before Congress on 28 July 2021. Despite Castillo's victory in the presidential elections, he was unable to obtain a majority in Congress. His party obtained 37 parliamentary seats out of 130. Right-wing parties gained a total of at least 44 seats, with the remaining seats won by parties that can be considered 'moderate'. Nevertheless, whether 'moderate', left-wing or right-wing, political parties in Peru do not necessarily defend a specific ideology, but rather focus on the interests of certain groups. It is important to note that the country faces a major crisis with its political parties, with these being vehicles to represent not the Peruvian people, but rather private interests.[41]

Castillo's government left a lot to be desired. He appointed four prime ministers in the space of less than one year and nominated at least 70 ministers. Many of the ministers were inexperienced and involved in corruption scandals. However, Congress did not submit a vote of no confidence for any of the cabinets proposed by the Executive, fearing a possible future Congressional dissolution. As mentioned before, according to Article 134 of the Constitution, if two consecutive cabinets are denied confidence by Congress, then the President is allowed to dissolve Congress. With the passing of time, the opposition bloc gained strength and a first motion of vacancy was introduced; however, it was based on weak grounds, the declarations of President Castillo affirming that he would consider calling a referendum to decide whether to cede land to Bolivia for access to the Pacific Ocean. As time went on, Congress achieved an important Act, Law 31355, which limited votes of confidence to general policy issues, granting Congress the power to declare a motion of confidence as inadmissible without losing its first 'silver bullet'. It also mandated that a negative vote of confidence is always explicit and not liable to be interpreted as implicitly denied by the Executive.[42] The Executive filed a writ of unconstitutionality against this law, but the Tribunal did not gain the necessary votes to declare its unconstitutionality, so it was ratified.[43] In total, three motions of vacancy against Castillo were filed by members of congress. Even the General Attorney lodged a constitutional complaint indicting Castillo for corruption crimes, despite the locks of presidential responsibility prescribed by Article 117. On 7 December 2022, Castillo intended to stage a coup d'état, fearful of being ousted by Congress after the debate of a third motion of vacancy for permanent moral incapacity. Later that day, he was ousted for perpetrating a coup d'état in flagrante and captured by his own personal guard while fleeing to request asylum at the Mexican Embassy. Dina Boluarte, the first vice president, was sworn in as the first female President of the Republic later that day.

[41] M Campos, 'De nuevo, crisis política (no importa cuando lo leas)' (Instituto Peruano de Economía 10 February 2022) www.ipe.org.pe/portal/de-nuevo-crisis-politica-no-importa-cuando-lo-leas/ (accessed 15 December 2022).

[42] Ley que desarrolla el ejercicio de la cuestión de confianza regulada en el último párrafo del artículo 132 y en el artículo 133 de la Constitución Política del Perú of 21 October 2021.

[43] *Caso Cuestión de Confianza II* [2022] Peruvian Constitutional Tribunal 0032-2021-PI/TC.

The various political crises that occurred in the middle of the pandemic reveal the need for a reform of the Constitution of 1993. The Constitution no longer offers an exit from political crises; on the contrary, the political actors in charge of interpreting it manipulate its grey areas, thus intensifying the conflicts. A major reform of constitutional checks and balances needs to be executed. Ousting a President should not only be a matter of obtaining 87 votes. Equally, however, it should not be possible for the President to shoot someone in the middle of the street without risk of being impeached or removed due to the limitations outlined in Article 117.

C. Legislative Wars

As mentioned, legislative elections were held in January 2020, just two months before the pandemic. The elections were the consequence of the dissolution of Congress in September 2019 following a very controversial interpretation of Article 134 of the Constitution by then-President Vizcarra. These elections were the first ones after the incorporation of Article 90-A into the Constitution, which prohibits immediate congressional re-election, so it was therefore an election in which most contenders were amateur politicians. Moreover, a sort of anti-establishment feeling was prevalent in Peruvian voters before the pandemic, steering them towards unpopular and marginal political options. This is one plausible explanation for the 28 congressional seats obtained by FREPAP, the political arm of a religious organisation named 'Israelitas del Nuevo Pacto Universal'.[44] The newly-elected Congress began operations on 16 March 2020. A series of modifications were made to Congress regulations to allow for remote voting procedures.[45]

The newly elected Congress soon opted for a populist position and enacted controversial laws. One of the first measures introduced mandated the suspension of toll collections by highway concessionaires.[46] The Executive brought a writ of unconstitutionality against this act. The Constitutional Tribunal sided with the Executive position and declared the unconstitutionality of this measure for its violation of the economic system principles, particularly Article 62, which protect 'contract law'. Some time later, Congress enacted a law that allowed the

[44] Peru 21, 'Carlos Melendez: 'Lo de Frepap es un voto de protesta' *Peru21* (Lima, 27 January 2020) peru21.pe/politica/carlos-melendez-lo-de-frepap-es-un-voto-de-protesta-noticia/ (accessed 14 December 2022).

[45] Resolución legislativa del Congreso que modifica el Reglamento del Congreso de la República, con la finalidad de implementar, en circunstancias de gravedad, el desarrollo de sesiones virtuales de la organización parlamentaria y del servicio parlamentario of 04 February 2021 (R.L. No 002-2020-2021-CR).

[46] Ley que suspende el cobro de peajes en la red vial nacional, departamental y local concesionada, durante el Estado de Emergencia Nacional declarado a causa del brote del COVID-19 of 7 May 2020 (Law No 31018).

withdrawal of public pensionary funds. Again, the Executive Branch successfully filed a writ of unconstitutionality before the Constitutional Tribunal since the law represented a violation of the public budget constitutional regulations.[47]

Despite the emergency occasioned by the pandemic and Congress's transitory role (as it would operate only from March 2020 to July 2021), a series of important legislative and constitutional amendments were passed. Congress modified many electoral laws to adapt their regulations to the pandemic scenario.[48] Regarding constitutional amendments, Congress approved the elimination of parliamentary immunity and consequently the modification of Article 93 of the Constitution, which now regulates a special jurisdiction privilege, since common crimes committed by members of congress during their period in office shall be prosecuted before the Supreme Court, which shall judge whether the charges are justified or simply part of a political persecution.[49] Another important constitutional amendment approved by Congress modified Articles 34-A and 39-A of the Constitution.[50] The first amendment forbade those sentenced in first instance for committing an intentional crime from running for positions of public election. The second one prevented convicted persons from exercising public functions. Although these amendments can be considered reasonable, Congress insisted on passing three other constitutional amendments whose suitability was doubtful, and which were declared to be formally unconstitutional by the Constitutional Tribunal. Among these constitutional amendment laws, we find Law 31280, which modified Articles 99 and 100 of the Constitution, forbidding the President to leave the territory of the Republic after his mandate;[51] and Law 31305, which authorised the Comptroller General to lift banking and taxing secrecy.[52] In its ruling, the Tribunal declared the unconstitutionality of Legislative Resolution 021-2020-2021-CR that authorised the splitting of the third legislature into two. This fourth legislature lasted less than a month. In the opinion of the Constitutional Tribunal, Congress made improper use of the fourth legislature that disrupted the requirements demanded by the Constitution to approve a constitutional reform, which are the ratification via referendum or a reasonable discerning process for constitutional amendments in two successive ordinary legislatures.[53]

[47] *Caso de la ley que suspende el cobro de peajes* [2020] Peruvian Constitutional Tribunal 006-2020-PI/TC.

[48] J Naupari, 'Reforma Electoral En Tiempos de Pandemia: El Caso Peruano' (2020) 19 *Elecciones* 143.

[49] Ley de Reforma constitucional que elimina la inmunidad parlamentaria of 6 February 2021 (Law No 3118).

[50] Ley de Reforma Constitucional que incorpora el artículo 34-A y el artículo 39-A sobre impedimentos para postular a cargos de elección popular o ejercer función pública of 11 September 2020 (Law No 31042).

[51] Ley de Reforma Constitucional que establece el régimen de residencia temporal del expresidente de la República of 15 July 2021 (Law No 31280).

[52] Ley de Reforma Constitucional que fortalece la lucha anticorrupción en el marco del levantamiento del secreto bancario y la reserva tributaria of 22 July 2021 (Law No 31305).

[53] *Caso del desdoblamiento de las legislaturas ordinarias* [2021] Peruvian Constitutional Tribunal 00019-2021-AI/TC,00021-2021-AI/TC and 00022-2021-AI/TC.

The inexperience of the members and the lack of authentic representation by political parties were the cause of several defects in Congress's performance. The prohibition of members of congress standing for re-election, brought on by the 2019 referendum, was a very impulsive decision. The context of the pandemic impeded the application of a series of electoral reforms that could have improved the quality of political representation, at least to an extent. Congress did not have a starring role in dealing with the pandemic nor did it control the measures adopted in the context of the state of emergency. Congress had above all a political role, as if it were acting in normal times rather than exceptional times.

V. Conclusions

The analysis carried out in this work brings to light three important aspects of Peruvian constitutional design that need a thorough and reflexive reform.

First, the state of emergency regulations should be modified to allow for a greater degree of Congressional participation. Congress should not only be informed of the declaration of a state of emergency; it should grant its authorisation for such an emergency regime and should adequately define which rights will be limited and in which way.

Second, it is important for the Legislative and Executive branches to bring about a real process of decentralisation. Regional governments have not been able to implement basic levels of access to health and are unable to execute the budget assigned by the national government. Regional governments need not only budget transfer, but also capacity and transfer of skills.

Third, a revision of the political regime based on the Constitution of 1993 is needed. There are many clauses which are open to controversial interpretations and which in the hands of the wrong political actors can lead to major crises. The Constitution should contain the possibility to impeach the President, vacancy should be limited to objective and verifiable premises, not subjective ones like 'permanent moral incapacity'. Congressional re-election should not be forbidden. Congress in transitory roles and during emergency regimes should cooperate with the management of the crisis at hand, instead of proposing political reforms, which should come from a reflexive and calm process, not one of urgency.

8

Venezuela: Effects of the Pandemic in a State Already Lacking Constitutional Democracy and Immersed in a Complex Humanitarian Crisis

DANIELA UROSA AND JOSÉ IGNACIO HERNÁNDEZ

I. Introduction

The COVID-19 pandemic posed several global challenges to constitutional democracy due to the sudden and temporary concentration of power in the Executive Branch, commonly triggered through states of emergency.[1] A technical reason is behind the proliferation of such exceptional measures: as the Global Preparedness Monitoring Board concluded in September 2019, the World Health Organization Member States were not prepared for a global health emergency.[2] Without a proper legal framework, declaring a state of emergency was the method used to adopt extraordinary restrictive sanitary measures.

Latin America was no exception,[3] particularly considering the region's tradition of having states of emergency and the presidentialism that dominates there.[4] The evolution of constitutional democracy in the region has helped to

[1] K Lachmayer, 'Democracy, Death, and Dying: The Potential and Limits of Legal Rationalisation' in MC Kettemann and K Lachmayer (eds), *Pandemocracy in Europe. Power, Parliaments, and People in Times of COVID-19* (Oxford, Hart Publishing, 2021) 52.

[2] *A world at risk. Annual report on global preparedness for health emergencies*. Global Preparedness Monitoring Board, 2019: www.gpmb.org/docs/librariesprovider17/default-document-library/annual-reports/gpmb-2019-annualreport-en.pdf?sfvrsn=d1c9143c_30.

[3] JI Hernández G., *La pandemia de la covid-19 y el Derecho Administrativo en América Latina. Un estudio sobre la fragilidad de las Administraciones Públicas* (Bogotá, Tirant Lo Blanch, 2021) 114.

[4] DL Palacios, 'América Latina y El Perú: cuarentena, estado de emergencia, fuerzas del orden y pandemia' in CL Arroyo (ed), *Constitución y emergencia humanitaria* (Lima, Palestra Editores 2020) 28.

narrow the scope of these exceptional regimes, whose main effect is to temporarily enable the Presidency to enact legislative decrees – diminishing, in consequence, the Legislative's scope of authority.[5] Also, the *Inter-American Corpus Iuris* has established standards of human rights protection that constrain these exceptional presidential powers from the human dignity perspective.[6] To be precise, the Inter-American Commission and the Inter-American Court issued general guidelines to moderate the exercise of a state of emergency as an exceptional measure to effectively implement the economic and health policies aimed at tackling the crises triggered by the pandemic.[7]

The situation in Venezuela was different. When the pandemic was declared on 11 March 2020, Venezuela had been in a continuous state of emergency for more than four years. The pandemic did not really pose a new threat to constitutional democracy simply because democracy had already been formally dismantled. Therefore, the legislative decrees adopted during the pandemic were not *exceptional* and rather were ordinary measures derived from the de facto political situation in Venezuela, characterised by the absolute concentration of powers in the Presidency and the decimation of the Legislative Branch's authority.

Therefore, while in the rest of the Latin American countries, the pandemic created risks for constitutional democracy, in Venezuela, it created favourable conditions for the stabilisation of the authoritarian regime of Nicolás Maduro. The stability of that regime was threatened when more than 60 countries recognised the speaker of the Legislative Branch – the National Assembly – as interim president on 23 January 2019.[8] One year later, the interim president visited several countries, including the US. In February 2020, during the State of the Union Address – attended by Venezuela's interim president – the President of the US – with rare bipartisan support – promised that Maduro's tyranny would be 'smashed and broken'.[9]

But just a few weeks later, the pandemic changed the priorities of the international coalition that supported the interim president. In Venezuela, the lockdowns impeded social mobilisation, while the Maduro Government increased its social control over the population – taking advantage of the complex humanitarian

[5] A Bogdandy et al., *La resistencia del Estado Democrático de Derecho en América Latina frente a la pandemia de COVID-19. Un enfoque desde el ius commune* (Caracas, Max Planck Institute-Universidad Católica Andrés Bello, CIDEP, 2020).

[6] M Morales, 'El mandato transformador del Sistema Interamericano como respuesta a la pandemia a la luz del test democrático. The Inter-American System's transformative mandate as a response to the pandemic in light of the democratic test' (2021) 19 *International Journal of Constitutional Law* 4, 1229.

[7] D Urosa M., 'Sistema Interamericano de Derechos Humanos y COVID-19: reforzando la protección de los derechos humanos en tiempos de pandemia' in AR Brewer-Carías and H Romero-Muci (eds), *Estudios Jurídicos sobre la Pandemia del Covid-19* (Caracas, Academia de Ciencias Políticas y Sociales-Editorial Jurídica Venezolana Internacional, 2020) 315.

[8] JI Hernández G., *Bases fundamentales de la transición en Venezuela* (Caracas, Editorial Jurídica Venezolana, 2020).

[9] See the transcript here: www.nytimes.com/2020/02/05/us/politics/state-of-union-transcript.html.

emergency. Therefore, the pandemic did not threaten constitutional democracy in Venezuela but did contribute to removing the probability of a democratic transition, with incentives now in place for consolidating the de facto rule of Nicolás Maduro.

To develop this conclusion, this chapter is structured as follows. The first part summarises the constitutional framework of the state of emergency in Venezuela, which was adopted in an abuse of power in 2016. The second part explains how the authoritarian government of Venezuela reacted to the pandemic and how this emergency hindered the democratic transition. The third part describes the pandemic's aftermath in terms of stabilising Maduro's regime amidst the increasingly complex humanitarian crisis. Conclusions will follow.

II. The Continuous State of Emergency in Venezuela

After the election of Hugo Chávez in December 1998, Venezuela started a slow-motion process of democratic backsliding that accelerated after Chávez's death and the rigged election of his Vice President – Nicolás Maduro – as President in April 2013.[10] The consequences of the predatory economic policies adopted by Chávez could already be felt at that time, in terms of a shortage of essential goods and services – such as food and medicines – and inflation. Instead of tackling the root causes of that crisis, Maduro decided to continue those predatory policies, aggravating the economic situation and social unrest.[11]

The increasing economic and social crisis favoured the electoral triumph of the democratic opposition in the parliamentary elections held in December 2015. Unexpectedly, the opposition won two-thirds of the seats in the fourth legislature of the National Assembly – a super majority that allowed any constitutional decision to be taken to promote a democratic transition. However, the foundations of constitutional democracy were already severely hindered at that time, mainly through the political control of the Supreme Tribunal and the Constitutional Chamber, which in Venezuela exerts the concentrated judicial review.[12] Consequently, in January 2016, Maduro took two measures to block the authority of the National Assembly. The first one was to enact a legislative decree that declared a state of emergency, extended over the following years. The second one was to use the Constitutional Chamber to review and block the legislative functions of the National Assembly.[13] To consolidate his de facto power, Maduro

[10] AR Brewer-Carías, *Dismantling Democracy in Venezuela: the Chávez Authoritarian Experiment* (New York, Cambridge University Press, 2010) 31.

[11] R Balza et al., 'Economía', in B Alarcón, *La consolidación de una transición democrática. El desafío venezolano III* (Caracas, Universidad Católica Andrés Bello, 2018).

[12] R Badell, *Asalto al parlamento* (Caracas, Academia de Ciencias Políticas y Sociales, 2021).

[13] AR Brewer-Carías, *La dictadura judicial y la perversión del Estado de Derecho* (Caracas, Editorial Jurídica Venezolana, 2017).

convoked a fraudulent constituent assembly in 2017 that also exerted legislative functions – transforming the newly elected National Assembly into a powerless institution.[14]

A. The State of Emergency in the Venezuelan Constitutional Law and its Continuity Since 2016 – An Example of Constitutional Authoritarian Populism

A distinctive characteristic of the presidential system in Venezuela is the constitutional predominance of the Presidency. This predominance can be understood from two perspectives: vertically, the national level tends to predominate over the subnational levels (states and municipalities); horizontally, relevant competencies are concentrated in the Presidency, compared with the Judiciary and the Legislative.

One of the core institutions of this predominant presidentialism is the state of emergency, according to which the Presidency can temporarily assume the exercise of the legislative functions through decrees with the rank, force, and value of law, usually known as legislative decrees. Following the Romanist tradition of the Venezuelan Constitutional Law, these emergency powers have been characterised as a constitutional dictatorship because they concentrate legislative power in the Presidency, but under constraints that are designed to ensure the exercise of these powers towards the common good. But in the Venezuelan Constitutional Law, these powers have not been exceptional: the day the democratic Constitution of 1961 was published, the President issued decrees that declared a state of emergency. This supposed exceptional state was the cornerstone of the economic policies based on centralised controls and was maintained until the 1990s. Rather than extraordinary measures, the legislative decrees were an ordinary tool – demonstrating the fragility of the separation of powers system.[15]

To avoid the abusive exercise of exceptional powers, the 1999 Constitution established a narrower framework. According to this, the state of emergency can only be declared under specific circumstances and based on the concrete regulation that, exceptionally, is required to address these extraordinary circumstances when the ordinary legal framework is insufficient. In that sense, the Constitution provides different types of state of emergency: (i) the state of alarm 'when catastrophes, public calamities or other similar events occur, seriously endangering the security of the Nation or its citizens'; (ii) the state of economic emergency 'when

[14] AR Brewer-Carías and C García (eds), *Estudios sobre la Asamblea Nacional Constituyente y su inconstitucional convocatoria* (Bogotá, Temis, 2017).

[15] JM Casal, *Dictadura constitucional y libertades públicas* (Caracas, Editorial Jurídica Venezolana, 1993) 24; G Sira, *El estado de excepción a partir de la Constitución de 1999* (Caracas, Editorial Jurídica Venezolana, CIDEP, 2017).

extraordinary economic circumstances arise, such as to affect the economic life of the Nation'; and (iii) the state of internal or external commotion, based on events 'of an internal or external conflict seriously endangering the security of the Nation'. The length of any such state of emergency is limited (from 30 to 90 days) and could be extended.[16]

The legislative decree that declares the state of emergency and adopts the extraordinary regulation could be overruled by the National Assembly. In addition, it is automatically reviewed by the Constitutional Chamber, which has developed a jurisprudence that restricts the state of emergency based on general principles, such as proportionality. Finally, the legislative decree must be communicated to international bodies, including the Organization of American States.

This constitutional framework was not implemented until the Presidency of Nicolás Maduro. Notably, after the election of the fourth legislature of the National Assembly, the Maduro regime declared an economic state of emergency in January 2016.[17] Although that exceptional regime cannot be extended for more than 60 days, the legislative decree was continually renewed. Rather than deal with this evident abuse of power, the Constitutional Chamber, under the political control of the authoritarian government, confirmed the constitutionality of the decree.[18] The fourth legislature of the National Assembly rejected the emergency decree, which should have impaired its validity. However, the National Assembly's legislative functions were already stripped down. Consequently, the effectiveness of the emergency decree was not affected.[19]

As a result, the legislative function was unconstitutionally transferred from the newly elected National Assembly to the Presidency. And the legislative functions that could not be transferred were fraudulently assumed by the Constitutional Chamber.[20] The General Secretary of the Organization of American States considered these measures a violation of the general principles embedded in the Inter-American Democratic Charter because the regime fraudulently disowned the parliamentary election and usurped the legislative function.[21]

The abusive exercise of the state of emergency was justified with populist rhetoric.[22] Therefore, this abuse of power can be characterised as constitutional

[16] Art 338, Venezuelan Constitution. The main difference is the extension of the state of emergency: 30 days in the case of the state of alarm, 60 days in the case of the state of economic emergency, and 90 days regarding the state of internal or external commotion.

[17] Decree No 2184, published in the Official Gazette No 6214 extraordinary, dated 14 January 2016.

[18] Constitutional Chamber, Supreme Tribunal of Justice, ruling No 04, 20 January 2016.

[19] National Assembly Resolution dated 22 January 2016. The Resolution was declared null by the Constitutional Chamber of the Supreme Tribunal of Justice, ruling No 7, 11 February 2016.

[20] For instance, legislative control over the national budget. See AR Brewer-Carías, 'El reparto de despojos' (2018) 149–150 *Revista de Derecho Público* 292.

[21] AR Brewer-Carías, *The Collapse of the Rule of Law and the Struggle for Democracy in Venezuela Lectures and Essays (2015–2020)* (Miami, Ediciones EJV International, 2020), 116.

[22] According to Norris and Inglehart, populism is rhetoric based on the exaltation of the will of 'the people' instead of the elites. But this rhetoric does not consider second-order issues, such as antipluralist values. See P Norris and R Inglehart, *Cultural Backlash. Trump, Brexit, and Authoritarian Populism* (Cambridge, Cambridge University Press, 2019) 3, 65.

authoritarian populism, that is, authoritarian measures covered with a veneer of constitutionality, purportedly adopted in defence of the people.[23] The pandemic, as will be analysed later, boosted this rhetoric.

B. The Complex Humanitarian Emergency and the 2019 Democratic Transition

Rather than tackle the root causes of the economic crisis created by the predatory policies adopted by Chávez, Nicolás Maduro decided to continue those policies based on the state of emergency declared in January 2016. As a result, the economic crisis degenerated into a complex humanitarian emergency. Wide sections of the population were excluded from essential goods, such as food and medicine, while public services – such as electricity – began to collapse. Inequality and poverty increased, particularly when inflation became hyperinflation in 2017. The poster child of this emergency is the gross domestic product collapse, estimated at more than 80 per cent. Only countries facing terrible wars – such as Germany during the Second World War – have suffered such a collapse.[24]

Amidst this increasingly complex humanitarian emergency and constitutional breakdown, Nicolás Maduro was re-elected President in a rigged ballot held in May 2018 that was rejected by tens of countries. Therefore, when the new presidential term began on 10 January 2019, those countries decided not to recognise Maduro as President but instead recognise the speaker of the National Assembly as interim president until free and fair presidential elections were called. That recognition was intended to create incentives for a democratic transition, mainly because the capacity of Nicolás Maduro to represent Venezuela abroad was severely diminished.[25]

However, in Venezuela itself, that recognition was useless because Maduro retained control of the country – or at least, part of it, considering the gradual collapse of the state.[26] Consequently, Maduro continued to exercise absolute de facto powers based on the state of emergency declared in 2016. The imposition of international sanctions – particularly by the US – created additional excuses

[23] JI Hernández G., 'Towards a Concept of Constitutional Authoritarianism: The Venezuelan Experience', Iconnectblog at: www.iconnectblog.com/2018/12/towards-a-concept-of-constitutional-authoritarianism-the-venezuelan-experience/.

[24] D Barrios et al, '¿Cuánto puede tomarle a Venezuela recuperarse del colapso económico y qué debemos hacer?' in R Balza and H García (eds), *Fragmentos de Venezuela. 20 escritos sobre economía* (Caracas, Fundación Konrad-Adenauer-Stiftung, 2019) 91.

[25] AR Brewer-Carías, *Transición a la democracia en Venezuela. Bases Constitucionales* (Caracas, Editorial Jurídica Venezolana, 2019).

[26] The collapse of the state has resulted in a weak capacity to exert territorial control. JI Hernández G., *Control de precio y de cambio. Auge y colapso institucional* (Caracas, Editorial Jurídica Venezolana, 2022).

to prolong this state of emergency.[27] At the same time, the authoritarian regime increased its political control over the population based on political conditions regarding social programs.

Although the liberation from the regime was envisioned as a short-term objective in 2019, the process looked to have stalled one year later. To renew the transition movement, the interim president visited several countries in the Americas and Europe during January and February 2020. And the transition did indeed gain new traction, creating expectations that mass protests could resume and, as in 2017 and 2019, jeopardise the regime. However, the COVID-19 pandemic unexpectedly changed the political situation.

III. The Pandemic and the Consolidation of the Authoritarian Regime

When the pandemic was declared, Venezuela was one of the worst countries in Latin America in terms of capacity to address fiscal and sanitary emergencies because of the complex humanitarian crisis already in existence.[28] And simultaneously, the country was in a state of transition, with the ongoing political battle between the authoritarian regime and the opposition. Both groups redesigned their political strategies to maximise the pandemic's political benefits.

A. The Continuance of the State of Emergency as a Result of the Pandemic

As the World Bank concluded, 'during times of crisis, the public administration is called upon to take a stronger role'.[29] There is a technical reason to explain this outcome: within the government, only the Executive Branch can enter into direct relations with the persons to handle collective necessities.[30] Therefore, only the Executive Branch has the authority to design and implement policy measures to impose lockdowns and other coercive measures to prevent the spread of the coronavirus. Also, only the Executive Branch can provide direct subsidies to

[27] A Ayuso and S Gratius, 'Sanciones como instrumentos de coerción: cuán similares son las políticas de Estados Unidos y la Unión Europea hacia Venezuela?' in S Gratius and JM Puente (eds), *Venezuela en la encrucijada. Radiografía de un colapso* (Caracas, AB Ediciones-IESA-Konrad Adenauer Stiftung, 2021).

[28] E Abuelafia and JL Saboin, *Los desafíos para la recuperación de Venezuela y el impacto del COVID-19* (Washington, D.C., Inter-American Development Bank, 2021).

[29] World Bank Group, *Protecting people and economies: integrated policy response to COVID-19* (Washington, DC, The World Bank, 2020) 33.

[30] C Delpiazzo, 'Bien común, sociedad y Estado' (2012) 11 *Revista de Derecho de la Universidad de Montevideo* 83.

households and businesses to compensate for the economic losses derived from the pandemic. Because the recession triggered by the pandemic was not based on a supply and demand imbalance, anti-cyclical economic policies were not appropriated: expanding economic activities would increase the risk of contagion. Therefore, the Executive Branch was forced to impose coercive measures that increased the social and economic damages of the pandemic, particularly in vulnerable sections of the population.[31]

From a Latin American comparative perspective, the Executive Branch adopted those coercive measures under three frameworks.[32] Some countries implemented coercive measures based on ordinary health legislation. That legislation tends to include technical and undetermined concepts that enable the administrative powers to adopt 'any necessary measure' to protect the right to health, a social right in Latin American Constitutional Law and Inter-American Law. Other countries declared a state of emergency, enabling the Executive Branch to issue legislative decrees that adopted such coercive measures. In some countries, the emergency decrees created a conflict with constitutional courts, which applied the standards of review, declaring the unconstitutionality of some decrees due to their excessive nature. Finally, some countries interchanged ordinary administrative measures based on health legislations with states of emergency.

The study of the pandemic consequences on constitutional democracy – or *pandemocracy*[33] – is particularly relevant in countries that are considered free or, at least, partially free.[34] In autocracies or non-competitive authoritarian states like Venezuela, these consequences could be different. In that sense, there has been an academic discussion about whether democracies or autocracies perform better during a crisis such as the pandemic.[35] From the point of view of constitutional democracy, in any case, the type of regime could lead to different situations as a result of the pandemic state of emergency: while in democratic regimes the state of emergency could be subject to effective constraints, in non-democratic regimes, the pandemic could increase de facto powers and, eventually, stabilise the government. Particularly in non-democratic regimes, the ruling government does not face any challenge from free and fair elections that tend to disfavour the incumbent government.[36]

[31] V Nuguer and A Powell, *Políticas para combatir la pandemia. Informe macroeconómico de América Latina y el Caribe 2020* (Washington, D.C., The Inter-American Development Bank, 2020).

[32] Hernández (n 3).

[33] K Lachmayer and MC Kettemann, 'Conclusions: Pandemocracy-Governing for the People without the People?' in Lachmayer and Kettemann (n 1) 329.

[34] 'While most countries with stronger democratic institutions ensured that any restrictions on liberty were necessary and proportionate to the threat posed by the virus, a number of their peers pursued clumsy or ill-informed strategies, and dictators from Venezuela to Cambodia exploited the crisis to quash opposition and fortify their power'. Freedom House, *Freedom in the World 2021. Democracy Under Siege* (Washington DC, The Freedom House, 2021) 2.

[35] K McMann and D Tisch, *Democratic Regimes and Epidemic Deaths* (Sweden, V-Dem Institute, 2021).

[36] The coercive measures adopted during the pandemic increased social unrest and threatened political stability. While democracies offer civil rights guarantees, they also face major obstacles to

Precisely this happened with the Venezuelan Government. In March 2020, the government faced no challenges regarding checks and balances or elections. As a result of the de facto powers assumed in 2016, Maduro's administration had already dismantled the checks and balances system and the conditions for electoral integrity. Under these political conditions, the pandemic increased the actual powers for social control regarding economic and social policies. More importantly, the pandemic arrived just in time for the government because, as has been explained, the political transition was gaining new momentum in February 2020. Therefore, the pandemic created the perfect conditions for Maduro to stall this momentum and regain control over the population.

To that end, and like many other countries, Venezuela adopted the state of emergency strategy. For that purpose, the government declared a state of alarm, justifying this with the necessity to protect the people against the perils of the pandemic. According to the Constitution, the legislative decree that declared the state of alarm needed to specify the applicable regulations. However, the state of alarm was adopted indefinitely, enabling regulations that invested in the Presidency unlimited legislative powers.[37] The Constitutional Chamber ratified the decree's constitutionality, despite its clear violations of the Venezuela Constitution and the Inter-American standards applicable to the state of emergency.[38]

But this state of alarm had no practical consequences because, due to the continuing state of emergency declared in 2016 and the dismantling of the National Assembly's authority, the Presidency had already assumed the legislative function, exercising de facto powers to impose coercive measures. Nor did the state of alarm affect the budgetary controls because those controls had already been dismantled in 2016. As a result, the President had de facto powers to design and redesign the fiscal expenses.[39] Rather than momentarily expand the scope of authority of the Executive, the pandemic state of emergency ratified the de facto powers derived from the continuing state of emergency declared in 2016.

implementing such measures, considering the checks and balances system. Authoritarian regimes, on the contrary, did not meet those obstacles, although they were exposed to risks in terms of inefficiency, corruption and distrust. See R Wood et al., 'Resisting Lockdown: The Influence of COVID-19 Restrictions on Social Unrest' (2022) 66(2) *International Studies Quarterly* 1.

[37] Decree No 4160, published in Official Gazette No 6519, dated 13 March 2020. See AR Brewer-Carías, 'El decreto del estado de alarma en Venezuela con ocasión de la pandemia del coronavirus' (2020) 161–162 *Revista de Derecho Público* 385. See also G Sira 'Venezuela y el Estado de alarma por el COVID-19' in Brewer-Carías and Romero-Muci (n 7) 58.

[38] Constitutional Chamber of the Supreme Tribunal of Justice, ruling No 2, dated 14 January 2020.

[39] Because during the pandemic the regular budgetary controls were not adequate to implement fiscal policies aimed at addressing the economic shock created by the pandemic, the Executive tended to concentrate exceptional authority on budget management. The diminishing of the checks and balances regarding the budget increased the risk of corruption and other malpractices, aggravating the citizens' lack of trust. In any case, in Venezuela, those fiscal controls had been dismantled in 2016. See H Romero-Muci, 'Desinstitucionalización tributaria en Venezuela. Entre la distopía y la anomia social' in AR Brewer-Carías and H Romero-Muci (eds), *El falseamiento del Estado de Derecho* (Caracas, Academia de Ciencias Políticas y Sociales, 2021).

It could be concluded that when the pandemic was declared, Maduro did not face any political costs regarding negotiations with the other branches. The National Assembly's authority was already dismantled, and the other branches – particularly the Judiciary – were coopted by him. Why, then, did Maduro decide to declare a pandemic state of alarm?

Modern dictators – wrote Heinrich A Rommen – are masters of legality.[40] Moisés Naím has explained how modern autocracies simulate their authoritarian measures within the formalities of the law. Naím called these rigged formalities 'pseudo-law'.[41] It is important to remember that the Constitution and the Law are not only constraints to the government but also sources of legitimacy. Due to the expansion of constitutionalism as the accepted form of government, autocracies have decided to base their authoritarian regimes on non-democratic constitutions, as Manuel García-Pelayo observed during the 1950s.[42] Non-democratic regimes have constitutional law, not inspired by the values of constitutional democracy but by authoritarian values.[43] Also, non-democratic regimes could rely on populist rhetoric to justify authoritarian measures to protect 'the people' that are covered by constitutional formalities based on 'popular sovereignty'.[44]

Back in 2016, Maduro could have chosen to assume de facto powers with a military coup against the newly elected National Assembly. Instead, he opted for constitutional disguises boosted by popular rhetoric. These disguises were the Constitutional Chamber rulings, the constituent assembly, and the state of emergency. When the pandemic occurred, he decided to continue this 'pseudo-law', declaring the state of alarm that had no practical effects because the legislative powers were already concentrated in the Presidency. However, the state of alarm provided a constitutional cover, while the pandemic offered the perfect excuse to justify the state of alarm in terms of protecting the people. But even more importantly, the pandemic demonstrated that the authoritarian regime – not the interim president – was the one that controlled the country.

B. Social Control and the Vaccines: How the Pandemic Helped to Make the Democratic Transition Disappear

From the perspective of the Venezuela democratic transition, the pandemic created challenges for the National Assembly and the interim president: particularly in

[40] R Hittinger, 'Introduction', in H Rommen, *The Natural Law* (Indianapolis, Liberty Fund, 1998) xi.

[41] M Naím, *The Rrevenge of Power* (New York, St. Martin's Press, 2022) 7.

[42] M García-Pelayo, *Derecho Constitutional Comparado* (Madrid, Alianza Editorial, 1993) 109. The first edition was published in 1951.

[43] M Tushnet, 'Authoritarian Constitutionalism: Some Conceptual Issues', in T Ginsburg and A Simpser (eds), *Constitutions in Authoritarian Regimes* (Cambridge, Cambridge University Press, 2018) 36.

[44] P Blokker, 'Populism as a Constitutional Project' (2019) 17(2) *International Journal of constitutional Law* 535.

terms of how to demonstrate that, despite the lack of control over the country, the interim president was able to provide relief. This led to implementing a strategy based on the external assets under the interim president's control. Therefore, the pandemic became a sort of competition between Maduro's government and the interim president. And as Francis Fukuyama predicted, the competition was decided in favour of the government that demonstrated the highest degree of efficiency.[45]

As explained, the primary legal consequence of the international recognition of the speaker of the National Assembly as interim president was that the international representation of the Government of Venezuela shifted from Maduro's regime to the interim president in the jurisdictions that recognised him as the de jure Government of Venezuela, as mainly happened with the US and the UK.[46] Based on the control of the Central Bank's accounts in the US, the interim president announced in March 2020 the intention to use part of those resources to provide economic relief to medical doctors and nurses during the pandemic.[47] In response, Maduro's government filed a claim against the Bank of England, requesting the transfer of part of the Central Bank's gold deposits to provide humanitarian relief after the UK Government recognised the interim president as the exclusive representative of the Central Bank.[48]

The social program designed by the interim president was impaired because of political differences between members of the National Assembly. From a legal perspective, these differences resulted in a controversy about how the economic resources could be used. According to the Democratic Statute approved by the National Assembly in 2019, the National Assembly had to authorise, by law, any public expenses. The discussions to approve a special budgetary Law began in March 2020. However, as a result of the political debates within the National Assembly and the administrative controls derived from the US economic sanctions, the social program was only implemented six months later.[49] In the meantime, Maduro's government was able to implement economic relief without facing any

[45] F Fukuyama, 'The Thing That Determines a Country's Resistance to the Coronavirus' (2020) *The Atlantic*, 30 March 2020: www.theatlantic.com/ideas/archive/2020/03/thing-determines-how-well-countries-respond-coronavirus/609025.

[46] AR Brewer-Carías and JI Hernández, *The Defense of the Rights and Interest of the Venezuelan State by the Interim Government before Foreign Courts, and its International Recognition 2019–2020* (New York, Editorial Jurídica Venezolana International, 2021).

[47] 'Guaidó busca retomar la iniciativa en medio de la pandemia', *El País*, 30 March 2020: elpais.com/internacional/2020-03-30/guaido-busca-retomar-la-iniciativa-en-medio-de-la-pandemia.html.

[48] Brewer-Carías and Hernández (n 46).

[49] See the press release of National Assembly dated 5 September 2020: asambleanacionalvenezuela.org/noticias/guaido-cumplimos-con-nuestra-palabra-desde-hoy-los-heroes-de-la-salud-recibiran-el-pago-de-100-dolares-por-tres-meses. The social program, called 'Héroes de la Salud' (Health Heroes) was based on technological and legal innovations because it was necessary to design direct transfers avoiding Maduro's controls. See 'Digital scheme pays Venezuela health workers from frozen funds', *Financial Times*, 9 December 2021: www.ft.com/content/2a271032-35b4-4969-a4bf-488d4e9e3d18.

delays based on democratic controls.[50] In addition, the government, with its populist rhetoric, blamed international sanctions and the interim president for blocking access to the means necessary to fight the pandemic, particularly regarding the Central Bank's deposits.[51]

The vaccine program was also the subject of a political struggle. Initially, the Maduro government blamed international sanctions and the interim president for blocking resources needed to cover the expenses of the vaccines program, particularly under the COVAX agreement.[52] The interim president saw an opportunity to increase his leverage and offer a political agreement to use assets under his control to finance vaccines under the supervision of international organizations.[53] Ultimately, Maduro rejected any negotiation with the opposition and decided to pay for vaccines from the COVAX initiative using assets under his control.[54] Once again, he showed that his government was the one in charge.

C. The Rigged Election of the Fifth Legislature of the National Assembly

During the pandemic, the authoritarian regime organised a rigged election of the National Assembly's fifth legislature in December 2020. As expected, Maduro's political coalitions won almost all the seats in the new legislature, which began operations in 2021 – at the same time that the fraudulent constituent assembly was dissolved. With the National Assembly on his side, Maduro no longer needed to implement a state of emergency to justify the authoritarian exercise of legislative power.

The economic state of emergency declared in January 2016 was fraudulently renewed until February 2021. The pandemic state of alarm declared in 2020 was also renewed until February 2021. After the rigged parliamentary election, it was not necessary to hide the populist authoritarian measures beneath the formalities

[50] For instance, in March 2020, the government implemented a social bonus to alleviate the economic costs of the pandemic. See 'Maduro entrega nuevo bono en medio de cuarentena por coronavirus', *Tal Cual*, 20 March 2020: talcualdigital.com/maduro-entrega-nuevo-bono-en-medio-de-cuarentena-por-coronavirus/.

[51] 'Exclusive: Venezuela asks Bank of England to sell its gold to UN for coronavirus relief – sources', *Reuters*, 20 April 2020: www.reuters.com/article/us-health-coronavirus-venezuela-gold-exc-idUSKBN22B30X.

[52] Regarding the COVAX program, see A Bogdandy and P Villarreal, *The Role of International Law in Vaccinating Against COVID-19: Appraising the COVAX Initiative* (Heidelberg, MPIL Research Paper Series No. 2020-46).

[53] 'Venezuelan government and opposition begin talks on vaccine financing', *Reuters*, 11 February 2021: www.reuters.com/world/americas/venezuelan-government-opposition-begin-talks-vaccine-financing-2021-02-12/.

[54] 'Venezuela to receive COVAX vaccines in coming days, Maduro says', *Reuters*, 1 August 2021: www.reuters.com/world/americas/venezuela-receive-covax-vaccines-coming-days-maduro-says-2021-08-02/.

of the state of emergency: the fifth legislature of the National Assembly provided the means to carry out those measures. The pandemic state of emergency ended not because of technical reasons but because it was no longer necessary to camouflage authoritarian measures beneath a state of emergency.

The fifth legislature did not enact any legislation related to the pandemic, though.[55] This demonstrates that the alarm decrees were not technically necessary to enact health and economic measures not established in the Law, but rather served to camouflage the concentration of powers in the Presidency. The legality principle was not a constraint during the pandemic because, under the de facto prevalent conditions, the Law no longer limited the Executive. Therefore, the same administrative pandemic measures that were formally justified in the state of alarm due to the lack of legal framework continued after February 2021 without a state of emergency.

D. Venezuela: Pandemocracy or 'Pandeautocracy'?

As a result of the COVID-19 pandemic, Maduro demonstrated that his government – despite the lack of legitimacy and increasing corruption – was in a better position to address the pandemic than the interim president. The fourth legislature and the interim president were trapped in political debates, with additional constraints derived from sanctions that, in the US, restricted the use of external assets. In comparison, Maduro did not face any decision-making obstacles to implementing policies.[56] Also, the lockdowns disincentivised mass gatherings and, in sum, increased the population's dependence on Maduro's government, particularly regarding the provision of food and medicine.

Despite the collapse of the Venezuelan state, the public services debacle, and the pervasive corruption, the government achieved its strategic aims. Maduro was by no means the best government head possible, but compared with the interim presidency, he was the lesser evil. He administered, with opacity, the vaccine programs, along with the other health and economic measures related to the pandemic. But in the end, his government did deliver much more than the interim presidency.

The pandemic was, in that sense, the final blow against the transition strategy initiated in 2019. For instance, according to *Latinobarómetro*, Maduro's popularity

[55] The legislative agenda of the fifth legislature has been quite erratic. In any case, the main legislative topic has been the reform of criminal legislation to demonstrate that the investigation initiated by the International Criminal Court's Prosecution Office is not necessary. G Sira 'Leyes, Decretos Normativos, Reglamentos y Resoluciones de efectos generales dictados durante el segundo semestre de 2021' [2021] *Revista de Derecho Público* 167–168, 228.

[56] While the external assets under the control of the Interim Government were in the US, the regime had several accounts in Europe and Asia, not subject to US sanctions. Also, the Maduro regime was – and still is – in control of the national budget.

rating *slightly increased* between 2018 and 2020.[57] The liberal component index of the Liberal Democracy Index prepared by V-DEM demonstrated that the Venezuela index *improved* between 2020 and 2021, while in South America in general, the index decreased:

Figure 1 Liberal Component Index-South America and Venezuela, 2021–21[58]

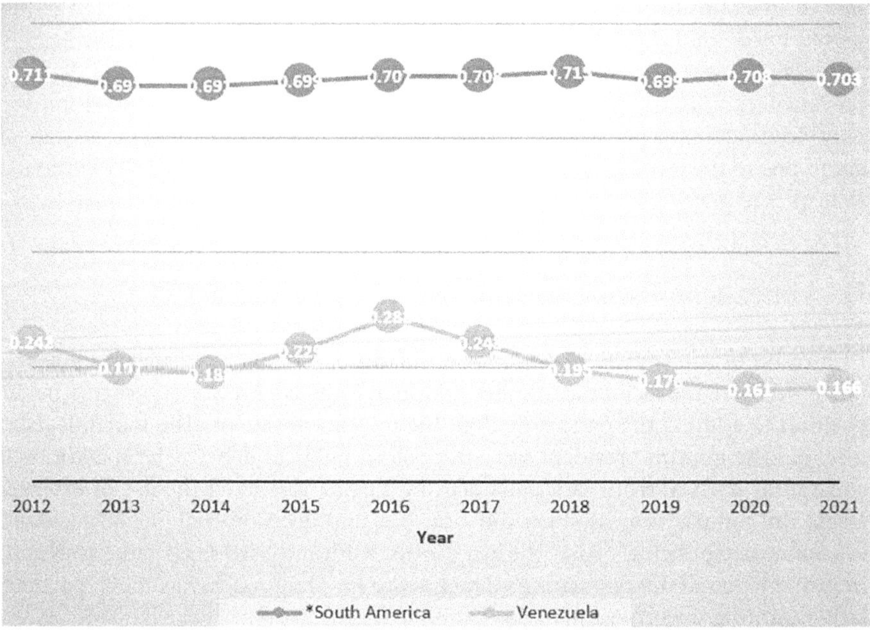

Source: V-DEM Institute.

This data must be carefully interpreted. Constitutional democracy certainly did not improve in Venezuela between 2020 and 2021 as a result of the pandemic. But considering the collapse of constitutional democracy, particularly since 2016, the pandemic favoured an autocratic stabilisation, reducing social pressure and, therefore, the need to fight repression. In particular, the pandemic did not concentrate the Presidency's powers simply because that concentration had already been consolidated in 2016. Another variable to consider is that the rigged election of the National Assembly's fifth legislature in December 2020 created the illusion of executive oversight. However, as explained, the fifth legislature has not exerted any real control over the Executive.

An additional factor that should be considered is how the pandemic affected the Venezuelan population. While COVID-19 caused devastation in Latin America as

[57] In 2018, 24% of Venezuelans approved of Maduro, while 71% disapproved of his government. In 2020, the approval rating increased to 25%, while the disapproval rating fell to 68%. See www.latinobarometro.org/latOnline.jsp.

[58] Chart prepared by the authors analyzing the data from the Liberal Component Index regarding South America and Venezuela, 2021–202, Liberal Democracy Index, V-DEM https://v-dem.net.

a whole with regard to cases, deaths, and economic collapse, the pandemic's impact on Venezuela was moderate in comparison. For instance, Venezuela has the lowest number of cases reported per 100k inhabitants compared with the Andean countries and the Latin American and Caribbean average:

Figure 2 Charter No 1. Cases reported by 100k inhabitants. 26 October 2022

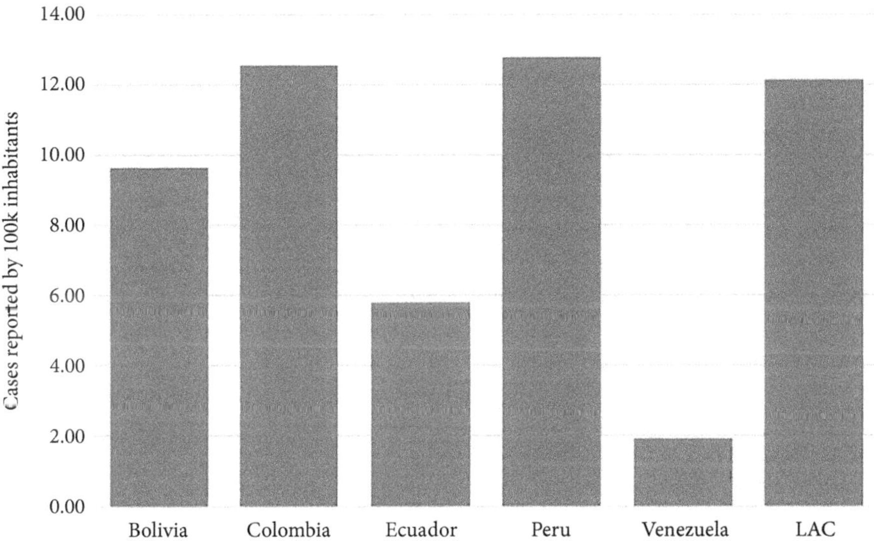

Source: Inter-American Development Bank.

Venezuela also has the lowest deaths reported per 100k inhabitants compared with the Andean countries and Latin America and the Caribbean average:

Figure 3 Charter No 2. Death reported by 100k inhabitants. 26 October 2022

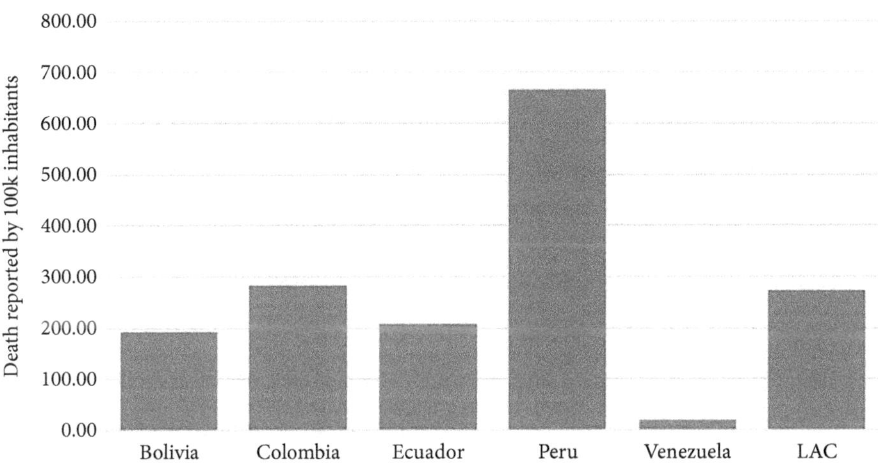

Source: Inter-American Development Bank.

In economic terms, and according to the International Monetary Fund, in 2022, the Venezuelan GDP grew 6 per cent (compared to the estimated GDP growth of 2.3 per cent in the western hemisphere). This figure demonstrates that the post-pandemic economic performance in Venezuela could be much better than the regional average,[59] which could eventually also favour the regime.

Another interesting factor to compare is trust in government. According to Latinobarómetro, in 2018, the country with the lowest distrust value was Chile (25 per cent), while Venezuela had the highest distrust value (63 per cent).[60] In 2020, meanwhile, distrust in Chile increased to 52 per cent, while in Venezuela it *decreased* to 61 per cent.[61]

The pandemic did not impair constitutional democracy in Venezuela simply because, when it started, Venezuela was already a non-democratic country. Therefore, the pandemic allowed Maduro to consolidate his power, despite the democratic transition initiated in that country in 2019 with the international recognition of the interim president. During the pandemic, Venezuela had a sui generis situation with the coexistence of two parallel governments: the de facto regime and the de jure interim president. However, the de facto regime performed much better, which resulted in an increase in its political support.

On the whole, this 'autocracy stabilisation effect' of the pandemic, far from improving constitutional democracy, contributed to its progressive deterioration. Powers remained under the de facto control of Maduro's government, and human rights violations continued and even increased (in any case, at a lower pace than the massive violations registered during 2017). According to the UN Human Rights Council Independent International Fact-Finding Mission report on the Bolivarian Republic of Venezuela of September 20, 2022,

> the human rights situation in the Bolivarian Republic of Venezuela remains grave. The country has endured a decade of spiraling humanitarian, social, economic, and human rights crises, coupled with a breakdown of State institutions, all of this exacerbated by the impact of COVID-19. Stark evidence of this is the more than six million people who have felt compelled to leave the country.[62]

IV. Conclusion

The COVID-19 pandemic has been one of the greatest recent global threats against constitutional democracy. 'Pandemocracy' is a term used to describe how

[59] The GDP growth in Venezuela is mostly a consequence of the collapse of centralised controls. Also, the economic crisis tended to stabilise after an unprecedented collapse of more than 80% of GDP growth between 2013 and 2021. See: Hernández (n 31).

[60] The value measures the percentage of the population without trust in the government.

[61] 'Autocracies outdo democracies on public trust – survey', *Reuters*, 18 January 2022: www.reuters.com/business/autocracies-outdo-democracies-public-trust-survey-2022-01-18/.

[62] A/HRC/51/43: Report of the independent international fact-finding mission on the Bolivarian Republic of Venezuela, 20 September 2022: www.ohchr.org/en/hr-bodies/hrc/ffmv/report-ffmv-september2022.

the pandemic promoted democratic erosion, primarily due to the extension or increase of extraordinary powers of the Executive Branch, the weakening of the separation of powers, and the limitations on human rights, both fundamental freedoms and economic and social rights. In Latin America, the initial concern was to prevent the abuse of power and the unjustified or disproportionate limitation of human rights, mainly based on Inter-American standards. However, in the end, it was not the abuse of power that created the most significant problem in the region but the lack of power in terms of the state's inability to fulfil the increasing number of tasks that COVID-19 brought about.

The case of Venezuela is somewhat different. Instead of analysing the democratic setback in that country due to COVID-19, it should be studied how the pandemic made it easier for the authoritarian regime to stay in power, basically, due to three reasons: (i) fewer anti-government protests to repress; (ii) the continuance of the state of emergency regime that had already been established for years, and (iii) a diminishing interest in the democratic transition initiated in 2019 with the international recognition of the interim president. Venezuela has been ranked bottom of the WJP Rule of Law Index for years before and after the pandemic.[63] However, political support for Maduro's government improved slightly after the pandemic, while his regime seems more stable, at least from the perspective of a democratic transition that, after the pandemic, now seems highly unlikely.

[63] According to the World Justice Project Rule of Law Index 2019, Venezuela was 126/126 in the global ranking: worldjusticeproject.org/sites/default/files/documents/ROLI-2019-Reduced.pdf. In the 2022 index, the country is still in last place, ranking 140/140.

PART III

Beyond States

9

COVID, Corruption, and Democratic Institutions

DELIA M FERREIRA RUBIO

I. Emergencies: An Excuse for Abuse

Emergencies generally increase corruption risks and COVID was no exception. In March 2020, the Latin American Chapters of Transparency International published a document highlighting the main areas and types of corruption risk that governments would face in their response towards the pandemic.[1]

The COVID-19 pandemic was a combination of factors particularly prone to corruption. The emergency itself on the one hand, and the fact that it affected mainly the health sector, one of the areas of public policies and public services which normally shows high levels of corruption. In a non-pandemic situation, an estimated U$500 billon is lost to corruption in the sector every year.[2]

When emergencies affect the people so directly and in such a dramatic way, as COVID did, the institutional reaction is to resort to urgent measures and exceptional rules.[3] The standard transparency and accountability mechanisms are weakened or completely bypassed. The decision-making power is concentrated on the executive, particularly through decree authority (in Latin American countries, '*decretos de necesidad y urgencia*', '*medidas provisorias*', etc).[4] During the pandemic, many governments operated with lower standards of consultation, transparency,

[1] Transparency International, 'Coronavirus sparks high risk of corruption across Latin America', March 2020, available at: www.transparency.org/en/press/coronavirus-sparks-high-risk-of-corruption-across-latin-america.

[2] Transparency International – Health, 'The Ignored Pandemic', March 2019, available at: ti-health.org/wp-content/uploads/2019/03/IgnoredPandemic-WEB-v3.pdf.

[3] KD Ewing, 'COVID-19: Government by Decree' (2020) 31(1) *King's Law Journal* 1–24, published online May 2020, available at: www.tandfonline.com/doi/pdf/10.1080/09615768.2020.1759398?needAccess=true. See also T Ginsberg and M Versteeg, 'The Bound Executive: Emergency Powers during the Pandemic', posted May 2020, available at: papers.ssrn.com/sol3/papers.cfm?abstract_id=3608974.

[4] Idea International, 'Emergency Law Responses and the COVID-19 Pandemic', 2021, available at: www.idea.int/gsod/sites/default/files/2021-11/emergency-law-responses-covid19-pandemic-gsod2021.pdf.

oversight, or control in their processes, and they issued hundreds of emergency regulations, often on a fast track.[5] On the other hand, people demand rapid and efficient responses to the crises without caring much about their institutional consequences. At the same time, because of fear and uncertainty, people tend to accept this move to a more authoritarian and discretionary decision-making process and tolerate the restrictions of freedoms, even in cases of clear abuses.

Although there are international standards on the limits that – even in time of emergencies – shall be respected to protect the rule of law and civil rights, these standards were not complied with in some countries. These standards refer to: a) the respect of the legality; b) the proportionality and reasonableness between the threat faced and the restrictions on civil rights and freedoms; c) the limited duration of the exceptional restrictions; d) the transparency and access to information about the decisions made; e) the existence of effective accountability mechanisms; and f) the effective legislative and judicial oversight.[6] The reality was quite different: the pandemic was used as an excuse for abuse.

The measures adopted in Latin America – as in most of the countries around the world – included curbing some human rights, restricting travel, closing classrooms, suspending government services, ordering the temporary closure of businesses, controlling or curtailing news reporting, delaying elections, establishing extended quarantines, lockdowns, and curfews. In some countries the role of police, security and military forces in civilian governance increased with the pandemic response. This securitisation of the COVID response came at the expense of the abuse of human rights.[7] In November 2020, Human Rights Watch denounced the abuses committed by police forces in Argentina.[8]

During the pandemic, unparalleled numbers of resources were mobilised including national budgets and stimulus packages from multilateral institutions which made efficient controls more important than ever. However, accountability mechanisms were reduced or paralysed, in part because of the reduction in bureaucratic activity but mainly based on the argument that the urgent situation demanded agile decision-making so there was no time for oversight. Not only the executive concentrated power at the expense of the legislative, but also

[5] OECD, 'Government at a Glance2021', July 2021, available at: www.oecd.org/gov/government-at-a-glance-22214399.htm.

[6] UN International Covenant on Civil and Political Rights (1976) Art 4, available at: www.ohchr.org/en/instruments-mechanisms/instruments/international-covenant-civil-and-political-rights; International Commission of Jurists, 'Siracusa Principles on the Limitation and Derogation Provisions on the International Covenant on Civil and Political Rights' (1985) available at: www.icj.org/wp-content/uploads/1984/07/Siracusa-principles-ICCPR-legal-submission-1985-eng.pdf. See also UN OHCHR, 'Emergency Measures and COVID-19: Guidance', April 2020, available at: www.ohchr.org/sites/default/files/Documents/Events/EmergencyMeasures_COVID19.pdf.

[7] Amnesty International, 'COVID-19 Crackdowns. Police Abuse and the Global Pandemic', December 2020, available at: www.amnesty.org/en/documents/act30/3443/2020/en/.

[8] Human Rights Watch: www.hrw.org/es/news/2020/11/20/la-pandemia-ha-dejado-al-descubierto-la-brutalidad-de-la-policia-argentina#:~:text=La%20Secretar%C3%ADa%20de%20Derechos%20Humanos,2019%20y%20marzo%20de%202020.

some special commissions were created with decision-making authority based on opaque delegation, no clear remit, and no clear accountable lines. Obviously, all these elements created fertile ground for corruption to flourish.

The second element of this combination which favoured corruption was the fact that the emergency was a pandemic. The health sector is one of the public policy areas most affected by corruption in normal times.[9] According to the UN Office on Drugs and Crime (UNODC), approximately 10 to 25 per cent of all money spent on procurement globally in the health sector is lost to corruption yearly.[10] The health service is identified as one of the more likely to be affected by bribery, which includes access to attention, beds in hospitals, tests, treatments, medicines, ventilators, and vaccines. Both these factors, corruption related to public procurement in the health sector and bribery or petty corruption in health services were documented in many countries in the region. Proética – Transparency International's chapter in Perú – opened a special channel to collect reports of bribery and corruption and provided legal assistance to the complainants or whistleblowers.[11] Transparencia Venezuela organised a similar reporting channel.[12] In 2020, more than 1,800 people around the world contacted Transparency International's Advocacy and Legal Advice Centres to report corruption and seek support for issues related to COVID-19.[13]

The main areas of corruption risks that could be anticipated were clear: public procurement of elements needed for the COVID response; management of subsidies, loans, and stimulus packages from multilateral bodies;[14] use of special trusts and endowments to address the emergency; the distribution of special financial aid, credits, subsidies and loans to individuals and businesses to cover economic losses, and the access to the health care system. The consequences of corruption in these different areas undermined not only the effective response to the pandemic, but also affected people's health and even lives.

[9] USAID, 'Global Health Anti-Corruption Integration Handbook', October 2022, available at: www.usaid.gov/documents/usaid-global-health-anti-corruption-integration-handbook.

[10] UNODC, 'Guidebook on Anticorruption in Public Procurement and the Management of Public finances', September 2013, available at: www.unodc.org/documents/corruption/Publications/2013/Guidebook_on_anti-corruption_in_public_procurement_and_the_management_of_public_finances.pdf.

[11] *Proética*, 'Orientación legal anti-corrupción': www.proetica.org.pe/orientacion-legal-anticorrupcion-durante-la-pandemia-del-covid-19/.

[12] Transparencia Venezuela, 'Working in One of the World's Most Dangerous Hospitals during COVID-19', January 2021, available at: www.transparency.org/en/news/working-in-one-of-the-worlds-most-dangerous-hospitals-during-covid-19.

[13] See some stories on reported cases at: www.transparency.org/en/citizens-report-covid-19-corruption.

[14] UNODC, 'COVID 19 Fiscal Response and the Prevention of Corruption', available at: www.unodc.org/pdf/corruption/COVID-19fiscal_response.pdf; and D Santoro, 'COVID: Duras objeciones de la Auditoría General de la Nación', *CLARIN*, June 2022, available at: www.clarin.com/politica/covid-duras-objeciones-auditoria-general-nacion-compras-ministerio-salud-s-35-millones_0_eyW44dnVsr.html. See also, on the situation in El Salvador: Fund, 'El Salvador: A Recipe for Corruption', August 2020, availableat: www.transparency.org/en/blog/el-salvador-bloated-budgets-and-little-oversight-a-recipe-for-disaster.

Information was one of the victims of the pandemic which exacerbated the risk of corruption. Access to information is essential to prevent, detect, and punish corruption. The 'infodemic' – reported by the World Health Organization[15] – was of serious concern as well as misinformation and manipulation of the data about the illness and its consequences, the treatments, the statistics of affected people, etc, because they undermined people's trust and public support of the response to the pandemic. At the same time, freedom of expression and freedom of the press suffered unreasonable restrictions,[16] and criticism of governments' decisions was suppressed in many countries.[17] The right of access to information was formally suspended or the governments simply disregarded and did not answer the petitions.[18] The role of civil society organisations, the press, and particularly investigative journalists was crucial in the fight for transparency and accountability.

Corruption is not just a financial crime and transparency is not just access to information. Integrity is a key element in the fight against corruption and what was not highlighted at the beginning of the pandemic but was then detected in many countries was the violation of public ethics rules and integrity standards by the authorities who allowed themselves to special treatment and behaved in clear contradiction with the rules and restrictions they had imposed on their fellow citizens. When these cases of misconduct (Partygates, VIP access to treatment and vaccines, the so-called Vaccinegates) were made public, the result was a decrease in the already low trust in institutions and leadership, that also contributed to the weakening of democratic institutions.

To mitigate the identified corruption risks, Transparency International and its national chapters in Latin America recommended the adoption of certain measures to address the pandemic: a) the decision-making process should be transparent, open and evidence-based; b) public procurement should be transparent and open contracting mechanisms should be implemented; c) prevention of

[15] PAHO-WHO, 'Understanding the Infodemic and Misinformation in the Fight Against COVID-19', available at: iris.paho.org/bitstream/handle/10665.2/52052/Factsheet-infodemic_eng.pdf?sequence=16.

[16] *Open Society*, 'How COVID-19 Threatens Independent Journalism', July 2020, available at: www.opensocietyfoundations.org/explainers/how-covid-19-threatens-independent-journalism.

[17] *Freedom House*, 'Democracy Under Lockdown', October 2020, available at: freedomhouse.org/sites/default/files/2020-10/COVID-19_Special_Report_Final_.pdf. See also, UNESCO, 'Journalism, press freedom and COVID-19', 2020, available at: unesdoc.unesco.org/ark:/48223/pf0000373573; Coalition for Human Rights, Art 19 and Ifex, 'Unhealthy Silence', July 2021, available at: /rightsindevelopment.org/unhealthy-silence/; and Committee to Protect Journalists, 'COVID-19 and Press Freedom' (several reports), available at: unesdoc.unesco.org/ark:/48223/pf0000373573.

[18] *Alianza Regional*, 'Acceso a la información en contexto de emergencia sanitaria', May 2020, available at: www.alianzaregional.net/wp-content/uploads/2020/05/Estudio-regional_-AIP-en-contexto-de-emergencia-sanitaria-final-.pdf; and 'Segundo informe', July 2020, available at: www.alianzaregional.net/wp-content/uploads/2020/07/II-Estudio-Regional-AIP-en-contexto-de-emergencia-sanitaria.pdf.

conflict of interests and undue influence should be reinforced; d) accountability and control mechanisms should be in place and made more agile; e) due-diligence processes should be fulfilled; f) access to health care should be granted on an equal basis, avoiding privileges, discrimination and discretional decision-making, and people should be clearly informed on the criteria applied to access them; g) access to economic aid, subsidies and credits should be distributed on the basis of equal, fair, and transparent criteria; and h) loans and stimulus packages from multilateral organisations should be accompanied by accountability and transparency mechanisms.

One significant difference in terms of corruption between COVID-19 and previous emergencies like the Ebola pandemic in 2014–16, the tsunami that affected Indonesia and Thailand in 2004, or the 1985 earthquake in Mexico was the fact that from the very beginning of the COVID pandemic there was a clear awareness of the corruption risks that the world would face and that reports on corruption cases were concomitant with the emergency and covered the whole world.

The increasing risk of corruption, the decline in democratic institutions and the loss of trust in institutions and leadership during the pandemic is clearly shown in different reports, surveys, and indexes. The emergency reinforced already registered trends towards authoritarianism, the deterioration of democratic governance, the undermining of rule of law, as well as the pervasive presence of corruption. These trends are still predominant in the region.[19]

According to Transparency International's Corruption Perception Index 2021, the fight against corruption has been stagnant in the Americas for three consecutive years with an average of 43 points out of 100 possible, and if we consider only Latin American countries the average drops to 37 points.[20] The situation is not better in terms of the state of democracy. The results of the EIU Democracy Index 2021 reflect the continuing negative impact of the COVID-19 pandemic on democracy and freedom for a second successive year.[21] Latin America suffered a big setback in 2021. The change in the region's score in 2021 was the biggest year-on-year decline experienced by any region. Only two countries – Uruguay and Costa Rica – qualified as 'Full' democracies. The WJP Rule of Law Index 2022 offers consistent results with the status of the rule of law weakening around the world for the fifth consecutive year. In Latin America, 11 countries registered a decline in their rule of law scores.[22]

[19] DF Rubio, 'La corrupción en Las Américas: Un desafío para la democracia', NDI, Summit of the Americas, Los Angeles, US, June 2022 (printing in process).

[20] Transparency International, 'Corruption Perception Index 2021', January 2022, available at: www.transparency.org/en/news/cpi-2021-americas-a-region-in-crisis.

[21] *The Economist Intelligent Unit*, 'Democracy Index 2021', February 2022, available at: www.eiu.com/n/democracy-index-2021-less-than-half-the-world-lives-in-a-democracy/.

[22] *World Justice Project*, 'Rule of Law Index 2022', October 2022, available at: worldjusticeproject.org/rule-of-law-index/insights?s=09#two-year-trend-.

II. Risk Zones

The deterioration of rule of law, checks and balances, transparency and accountability opened a window of opportunity for corruption in a wide range of areas. As for the type of corruption reported, bribery, conflicts of interest, undue influence, clientelism, cronyism, and petty corruption were prevalent.

Public Procurement was a major area of concern from the start of the pandemic. The whole world simultaneously demanded the urgent supply of the same kind of products. This massive demand determined the shortage of goods, a huge increase of prices, and the surge of new and improvised providers.

To face the emergency, one of the first measures adopted by governments was to resort to direct contracting, avoiding the relative long and competitive bidding processes, and bypassing normal checks and oversight. Unknown providers were hired without the most elementary due diligence, many of whom had conflicts of interest with government officials. Overprices, substandard supplies, lack of contract fulfilment, goods paid in advance and never delivered, fraud and money laundering were some of the facts reported.

Transparency was one of the victims of the pandemic. In many countries the government stopped publishing information about public contracts, open contracting portals were disabled, and access to information petitions were not answered. In Latin America, the media,[23] mainly investigative journalists,[24] and civil society organisations – among them all Transparency International's chapters – played a key role in monitoring, sharing information, and reporting suspicious cases.

In Honduras, Colombia, Argentina, México, Perú and Chile, Transparency International chapters created publicly accessible COVID-Contracts Monitors which collected disperse or unavailable information about the use of public resources in response to the pandemic. These monitors disclosed hidden or opaque information and facilitated the assessment of the processes followed and the decisions made. A few examples are enough to show the importance of the organisation's work.

In Perú, the government facilitated access to information related to the resources transferred to local governments and Proética created two, user friendly monitors to inform about the resources devoted to the COVID response and to follow the effective use of these resources with weekly updates,[25] and published

[23] *DW*, 'COVID-19 en América Latina: Escándalos de corrupción no dan tregua', July 2021, available at: www.dw.com/es/covid-19-en-am%C3%A9rica-latina-esc%C3%A1ndalos-de-corrupci%C3%B3n-no-dan-tregua/a-58181894.

[24] *Redpalta*, 'Las Compras en pandemia', available at: www.redpalta.org/compras-pandemia/, and 'Los beneficios a farmacéuticas en compras de vacunas COVID', available at: www.redpalta.org/post/los-beneficios-a-farmaceuticas-en-compra-de-vacunas/. See also, *Connectas*, 'Huellas de la pandemia. Pandemia de corruptos', available at: www.connectas.org/coronavirus-corrupcion/.

[25] *Proética*, 'Lupa en las transferencias. Monitoreo al gasto público' available at: www.proetica.org.pe/lupa-sobre-las-transferencias-monitoreo-ciudadano-al-gasto-publico-en-estado-de-emergencia/, and

several analysis on the open data provided through the official platforms (which covered only 10 per cent of the total amount of resources used for coping with the emergency), including those referring to conflicts of interest and overpricing.[26] Additionally, Proética conducted social audits to detect and report any wrongdoing in public procurement, misuse of funds, any problem related to the providers, lack of reporting, and discrepancies in the information provided through the official channels.[27] Another interesting initiative of Proética was the Monitor of Corruption cases.[28]

In Honduras, ASJ (Asociación para una Sociedad más Justa) produced a series of audits and reports on the use of public resources in the response to COVID.[29] The results of these investigations were published by *Revistazo*.[30] One of the corruption scandals disclosed – an authentic paradigmatic case – was the suspicious purchase of nine mobile hospitals.[31] The intermediary was an unknown company with just a mailbox address in the US, but the manufacturer was a Turkish company that was not a party to the agreement. The purchase order was signed although the Public Health Secretary had expressly stated that there was no need to buy this type of hospital. Significant overpriced was reported. The ASJ team quoted the same mobile hospitals directly with the same manufacturing company from which the government bought the hospitals, at a price of US$2 million less, and with other companies, very similar hospitals were quoted for US$4 million less each. Despite the urgency adduced to justify the purchase of nine hospitals, the provider did not deliver the hospitals on time.[32] The contract did not include any guarantee in case of unfulfillment or defective products.

Although, in Argentina, the emergency direct procurement regulation ordered that the information should be published, the official data platforms were not providing complete and up-to-date information about the contracts signed by

'Seguimiento de la ejecución del gasto', available at: www.proetica.org.pe/seguimiento-al-avance-de-la-ejecucion-presupuestal-destinado-al-estado-de-emergencia-por-covid-19/.

[26] *Proétca*, 'Analisis de datos abiertos sobre contrataciones públicas en el marco de la emergencia sanitaria contra el COVID', available at: www.proetica.org.pe/contenido/analisis-de-los-datos-abiertos-sobre-contrataciones-publicas-en-el-marco-de-la-emergencia-sanitaria-contra-el-covid-19/, and 'Reporte #2', available at www.proetica.org.pe/contenido/reporte-n-02-que-nos-dicen-los-datos-abiertos-sobre-las-contrataciones-publicas-para-atender-la-emergencia-sanitaria/.

[27] *Proética*, 'Reporte de veeduría ciudadana', available at: www.proetica.org.pe/wp-content/uploads/2020/10/476154892-OPERATIVO-VIRTUAL-EN-EL-ESTADO-DE-EMERGENCIA-COVID-19.pdf.

[28] *Proética*, 'Observatorio de casos de corrupción', available at www.proetica.org.pe/contenido/observatorio-de-casos-de-corrupcion-en-medio-de-la-pandemia-mas-de-1400-investigaciones-en-fiscalias-en-todo-el-pais/.

[29] *ASJ*, 'Auditoría y veeduría de las compras por emergencia para combatir el COVID-19', available at asjhonduras.com/covid19/index.html.

[30] *Revistazo*, 'Especial COVID-19. Transparencia salva vidas', available at: revistazo.com/covid-19/.

[31] *ASJ*, 'Auditoría y veeduría de las compras por emergencia para combatir el COVID-19 – Informes hospitales móviles', available at asjhonduras.com/covid19/informe_hospitales.html.

[32] *Revistazo*: revistazo.com/al-menos-57-defectos-reclamo-invest-h-a-fabricante-de-hospitales-moviles/, and revistazo.com/mr-hispanopreneur-el-hombre-detras-del-covid-desastre-de-47-millones-de-dolares-en-honduras/.

the government.[33] Poder Ciudadano created the 'ComprasCOVID' monitor – an open and usable database – which included all the information about COVID contracts, which rapidly became the to-go site to find information,[34] and mapped the risks in emergency contracting.[35]

Transparencia por Colombia monitored and audited the use of public resources and contracts signed by the government during the pandemic. Several problems were detected and reported, from overpricing, to lack of capacity of some providers, undue use of the emergency framework for purchases not related to COVID, the resort to private law agreements to avoid public law controls, and possible conflicts of interest in contracts that benefited campaign donors.[36] Chile Transparente monitored COVID-contracts with similar results.[37]

The lack of transparency was almost absolute in relation to the purchase of COVID vaccines. Open Contracting Partnership and Transparency International highlighted the data that should be shared during the vaccine procurement cycle. Publicly collecting and sharing this information would have supported (and it will support in the long term) governments and civil society in strengthening the planning, implementation, and monitoring of the related contracting processes in a way that builds public trust.[38] Unfortunately, opacity was the rule, and it created the opportunity for dubious negotiations.[39] The arguments in favour of secrecy were the defence of patent rights and commercial interests of the developer labs. These were not valid grounds on which to deny information. The people were not interested in the vaccines' formulas but had – and have – the right to know

[33] *Poder Ciudadano*, 'Observatorio de compras y contrataciones públicas en el marco del COVID-19', May 2020, available at: poderciudadano.org/wp-content/uploads/2020/12/ROCC-Contrataciones-publicas-en-Argentina-durante-el-estado-de-emergencia.pdf.

[34] *Poder Ciudadano*, 'ComprasCOVID19', available at: comprascovid19.poderciudadano.org/. See also, Poder Ciudadano – ROCC, 'Contrataciones públicas en Argentina durante el estado de emergencia', June 2022, available at: poderciudadano.org/wp-content/uploads/2020/12/ROCC-Contrataciones-publicas-en-Argentina-durante-el-estado-de-emergencia.pdf.

[35] *Poder Ciudadano*, 'Mapa de riesgos normativos en los procesos de compras de emergencia en Argentina. Transparencia, rendición de cuentas y control social para combatir el COVID-19', December 2020, available at <https://poderciudadano.org/wp-content/uploads/2020/12/Mapa-de-riesgos-normativos-COVID19.pdf>.

[36] *Transparencia por Colombia*, 'Balance del monitoreo a la contratación pública COVID-19', September 2022, available at <https://www.redpalta.org/compras-pandemia/>.

[37] *Chile Transparente*, 'Análisis de compras públicas en el contexto de la crisis sanitaria del COVID-19', June 2020, available at: www.chiletransparente.cl/analisis-de-compras-publicas-en-el-contexto-de-la-crisis-sanitaria-del-covid-19-mayo-2020/.

[38] Open Contracting Partnership and Transparency International – Health, 'Open Contracting for the COVID-19 Vaccine. A Good Practice Guide', July 2021, available at: www.open-contracting.org/wp-content/uploads/2021/07/OCP2021-C19-vaccine-guide.pdf.

[39] Transparency International – Health, 'For Whose Benefit', May 2021, available at: ti-health.org/wp-content/uploads/2021/05/For-Whose-Benefit-Transparency-International.pdf; *Poder Ciudadano*, 'Observatorio de vacunas COVID-19. Primeros hallazgos y recomendaciones', June 2022, available at: vacunas.poderciudadano.org/wp-content/uploads/2022/06/Observatorio-Vacunas-COVID-19-Informe-Primeros-Hallazgos-VF.pdf, and 'Análisis de disponibilidad de la información', September 2022, available at: vacunas.poderciudadano.org/wp-content/uploads/2022/09/Inf.-Analisis-de-Disponibilidad-de-la-Informacion.pdf.

which vaccines were bought, how many doses were purchased, what was the price paid, when the supplies would arrive and which conditionalities were attached to the agreements.[40] In Latin America, the scarce information available was the result of the work of Transparency International's chapters which, in some cases, had to file lawsuits to get information.[41] Transparencia Mexicana led the work on vaccine contracts in the region, coordinating the access to information petitions and centralising the information about the contracts.[42]

Social aid packages, public subsidies, and loans were distributed by governments to support the population as the lockdowns produced a parallel economic pandemic.[43] The criteria to access this aid were not always clear and transparent and as the situations were so different and unprecedented the regulations approved were subjected to continuous modifications and presented several loopholes and inconsistencies. This created the space for clientelism, favouritism, and other forms of discretionary and discriminatory decision-making. This affected not only individual persons but also the business sector.[44]

Bribery risk in the health care system was detected as soon as the pandemic was declared. The problem of 'informal payments' is pervasive in the health sector.[45] The 2019 Global Corruption Barometer – Latin American edition – reported that

[40] K Husmann, 'Global access to COVID vaccines. Lifting the veil of opacity', *U4*, October 2021, available at: www.u4.no/publications/lifting-the-veil-of-opacity-in-covid-19-vaccines-to-combat-the-pandemic.pdf.

[41] More information can be found at the following links: *ASJ-Revistazo* (Honduras), 'Vacunas abiertas': revistazo.com/vacunasabiertas/; *Chile Transparente*, 'Análisis de las negociaciones que el estado chileno ha realizado para la adquisición de Vacunas contra el COVID-19', July 2021, available at: www.chiletransparente.cl/antecedentes-de-las-negociaciones-que-el-estado-chileno-ha-realizado-para-adquirir-vacunas-contra-la-covid-19/; *Poder Ciudadano* (Argentina), 'Observatorio vacunas COVID-19': vacunas.poderciudadano.org/, and poderciudadano.org/poder-ciudadano-presento-un-amparo-para-que-el-ministerio-de-salud-de-la-nacion-haga-publicos-los-contratos-de-compra-de-vacunas-contra-el-covid-19/; *Proética* (Perú), 'Que la falta de transparencia y el abuso del poder no pongan en riego el proceso de vacunación', February 2021: www.proetica.org.pe/wp-content/uploads/2020/10/476154892-OPERATIVO-VIRTUAL-EN-EL-ESTADO-DE-EMERGENCIA-COVID-19.pdf; *Transparencia por Colombia – Revista Destapate*, 'Un grito por la transparencia: vacunas y movilización social', September 2021, available at:transparenciacolombia.org.co/2021/09/29/publicacion-numero-3-de-la-revista-destapate/.

[42] *Transparencia Mexicana*, 'Análisis de la transparencia en 39 contratos de vacunas contra el COVID-19 en el mundo', February 2022, available at: www.tm.org.mx/transparencia-en-contratos-vacunas-contra-covid-19-en-el-mundo/.

[43] *Oxfam*, 'Shelter from the Storm', December 2020, available at: www.oxfamargentina.org/2-700-millones-de-personas-no-han-recibido-proteccion-social-frente-a-la-crisis-economica-derivada-de-la-covid-19/.

[44] *El Economista* (Argentina), 'El gobierno detectó irregularidad en los beneficiarios del ATP – COVID stimulus program for the business sector', February 2021, available at: eleconomista.com.ar/economia/el-gobierno-detecto-irregularidad-beneficiarios-atp-n41237. See also *El Destape*, 'El gobierno define sanciones a empresas por irregularidades en el ATP', July 2021, available at: www.eldestapeweb.com/economia/programa-atp/el-gobierno-define-sanciones-a-empresas-por-irregularidades-en-el-atp-202111915560.

[45] C Incaltarau, AV Horodnic, CC Williams and L Oprea, 'Institutional Determinants of Informal Payments for Health Services: An Exploratory Analysis across 117 Countries' (2021) 18 *International Journal of Environmental Research and Public Health* 12421, available at: www.mdpi.com/1660-4601/18/23/12421/pdf.

an average of 10 per cent of the respondents said that they had had to pay bribes to receive attention at public clinics and hospitals.[46] The scarcity of resources created the opportunity for petty corruption mainly at hospitals that struggled to cope with COVID-19 and faced increasing shortages in staff, beds, ventilators, and other equipment. People were asked to pay for a bed, or for the possibility to be connected to a ventilator. Healthcare staff reported that they were bribed to get personal protective equipment. When vaccines were available at the end of 2020, the cases of bribery to get priority access to the vaccine were also reported.

Public integrity standards constitute a central piece in the public ethics ecosystem. presidents, ministers, parliamentarians, government officials and public servants shall behave honestly; they must not abuse their position for their private benefit or for that of their families, friends, followers, and cronies; they shall declare their interest and assets and avoid conflict of interests. The violation of these duties is a form of corruption that is unfortunately common. The concentration of power and the weakening and bypassing of accountability mechanisms generated a window of opportunity for those in power who – having access to inside information, and the unrestricted authority to create and modify the rules – believed that because there was an exceptional and urgent situation, they had been graciously granted a status of privilege and impunity. The 'Olivosgate', in Argentina, was a scandal related to the visits and parties organised by the presidential family at the official residence in violation of lockdown regulation.[47] Other scandals were related to the privileged access to vaccines for public officials, cronies and VIPs in violation of the established priority criteria ('Vacunasgate'; 'VacunatorioVIP), in Perú,[48] Argentina,[49] Chile,[50] and Ecuador.[51]

III. The Aftermath

The detrimental effect of the pandemic on the status of democracy has not been reversed in Latin America. The economic crisis that followed the pandemic with its consequence of recession, inflation, unemployment, and debt crisis has given governments another emergency to justify the concentration of power and to

[46] Transparency International, 'Global Corruption Barometer – Latin America – 2019', available at: www.transparency.org/en/gcb/latin-america/latin-america-and-the-caribbean-x-edition-2019.

[47] *La Nación*: www.lanacion.com.ar/politica/alberto-fernandez-habla-por-primera-vez-tras-la-confirmacion-de-los-festejos-en-olivos-nid13082021/; <https://www.lanacion.com.ar/politica/la-dura-respuesta-de-la-periodista-que-revelo-la-foto-de-olivos-a-un-colega-de-c5n-nid14082021/>; and www.lanacion.com.ar/lnmas/hablo-guadalupe-vazquez-la-periodista-que-difundio-la-foto-del-escandalo-de-olivos-nid15082021/.

[48] *El Pais*: elpais.com/internacional/2021-02-17/el-vacunagate-convulsiona-peru-mas-de-460-personas-influyentes-recibieron-en-secreto-dosis-de-sinopharm.html.

[49] *DW*:www.dw.com/es/llueven-denuncias-sobre-vacunaci%C3%B3n-vip-en-argentina/a-56638653.

[50] *France 24*: www.france24.com/es/am%C3%A9rica-latina/20210220-america-latina-desigualdad-vacunacion-escandalos.

[51] *BBC*: www.bbc.com/mundo/noticias-america-latina-56218624.

keep enforcing some of the exceptional rules approved during the pandemic. The permanent emergency is not new in Latin America and generates the normalisation of what shall be an exceptional and temporary legal arrangement. This is the case particularly of some populist governments in the region.

Lack of trust in democratic institutions and leadership and the prevailing social discontent contribute to weaken democracy and undermine rule of law. According to the 2021 report of the Latinobarómetro, less than half of Latin Americans are committed democrats and a growing number say it is the same to live in a democracy or an authoritarian regime.[52] The dissatisfaction with the performance of democracy has increased too. The region's average of satisfaction with the way in which democracy works is only 25 per cent and has constantly declined in the last seven years.

As Winston Churchill is credited with saying, one should 'never allow a good crisis go to waste'. To strengthen democracy, prevent corruption, and rebuild trust there are some lessons that should be learned after this pandemic to be better equipped to face similar emergencies in the future. It would be advisable to review the rules, standards, procedures, and institutional arrangements applicable in case of emergency, particularly the following principles should be guaranteed: a) access to information shall be guaranteed; b) exceptional and concomitant accountability mechanisms and tools shall be applied to oversee the decision-making process; c) public procurement procedure shall guarantee transparency, elementary due-diligence, and robust contractual arrangements to avoid fraud; d) justice service shall be considered essential and shall not be discontinue or suspended; e) freedom of expression shall not be censored – this includes opinion, press, media and social media; and f) all restrictions on civil liberties shall be reasonable, proportional, transparent, accountable, and of limited duration.

Strengthening democracy and democratic values is our collective responsibility to prevent future abuse of emergency powers. Constitutions, rule of law, checks and balances, transparency, accountability, and integrity systems must never be put in quarantine again.

[52] *Latinobarómetro*, 'Informe 2021', available at: www.latinobarometro.org/latContents.jsp.

10

Hyper-Presidentialism versus Federalism During the COVID-19 Emergency in Argentina, Brazil and Mexico

ANTONIO MARÍA HERNÁNDEZ

I. Introduction

The chapter analyses the institutional and political impact produced in Argentina, Brazil and Mexico by the COVID-19 emergency. These three countries have an institutional pathology that is hyper-presidentialism, which means the President's control over the competencies of the other powers. During the emergency, this phenomenon affected the respective republican systems, with presidents governing by executive orders and decrees, and weak participation by Congresses.

Likewise, the centralist style of the presidents has been another characteristic in common which has damaged the functioning of the respective federal systems. It should not be forgotten that subnational governments exercise important concurrent powers in health.

Consequently, intergovernmental conflicts arose over this issue, since there were state governors who confronted their respective presidents due to the pandemic. In Brazil and Argentina in particular, the highest courts of justice issued very important rulings to affirm state and provincial powers.

In addition, there were severe violations of fundamental rights, which led to complaints against Argentina, before the Inter-American Commission on Human Rights, among other consequences. There was no adequate compliance with the jurisprudential principles of the Inter-American Court of Human Rights regarding the limitation of rights during the emergency. These unconstitutional measures were not only dictated by the federal government but also by provincial and municipal governments.

II. Hyper-Presidentialism in Argentina and Other Latin American Countries

It is necessary to clarify the concept of 'hyper-presidentialism', both in Argentina and in other countries in the region.

This phenomenon is characterised by the concentration of power in the President, beyond the powers established by the Constitution, to the detriment of the division and balance of powers and the principles of constitutional democracy.

Carlos Santiago Nino has studied this serious institutional pathology, which produces immeasurable negative effects for political and legal systems and for an open society.[1]

Referring to the hypertrophied presidency in Argentina, according to the original constitutional text of 1853 – that is, before the 1994 reform – he maintained:

> This brief review of the powers that the Presidents were acquiring by an extensive interpretation of constitutional clauses, by claudication of the other powers of the State, or by a plain and simple exercise of political muscle, shows that, from the normative point of view, the Argentine president is, as Alberdi foresaw, a true monarch, although his powers have not been an obstacle to the instability of governments and abuses of power against the rights of citizens. It is also confirmed that, with the distortion of the spirit and often of the constitutional texts, in granting and assumption of extraordinary powers by the President, the tendency to illegality has been a constant in our political-institutional practice, even in periods de jure.[2]

Nino also drew attention to corporatism, which he considered very important to understand Latin American politics, due to its link with political regimes such as bureaucratic authoritarianism and with ideologies such as populism. He wrote: 'in Argentina the corporatization of the State has been obvious', noting the actions of the Armed Forces for the seizure of power, the Catholic Church, the unions and certain groups of state contractors in the economic system for the granting of privileges, monopolies and subsidies.[3] In opposition, he defended the model of 'deliberative' democracy.[4]

I affirm that many of his concepts are fully valid today, and I would particularly point out that the problem of corporate hyper-presidentialism

[1] In his book *Fundamentos de Derecho Constitucional* (Buenos Aires, Astrea, 2002) Carlos Santiago Nino exposed with an interdisciplinary vision in ch III dedicated to the 'Organization of Power' these 3 sections: a) 'Current organization of power in Argentina', with emphasis on the legal-constitutional; b) 'Evaluation of Argentine hyper-presidentialism from the point of view of its democratic legitimacy', with emphasis on the philosophical; and c) 'Evaluation of Argentine hyper-presidentialism from the point of view of its stability and effectiveness', with emphasis on political science.

[2] *Cf*, Nino ibid 529.

[3] ibid 562–66.

[4] ibid 605.

continues to be one of the most serious issues in our country. Since the 1994 Constitutional reform, which incorporated institutions to mitigate it, the violation of the letter and spirit of the Supreme Law can be more clearly observed.[5]

Our 'hyper-presidentialism', based on Alberdi's model – of presidentialism stronger than the North American model due to the influence of the Chilean Constitution of 1833 – was accentuated by political practices, emergencies, the weakening of Congress, the inadequate exercise of control of constitutionality – especially of the Supreme Court – and the coups d'état, between 1930 and 1983.

The constitutional reform of 1994 adopted the following main modifications in order to reduce the powers of the President:[6]

(1) Deprivation of the competence to appoint the Mayor of the City of Buenos Aires.
(2) Strengthening of Congress through different reforms, which seek a better balance of powers within our republican system. It is important to mention: the extension of the ordinary session period, the power for the declaration of federal intervention, and other institutions which will be explained later.
(3) Reduction of the powers of the President in the designation of the members of the Judiciary through the creation of the Council of the Magistracy.
(4) Strengthening of provincial and municipal autonomy, to reduce the powers of the federal government and affirm the vertical control of power, as another objective of federalism.[7]
(5) Constitutional hierarchy of control bodies such as the National Audit Office, the Ombudsman and the Public Ministry, in order to increase the control of the republican system.
(6) Reduction of the President's mandate to four years, with the possibility of immediate re-election and direct election, as had been demanded for years by most of the political parties.
(7) Incorporation of the decrees of necessity and urgency and the delegated legislation, as emergency institutes validated by the jurisprudence of the Supreme Court of Justice from the cases '*Peralta*' (1990) and '*Delfino*' (1927), with the purpose of limiting the powers of the Executive Branch, according to Artsicles 99 inc. 3 and 76.
(8) Creation of the Chief of the Cabinet of Ministers, as an institution of a certain hybridity due to its parliamentary origin in a presidential system and in

[5] See AM Hernández (dir) and PRC Castro (coord), 'El Poder Ejecutivo- Ch. XVII' in *Derecho Constitucional*, Vol 2 (Buenos Aires, La Ley, 2012) 1279ff. and AM Hernández, *Constitutional Law in Argentina*, 4th edn (The Netherlands, Wolters Kluwer, Kluwer Law International, 2022). Regarding the hegemonic presidency, as Natalio Botana has also pointed out, see his book *Poder y hegemonía* (Buenos Aires, Emecé Editores, 2007).

[6] See AM Hernández, *A veinticinco años de la reforma constitucional de 1994-Legitimidad, ideas fuerza, diseño constitucional, modernización e incumplimiento* (Cordoba, National University of Cordoba Press, 2019).

[7] As argued by Madison and Hamilton in the Federalist Papers.

> order to moderate hyper-presidentialism and serve to ensure governability in situations of political crisis.[8]

I maintain that there is a notorious contrast between the republican and federal democracy established in the Constitution and reality, characterised by a hyper-presidentialism that does not respect the division and balance of powers and tends towards centralisation, affecting the autonomy of provinces, of the City of Buenos Aires and of the local governments. Despite the great advances achieved in the constitutional reform of 1994, the anomie has prevented the modification of the centralist and unitary policies that have led us to this backwardness and decadence.[9]

Hyper-presidentialism is exercised through the arbitrary management of financial resources, which subordinates the provincial and municipal governments, creating a notable political, economic and social dependence. Twenty-six years ago, the tax co-participation agreement law had to be sanctioned, according to the constitutional reform of 1994. Constitutional non-compliance in this aspect has very serious institutional consequences, because it deeply affects the federal republic.

Indeed, instead of federal finance, the reality is that of fiscal unitarism, because the federal government manages more than 80 per cent of the fiscal resources.[10]

Another very serious expression of the aforementioned pathology, and one which substantially affects Congress, is linked to the national budget, in accordance with the provisions of Law 26,124 of 2006 – which modified Article 37 of the Financial Administration Law – to grant special powers to the Head of Cabinet of Ministers, for the possibility of restructuring the budget.

Government by Decrees of the Executive Branch is one of the greatest expressions of hyper-presidentialism. The number of Necessity and Urgency Decrees issued by the presidents has been recorded: Menem, 550; De la Rua, 51; Rodriguez Saa, 6; Duhalde, 152; Kirchner, 237; Fernandez de Kirchner, 81; Macri, 45; and Fernandez, 39.[11]

[8] This has been the trend enshrined in the 14 constitutional reforms produced in a total of 18 Latin American countries, as analysed in particular by D Valadés, *El Gobierno de Gabinete* (Rubinzal Culzoni and the Autonomous University of Mexico, Santa Fe, Argentina, 2008), with my Prologue, and *La parlamentarización de los sistemas presidenciales* (Legal Research Institute of UNAM and the National College of Mexico, Mexico, 2007). In these books, the distinguished constitutionalist reopens the debate that political scientists such as Linz, Valenzuela, Sartori and Nohlen had started around presidentialism and parliamentarism in Latin America. Valadés pointed out the renewal of presidentialism through the incorporation of institutions of parliamentarism, in order to moderate the concentration of presidential power and rationalise the exercise thereof.

[9] See AM Hernández, D Zovatto and E Fidanza, *Segunda Encuesta de Cultura Constitucional: Argentina una sociedad anómica* (Buenos Aires, University of Buenos Aires Press, 2016).

[10] See AM Hernández and G Krivocapich, *Autonomía municipal en su aspecto tributario* (Buenos Aires, La Ley, 2021).

[11] See A Santiago, 'Las tres generaciones de DNU (1983–2018)' (2019) 20(2) *Revista Argentina de Teoría Jurídica (RATJ)*, Law School, Torcuato Di Tella University, Buenos Aires. But at the end of 2022, those dictated by the current President Fernández exceeded 130.

The serious institutional responsibility of Congress in this matter cannot be ignored, and there has been a notable decline of its constitutional obligations of control. I also draw attention to the slowness in enacting the Law No 26,122, regulating Article 99 inc. 3, sanctioned in 2006. Another unconstitutional step involved, establishing that the decrees have no expiration period and that the approval of only one of the Chambers is necessary for their ratification.[12]

In addition, it is important to observe the almost non-existent controls carried out by Congress through the Permanent Bicameral Commission, and later in the Plenary Sessions of both Chambers, which never declared any DNU or any Delegate Decree invalid.[13]

In relation to Latin America, the de facto governments contributed to the consolidation of hyper-presidentialism. But this pathological deformation of institutions can also be observed in governments elected by the people. This is what has been happening in our country for a long time and can also be seen in other Latin American countries, such as Brazil and Mexico, among others.[14]

It is essential to point out the trend towards rational and controlled presidentialism that can be observed in most of the constitutional reforms introduced in Latin America, as well as the need to consolidate the proper functioning of republican systems, with division and balance of powers, for the achievement of open and democratic societies with an increase in constitutional culture and legality.[15]

Our problems are linked not so much to the normative design of our institutions,[16] but to our political behaviour, which exhibits a deficient democratic culture.

Two phenomena that also show the low institutional quality in some countries of the region are the aforementioned corporatism and the concept of delegative democracies. These differ from the representative ones, since broad powers are

[12] See AM Hernández, 'Balance of the Constitutional Reform of 1994', *La Ley*, 22 August 2009. That same year, 2006, should be especially remembered for the constitutional violations and for the deepening of hyper-presidentialism, since in addition to this Law, the Presidency of Néstor Kirchner achieved the approval of two other laws: No 26,080 for the modification of the Council of the Magistracy, which facilitated the influence of the ruling party in the management of the organism affecting the independence of the Judiciary and No 26,124 for the modification of the state Financial Administration, because Art 37 empowered the Chief of the Cabinet of Ministers to change the destination of the items, destroying the indisputable and non-delegable powers of Congress in said budgetary matters.

[13] See A Santiago, SVeramendi and SC Videla, *El control del Congreso sobre la actividad normativa del Poder Ejecutivo* (Buenos Aires, La Ley, 2019) and Santiago (n 11).

[14] See S Levitzky and D Ziblatt, *How Democracies Die* (Cambridge, MA, Harvard University Press, 2018) and MV Murillo, S Levitzky and D Brinks, *La ley y la trampa en América Latina* (Siglo XXI, Colombia, 2021).

[15] See AM Hernández, 'Reflexiones sobre transición democrática y reformas constitucionales en América Latina' in *Cadernos de Solucoes Constitucionais*, No 4 (Asociación Brasileira de Constitucionalistas democratas and Malheiros Editores, San Pablo, Brasil, 2012).

[16] Roberto Gargarella has developed a thesis about the inadequate design of the constitutional reforms introduced in Latin America. Although the recognition of rights has been expanded, the 'machine room', as he calls the operation of the organic part, has been neglected, which has allowed the concentration of power. *Cf*, R Gargarella *La sala de máquinas de la Constitución en el constitucionalismo latinoamericano* (Buenos Aires, Katz Editores, 2014).

granted by the electorate to the presidents, who govern practically alone or with the involvement of a small circle and without the controls of the other legislative branches.[17]

III. Hyper-Presidentialism in the Federations of Argentina, Brazil and Mexico in Times of Covid-19

Faced with the coronavirus pandemic that has affected the country, the President of the Argentine Republic, with the support of legislative authorities and governors of different political parties, announced the issuance of Decreto de Necesidad y Urgencia (Necessity and Urgency Decree) 297/2020, dated 19 March 2020, which implemented preventive and mandatory social isolation, among other measures.[18]

This attitude contrasted with what had happened throughout our history. In the last 100 years, Argentina has moved from emergency to emergency, with profound violations of the constitutional order, its republican and federal system and individual rights and guarantees. All this has increased the anomie, the low institutional quality, the hyper-presidentialism and the underdevelopment that characterises the country.[19]

But the initial attitude of the President changed after a few days, since Congress was not in operation, and the country began to be governed by Decrees.

As I argued:

> In the emergency, the functioning of the legislative bodies is essential, for the approval of measures and for the control of the decrees of the Executive Power issued by the legislative delegation due to the health emergency and those decrees of necessity and urgency'... To face the emergency, the State must respond in its entirety with the full functioning of its powers, where the Legislative and the Judiciary also have obligations to fulfill. I insist that the emergency is not above the Constitution nor does it suspend it. This is what differentiates democracies from autocracies. Nor can it be believed that this emergency will turn us into a unitary state, where the autonomy of the Provinces, the Autonomous City of Buenos Aires and the Municipalities ceases.[20]

[17] GO·Donnell, 'La democracia delegativa', *La Nación Newspaper*, Buenos Aires, 28 May 2009.

[18] The health emergency was previously declared by Law No 27,541 enacted for Congress in December 2019.

[19] See my books titled *Emergencias y el orden constitucional*, with their two editions by (Buenos Aires, Rubinzal-Culzoni, 2002), and (Mexico, Legal Research Institute of UNAM, 2003) and R Culzoni, 'Emergencias, orden constitucional y COVID-19' (Buenos Aires, 2020). And also my ch XII, 2nd part, on 'Limitaciones Excepcionales a los derechos' (Exceptional Limitations to Rights) in the book *Derecho Constitucional* (Constitutional Law), which I edited, (Buenos Aires, La Ley, 2012). See also my journalistic articles titled 'Emergencias y orden constitucional', published in *Clarín digital*, on 23 March 2020 and in *La Voz del Interior* on 1 April 2020, and in *Clarín online*, from 27 March where I pointed out the closure of Congress and the affectation of Argentine federalism.

[20] See AM Hernández, 'Federalismo y COVID19', in the *Clarín online* newspaper, Buenos Aires, 24 April 2020.

Although the governors and the head of government of the Autonomous City of Buenos Aires (CABA) were consulted, as well as some mayors, the principles of our Federation have not been fully respected.

In the first place, this was because Congress did not sit for 60 days. I believe, however, that the main decision made, which was to order the quarantine, was initially successful,[21] because it had the support of the provincial, the CABA and municipal governments.[22]

I believe that the Federation as a state and government system has been very important on this occasion, as other examples in comparative law also indicate, particularly that of Germany.[23]

Pointing out the importance of coordination federalism, I indicated that in some DNU (Necessity and Urgency Decrees) such as 355/2020, in Article 3 adequate reference was made to coordination with the different orders of government for the execution of various measures.[24]

But in that same decree in Article 2, the subnational governments were practically subordinated, since only the Chief of the Cabinet of Ministers was empowered to provide exceptions for the orderly exit from quarantine, at the request of those governments.[25]

The same thing happened with the Single Enabling Certificate for Circulation throughout the country, with the Ministry of the Interior responsible here, thus creating a very high degree of centralisation.[26]

I argued that the decisions regarding these aforementioned issues corresponded to the provincial and municipal governments, due to the differing situations that the pandemic presented in the provinces and in the municipalities.

[21] Although I expressed my concern about its extension, with the serious problems that this produced in the economy and in other aspects of people's psychosocial health. Keep in mind that models such as those in Sweden and Uruguay did not establish a mandatory quarantine, showing maximum respect for personal liberties, although they advised social distancing and other measures. See also S Rhodes, 'Freedom of movement after COVID-19', *CADAL*, online, 19 May 2020.

[22] See A Porto and L di Gresia, 'El rol de los gobiernos subnacionales (provinciales y municipales) en la pandemia COVID19' in Asociación Iberoamericana de financiación local (ed), *Los desafíos de las finanzas intergubernamentales ante el COVID-19* (Universidad Nacional de La Plata, 13 April 2020).

[23] See the article by A Carbajosa and M Bassets, 'The Pandemic Examines German Federalism and French Centralism', *El País online*, 17 April 2020, where the efficiency of the German decentralised system is highlighted, based on the Merkel agreements with the heads of government of the Lander for the big decisions, while the execution of the same falls to the Lander. The fact that citizens could relate to the decisions, these being based on the reality in their region, enabled the country's success in these matters. This is contrasted with the French system, based on the centralism of the President's power and his technocratic elite.

[24] Art 3 expresses with adequate federal technique that the federal authorities '... in coordination with their peers from the provincial jurisdictions, the Autonomous City of Buenos Aires and the municipal authorities, each one within the scope of their powers, will order the measures ...'.

[25] Along the same lines, DNU 408/2020 grants the provinces the determination of activities and the preparation of the respective protocols, but reaffirming federal competence, since ultimately the Ministry of Health and the Chief of the Cabinet of Ministers decide. And the same was provided for in the most recent DNU 493/2020 of 24 May 2020, for the extension of the quarantine.

[26] See Resolution 48/2020 of the Ministry of Interior, 28 March 2020.

I also remembered that, in this health emergency, the powers corresponded concurrently to the four government orders: federal government, provinces, the CABA and municipalities.[27]

In addition, the public services in this matter were mainly in charge of the provinces, the CABA and the municipalities.

Consequently, a joint and coordinated participation of the various government orders should have been adopted in major decisions during the emergency, instead of those being made only by the Executive Branch through decrees.

Likewise, a more pronounced development of interjurisdictional relations and a greater emphasis on decisions and execution by subnational governments would have been convenient.[28]

Hyper-presidentialism of the Executive Power also produced two serious interjurisdictional conflicts with the CABA, governed by the political opposition.

The first was caused by a DNU that prohibited teaching classes during the pandemic in the Autonomous City and the second by another DNU that reduced its tax co-participation funds. The Supreme Court of Justice of the Nation finally resolved both cases, as I will analsze later.

Continuing with this analysis, I must briefly consider the nature of the institutional functioning of subnational governments during the emergency. In this aspect, the phenomenon of hyper-presidentialism has also been observed, with a lack of functioning of legislatures and deliberative councils,[29] albeit with some exceptions.[30]

Regarding the exercise of emergency powers in this matter, there was full agreement between the various governments in the country in terms of applying mandatory social distancing as the main measure.[31]

In other federations this did not happen, such as in Brazil, Mexico and the US, where the presidents were reluctant to order quarantines. For this reason, the Governors of São Paulo and Rio de Janeiro, of Jalisco and Nueva León and of

[27] See AM Hernández, 'El federalismo argentino', chs II and IV in AM Hernández and B Buteler (eds), *Derecho Público Provncial* (Buenos Aires, Abeledo Perrot, 2020); *Federalismo y Constitucionalismo Provincial* (Buenos Aires, Abeledo Perrot, 2009) and *Municipal Law* (Mexico, UNAM, 2003). With regard to concurrent municipal powers, see E Marchiaro, 'Municipal Closures and Pandemic' [2020] *DPI, Administrative Journal* 273, which highlights the important role of local governments.

[28] Although the functioning of the Federal Health Council should be highlighted. In my 20 proposals to strengthen Argentine federalism, I raise the need to establish a National Association or Conference of Governors, as in the US and Mexico. See AM Hernández, *La Ciudad Autónoma de Buenos Aires y el fortalecimiento del federalismo argentino* (Buenos Aires, Iusbaires, 2017).

[29] The model observed in the federal government has been repeated in general in the provinces and municipalities, through government by Decrees of the governors and mayors.

[30] See J Brugge, in his article entitled 'Congreso Nacional, sesiones virtuales y su constitucionalidad' *Perfil*, online, 17 April 2020. The state legislatures of Chiapas, Sinaloa and Zacatecas also functioned virtually in the Mexican Federation For their part, see the legislative activity of 35 North American states on the website of the National Conference of State Legislatures, www.ncsl.org, with all the information about COVID-19.

[31] See AM Hernández, 'Federalismo y COVID 19', in *Clarin Newspaper* online, 24 April 2020, Buenos Aires and the book *Emergencias, orden constitucional y COVID19* (n 19).

New York and California, among other states and municipal authorities, made decisions to do so in advance of the presidents' announcements, since there are concurrent faculties between the various government orders.[32]

Regarding the brief analysis of the fundamental rights restricted or violated during this emergency,[33] I note in the first place the freedom of movement, the freedom of assembly and the freedom to work, these being restricted as a consequence of the preventive and compulsory isolation.[34] However, due to excessive measures, the rights to equality and privacy, the right to information and freedom of the press, enshrined in the national Constitution and various international treaties with the same hierarchy, have in some cases been violated.[35]

The worst offender in this matter was the province of Formosa, which established prohibitions beyond the national DNU, and which caused Argentina to be denounced before the Inter-American Commission on Human Rights by organisations such as Human Rights Watch and Amnesty International. For months, thousands of citizens from Formosa were prevented from entering the province, while the isolation centres operated under deplorable conditions.[36]

Finally, with the intervention of the Supreme Court of Justice of the Nation in the cases '*Lee Carlos Alberto*' (2020), where reports were requested from the Province of Formosa,[37] and '*Petcoff Naidenoff*' (2021), where the same was done,

[32] See J Kincaid and JW Leckrone, 'Federalism and the COVID-19 crisis in the United States of America', *Forum of Federations*, who report that 10 of the governors ordered the quarantine, 9 of them Democrats, before the decision by the President. The authors criticise the official federal action in the face of the pandemic, mindful of the marked political polarisation that exists and the serious effects produced. For an analysis of what happened in the North American States, see A Artiles, M Gandur and A Driscoll, 'The (un)United States: Federalism and Decentralization in Times of Pandemic' in E Nader and M-C Fuchs (eds), *COVID-19 and States in Action: A Comparative Constitutional Study Between Federal and Non-Federal Countries* (Colombia, IIDP and Konrad Adenauer Stiftung, Tirant lo Blanch, 2021) 278ff. The authors maintain that the states should have taken charge of the fight against the pandemic, given the denialist attitude of President Trump, and that this meant a decentralisation of power in the US, although, on the other hand, the governors did not adequately respect municipal powers, they cite as an example the conflicts between Governor Cuomo of the State of New York and Mayor Di Blasio of the City of NY.

[33] In my article 'Restrición de Derechos por Decreto', *Clarín*, Buenos Aires, 15 April 2021, I analyse the unconstitutionality of the limitation of rights carried out by DNU, since the national Constitution by Arts 14, 19 and 28 requires laws. And the same is required by International Human Rights Law, and in particular by Advisory Opinion 6 of the Inter-American Court of Human Rights, in relation to Art 27 of the American Convention on Human Rights.

[34] Ordered by DNU 297/2020 already mentioned above, which was followed by a multiplicity of other DNU. More than 130 have been issued to date and, in quite a few cases, they deal with other issues that go beyond the health issue. In short, another expression of hyper-presidentialism and government by decree.

[35] For an analysis of these issues, see Hernández (n 19) and the articles published in *Clarín*, Buenos Aires: 'Emergencias y orden constitucional', of 23 March from 2020; 'Federalismo y COVID19', 25 April 2020; 'Restricción de derechos por Decreto', *Clarín*, Buenos Aires, already mentioned and 'El proyecto de superpoderes es mas del mismo hiperpresidencialismo', of 12 May 2021.

[36] There were also other very serious cases in the provinces of Tucumán, Córdoba, Santiago del Estero, Corrientes and San Luis, among others and also in municipal governments.

[37] By the judgment of 29 October 2020, issued unanimously by the justices, where a report was requested from the province for a period of three days, among other warnings.

the order was made for entry into the province to be permitted and the restrictions implemented were lifted.[38]

In the '*Maggi Mariano*' case (2021), the High Court permitted the entry into the Province of Corrientes for the plaintiff.[39]

With respect to Brazil, Marcelo Figueiredo maintained that this phenomenon of hyper-presidentialism also occurs there, since the President is not adequately controlled by Congress, and enjoys enormous legal, financial and administrative powers in a patrimonial state.[40]

Luis Guilherme Arcaro Conci affirmed that, historically, there was a highly centralised federalism, based on systems of hyper-presidentialism, as in the cases of Argentina and Mexico. The transition from the monarchy to a republican and federal regime only took place in 1889, being specified in the Constitution of 1891. But the routed to decentralisation was very complex, held up by the Presidencies of Getulio Vargas and the military governments during the twentieth century. This trend has continued to the present day.[41]

The current constitutional text is from 1988, and established a coordination federalism, with concurrent powers in health matters, according to Article 23, for the different governmental orders: federal, states, federal district and municipalities.

The author maintained that, despite this, there were centralised decisions in the federal government during the pandemic, albeit with decentralised execution.[42] It was also notable that, as per data from 2013, 58 per cent of the national income corresponded to the federal government, 22 per cent to the states and 20 per cent to the municipalities, as a sign of the existing centralisation. The actions of the national political parties also contribute to this.[43]

During the pandemic, by a Resolution of the Ministry of Public Health of 3 February 2020, a Public Health Emergency of National Importance was declared. By Law No 13,979 of 6 February, measures were taken to face the pandemic.

In comparison with Argentina, the Brazilian Congress had much greater legislative activity during the pandemic, beyond the permanent conflicts with

[38] This judgment was issued on 25 February 2021. It should be taken into account that the Court, in addition to requesting reports, urged the province to respect constitutional and conventional standards regarding the restriction of rights during the pandemic and according to the Resolution 1/2020 of the Inter-American Court of Human Rights.

[39] The Supreme Court, in a Resolution of 10 September 2020, required reports from the Province of Corrientes, but also permitted to the plaintiff to enter into the province, in order to allow him to attend to his mother, who was sick with cancer.

[40] See M Figueiredo, 'A reeleicao do titular do Poder Ejecutivo nas Americas – La situacao do Brasil' in M Figueiredo (ed), *Novos rumos para o Direito Publico* (Belo Horizonte, Editora Forum, 2012) 290.

[41] See LGA Conci, 'La federación brasileña en movimiento: oportunismo y descentralización frente a la pandemia' in E Nader and M-C Fuchs (eds), *COVID 19 y Estados en acción: un estudio constitucional comparado entre países federales y no federales* (Colombia, Tirant lo Blanch, IIDP y Konrad Adenauer Stiftung, 2021) 144ff.

[42] *Cf* Conci ibid 153.

[43] ibid 155.

the Executive Branch. Conci claimed that, historically, President Bolsonaro had the fewest number of Provisional Measures turned into laws. The lack of coordination between the different governmental orders was a constant, beyond the provisions of the Constitution. The author also highlighted in particular the role played by the Judiciary and especially by the Federal Supreme Court, which will be analysed later.[44]

In relation to presidentialism in Mexico, Diego Valadés referred to the model adopted from the Philadelphia Constitution of 1787, which had the objective of overcoming the problems of the confederate government and avoiding atomisation, and producing other results in his country: the concentration of power in the President, through the subordination of the state governments. He maintained that 'a kind of presidential absolutism was created from the very moment at which the constitutional republic was founded'.[45] The Mexican jurist then explained the expansion of presidentialism through the Institutional Revolutionary Party, with the 'meta-constitutional' powers, which consisted of the leadership of the hegemonic party and the election of the successor, in addition to the rest of the competencies.[46]

The author mentioned that former President Adolfo Ruiz Cortines is attributed with having said that 'the governors and senators belong to the President; the federal deputies are from the sectors; the local deputies belong to the governors and the municipal presidents belong to the people'.[47] Then Valadés said that 'the meta-constitutional' powers that run parallel to the norm became 'para-constitutional' because they operated against the Constitution, perverting the elections and multiplying corruption. Consequently, there is no doubt that the transition to hyper-presidentialism had taken place.

Although some institutional reforms were attempted through the creation of autonomous institutes, between 1977 and 2012, with the electoral ones particularly noteworthy, leading to a greater balance of powers,[48] during the Presidencies of Peña Nieto and later with López Obrador, the pathology of hyper-presidentialism had deepened.

Valadés noted another characteristic of Mexican hyper-presidentialism:

> 'verticalism', which referred to a government in which some elements of authoritarianism, such as the concentration of presidential power and the political irresponsibility of those who help him in the task of government, coexisted with some democratic

[44] ibid 161.

[45] D Valadés, *Constitucionalismo crítico-Ideas para la transición constitucional en la era post COVID-19* (Mexico, Siglo Veintiuno Editores, 2021) 61. This was established by the Constitution of 1824 and ratified by those of 1857 and 1917.

[46] Valades ibid 63 and ff. The term 'meta-constitutional' was coined by J Carpizo in his book *Presidencialismo mexicano* (Mexico, Siglo Veintiuno Editores, 1978).

[47] Valadés (n 45) 65–6.

[48] See P Salazar, *El Poder Ejecutivo en la Constitución mexicana. Del metaconstitucionalismo a la constelación de autonomías* (Mexico, Fondo de Cultura Económica, 2017).

elements, such as free elections and open pluralism. Although the manifestations of this type of regime had been registered for decades in the Mexican political system, due to the 2020 health crisis they were revealed through multiple decisions.[49]

Valadés maintained that 'the health emergency measures imposed limitations on the freedom of movement, work and commerce, without the constitutional provisions provided for this type of case having been applied', that is, the state of exception provided for in Article 29 of the Constitution. This regime implies the convening of Congress, with guarantees of fundamental rights, but instead they opted for unilateral administrative decisions by the President.[50] He described this as a progressive deconstitutionalisation, since the Constitution was violated to impose the hegemony of the Executive in handling the pandemic. Even the constitutional text on health was modified, dated 8 May 2020, by including three paragraphs that the author qualified as confusing and that increased the benefits that the state cannot fulfil, to the detriment of the Constitution.[51]

Following the same line of thought, José María Serna de la Garza explained that, although the Constitution of Mexico and the General Health Law provided for the action of a General Health Council, the measures of the federal government were centralised in the Ministry of Health, dependent on the President. He also stressed that there is a concurrence of powers in this matter among the various levels of government.[52] In another article, the author highlighted that, by Article 4 of the Constitution of Mexico, subnational governments are empowered to guarantee the right to health and, in this regard, he cited a decision of the Supreme Court of Justice in a case of the State of Baja, California.[53]

Carla Huerta Ochoa pointed out the powers that the Constitution allocates to the states that make up the Federation of Mexico in Article 124, to Mexico City in Article 122 and to the municipalities in Article 115, and that, together with the powers of the federal government, make up a coordination federalism. Consequently, general health must be dealt with by the federal government, with the concurrence of the states, while the execution is especially down to the subnational governments.[54]

[49] *Cf* Valadés (n 45) 92–3.

[50] ibid 95.

[51] ibid. 94–8.

[52] See JM Serna de la Garza, 'COVID-19 y Constitución en los Estados Unidos Mexicanos' in NG Martin and D Valadés (eds), *Emergencia sanitaria por COVID-19: Derecho Constitucional Comparado* (Mexico, Instituto de Investigaciones Jurídicas de la UNAM, 2020) 139ff.

[53] *Cf* JM Serna de la Garza, 'Facultades de las entidades federativas para dictar medidas de seguridad sanitaria ante epidemias como el COVID-19' in NG Martin (ed), *Emergencia sanitaria por COVID19-Federalismo* (Mexico, Instituto de Investigaciones Jurídicas de la UNAM, 2020). Sentence was passed in the case before the Supreme Court of Justice in 1972 ('Amparo en revisión 5465/71. Rubén Núñez de la Paz').

[54] *Cf* CH Ochoa, 'Emergencia sanitaria y la distribución de competencias en el Estado Federal Mexicano' in NG Martin (ed), *Emergencia sanitaria por COVID-19-Federalismo* (Mexico, Instituto de Investigaciones Jurídicas de la UNAM, 2020).

Daniel Barceló Rojas drew attention to another very significant factor to explain the extension of the President's powers: budgetary management, which implies that he can order the modification of the items approved by Congress. The same thing happened with the governors in their states. He also considered that, during the pandemic, there were no adequate controls by the legislative bodies, and the Senate in particular, which led to a deepening of hyper-presidentialism.[55] Likewise, in another article, he analysed the measures adopted by the different state governments, in particular those of Nueva León and Mexico City, since President López Obrador did not assume a responsible attitude in the face of the pandemic.[56]

Finally, Francisco Tortolero Cervantes carried out a brief comparative analysis of different countries, emphasising the important role that subnational governments played in this emergency.[57]

IV. Intergovernmental Conflicts and Judicial Review

In Argentina, the conflicts between the federal state and the CABA should be highlighted, for the exercise of concurrent matters on health and education and for tax co-participation and the transfer of security functions.

On 16 April 2021, the Government of the CABA presented before the Supreme Court of Justice of the Nation a Declarative Action of Unconstitutionality against the federal state, requesting the declaration of unconstitutionality of Article 2 of said DNU of the Executive Power, which had ordered the suspension of face-to-face classes in the Buenos Aires Metropolitan Area[58] between 19 and 30 April 2021.

The CABA pointed out the violation of Articles 5 and 129 of the Supreme Law of the Nation, which guarantee the autonomy of the provinces and of the CABA in their educational function. Likewise, it maintained the unconstitutionality of the DNU cited due to ignorance of Article 99 inc. 3. It defended the importance of

[55] *Cf* DB Rojas, 'Controles constitucionales sobre los Gobiernos Federal y de los Estados en emergencias sanitarias' in NG Martin (ed), *Emergencia sanitaria por COVID19-Federalismo* (Mexico, Instituto de Investigaciones Jurídicas de la UNAM, 2020) 52ff.

[56] *Cf* B Rojas, 'Retos del federalismo ante la pandemia. La experiencia de Mexico' in E Nader and M-C Fuchs (eds), *COVID-19 y Estados en acción: un estudio constitucional comparado entre países federales y no federales* (Colombia, Tirant lo Blanch, IIDP and Konrad Adenauer Stiftung, 2021) 406ff.

[57] *Cf* FT Cervantes, 'La pandemia como oportunidad para relanzar el rol de las entidades subnacionales latinoamericanas' in NG Martin (coord) *Emergencia sanitaria por COVID-19-Federalismo* (Mexico, Instituto de Investigaciones Jurídicas de la UNAM, 2020) 63ff.

[58] Previously, by DNU 125/2021 said Metropolitan Area had been created. The Supreme Court, when referring to it in this ruling, emphasises that for said creation, as for that of the regions of Art 124 of the Constitution, the will of the respective government entities is always necessary. Yet here this was not the case. It was a decision made solely by the federal government and by Decree.

education recognised in the constitutional texts and in the International Treaties of Human Rights and the competence of the CABA in this matter.

In a historic ruling of special relevance for Argentine federalism,[59] the Supreme Court on 4 May 2021 resolved 'that in the specific case the autonomy of the Autonomous City of Buenos Aires was violated'.

It is argued that it is a constitutionally federated city and that it is no longer a federalised territory as it was before the Constitutional Reform, in Recitals 9 and 10 of the Majority Vote. In Recital 10 of the Majority Vote, Maqueda and Rosatti, who were Members of the Constituent Convention of 1994, explained that Buenos Aires being the capital is the exception, since now the CABA is a full member of the Federation whether or not it continues to be the seat of the federal authorities.

Likewise, it is clearly reaffirmed that, as a result of said Constitutional Reform, there are now four governmental orders, with their respective powers: federal, provinces, the CABA and municipalities.[60]

The judgment insisted on the concurrent nature of the powers in these matters and on the need to affirm a concerted federalism, emphasising the role of the Federal Council of Education, which had recognised the powers of local governments, to resolve on face-to-face attendance or not in schools.

This ruling consolidated a change in jurisprudence tending to comply with a modern concerted federalism, within the framework of a profound decentralisation of power, which was one of the main ideas of the 1994 Constitutional Reform.[61]

Regarding the second conflict, on 21 December 2022, the Supreme Court of Justice issued a unanimous ruling by its members, in '*Gobierno de la Ciudad de Buenos Aires c. Estado Nacional – Acción Declarativa de Inconstitucionalidad*' ('*Government of the City of Buenos Aires v National State-Declarative Action of Unconstitutionality*'), giving rise to a precautionary measure requested by the City against the national state, in the conflict caused by the reduction of the tax co-participation. The High Court ordered that, during the processing of the case, the federal government should deliver to the Autonomous City 2.95 per cent of the

[59] See my comments in 'Trascendente fallo sobre la Ciudad Autónoma de Buenos Aires y otras cuestiones federales', *Revista de Derecho Administrativo*, Abeledo Perrot, Buenos Aires, July–August, 2021, No 136, 207ff.

[60] As I wrote in my books on the constitutional reform of 1994: *Federalismo,autonomía municipal y Ciudad de Buenos Aires en la reforma constitucional de 1994* (Buenos Aires, Depalma, 1997); *Federalismo y Constitucionalismo Provincial* (Buenos Aires, Abeledo Perrot, 2009); *La Ciudad Autónoma de Buenos Aires y el fortalecimiento del federalismo argentino* (Buenos Aires, Iusbaires, 2017); *A veinticinco años de la reforma constitucional de 1994* (National University of Cordoba Press, 2019) and *Derecho Público Provincial*, chs 3 and 4 on *Federalismo Argentino* (Buenos Aires, Abeledo Perrot 2020) ibid.

[61] For an analysis of the affirmation of this jurisprudence in defence of the decentralisation of power, see AM Hernández, *A veinticinco años de la reforma constitucional de 1994* (National University of Cordoba Press, 2019) and AM Hernández and G Krivocapich, *La autonomía municipal en su aspecto tributario* (Buenos Aires, La Ley, 2021).

co-participating amount of Article 2 of Law No 23,548, daily and automatically by Banco Nación and that it refrain from applying Law No 27,606.

The serious conflict originated from the DNU 735/2020 of the federal government that ordered a reduction of 1.18 per cent to the 3.50 per cent that the Autonomous City had. It should also be noted that the amount deducted from the CABA was destined directly for the province of Buenos Aires, which undoubtedly demonstrated the arbitrariness and political intent of the President.[62]

For this reason, the City sued the national state, maintaining the unconstitutionality of said DNU, which also affected financial autonomy and violated the federal principles of co-participation. Subsequently, Law No 27,606 of 2020, finally provided that the co-participation of the CABA returned to 1.40 per cent, as set in the Duhalde Presidency. The amount corresponding to said security transfer will be set each year in the budget. As a consequence, the CABA presented this Unconstitutionality Action before the Supreme Court, in which the precautionary measure was issued, which means that the merits of this action and the one linked to DNU 735 must still be ruled on.

In Recital 5 of the judgment, one of special importance, a historical analysis of the co-participation and the modifications operated by the Constitutional Reform of 1994, which changed the status of the City, with the recognition of full autonomy, is carried out. It is argued that, due to the lack of sanction of the Tax Co-participation Agreement Law, the financial aspects of said autonomy could not be specified. Consequently, by continuing to govern Law No 23,548 of 1988, the Court pointed out that the co-participation of the City continues to correspond to the primary distribution of the federal government, and therefore the co-participation of the provinces is not affected. It is specified with great clarity that Article 75 inc. 2, which establishes the constitutional bases of the tax co-participation, as well as what is linked to the transfer of powers, services or functions, is based on the concurrence of wills of the different governmental orders.

In Recital 8, Article 75 inc. 2 on co-participation is analysed and it is highlighted that neither DNU 735 nor Law No 27,606 had the approval of the CABA, and that there was also no agreement regarding the transfer provided for by Law No 27,606, as required by Law No 24,588.

Consequently, having verified the abrupt decrease in the City's resources, the plausibility of the right invoked and the danger in the delay, the precautionary measure is granted, and with equitable criteria the co-participation is set at 2.95 per cent and not at the 3.50 per cent that was claimed.

It is a ruling of enormous importance, since it consolidates a jurisprudence in defence of autonomies, in this case of the CABA, unquestionably enshrined in Article 129, which is decisive for the decentralisation of power.

[62] See AM Hernandez, 'Del unitarismo fiscal al falso federalismo' *La Nación Newspaper*, Buenos Aires, 24 December 2022.

Likewise, the importance of concerted federalism is highlighted, as ordered by the Supreme Law in Article 75 inc. 2, because the agreement of the different governmental orders is essential, in tax co-participation.

Regarding this, it is unfortunate that the debate on the tax sharing agreement law, which had to be sanctioned on 31 December 1996, has not begun, as the Court also recalls in its ruling, an expression of our weak constitutional culture.

I especially emphasise that nowadays the Highest Court is fulfilling its essential role of defending the national Constitution by limiting the hyper-presidentialism exercised through DNU 735.

There was also a conflict between federal judges of different provinces due to the road blockades ordered by the Governor of the Province of San Luis, in the case '*Sociedad Rural de Río Cuarto y otros c. Provincia de San Luis-Poder Ejecutivo-Amparo*', which concluded after the request for reports made by the Supreme Court of Justice to the province.[63]

The interjurisdictional conflict was raised between the federal courts of Río Cuarto and San Luis, since, in view of the precautionary measure of the former that ordered the termination of the blockade ordered by the Province of San Luis of National Route 8 and other routes that unite the Río Cuarto Department of the Province of Córdoba with the Province of San Luis, the federal judge of San Luis upheld a precautionary measure to the contrary requested by said provincial government.[64]

It was an *Amparo* (judicial protection of fundamental rights) presented before the federal judge of Río Cuarto on behalf of four entities that represent thousands of citizens of the South of the Province of Córdoba, given the extreme seriousness of the rights violated by the complete closure of said routes provided by the provincial government of San Luis.[65]

Given the conflict of competence raised, the judicial files went to the Supreme Court of Justice of the Nation. It does seem incredible that this happened, because the Province of San Luis prevented interprovincial traffic on a National Route like number 8 for months, in violation of Articles 9 to 12 of the national Constitution and elementary principles of Argentine federalism, with major effects on fundamental rights. And this situation only ceased when the aforementioned report was requested by the Supreme Court.

In the same way as the Supreme Court in Argentina, the Supreme Federal Court of Brazil has stood out for its rulings, since it modified the previous centralist jurisprudence that benefited the federal government.

[63] By Resolution of 10 September 2020, which requested reports within 3 days on the reasons for preventing transit. In said case, I acted as lawyer for the plaintiff.

[64] See Hernández (n 19) 167ff.

[65] In the judicial file there are photographs of the complete closure of said routes, and in the case of the local roads, of the embankments built almost 4 meters high and with trenches that reach 20km, to prevent any access to the province. Unfortunately, it was not the only province to carry out these unconstitutional measures.

In this emergency due to COVID-19, in 33 collegiate judgments on conflicts between the federal government and the states, a recognition of the competences of the states and municipalities in health matters has been observed, as maintained by Bessa Fernandes and Mafort Ouverney[66]

The researchers have analysed these 33 collegiate rulings, constituting nine on issues of health policy and services, nine on territorial regulation and management, nine on employment and income, three on public finances and three on other issues, and of which 32 were issued between March and May 2020.

The Federal Supreme Court declared the unconstitutionality of the Provisional Measures issued by the federal government in different actions of unconstitutionality or unconstitutionality by omission, presented by opposition political parties.[67]

Luis Guilherme Arcano Conci maintained that the most important ruling was in the Direct Action of Unconstitutionality 6341, regarding the concurrent nature of health powers between government orders, which consolidated a federalist jurisprudence in favour of the powers of states and municipalities.[68]

V. Brief Conclusions

In the first place, it is evident that hyper-presidentialism is a serious pathology that affects Argentina, Brazil and Mexico, among other countries in the region.[69]

This leads to an inadequate functioning of the republican and federal system, in violation of the respective Supreme Laws.

Hyper-presidentialism is also a cause of the highly centralised character of Latin American federalisms. This is the case in Venezuela, Argentina, Brazil and Mexico, although these last three countries cannot be compared with the first, where it is already very difficult to classify said country as federal.[70]

The cases of the Presidents Fernandez, Bolsonaro and Lopez Obrador were clear examples of hyper-presidentialism during the pandemic, with the issuance of Decrees, without adequate controls by the Legislative Power.

The control of constitutionality carried out by the Supreme Court of Justice of the Nation of Argentina and the Federal Supreme Court of Brazil should be

[66] See FMB Fernandes and ALM Ouverney, 'Decisoes do Supremo Tribunal Federal no inicia de la pandemia de COVID 19: impactos no federalismo brasileiro?'(2022) 46(1) *Saude Debate*, Rio de Janeiro, 48–61.

[67] See VElias de Oliveira and LM Madeira 'Judicializasao de la política no enfrentamento COVID 19: un novo padrao decisorio do STF?' (Judicialization of politics in the fight against COVID-19: a new STF decision-making pattern?) (2021) 35 *Revista Brasileira de Ciencia Politica* 1–44, with the same conclusions as the previous article.

[68] See Conci (n 41) 162.

[69] See AM Hernández, *Studies in Comparative Federalism: Argentina, The United States and Mexico* (Universidad Nacional de Córdoba, 2019) and *Estudios de Federalismo Comparado: Argentina, Estados Unidos y Mexico* (Mexico, UNAM, 2019).

[70] See Hernández ibid.

highlighted, because in specific cases it defended the provincial and state autonomies, in the face of the presidential measures. The situation was different in Mexico, where the intervention of the Judiciary was through federal judges, but not by the Supreme Court.

A greater decentralisation of power has also been observed in Brazil and Mexico, since, given the attitude of Presidents Bolsonaro and López Obrador, the state governors had to take charge of concrete measures to face the COVID-19 pandemic.

11

Environmental Democracy under Quarantine? Access to Information and Public Participation During the COVID-19 Pandemic

MARÍA FLORENCIA SAULINO*

I. Introduction

The aim of environmental law is not to eliminate all risk, but to decide what level of risk is acceptable. Environmental decision-making is therefore a complex process.[1] Economic, social, political, aesthetic, spiritual and environmental interests frequently conflict with each other. What priority is given to each of them and how they ought to be balanced depends on value judgments that differ from person to person. These conflicts arise not only between environmental advocates and those who have economic motivations, but also between environmental groups themselves.[2] On top of conflicting interests, decision-makers must also deal with scientific uncertainty, technical judgments, and an expanded range of affected parties, which may include not only people living outside the community but also future generations, animals, and nature as a whole.[3]

Since the environment is a public good, shared by all the members of the community, it is only logical that all of them should have a seat at the table when these complex decisions are being made. Environmental democracy is therefore rooted in the idea that people must be involved in those decisions that affect their

* I am grateful for the suggestions and comments of Eduardo Bertoni, Florencia Lacapmesure, and Inés Rivera, and for the excellent research assistance of Patricio Kenny.

[1] E Barritt, *The Foundations of the Aarhus Convention: Environmental Democracy, Rights and Stewardship* (Oxford, Bloomsbury Publishing, 2020) 50.

[2] ibid 52. Take for example the case of the construction of a wind farm that leads to a choice between sustainable energy and landscape preservation. It is easy to see how different environmental groups may advocate for either sustainable energy or the protection of the rural landscape.

[3] Barritt (n 1) 52–53. See also MV Berros and MC Carman, 'Los dos caminos del reconocimiento de los derechos de la naturaleza en América Latina' (2022) 13 *Revista Catalana de Dret Ambiental* 1.

environment.[4] Although there is no single definition of 'environmental democracy', it is generally agreed that the core concept is the idea that environmental decision-making needs to be participatory, open, and inclusive.[5] In the last decades, procedural environmental rights have emerged as a cornerstone of environmental democracy, protecting public participation, access to information, and access to justice in environmental matters.[6]

Indeed, the right to public participation privileges collective decision-making over decisions based solely on administrative, professional, or scientific expertise, by allowing broad access to the decision-making process.[7] From a practical point of view, public participation facilitates trust, legitimacy and mutual learning, by incorporating people's points of views and values into the decision.[8] It also contributes to a better substantive decision, by providing decision-makers with relevant and accurate information, engaging participants in the assessment and monitoring alternatives.[9]

The right to access to environmental information complements and reinforces public participation by ensuring that members of the public understand what is happening around them and participate in an informed manner.[10] Well-informed stakeholders are in a better position to allay concerns, mitigate impacts and make decisions regarding their environment.[11] Moreover, access to information also enhances the capacity of citizens to check for compliance with environmental laws and regulation, and uncover abuses by public or private actors.[12]

[4] G Parola, *Environmental Democracy at the Global Level: Rights and Duties for a New Citizenship* (London, Versita, 2013).

[5] Economic Commission for Latin America and the Caribbean (ECLAC), 'Access to Information, Participation, and Justice in Environmental Matters in Latin America and the Caribbean: Towards Achievement of the 2030 Agenda for Sustainable Development' (LC/TS.2017/83, Santiago, 2018) repositorio.cepal.org/handle/11362/43302?locale-attribute=en 14.

[6] G Bándi, 'Introduction into the Concept of 'Environmental Democracy'' in G Bándi (ed), *Environmental Democracy and Law: Public Participation in Europe* (Groningen, Europa Law Publishing, 2014) 3, Barritt (n 1) 63, and F Fischer, 'Environmental Democracy: Participation, Deliberation and Citizenship' in M Boström and DJ Davidson (eds), *Environment and Society. Concepts and Challenges* (Cham, Palgrave MacMillan, 2018) 257. However, as Bell points out their aim is not to replace but to supplement representative democracy: it 'is not the traditional 'green' vision of autonomous local communities making collective decisions in a non-discriminatory version of the Athenian assembly'. See DR Bell, 'Sustainability Through Democratization?' in J Barry, B Baxter, and R Dunphy (eds), *Europe, Globalization and Sustainable Development* (London, Routledge, 2004) 97–98.

[7] Barritt (n 1) 146 and JC Gellers and C Jeffords, 'Procedural Environmental Rights and Environmental Justice: Assessing the Impact of Environmental Constitutionalism' (2018) 18 *Global Environmental Politics* 99, 102.

[8] MB Mihaly, 'Citizen Participation in the Making of Environmental Decisions: Evolving Obstacles and Potential Solutions Through Partnership with Experts and Agents' (2009) 27 *Pace Environmental Law Review* 151, 164–65.

[9] Bándi (n 6) 18–20 and LH Berry et al, *Making Space: How Public Participation Shapes Environmental Decision-Making* (Stockholm Environment Institute, 2019) www.sei.org/wp-content/uploads/2019/01/making-space-how-public-participation-shapes-environmental-decision-making.pdf 2.

[10] S Stec and S Casey-Lefkowitz, *The Aarhus Convention: An Implementation Guide* (Economic Commission for Europe, 2000) www.unece.org/fileadmin/DAM/env/pp/acig.pdf 49.

[11] JR May, 'Constitutional Directions in Procedural Environmental Rights' (2013) 28 *Journal of Environmental Law and Litigation* 27, 31.

[12] Gellers and Jeffords (n 7) 103.

Finally, the right to access to justice protects environmental rights in the face of recalcitrant or improvident governments, by guaranteeing access to courts or administrative procedures.[13] Indeed, given that the environment is a public good, regular standing provisions make it difficult for communities to act in its defence. By relaxing standing requirements, access to environmental justice allows a broad range of citizens and organisations to take action to ensure that governments comply with their obligations. Assistance mechanisms to remove or reduce financial and other barriers also contribute to ensure access to justice in environmental matters.[14]

The 1992 Earth Summit recognised the importance of procedural environmental rights in principle 10 of the Rio Declaration, which provides that

> [e]nvironmental issues are best handled with the participation of all concerned citizens, at the relevant level. At the national level, each individual shall have appropriate access to information concerning the environment that is held by public authorities … and the opportunity to participate in decision-making processes.[15]

The Summit gave strong impetus to environmental protection in Latin America, fostering the creation of environmental legislation and institutions.[16] Since then, countries in the region have made substantial progress in the implementation of environmental democracy, expanding the demand for access to information and participation, and publicising access rights among the population.[17] However, much remains to be done. Many countries have yet to develop their domestic legal frameworks and address the barriers to the implementation of procedural environmental rights.[18] Moreover, as a recent report by the Economic Commission for Latin America and the Caribbean (ECLAC) highlights, people living in poverty and indigenous and Afro-descendant peoples still face significant barriers to the full enjoyment of procedural environmental rights.[19]

Significant progress was made in 2018, when countries in the region were invited to sign the Escazu Agreement on Access to Information, Public Participation, and Justice in Environmental Matters (Escazu Agreement). This landmark treaty was the first regional agreement on the environment and aims to guarantee human

[13] JR May and E Daly, *Global Environmental Constitutionalism* (New York, Cambridge University Press, 2014) 237.

[14] ECLAC (n 5) 124.

[15] General Assembly of the United Nations (UN), 'Report of the United Nations Conference on Environmental and Development (Río de Janeiro, 3–14 June 1992) Annex I Rio Declaration on Environment and Development' (A/CONF.151/26 (Vol I), 12 August 1992) www.un.org/en/development/desa/population/migration/generalassembly/docs/globalcompact/A_CONF.151_26_Vol.I_Declaration.pdf. See also principles 20 and 22 of the Rio Declaration.

[16] ECLAC (n 5) 33.

[17] ibid 38. However, despite the significant advances registered in the last 20 years, many countries of the region have not fully implemented this principle in their legal frameworks or encounter difficulties in its implementation.

[18] ECLAC (n 5) 103.

[19] ibid 99–103.

rights through the effective implementation of environmental democracy. Indeed, it fosters the generation of information, facilitates access to this information, and encourages the participation of all stakeholders in the decision-making process, with a special focus on local and indigenous communities.[20] The Escazu agreement is particularly keen on including those that have traditionally been underrepresented, excluded or marginalised[21] and it is also a pioneering instrument in establishing procedural safeguards to protect environmental activists from threat, restriction and insecurity.[22]

Although the Escazú Agreement represented a major step forward for environmental democracy in the region, two years later, even before the treaty could enter into force, the COVID-19 pandemic would put environmental democracy at great risk. Indeed, while extractive industries and infrastructure projects were allowed to continue during the health emergency, quarantines, lockdowns, travel restrictions and social distancing, together with the disruption of judicial and administrative proceedings, have delayed, hindered, and even prevented the normal exercise of procedural rights, with a consequential impact on the environment. In some cases, COVID-19 has been used as a pretext to weaken environmental protection by lowering environmental standards, suspending public hearings and monitoring requirements, and restricting public participation.[23]

Nevertheless, some states and local jurisdictions have been able to adapt to the challenges posed by the pandemic and have been able to continue to ensure the effectiveness of these rights, even in the context of this unprecedented public health emergency. This chapter discusses the impact of COVID-19 on environmental democracy and the solutions adopted by some Latin American countries. Section II summarises the impact of the COVID-19 pandemic on environmental democracy in the region. Sections III and IV highlight the difficulties and opportunities that this emergency has created for environmental democracy in the region, by focusing on access to information and public participation in the decision-making process. Both sections also highlight the role of access to justice in guaranteeing these rights. Section V discusses the situation of indigenous peoples and their right to be consulted. Finally, section VI concludes by drawing lessons from these experiences.

[20] S López-Cubillos et al, 'The Landmark Escazú Agreement: An Opportunity to Integrate Democracy, Human Rights, and Transboundary Conservation' (2022) 15 *Conservation Letters* 1, 2.

[21] Economic Commission for Latin America and the Caribbean (ECLAC), 'Regional Agreement on Access to Information, Public Participation and Justice in Environmental Matters in Latin America and the Caribbean (Escazú Agreement)' (Escazú, 4 March 2018) repositorio.cepal.org/bitstream/handle/11362/43583/1/S1800428_en.pdf 8. According to Art 4 of the Escazú Agreement, the parties are obligated to ensure that guidance and assistance is provided to the public, and particularly to those in vulnerable situations, in order to facilitate the exercise of their access rights.

[22] Art 9 of the Escazú Agreement.

[23] United Nations Human Rights Office of the High Commissioner, 'COVID-19: 'Not an excuse' to roll back environmental protection and enforcement, UN rights expert says' (15 April 2020) www.ohchr.org/en/press-releases/2020/04/covid-19-not-excuse-roll-back-environmental-protection-and-enforcement-un?LangID=E&NewsID=25794.

II. The Impact of the COVID-19 Pandemic on Environmental Democracy

Before the COVID-19 pandemic started, governments in the region relied heavily on face-to-face procedures and in-person gatherings to implement procedural environmental rights. With a few exceptions, people had to go to the administrative offices in person to access information; public participation was implemented through public hearings that were conducted at a physical location; and lawyers were required to appear in person before the courts to protect environmental rights.[24] By reducing people's mobility, government interventions to deal with COVID-19 severely affected the normal functioning of these procedures.[25] Offices of the national and local governments that did not provide COVID-related services were closed or operated with significant constraints. Many countries suspended all public gatherings and hearings. Court systems across the region either suspended their activities due to COVID-19 or lifted deadlines, implemented telework, limited work shifts, and established online hearings.

However, in countries like Argentina, Brazil, Chile, Colombia, Ecuador, Mexico and Panama, extractive industries and infrastructure projects were deemed essential activities and allowed to continue operating in spite of general restrictions.[26] This created a challenging situation for environmental democracy in the region, since sanitary measures affected public participation and the social control of these industries by prohibiting or limiting the movement of people and their participation in the hearings prior to the approval of new projects.[27] At the same time, public offices in charge of access to information were closed or reduced their operations, hindering the access to information that was essential for monitoring extractive industries and participating in decisions concerning new projects.[28]

[24] Inter-American Development Bank (IADB), 'Digitalización de los trámites reduciría la corrupción y los costos de la burocracia en América Latina y el Caribe' (11 June 2018) www.iadb.org/es/noticias/digitalizacion-de-los-tramites-reduciria-la-corrupcion-y-los-costos-de-la-burocracia-en.

[25] S Srinivasan et al., *Internet Access and Use in Latin America and the Caribbean. From the LAC High Frequency Phone Surveys 2021* (World Bank, September 2022) www.undp.org/sites/g/files/zskgke326/files/2022-09/undp-rblac-Digital-EN.pdf 2.

[26] *Bnamericas*, 'Mining in Latin America: An Essential Activity' (8 April 2020) www.bnamericas.com/en/features/mining-in-latin-america-an-essential-activity and ML Ossa Daza et al., *LATAM COVID-19 Task Force – Actions Affecting Energy and Infrastructure Projects in Latin America* (Willkie Farr & Gallagher LLP, 25 June 2020) www.willkie.com/-/media/files/publications/2020/06/update-3actionsaffectingenergyandinfrastructureproj.pdf. See also Radio Temblor, 'Panamá. Auxilio para los bosques de Darién' (9 June 2020) www.radiotemblor.org/panama-auxilio-para-los-bosques-de-darien/). See also G Rodríguez et al., *Situación de la defensa de derechos humanos y la libertad de expresión en México a partir de la pandemia por COVID-19* (Centro por la Justicia y el Derecho Internacional (CEJIL) 2020) www.cejil.org/wp-content/uploads/2021/05/Situacion-de-la-defensa-de-DDHH-y-LEX-en-MEX_Digital_ES.pdf 19).

[27] L Gómez and V Corral, 'Minería en pandemia: Avances sin restricciones, derechos restringidos' (Fundación Ambiente y Recursos Naturales 2022) www.farn.org.ar/wp-content/uploads/2022/06/DOC_MINERIA-BOELL_links-1.pdf.

[28] Organization of American States (OAS), 'IACHR and its SR FOE Express Concern about Restrictions on Freedom of Expression and Access to Information in States' response to the COVID-19 pandemic' (18 April 2020) www.oas.org/en/iachr/expression/showarticle.asp?artID=1173&lID=1.

As the pandemic progressed and endured, governments had to find new ways and modalities to work and, in the process, modernise environmental governance by channelling public participation, access to information and access to justice through digital technologies and social media. For some, the pandemic worked as a catalyst for further democratisation of environmental decision-making through improved use of the digital space and inclusive consultative processes.[29] In some countries, people were able to request access to information through online platforms, participate in public hearings through video calls and file their claims in court without leaving their houses. These digital tools proved so useful that some jurisdictions have continued to use them today.

However, these tools were not available for all. Although the Escazu Agreement clearly states that '[i]n no circumstances shall the use of electronic media constrain or result in discrimination against the public',[30] during the COVID-19 pandemic, the digital divide in the region hindered the exercise of procedural rights by indigenous and rural communities and those with limited economic resources.[31] When the COVID-19 pandemic started, only 60 per cent of the population in Latin America and the Caribbean used the Internet.[32] Mobile broadband was the primary means of internet access in the region,[33] while there were broad disparities in access to fixed internet connections, which were necessary to facilitate high-capacity data transactions such as video-calls.

Figure 1 Percentage of rural households with Internet connection in 2019. Elaborated on the basis of information from the Household Survey Data Bank (BADEHOG)

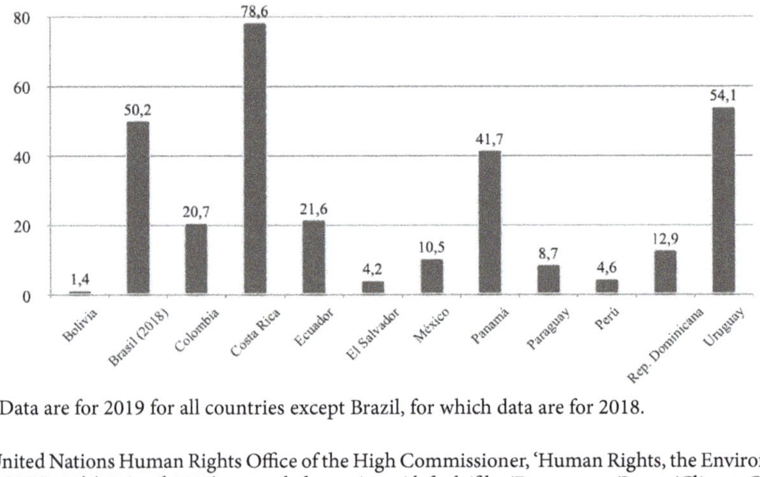

Note: Data are for 2019 for all countries except Brazil, for which data are for 2018.

[29] United Nations Human Rights Office of the High Commissioner, 'Human Rights, the Environment, and COVID-19' (15 April 2020) www.ohchr.org/sites/default/files/Documents/Issues/ClimateChange/HR-environment-COVID19.pdf.

[30] Art 4(9) of the Escazú Agreement. The Escazú Agreement entered into force during the second year of the COVID-19 pandemic.

[31] The Organization of American States highlighted the impacts of the internet access gap in the adequate guarantee of human rights during the pandemic. See Organization of American States (OAS), 'How to Promote Universal Internet Access during the COVID-19 Pandemic' www.oas.org/es/cidh/sacroi_covid19/documentos/03_guias_practicas_internet_ing.pdf.

[32] Srinivasan et al (n 25) 2.

[33] ibid 3.

Only 23 per cent of rural households had access to fixed Internet, compared to 67 per cent of the region's urban households.[34] In countries such as El Salvador, Paraguay, Peru, and Bolivia, more than 90 per cent of rural households did not have an internet connection.[35] But even in Chile, Costa Rica and Uruguay, only half of rural households were connected.[36] Low income was also a major limiting factor with regard to internet access. On average, 38 per cent of households in the lowest income quintile had an internet connection, while in Paraguay, Peru and Bolivia, only three per cent did.[37] Fifty per cent of those not connected at all to the Internet pointed to the high cost of data as the main obstacle to access.[38] Once online, internet users in the region faced low-quality connections, high service fees and frequent power outages.[39]

Figure 2 Households with an Internet connection, by income quintile, 2019 on the basis of information from the Household Survey Data Bank (BADEHOG)

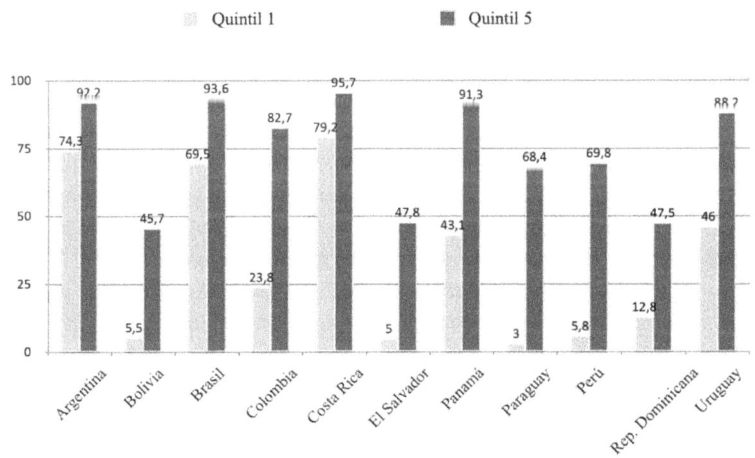

In this context, the Inter-American Commission on Human Rights (IACHR) and its Office of the Special Rapporteur for Freedom of Expression expressed their concern about the serious limitations posed by the lack of internet access on the exercise of other fundamental rights, especially by the most vulnerable sectors of the populations.[40] The IACHR Resolution 1/2020 recommended that governments

[34] Economic Commission for Latin America and the Caribbean (ECLAC), 'Universalizing Access to Digital Technologies to Address the Consequences of COVID-19' (26 August 2020) repositorio.cepal.org/bitstream/handle/11362/45939/S2000549_en.pdf?sequence=5&isAllowed=y 3.

[35] ibid 3.

[36] ibid 3.

[37] ibid 2.

[38] Srinivasan et al., (n 25) 7.

[39] ibid 8.

[40] Organization of American States (OAS), 'States of the Region must Accelerate Universal Internet Access Policies during the COVID-19 Pandemic and Adopt Differentiated Measures to Incorporate

should ensure that everyone has the broadest possible access to the internet and should quickly develop affirmative measures to close the digital divide facing vulnerable, low-income groups.[41] However, as will be shown in the next sections, the digital divide persisted during the pandemic despite government efforts, thus hindering the normal exercise of procedural environmental rights.

III. Access to Information

The right to access environmental information is key for environmental democracy, since meaningful public participation and effective access to justice are both dependent on it. Over the last decades, Latin American countries have made significant efforts to entrench environmental transparency within their governance frameworks.[42] Most countries in the region have recognised the right to access information in their constitutions, either explicitly or through the recognition of freedom of expression and the right to seek information.[43] Twenty-three countries have specific freedom of information laws that operationalise the right to access information, while Argentina and Brazil have also established specific procedures for assessing environmental information.[44] At the regional level, the Inter-American Court on Human Rights has recognised the right to access information as a fundamental right protected within the Inter-American System.[45] More recently, the Escazu Agreement recognised the public's right of access to environmental information, including the right to request and receive information from competent authorities without mentioning any special interest or explaining the reasons for the request.[46]

Despite these great efforts and successes, significant challenges remain to achieve the full implementation of this right. As highlighted in a recent ECLAC report, countries in the region need to improve their capacity to produce, process, and disseminate information on the state of the environment so as to ensure that people can play an informed role in environmental decision-making.[47] At the same time, they must ensure that access to information is provided to vulnerable

Groups in Vulnerable Situations' (31 August 2020) www.oas.org/en/iachr/expression/showarticle.asp?artID=1182&lID=1.

[41] Inter-American Commission on Human Rights (IACHR), 'Pandemic and Human Rights in the Americas, Resolution 1/2020' (10 April 2020) www.oas.org/en/iachr/decisions/pdf/Resolution-1-20-en.pdf.

[42] ibid 6.

[43] ECLAC (n 5) 45.

[44] Economic Commission for Latin America and the Caribbean (ECLAC), 'Observatorio del Principio 10' observatoriop10.cepal.org/en.

[45] *Claude Reyes y otros v Chile* (Fondo, Reparaciones y Costas) (Serie C No. 151, 19 September 2006).

[46] Art 5(2) of the Escazú Agreement.

[47] ECLAC (n 5) 67.

people and those who have traditionally been politically underrepresented, such as women, young people, indigenous peoples and Afro-descendants.[48]

During the COVID-19 pandemic, access to environmental information was affected by the administrative restrictions in place. Deadlines to respond were lifted or extended, as administrative agencies in charge worked with reduced personnel or were closed.[49] Indeed, at the beginning of the pandemic, Argentina,[50] Brazil, Colombia, El Salvador, Honduras, and Mexico extended or suspended the time limits for processing administrative requests, thus hampering access to environmental information.[51] In some countries, requests related to the pandemic were prioritised by the agencies, delaying access to information in other areas, such as the environment.[52] However, since access to information is protected within the Inter-American System, the IACHR recommended that, when deadlines were extended, governments should explain the denial, set a time period in which the obligation would be met, and allow for appeals against such decisions.[53]

Faced with this challenging scenario, some agencies in the region used digital media to provide access to environmental information. The implementation of digital channels to request information has several advantages. It promotes wider access by reducing distance and travel barriers. It also makes it easier and cheaper to access information for those with an internet connection.[54] To implement access to environmental information online, it was not necessary to carry out a complex technological development. Public authorities only needed to publicise an email address for requesting information and generate an automatic response to issue the receipts.[55]

Nevertheless, providing access to non-digitalised information while the restrictions were in place ended up being a challenge for agencies in the region. The previous level of implementation of online procedures was a key factor in determining the possibility to provide access to information online.[56] In countries like

[48] ibid 67.

[49] Economic Commission for Latin America and the Caribbean (ECLAC) et al, 'The Impact of COVID-19 on Indigenous Peoples in Latin America (Abya Yala). Between Invisibility and Collective Resistance' (LC/TS.2020/171, 2021) www.cepal.org/sites/default/files/publication/files/46698/S2000893_en.pdf 10.

[50] On 19 March 2020, Presidential Decree 298/2020 suspended the time limits for processing administrative requests. However, on 15 April 2020, an exception was granted for access to information requests by Resolution 70/2020. For a more detailed discussion, see E Bertoni, *El impacto por las medidas de salud pública en torno a la pandemia de COVID-19* (Instituto Interamericano de Derechos Humanos, 2022) www.iidh.ed.cr/iidh/media/10498/iidh_pandemia_eduardo_bertoni.pdf.

[51] Organization of American States (OAS), 'IACHR and its SR FOE Express Concern about Restrictions on Freedom of Expression and Access to Information in States' response to the COVID-19 pandemic' and Rodríguez et al., (n 26).

[52] ECLAC (n 5) 10.

[53] IACHR (n 41) para 32.

[54] U Etemire, 'The Escazú Agreement: Public Access to Environmental Information and the Goal of a Sustainable Future' (2023) 41 *Journal of Energy and Natural Resources Law* 12.

[55] ibid 12.

[56] I Montero de Espinosa Candau et al., *Transparencia, el acceso a la información y la protección de datos personales ante la emergencia sanitaria COVID-19* (Programa Eurosocial, 2020) www.eurosocial.eu/wp-content/uploads/2021/02/HERRAMIENTA_46-Transparencia-el-acceso-a-la-informacion.pdf 36.

Argentina, Costa Rica, Guatemala, Peru and Paraguay, the authorities in charge of providing access to information have pointed out the difficulties they encountered in accessing non-digitised information while teleworking.[57] On the other hand, countries like Brazil and Uruguay, where administrative procedures were largely carried out online prior to the crisis, seemed to have a comparative advantage in answering information requests through online channels.[58]

Even when the transition to digital media was successful, the use of digital channels affected the right to access to information by those who had limited or no access to the Internet.[59] Some countries in the region implemented multi-channel strategies that included the setting up of telephone lines, television broadcasting, and on-site personnel that received and responded to requests for information.[60] Nevertheless, as a recent report highlights, these initiatives were marginal and played only a token role in ensuring access to public information during the pandemic.[61]

Once the agencies resumed their operations, travel restrictions and social distancing continued to make it difficult to access environmental information. For instance, in Argentina, environmental groups have denounced the fact that information concerning mining projects was only available in print and necessarily had to be consulted in the governmental offices located in the provincial capital.[62] For many communities, this meant travelling 150 or 200km during a period of movement restrictions, with the risk of contracting COVID 19 while traveling.[63] The centralisation of information in the provincial capitals therefore negatively affected the right of access to public information for those residing outside those cities. Moreover, due to the sanitary measures in place, some provinces required their citizens to obtain a previous appointment via email, which constituted an additional barrier for indigenous and rural communities, due to the limited access to the internet and the lack of telephone signals in their territories.[64]

A. Access to Justice to Ensure the Right to Access Information

Some of these restrictive measures were challenged in court. For instance, in Brazil, the Conselho Federal da Ordem dos Advogados do Brasil challenged Provisional Measure 928/2020, arguing that it unduly restricted the rights to information, transparency and disclosure of public information.[65] Provisional Measure

[57] ibid 38.
[58] ibid 37.
[59] ibid 40.
[60] ibid 40.
[61] ibid 41.
[62] Gómez and Corral (n 27) 14–15.
[63] ibid 12.
[64] ibid 12.
[65] For an English summary of the case, see globalfreedomofexpression.columbia.edu/cases/president-jair-messias-bolsonaro-vs-federal-council-of-the-brazilian-bar-association-oab/.

928/2020 had prioritised information requests related to the health emergency and had suspended all deadlines for responding to requests directed at entities whose employees were subjected to quarantine, teleworking or equivalent regimes.[66] Pending requests were to be presented again after the state of emergency was over, while negative responses could not be appealed.

The Federal Supreme Court granted an injunction against Provisional Measure 928/2020. As Justice Moraes pointed out, the Provisional Measure had turned the exception – confidentiality of information – into a rule and had damaged the public administration principles of disclosure and transparency, which were recognised by the Brazilian Constitution. The ruling highlighted that access to information was necessary for the full exercise of democratic rights and sustained that, except in exceptional situations, the Public Administration has a duty of absolute transparency in the conduct of public affairs. According to Justice Moraes, Provisional Measure 928

> [did] not establish exceptional and concrete situations that prevent access to information, on the contrary, it transforms the constitutional rule of publicity and transparency into an exception, inverting the purpose of constitutional protection of free access to information for the whole of society.

IV. Public Participation in Decision-Making Processes

As mentioned before, public participation in the decision-making process is key for environmental democracy. Most countries in the region have included public participation provisions in their environmental laws and regulations[67] and some of them have also recognised this right in their constitutions.[68] Permanent consultation mechanisms for environmental affairs have been instituted in several countries in the region, including Brazil, Chile, Colombia, Costa Rica, Ecuador, Guatemala, Jamaica, and Mexico.[69]

However, whether public participation delivers on its promises depends on its implementation. To improve democratic processes, the quality of decision making and its legitimacy, public participation must take place in the early stages of the decision-making process.[70] It should also be inclusive, and ensure that all affected stakeholders bring their information to the table and that the information and points of view of the public really are considered by the administration.[71] To that

[66] *Conselho Federal da Ordem dos Advogados do Brasil (CFOAB) v Presidente da República* (Medida Cautelar na Ação Direta de Inconstitucionalidade, ADI 6351 MC/DF) (Brasilia, 26 March 2020).
[67] ECLAC (n 5) 73.
[68] Venezuela, Colombia, and Ecuador have recognised this right in their constitutions. See ibid 74.
[69] ibid 77.
[70] ibid 103.
[71] Berry et al (n 9) 2.

end, public participation should be suited to the social, economic, geographical and gender characteristics of the affected communities.[72] When these conditions are not met, the public might perceive the process to be unfair, and the decision might end up breeding distrust and conflict.[73]

Under the recently adopted Escazu Agreement, states are obligated to ensure the public's right to participate in decision-making processes, revisions, re-examinations or updates with respect to projects and activities, and in other processes for granting environmental permits that have or may have a significant impact on the environment.[74] The Escazu Agreement also provides that participation must be guaranteed in the early stages, so that due consideration can be given to the observations of the parties;[75] and procedures must be organised so as to allow sufficient time to inform the public and for its effective participation.[76]

While Latin American countries have made significant progress in recognising the right to public participation, a number of challenges remain to be addressed to ensure its proper implementation. As a recent ECLAC report highlighted that:

> On occasion, there is no more participation than required to comply with formal requirements, it takes place when most decisions have already been taken, it is not suited to the social, economic, geographical or gender characteristics of communities, and there is no proper response to the contributions of individuals and organizations.[77]

Countries in the region also need to recognise the diversity of languages and cultures in the region and strengthen the capacity of traditionally underrepresented groups and persons to fully exercise their rights.[78]

In this context, the COVID 19 pandemic posed additional challenges to the proper implementation of this right. Indeed, a key factor in environmental participation is the legal recognition of the rights to peaceful assembly and association, as these rights play an essential role in the creation of spaces and opportunities for real and effective participation.[79] During the pandemic, the rights to assembly and association were suspended or severely restricted, as countries in the region imposed quarantines, forced isolation, or banned social gatherings and other meetings.[80]

To deal with the new conditions, approval procedures were simplified.[81] Public participation was carried out online or resumed with certain limitations

[72] ECLAC (n 5) 103.
[73] Berry et al. (n 9) 2.
[74] Art 7(1)-(2) of the Escazú Agreement.
[75] Art 7(4) of the Escazú Agreement.
[76] Art 7(5) of the Escazú Agreement.
[77] ECLAC (n 5) 103.
[78] ibid 105.
[79] ibid 78.
[80] *BBC News Mundo*, 'Coronavirus: el mapa interactivo que muestra las medidas o distintos tipos de cuarentena que adoptaron los países de América Latina' (15 April 2020) www.bbc.com/mundo/noticias-america-latina-52248497.
[81] Gómez and Corral (n 27).

in accordance with safety protocols.[82] In a sense, the pandemic of COVID-19 pandemic acted as a booster that accelerated the adoption of technology for public participation.[83] However, Internet access inequality excluded important groups from the debate, especially when digital technologies were the only channel for participation.[84] Those without a reliable Internet connection were not able to access online hearings and procedures and could not submit their comments to the agencies in charge of the decision. This was especially true for indigenous populations, as well as for people living in rural areas and those with limited economic resources.

In some cases, the simplification of administrative procedures meant that public participation requirements were lifted for certain projects. For instance, in Argentina, the Province of Salta exempted 'low impact' deforestation projects and those involving less than 1,500 hectares from holding public hearings.[85] According to environmental groups, besides restricting public participation, this resolution hid deforestation: '[s]ince there are no public hearings, all these projects will go unnoticed because there will be no way for people to find out'.[86]

In other cases, public participation was carried out online or resumed with certain limitations to comply with COVID protocols. For instance, the Argentinean Province of Salta modified its legal framework to allow for online hearings.[87] In January 2021, public hearings were convened to modify zoning regulations and allow the clearing of 28,000 hectares of native forest without considering the characteristics of the affected population that lived in areas with limited or no internet coverage. Environmental organisations claimed that the governor took advantage

[82] ECLAC (n 5) 10.

[83] A Hasan and EN Megantara, 'The Public Participation Shifting of Environmental Impact Assessment During Covid-19 Outbreak' (2021) 249 *E3S Web of Conferences* 1, 5.

[84] SC Slinger, MA Tigre, and N Urzola, 'Environmental Protection and Human Rights in the Pandemic' (2021) 1 *Legal Policy and Pandemics* 317, 332. The Escazú Agreement requires the parties to establish conditions that are adapted to the social, economic, cultural, geographical, and gender characteristics of the public and to support persons and groups in vulnerable situations so they can effectively participate (Art 7(13)-(14) of the Escazú Agreement).

[85] See Secretaría de Ambiente y Desarrollo Sustentable del Ministerio de Producción y Desarrollo Sustentable de la Provincia de Salta, 'Resolución 333' (25 September 2020) www.boletinoficialsalta.gob.ar/instrumento.php?cXdlcnR5dGFibGE9QXwxMDAwODE0NjVxd2VydHk=.

[86] *Página 12*, 'Al no haber audiencias los proyectos van a pasar desapercibidos' (20 October 2020) www.pagina12.com.ar/300389-al-no-haber-audiencias-los-proyectos-van-a-pasar-desapercibi. Although the resolution was modified after the National Minister for the Environment expressed concern for the possibility of arbitrary decisions (Resolution 411/2020), environmental groups considered that the modifications adopted by the Province of Salta were insufficient. See *Página 12*, 'La Corte de Justicia rechazó un pedido para frenar los desmontes' (20 March 2021) www.pagina12.com.ar/330703-la-corte-de-justicia-rechazo-un-pedido-para-frenar-los-desmo.

[87] Resolution 123/2020 provided that online public hearing will be broadcast live through the Ministry's website and that people could register via email to participate. See Ministerio de Producción y Desarrollo Sustentable de la Provincia de Salta, 'Anexo de la resolución 123; Reglamento de audiencias públicas' (29 September 2020) www.boletinoficialsalta.gob.ar/anexos2/SA100036428.pdf.

of the sanitary emergency to authorise more deforestation in a month than had taken place during the whole of 2020.[88]

However, online hearings not only posed an obstacle due to the digital divide. The technology chosen by the government also affected public participation procedures. For example, in Mendoza, Argentina, NGOs denounced irregularities in the virtual hearings convened for the approval of a fracking project.[89] According to the organisations, registered speakers could not participate in the hearings because the online platform used by the authorities did not allow for more than 100 participants at a time. Technical difficulties also prevented some citizens from speaking at the hearing. Moreover, some NGOs argued that the hearing should not be considered public, since it was not broadcast through official channels for the rest of the population to witness it, and only the 100 participants allowed by the platform were able to watch it.

A. Access to Justice to Ensure Public Participation

The use of virtual hearings was challenged before the Constitutional Court of Colombia in case T-413/21. The Constitutional Court considered that the right to public and deliberative participation of the affected communities had not been guaranteed. It reasoned that broadcast hearings did not guarantee environmental participation, especially in its deliberative component.[90] Moreover, the Court pointed out that the efforts to establish face-to-face spaces did not constitute a full guarantee of the right to participate, because this modality privileged a limited group of citizens who lived mainly in urban centres and excluded those who lived in rural areas.[91]

Likewise, regarding the use of information technologies, the Court stressed that radio and phone calls were forms of communication that prevented the perception of images and, therefore, the complete capture of all the visual information on aerial spraying. On the other hand, regarding the use of the Internet, it indicated that it was not possible to determine that the residents in affected municipalities had had sufficient connectivity to participate due to the existing digital divide.[92] The Court called the authorities to adapt to this material reality

[88] L Colombo, 'Salta busca autorizar en un mes más de lo que desmontó durante todo el año pasado' (Greenpeace, 20 January 2021) www.greenpeace.org/argentina/story/issues/bosques/salta-busca-autorizar-en-un-mes-mas-de-lo-que-desmonto-durante-todo-el-ano-pasado/.

[89] *Observatorio Petrolero Sur*, 'Hoy continúa la audiencia pública por el fracking en Tupungato' (16 July 2021) www.opsur.org.ar/2021/07/16/hoy-continua-la-audiencia-publica-por-el-fracking-en-tupungato/.

[90] *Acciones de tutela presentadas por José Ilder Díaz Benavides y otros contra la Autoridad Nacional de Licencias Ambientales (ANLA) y otros* (Sentencia T-413/21) (Bogotá, 29 November 2021) para 90.

[91] ibid para 88.

[92] ibid para 92.

and design strategies that guaranteed the effective participation of the affected communities, even if that meant waiting for the sanitary measures to be lifted.[93]

Similarly, the Supreme Court of the province of Córdoba in Argentina, provided the provincial government with some guidelines on how to conduct virtual hearings.[94] According to the Court, for digital hearings to be legitimate, it is essential to provide prior training and advice to the affected population, so that they know how to register and are aware of the technological requirements to attend or participate in the hearing. In other words, the government must not start off from the premise that all the inhabitants are digital natives endowed with the necessary knowledge and means. Moreover, all documentation related to the project in question must be available on the agency's website. Where possible, the information should be presented in language that is easy to understand. The Supreme Court of Cordoba highlighted that if the predominant modality became digital, then there could be no room for opacity, parallel websites or overlapping links. Search engines must be suitable so that access was direct, easy, simple, immediate and without overlaps. In short, the possibilities offered by virtual hearings must be exploited through proper design and organisation that enhance the transparency of environmental information. Otherwise, the Court sustained, there was a risk that, 'by action or omission, the digital becomes an ambush that hinders – instead of facilitating – participation'.

B. The COVID-19 Pandemic as a Catalyst for Change

The COVID-19 pandemic did have a positive impact on the adoption of technologies for public participation. The need to carry out these procedures while complying with the sanitary measures in place prompted governments in the region to develop and implement technological tools. Both one-way communication through social media[95] and two-way interactive consultation through video-call technologies were used by different governments in the region to ensure public participation during the pandemic.[96] In some cases, these tools were combined with access points, which allowed those without a reliable internet connection to participate in the procedures.

[93] ibid para 95.

[94] *Islyma y otros contra Superior Gobierno de la Provincia de Córdoba y otros sobre amparo* (6513191) (Córdoba, 8 April 2021).

[95] *Dejusticia*, 'Gobierno Nacional responderá en audiencia pública a los reclamos históricos del campesinado' (18 July 2020) www.dejusticia.org/gobierno-nacional-respondera-en-audiencia-publica-a-los-reclamos-historicos-del-campesinado/.

[96] For instance, in Argentina the federal government used this technology to allow for participation in the approval of offshore oil exploration. See Ministerio de Ambiente y Desarrollo Sostenible de la Nación, 'El Ministerio de Ambiente inició la audiencia pública para la campaña de exploración de la cuenca argentina norte' (1 July 2021) www.argentina.gob.ar/noticias/el-ministerio-de-ambiente-inicio-la-audiencia-publica-para-la-campana-de-exploracion-de-la.

In areas with wide internet access,[97] the use of online hearings ended up boosting public participation. For instance, the City of Buenos Aires held online public hearings for the rezoning of 32 hectares of coastal zone.[98] The virtual hearing lasted for more than 30 days, 7,053 people registered and 2,057 speakers participated. People could also submit comments in writing that were read during the hearing. Those without internet access could take part in person at the legislative headquarters. It was the longest public hearing with the greatest participation in the history of the City.[99] Newspaper reports highlighted that the proceedings caught the attention of the public and that many young people participated for the first time.[100] The hearing was also broadcast through the legislature's YouTube channel to ensure its publicity.

The use of online platforms also contributed to broadening the geographic scope of those participating in the public hearings. For instance, in Argentina, the Federal Ministry of the Environment used an online platform to hold a public hearing before the approval of the environmental impact assessment of an offshore hydrocarbon exploration scheme.[101] The project information and the environmental impact study were available for consultation on the Ministry's website.[102] Those who wanted to participate as speakers had to register in advance.[103] However, the hearing was broadcast through the Ministry's YouTube channel and everyone could submit questions or documentation through a form enabled on the government website.[104] Although the use of the online platform had room for improvement,[105]

[97] The City of Buenos Aires has 7.2% of the total population of Argentina and 13.33% of all fixed broadband internet access in Argentina. These percentages seem to suggest that in the City of Buenos Aires there is more fixed broadband Internet access than the average for the rest of the country. See Dirección General de Estadística y Censos (Ministerio de Hacienda y Finanzas del Gobierno de la Ciudad de Buenos Aires), 'Accesos fijos a internet por tipo de banda, jurisdicción y participación relativa de la Ciudad en el total del país. 1er. trimestre 2014/1er. trimestre 2022' (2022) www.estadisticaciudad.gob.ar/eyc/?p=106173 and Instituto Geográfico Nacional de la República Argentina, 'Población en los principales centros urbanos (localidades de más de 500.000 habitantes)' (2022) www.ign.gob.ar/NuestrasActividades/Geografia/DatosArgentina/Poblacion2.

[98] L Cargnelutti, 'Terminó la audiencia por Costa Salguero y más del 97% de los oradores rechazó la privatización' (Telam, 28 January 2021) www.telam.com.ar/notas/202101/542917-audiencia-publica-costa-salguero-legislatura-portena.html.

[99] ibid.

[100] *Página 12*, 'Quiénes y cómo participan de las audiencias por la venta de Costa Salguero' (20 December 2020) www.pagina12.com.ar/312906-quienes-y-como-participan-de-las-audiencias-por-la-venta-de-.

[101] R Bellato, 'Audiencia pública offshore: punto de partida para una campaña de exploración por casi US$ 1.000 millones' (2 July 2021) *EconoJournal* www.econojournal.com.ar/2021/07/audiencia-publica-offshore-punto-de-partida-para-una-campana-de-exploracion-por-casi-us-1-000-millones/.

[102] Secretaría de Cambio Climático, 'Desarrollo Sostenible e Innovación del Ministerio de Ambiente y Desarrollo Sostenible de la Nación, 'Resolución 7/2021' (RESOL-2021-7-APN-SCCDSEI#MAD, 10 June 2021) www.boletinoficial.gob.ar/detalleAviso/primera/245550/20210611.

[103] ibid.

[104] ibid.

[105] Some environmental NGOs pointed out that the time to participate was limited and that there were problems with the Internet connection. Other organisations highlighted that the use of the online platform was not inclusive enough. See *Tiempo Argentino*, 'Exploración offshore: cómo fue la primera audiencia pública en Mar del Plata' (30 May 2022) www.tiempoar.com.ar/informacion-general/exploracion-offshore-comenzo-la-audiencia-publica-en-mar-del-plata/.

more than 522 speakers from different parts of the country participated in the hearing and 373 presented their comments either orally or in writing.[106]

V. Indigenous and Tribal People and their Right to Consultation and Free, Prior and Informed Consent

The situation of indigenous peoples and their right to consultation deserves a special mention. There are more than 800 indigenous peoples in the region, accounting for a population of close to 45 million.[107] Both the International Labor Organization 169 Convention ('ILO 169 Convention')[108] and the United Nations Declaration on the Rights of Indigenous Peoples[109] recognise the importance of ensuring that indigenous peoples participate in the decisions concerning the management of their territories.[110]

According to Article 6 of the ILO 169 Convention, governments shall consult the peoples concerned, through appropriate procedures and through their representative institutions, whenever consideration is being given to legislative or administrative measures which may affect them directly.[111] Moreover, consultations shall be undertaken, in good faith and in a form appropriate to the circumstances, with the objective of achieving agreement or consent for the proposed measures.[112] In cases in which the state retains ownership of mineral or subsurface resources or rights to other resources pertaining to their lands, governments shall establish or maintain procedures through which they shall consult these peoples, with a view to ascertaining whether and to what degree their interests would be prejudiced, before undertaking or permitting any programs for the exploration or exploitation of such resources.[113]

[106] R Bellato, 'Audiencia pública offshore: punto de partida para una campaña de exploración por casi US$ 1.000 millones' and Dirección Nacional de Evaluación Ambiental del Ministerio de Ambiente y Desarrollo Sostenible de la Nación, 'Informe final de la audiencia pública N° 1/21' (IF-2021-65230741, 20 July 2021) www.argentina.gob.ar/sites/default/files/if-2021-65230741-apn-dneamad.pdf.

[107] Economic Commission for Latin America and the Caribbean (ECLAC), 'Summary. Guaranteeing Indigenous People's Rights in Latin America. Progress in the Past Decade and Remaining Challenges' (November 2014) www.repositorio.cepal.org/handle/11362/37051 6.

[108] International Labour Organization (ILO), 'Indigenous and Tribial Peoples Convention' (C169, 1989) www.ilo.org/dyn/normlex/en/f?p=NORMLEXPUB:55:0::NO::P55_TYPE,P55_LANG,P55_DOCUMENT,P55_NODE:REV,en,C169,/Document. Argentina, Bolivia, Brazil, Chile, Colombia, Costa Rica, Dominica, Ecuador, Guatemala, Honduras, Mexico, Nicaragua, Norway, Paraguay, Peru, and Venezuela ratified this convention.

[109] General Assembly of the United Nations (UN), 'United Nations Declaration on the Rights of Indigenous Peoples' (A/61/L.67 and Add.1, 13 September 2007) www.un.org/development/desa/indigenouspeoples/wp-content/uploads/sites/19/2018/11/UNDRIP_E_web.pdf.

[110] ECLAC (n 5) 99.

[111] Art 6 of the ILO 169 Convention.

[112] ibid.

[113] Art 15 of the ILO 169 Convention.

According to ECLAC, the right to consultation and free, prior, and informed consent has been one of the main demands of indigenous communities, even before the COVID-19 pandemic started.[114] Indeed, despite the adoption of international standards, there are still obstacles to the full enjoyment of these rights, both because of the lack of an adequate legal framework and because of its poor implementation.[115]

During the pandemic, the IACHR urged governments to refrain from introducing legislation and progressing production or extractive projects in territories of indigenous peoples, given the impossibility of conducting prior, informed and free consent procedures due to social distancing measures.[116] Likewise, the UN Special Rapporteur on the Rights of Indigenous Peoples recommended that states adopt moratoriums on extractive projects impacting the lands of these peoples during the COVID-19 recovery phase.[117]

Despite these recommendations, several governments in the region intended to move forward with extractive projects anyway, by using digital technologies to fulfil their duty to consult. As the following examples will show, those decisions proved problematic. Besides the limited connectivity and internet access in indigenous territories, online formats generally do not align with the cultural protocols or traditional forms of decision-making of these peoples.[118]

In Colombia, external circular CIR2020-29-DMI-1000 ordered the suspension of in-person activities and proceedings and promoted the use of digital technology and virtual channels to advance prior consultation procedures for the duration of mandatory preventive isolation.[119] Environmental and human rights defenders rejected these guidelines, considering them contrary to the nature and purpose of the right to prior consultation.[120] In particular, they pointed out that the proposed use of virtual consultation had not taken into account the real conditions of life in indigenous territories, where access to information technologies was the exception rather than the rule.[121] Moreover, they pointed out that prior consultation should

[114] ECLAC (n 5) 101.

[115] ibid 105.

[116] IACHR (n 41) para 32.

[117] United Nations Special Rapporteur on the Rights of Indigenous Peoples, 'Indigenous Peoples and Coronavirus Disease (COVID-19) Recovery' (A/HRC/48/54, 6 August 2021) www.ohchr.org/en/documents/thematic-reports/ahrc4854-indigenous-peoples-and-coronavirus-disease-covid-19-recovery 18.

[118] ibid 6. According to Art 34 of the United Nations Declaration on the Rights of Indigenous Peoples, '[i]ndigenous peoples have the right to promote, develop and maintain their institutional structures and their distinctive customs, spirituality, traditions, procedures, practices'. See also Art 6 of the ILO 169 Convention that requires that consultation procedures be carried out through institutions that are representative of indigenous peoples.

[119] ECLAC (n 5) 43.

[120] *Earth Rights International*, 'Carta abierta al presidente Iván Duque sobre medidas regresivas contra derechos humanos y territoriales de comunidades étnicas' (15 April 2020) www.earthrights.org/media_release/carta-abierta-presidente-duque-medidas-regresivas-derechos-humanos-territoriales-comunidades-etnicas/#_ftnref4.

[121] ibid.

take into account the forms of government and decision-making processes of the ethnic communities.[122] They called on the Colombian Government to suspend all prior consultation processes until the health crisis was over.[123] Faced with the opposition of indigenous and environmental groups, the Office of the Counsel called upon the Ministry of the Interior to suspend the effects of the circular, saying it was unconstitutional, unlawful and contrary to the jurisprudence of the Constitutional Court.[124] The measure was ultimately repealed on 22 April 2020.[125]

A. Access to Justice to Ensure the Right to be Consulted

In Chile, a group of indigenous communities judicially challenged the resolution of the Ministry of Energy that allowed consultations to be carried out on the Internet or by telephone. The representatives of the communities pointed out that the Ministry of Energy had asked members of the communities to answer a 20-minute cell phone survey, a practice that did not conform to international standards of culturally relevant dialogue or to the customs of the indigenous peoples.[126] The Court of Appeals suspended the 'consultations' and ordered that they should be carried out in accordance with the standards of the ILO Convention 169. The Third Chamber of the Supreme Court upheld the Court of Appeal's ruling.

VI. Conclusions

The COVID-19 pandemic created additional challenges for environmental democracy in Latin America, as isolation and quarantine measures made the normal exercise of procedural environmental rights difficult or even impossible. The suspension of assembly and association rights prevented the creation of spaces and opportunities for real and effective participation, while the closure of public offices and the extension of administrative deadlines conspired against the normal exercise of the right of access to information. The situation was especially concerning since regional experience demonstrates that the lack of adequate

[122] ibid.

[123] ECLAC (n 5) 43.

[124] ibid 43 and RM Rodríguez, 'Carta a la ministra del Interior' (Procuraduría Delegada para Asuntos Ambientales y Agrarios, 15 April 2020) media.business-humanrights.org/media/documents/62230d46113b65d169b9a2271fe431aec4e6abdc.pdf.

[125] ECLAC (n 5) 43 and Ministra del Interior, 'CIR2020-42-DMI-1000' (20 April 2020) www.acmineria.com.co/acm/wp-content/uploads/2020/04/CIR2020-42-DMI-1000.pdf.

[126] *Observatorio Latinoamericano de Conflictos Ambientales (OLCA)*, 'Suprema prohíbe al Ministerio de Energía realizar consulta indígena 'vía telefónica' para proyectos hidroeléctricos en el Bío Bío' (4 June 2021) www.olca.cl/articulo/nota.php?id=108674 and *Observatorio Latinoamericano de Conflictos Ambientales (OLCA)*, 'Alto Bio Bio: Interponen recurso contra Ministerio de Energía por eludir consulta indígena en zona crítica por pandemia' (16 July 2020) www.olca.cl/articulo/nota.php?id=108025.

information about the environmental impacts of extractive and infrastructure projects, coupled with a lack of participation, usually fosters socio-environmental conflicts.[127]

Faced with this scenario, governments in the region were forced to seek new strategies to channel public participation and guarantee access to information. In some cases, the pandemic served as a catalyst to promote changes and digitisation of environmental procedures. Without replacing face-to-face interactions and deliberation, digital technologies allowed governments to implement procedural environmental rights during the pandemic, both by one-way communication through social media and two-way interactive consultation through video-call technologies. In areas with wide internet access, the use of these technologies boosted public participation and led to a broader and more diverse audience.

However, when only digital channels were available, the digital divide in the region made it difficult or even impossible for the most vulnerable groups to exercise their rights. This was especially true for indigenous populations, people living in rural areas, and those with limited economic resources. These groups faced significant barriers to exercising their rights even before the pandemic, and their situation was exacerbated by the measures taken during the public health emergency. Access to environmental justice contributed to providing solutions to some of these problems by forcing governments to rethink their strategies when rural communities and indigenous peoples were involved.

As has been shown through this chapter, governments cannot start off from the premise that all citizens are digital natives who have the necessary knowledge and means to actively participate and they should offer prior training and advice on the technology adopted and how to use it. Connectivity conditions should also be guaranteed, especially when the projects affect large rural areas or have a significant impact on low-income households. Moreover, to truly be considered public, a hearing should be broadcast through official channels, so the entire population can witness it (and not only those who are registered to speak).

In some cases, digital strategies were successfully complemented by access points that allowed people without an internet connection to participate in the hearings, coupled with the possibility to submit comments in writing or by phone. However, it is important that tools and techniques be adapted to the particularities of each territory and to the scale of the problem. Organising an access point in a city is not the same as in a rural or mountainous area. In cases involving indigenous peoples, procedures should be aligned with their cultural protocols and traditional forms of decision-making.

[127] *CIVICUS*, 'Interview to Aída Gamboa; Escazú: 'The work of civil society made a huge difference'' (12 February 2019) www.civicus.org/index.php/media-resources/news/interviews/3728-escazu-the-work-of-civil-society-made-a-huge-difference. See also General Assembly of the United Nations (UN), 'Situation of Human Rights Defenders; Note by the Secretary-General' (A/71/281, 3 August 2016) documents-dds-ny.un.org/doc/UNDOC/GEN/N16/247/09/PDF/N1624709.pdf?OpenElement 23.

As a UN Policy Brief highlighted, '[r]ecovering better from the pandemic should be a whole-of-society effort requiring transparency, accountability and multi-stakeholder partnerships and dialogues.'[128] Countries in Latin America will be better placed to preserve their natural resources through more inclusive and community-oriented action that upholds the fundamental values of democratic life and fosters responsive public policies.[129]

[128] United Nations (UN), 'Policy Brief: The Impact of COVID-19 on Latin America and the Caribbean' (July 2020) unsdg.un.org/resources/policy-brief-impact-covid-19-latin-america-and-caribbean 20.
[129] ibid 19.

12

The Inter-American System and Constitutional Emergencies

IGNACIO COLOMBO MURÚA

I. Introduction

It can be argued that constitutional systems, by virtue of the republican and democratic principles intertwined in their construction, contain two types of institutional mechanism that operate internally and follow dissimilar logic. One mechanism, which will be called 'deliberative', is based on the democratic principle and tends to strengthen decisions that are made through consensus. For example, the process that is established for the creation of laws. The other mechanism, that of 'control', is based on the liberal-republican principle and seeks to monitor the reasonableness and constitutionality of the decisions adopted by government bodies. For example, the judicial control of constitutionality.[1] The first type of mechanism can be called 'positive', since it exists to enable us to come to legitimate and consensual decisions. The latter type can be described as 'negative', since it seeks to remove from the system those measures that are contrary to the constitution.

In order to understand constitutional emergencies, it will be argued here that this double institutional dynamic must be taken into consideration and used as a starting point.

One of the legal consequences of emergencies is that, in an emergency situation, urgent decisions are required to safeguard the constitutional order. The entire

[1] It has been remarked that the principles in question actually come from different traditions. The liberal-republican tradition supports the ideal of freedom, the protection of fundamental rights, and the limitation of power. The democratic one, on the other hand, prioritises the majority decision and the principle of equality. We can read Mouffe in this sense: 'On the one hand we have the liberal tradition constituted by the rule of law, the defense of human rights and respect for individual freedom; on the other, the democratic tradition whose main ideas are equality, identity between rulers and ruled and popular sovereignty. There is no necessary relationship between these two distinct traditions, only a contingent historical overlapping. Through this overlap, as C. B. MacPherson likes to emphasize, liberalism was democratized and democracy liberalized.' Chl Mouffee, *La paradoja democrática (The democratic paradox)* (Barcelona, Gedisa, 2013) 20.

system must be structured with that end in mind.[2] This leads us to the necessary conclusion that the mechanisms that could potentially delay the implementation of an emergency decision must also be aligned with that primary purpose of ensuring constitutional order.[3]

It is noted, then, that those devices that can be made more flexible – the absolute essential – are those that are in operation before the decision is made. That is to say, those that carry out the deliberation itself. On the contrary, procedures that operate *a posteriori* the decision and as control mechanisms – those no longer under deliberation – should not only not be relaxed, but should be strengthened. In this regard, there is an inverse relationship between the positive and negative mechanisms, in the sense that if some become more flexible the others become stronger. Thus, those decisions made in an emergency by a single subject, the President, will not be preceded by the necessary deliberation that gives them legitimacy and, therefore, all subsequent control mechanisms must be activated to 'compensate' the imbalance.[4]

The logic of emergency situations, therefore, makes it possible to relax the procedures prior to making decisions, in pursuit of efficiency and always with the aim of safeguarding the constitutional system; but this comes at a cost, since, lacking a democratic basis, the decision itself loses its presumption of legitimacy. As such, the control mechanism must be strengthened.[5] This also means discouraging the use, when not strictly necessary, of emergency mechanisms; so that decision-makers know that a measure taken in this way will have little democratic legitimacy and a high chance of being invalidated. Along the same lines, what can be decided through the emergency regulations must be very limited, it should not be possible to enter other legal fields such as criminal or tax, among others.

The same dynamic can be observed in the specific field of constitutional guarantees, as well. It is appropriate to differentiate between: i) a priori guarantees, those that are activated before the restriction of rights; and ii) a posteriori

[2] See generally: O Gross and FN Aolain, *Law in Time of Crisis: Emergency Powers in Theory and Practice, in International and Comparative Law* (Cambridge, Cambridge University Press, 2006). According to Tushnet: '"Emergency powers" describes the expansion of governmental authority generally and the concomitant alteration in the scope of individual liberty, and the transfer of important "first instance" law-making authority from legislatures to executive officials, in emergencies'. M Tushnet, 'The Political Constitution of Emergency Powers: Parliamentary and Separation-of-powers Regulation' (2007) 3(4) *International Journal of Law in Context* 275.

[3] IC Murúa, 'Dinámica fáctica y normativa de los momentos de emergencia' (Factual and normative dynamics in moments of emergency) (2020) 2 *Revista de Derecho Público*, Rubinzal Culzoni, 354.

[4] This is the structure that constitutionalism has designed to avoid the 'vicious circle' that Agamben warned about, 'by which exceptional measures that are used to justify the defense of the democratic Constitution are the same ones that lead to its ruin'. G Agamben, *Estado de excepción* (State of exception) 2nd edn (Buenos Aires, Adriana Hidalgo, 2005) 34.

[5] IC Murúa, 'Notas sobre el constitucionalismo y los estados de emergencia. Las garantías constitucionales y el Poder Judicial' (Notes on constitutionalism and states of emergency. Constitutional guarantees and the Judiciary) in R Barra (ed), *Emergencia Sanitaria Global: su impacto en las instituciones jurídicas* (Global Health Emergency: its impact on legal institutions) (Buenos Aires, RAP, 2020) 263.

guarantees, those that function as control mechanisms once the restriction has already occurred.

Indeed, some guarantees function, in the first instance, as a condition of possibility for the limitation of a right – for example, principle of legality, *nulla poena sine lege*, *nulla poena sine iuditio praevio*, presumption of innocence, etc. Nino, following Tribe, astutely pointed out that these guarantees base their foundation on the principles that are derived from liberal democracies and that establish the concept that, before restricting a right, procedures should be strictly followed and the potentially affected parties considered. As such, those affected by a decision should participate in the deliberations to establish it.[6]

However, there is also another group of guarantees that operate after the fact, that is, as remedies to restore rights that have been violated or are threatened by a decision already made. They serve to analyse the legitimacy of the measure and to maintain or revoke it, depending on the conclusion reached. As examples, we could mention constitutional control as a generic guarantee, along with particular constitutional processes, such as amparo, habeas corpus, and habeas data, among others.[7]

It should be noted that these guarantees do not refer directly to the decision-making process – whether the restriction has already been established, skipping a priori guarantees, or because, even if these guarantees have been upheld, a constant audit must be sought to ensure the validity of what was decided – but to the facet of control that constitutionalism also postulates. Once a decision has been made that affects or may affect the rights of a citizen, these guarantees are activated. It is here that the restrictive measure of the rights will be verified as legitimate, strictly necessary and proportional.

This classification is relevant at this point, since it follows that, in emergencies, guarantees that can be suspended or 'relaxed' are only some of those from the first group (especially those related to the decision-making process itself), but never, and this is fundamental, those of the second group. For example, in the Argentine system, the President can directly and unilaterally arrest, search and open correspondence during a state of siege,[8] but habeas corpus or any other constitutional

[6] CS Nino, *Fundamentos de Derecho Constitucional* (Fundamentals of Constitutional Law) 3rd edn (Buenos Aires, Astrea, 2005) 446 and 447. He affirms that: '… on the one hand, the fact that an act that may imply, *prima facie*, the infringement of a right must be done with the utmost care that the conditions that make it justifiable are met; on the other, the scenario in which the individual who is or may be the recipient of it must participate in the justification of this act of coercion, not only in the democratic debate that leads to the enactment of the law that allows it in general terms, but also in the discussion about the origin of the deprivation in the particular case.' ibid 447.

[7] Vermuele, referring the thought of Holmes, points out that: 'During emergencies courts should not practice judicial minimalism or passive virtues; they should reach out, if necessary, to declare the existence of an emergency as soon as possible and to declare the termination of an emergency as soon as possible.' A Vermuele, 'Holmes on emergencies' (2008) 61 *Stanford Law Review* 164.

[8] In s 23, the Argentine Constitution establishes: 'In the event of domestic disorder or foreign attack endangering the full enforcement of this Constitution and of the authorities hereby established, the province or territory which is in a turmoil shall be declared in state of siege and the constitutional

process as a way to control the legitimacy of the measure can never be suspended.[9] On the contrary, it is in those scenarios where these types of guarantees must be strengthened at the same time as those aforementioned are weakened. That the decision has not gone through a previous dialogue scheme[10] is why it has little democratic legitimacy – only that given by the emergency constitutional norms. Therefore, the lack of prior deliberation must be 'compensated', so to speak, with a strict control of reasonableness and subsequent constitutionality.[11]

It is argued that the Inter-American system accepts this distinction, stipulating, albeit implicitly, that although deliberative procedures can be made more flexible during constitutional emergencies, control mechanisms must always be strengthened. To carry out this analysis, the most relevant pronouncements of both the Inter-American Court of Human Rights[12] and the Inter-American Commission on Human Rights[13] in relation to the subject will be investigated.

As such, it will be analysed how the Inter-American pronouncements on the matter admit constitutional emergencies as legitimate – albeit exceptional – tools of the rule of law, but stipulate a strong control of guarantees in relation to the decisions made in this framework. For example, in Advisory Opinion (OC) 9/87,[14] on the scope of judicial guarantees in states of emergency, the Court states that:

> From Article 27(1), moreover, comes the general requirement that in any state of emergency there be appropriate means to control the measures taken, so that they are proportionate to the needs and do not exceed the strict limits imposed by the Convention or derived from it (para 21).

Thus it is clear that the Court is concerned with highlighting the validity of the judicial control mechanisms of the measures or provisions issued in those contexts during states of emergency.

guarantees shall be suspended therein. But during such a suspension the President of the Republic shall not pronounce judgment or apply penalties on his own. In such case, his power shall be limited, with respect to persons, to their arrest or transfer from one place of the Nation to another, should they not prefer to leave the Argentine territory.'

[9] The Argentine Constitution's s 43 specifies that: 'When the right damaged, limited, modified, or threatened affects physical liberty, or in case of an illegitimate worsening of procedures or conditions of detention, or of forced missing of persons, the action of habeas corpus shall be filed by the party concerned or by any other person on his behalf, and the judge shall immediately make a decision even under state of siege.'

[10] Nino tells us: '… there may be extreme situations in which the exercise of these protections may further endanger other rights. However, it is problematic to prefix such circumstances; the guarantees in question fundamentally have an epistemic value: that of allowing to determine, with an acceptable degree of reliability, that the factors exist that (…) justify the limitation of rights. When such guarantees are not fulfilled, it is as if we are taking a leap into the epistemic void and we have to trust in procedures that are *a priori* much less reliable to verify the facts that justify the limitation of rights.' Nino (n 6) 485.

[11] Against: C Sunstein, 'Minimalism at War' [2004] *The Supreme Court Review*.

[12] Henceforth, the Court.

[13] Henceforth, the Commission.

[14] *Judicial Guarantees in States of Emergency (Arts. 27.2, 25 and 8 of the American Convention on Human Rights)*, Advisory Opinion OC-9/87, (adopted 6 Oct 1987) Ser. A No. 9. In para 20, the Court states that 'The Court shall first examine what are, according to the Convention, the 'essential' judicial guarantees alluded to in Article 27 (2).'

II. 'Positive' and 'Negative' Functions of the Processes

Constitutionalism postulates a double function that institutional procedures fulfil: one 'negative' and one 'positive'. Thus, on the one hand, the structure prevents the concentration of power that could threaten the rights and freedoms of people; while, on the other, it legitimises decisions that are made in democratic contexts.

The 'negative' dimension has been discussed since the origins of constitutionalism. In this regard, one can recall Madison's well-known reflection, in The Federalist Papers 51, regarding the need for power to always be divided and controlled, since the appropriate methodology when building institutions, he affirms, is to assume that they are aimed at containing less virtuous rulers. Madison argued that 'if men were angels, government would not be necessary'. With this, he justified reciprocal control between powers, which was later incorporated by classical constitutionalism. Thus, the engineering of checks and balances has a structural sense and must always be present, even if the conjunctural decision is correct. As such, withdrawing controls in the face of virtuous leaders would leave the system without answers should subsequent rulers become tyrants and infringe on individual rights. One can also resort to the fallibility argument, even in the presence of virtuous rulers, that the concentration of power can aggravate errors that are committed even with good intentions.

Regarding the 'positive' dimension, some procedural mechanisms make it possible to legitimise decisions that are made. From the deliberative perspective, it has been established that institutional designs exist to allow the participation of as many voices as possible, especially those that would be most affected by the decision itself. This feature is what ultimately gives democratic value to the final resolution that is made.[15] Nino said that the deliberative vision of democracy based on its epistemic value resolves the tension between the process and the content, and this because the process is valuable in itself: 'its value lies in its ability to decide moral issues, such as the content, scope and hierarchy of rights'.[16]

Decisions made in emergencies must be subjected to strict scrutiny and constant vigilance so that they deviate as little as possible from existing and current constitutional engineering. In other words, the decisions that are made in this way have little legitimacy, which implies that their validity is, in a certain sense, precarious and that there are, on the other hand, certain sensitive branches, such as Criminal Law, that are barred from legal instruments of emergency.

[15] See generally: L Sun and L Sun 'Deliberative and Democratic Legitimacy' in J Bohman and W Rehg (eds), *Deliberative Democracy: Essays on Reason and Politics* (Cambridge, The MIT Press, 1997). See also: R Gargarella, *The Law as a Conversation Among Equals* (Cambridge, Cambridge University Press, 2022).

[16] Nino (n 6) 190.

In line with this, the American Convention on Human Rights[17] has determined that there are certain rights which cannot be suspended under any circumstances. The Court has stated that:

> Article 27.2 provides that certain categories of rights cannot be suspended in any circumstance. Consequently, far from adopting a favorable criterion to the suspension of rights, the Convention establishes the opposite, that is, that all rights must be respected and guaranteed unless very special circumstances justify the suspension of some, while others can never be suspended no matter how serious the emergency is.[18]

III. The Inter-American System and Emergencies

On 30 January 1987, the Inter-American Court of Human Rights issued OC 8[19] regarding the validity of habeas corpus during states of emergency. There it accepted that: 'It cannot be denied that under certain circumstances the suspension of guarantees may be the only way to deal with emergency situations and, thereby, to preserve the highest values of a democratic society' (para 20). However, it stressed that there must be a series of parameters, which can be summarised as the need to safeguard the constitutional order, which must prevail for the declaration of a state of emergency to be legitimate. In turn, it indicated that, 'even when these conditions are satisfied, Article 27.2 provides that certain categories of rights cannot be suspended under any circumstance' (para 27.1).

These standards and prerequisites anticipate the need to recognise the unrestricted validity of the subsequent control mechanisms. Along these lines, the following is stated:

> Article 27(2), as has been stated, limits the powers of the State Party to suspend rights and freedoms. It establishes a certain category of specific rights and freedoms from which no derogation is permitted under any circumstances[20] and it includes in that category the judicial guarantees essential for the protection of such rights (para 23).

Additionally:

> 'it is necessary that "the essential judicial guarantees for [their] protection" endure'. 'Article 27(2) does not link these judicial guarantees to any specific provision of the

[17] American Convention on Human Rights (San José, Costa Rica, 22 November 1969). Henceforth, ACHR.

[18] *Habeas Corpus in Emergency Situations* (Arts 27(2) and 7(6) of the American Convention on Human Rights), Advisory Opinion OC-8/87, (adopted 30 Jan 1987), Inter-Am. Ct. H.R. (Ser. A) No. 8.

[19] ibid.

[20] 'Some of these rights refer to the physical integrity of the person, such as the right to juridical personality (Art 3); the right to life (Art 4); the right to humane treatment (Art 5); freedom from slavery (Art 6) and freedom from ex post facto laws (Art 9). The list of non-derogable rights and freedoms also includes freedom of conscience and religion (Art 12); the rights of the family (Art 17); the right to a name (Art 18); the rights of the child (Art 19); the right to nationality (Art 20) and the right to participate in government (Art 23)' (para 23).

> Convention, which indicates that what is important is that these judicial remedies have the character of being essential to ensure the protection of those rights' (para 27). Therefore, the Court unanimously interprets 'That, given the provisions of Article 27(2) of the American Convention on Human Rights, the legal remedies guaranteed in Articles 7(6) and 25(1) of the Convention may not be suspended because they are judicial guarantees essential for the protection of the rights and freedoms whose suspension Article 27(2) prohibits' (concluding opinion).

Later, on 6 October 1987, the Inter-American Court on Human Rights issued OC 9,[21] where it analysed which are the fundamental guarantees that can never be suspended. It highlighted the validity of the necessary guarantees to control the declaration of an emergency and all the measures to be taken within this framework:

> From Article 27(1), moreover, comes the general requirement that in any state of emergency there be appropriate means to control the measures taken, so that they are proportionate to the needs and do not exceed the strict limits imposed by the Convention or derived from it (para 21).

In various paragraphs, the Inter-American Court of Human Rights insists on this notion and adds that the guarantees that persist must also be appropriate, even during an emergency:

> In that sense, it should be emphasized that, for such a remedy to exist, it is not sufficient that it be provided by the Constitution or by law or that it be formally recognized, but rather it must be truly effective in establishing whether there has been a violation of human rights and in providing redress. A remedy which proves illusory because of the general conditions prevailing in the country, or even in the particular circumstances of a given case, cannot be considered effective. That could be the case, for example, when practice has shown its ineffectiveness: when the Judicial Power lacks the necessary independence to render impartial decisions or the means to carry out its judgments; or in any other situation that constitutes a denial of justice, as when there is an unjustified delay in the decision; or when, for any reason, the alleged victim is denied access to a judicial remedy (para 24).

It continues to argue that the guarantees that make up the concept of due process cannot be suspended:

> Reading Article 8 together with Articles 7(6), 25 and 27(2) of the Convention leads to the conclusion that the principles of due process of law cannot be suspended in states of exception insofar as they are necessary conditions for the procedural institutions regulated by the Convention to be considered judicial guarantees. This result is even more clear with respect to habeas corpus and amparo, which are indispensable for the protection of the human rights that are not subject to derogation and to which the Court will now refer. (para 30).

[21] *Judicial Guarantees in States of Emergency (Arts. 27.2, 25 and 8 of the American Convention on Human Rights)*, Advisory Opinion OC-9/87, (adopted 6 Oct 1987) Inter-Am. Ct. H.R Ser. A No 9.

The paragraph explicitly outlines the framework that was established in the introduction. There, the Court maintains that it is necessary to activate the jurisdictional control mechanisms required to maintain the Rule of Law in states of emergency:

> Given that the 'guarantees … derived from representative democracy as a form of government' referred to in Article 29(c) imply not only a particular political system against which it is unlawful to rebel (ibid., para 20), but the need that it be supported by the judicial guarantees essential to ensure the legality of the measures taken in a state of emergency, in order to preserve the rule of law.[22]

In turn, during the pandemic due to the COVID-19 crisis, the Commission issued Resolution No 1/2020,[23] in which it addressed a series of recommendations to state parties based on the theoretical framework that was presented. It affirmed that:

> Bearing in mind that democracy and the rule of law are necessary conditions for achieving respect for human rights, and that the legal nature of limitations on those rights may have a direct impact on the democratic systems of States, the Commission reaffirms the fundamental role of the independence and of the actions of the public authorities and oversight institutions, in particular of the judiciary and the legislature, whose operations must be assured even in the context of a pandemic (p 5).

In the same vein, in point 16, it recommended that states: 'Ensure that there exist mechanisms for accountability and access to justice in the face of possible violations of human rights, including economic, social, cultural and environmental rights, in the context of the pandemic and its consequences' (p 10) and 'Ensure that there are appropriate means of monitoring arrangements made during an emergency situation. The authorities must reassess on an ongoing basis the need to keep in place each of the temporary suspensions or restrictions that have been adopted.' (p 13).

Similarly, it indicated that states must:

> Refrain from suspending appropriate legal proceedings to ensure the full exercise of rights and freedoms, including habeas corpus and amparo to monitor the actions of the authorities, including restrictions on personal freedom in that context. These guarantees must be exercised in the framework and under the principles of due process of law (p 11).

[22] The Court concludes: '1. That the "essential" judicial guarantees which are not subject to derogation, according to Article 27(2) of the Convention, include habeas corpus (Art 7(6)), amparo, and any other effective remedy before judges or competent tribunals (Art 25(1)), which is designed to guarantee the respect of the rights and freedoms whose suspension is not authorized by the Convention (…) 2. That the "essential" judicial guarantees which are not subject to suspension, include those judicial procedures, inherent to representative democracy as a form of government (Art 29(c)), provided for in the laws of the States Parties as suitable for guaranteeing the full exercise of the rights referred to in Article 27(2) of the Convention and whose suppression or restriction entails the lack of protection of such rights'. ibid.

[23] *Pandemic and Human Rights in the Americas*. Resolution 1/2020. IACHR (adopted 10 Apr 2020). www.oas.org/es/cidh/decisiones/pdf/Resolucion-1-20-es.pdf.

In turn, it established that they must:

> Immediately, in the event of a suspension of human rights, inform the other States Party to the American Convention, through the Secretary-General of the Organization of American States, of those provisions that have been suspended, the grounds for the suspension, and the date on which the suspension is to end. The Commission recommends to those States that are not Party to the American Convention that they adopt the same practice, as a safeguard against abuse of extraordinary powers during a suspension, and as a good means of demonstrating solidarity and cooperation among member states in respect of measures that may be adopted to deal with the emergency (p 11).

It reminds us that it is the states' duty to:

> Ensure that no arbitrary detentions are carried out during the time a state of emergency is in effect or when restrictions are placed on the movement of persons, and see to it that all arrests are made with proper judicial control, in accordance with the standards (p 13).

They must also

> Ensure that human rights defenders are able to perform their defense and information work during the pandemic. Refrain from going after or detaining human rights defenders on account of the oversight they provide of the State's actions regarding the pandemic and possible violations of fundamental rights; this includes not bringing civil or criminal actions against them because of their opinions, not detaining them on the basis of overly broad or ambiguous criminal charges, and not exposing them to the risk of being attacked, in person or online (p 12).

Last, in a 2007 proclamation regarding the case '*Zambrano Vélez v Ecuador*',[24] the Inter-American Court replied to these stipulations. There, faced with an emergency situation decreed in Ecuador, the Court recalled the state's obligation to check the reasonableness of the measures adopted and added that a subsidiary control by the Inter-American bodies should, in turn, apply. Consequently, it indicated that:

> It is the obligation of the State to determine the reasons and motives that lead the democratic authorities to declare a state of emergency and it is up to these authorities to exercise appropriate and effective control over this situation and to ensure that the suspension decreed is limited 'to the extent and for the period of time strictly required by the exigencies of the situation', in accordance with the Convention. States do not enjoy an unlimited discretion; it is up to the Inter-American system's organs to exercise this control in a subsidiary and complementary manner, within the framework of their respective competences (para 47).

IV. Final Reflections

To this point, the standards establishing the Inter-American system have been reviewed based on Article 27 of the ACHR. Both the Court and the Commission

[24] *Zambrano Vélez, et al. v Ecuador* Series C No 166 Inter-Am Ct. H.R. (adopted 4 July 2007).

have emphasised that situations of constitutional emergency can be legitimately established in cases deemed absolutely necessary. For them to be issued in the first place, basic provisions must be met: strict necessity, suitability, and proportionality. At the same time, there are rights and guarantees that can never be suspended, such as the right to life, and those that are essential and inherent to the democratic system of government. Finally, and this is what interests us the most here, the guarantees that control the declaration of the state of emergency itself and the measures that are taken during its validity should not only remain intact, but should also be strengthened in these scenarios.

To conclude, the following items must be taken into consideration:

(i) That the standards established by the Court and the Commission are projected and become effective with the control mechanisms – especially, the jurisdictional ones. In other words, by setting minimum standards that the states party to the Inter-American system must uphold, a control platform regarding their compliance is established at the same time. Otherwise, the implementation of applicable standards would only be an expression of good intentions.

(ii) That the Inter-American system is, precisely, an instance of international control of states behaviour. Based on the principle of subsidiarity, it is stipulated that if the internal control mechanisms are not adequate and, therefore fail, as in the '*Zambrano Vélez*' case, the Court will carry out 'conventionality control', eventually condemning the state that had failed to comply with the appropriate requirements, and the Court will, in turn, order the appropriate reparation measures it deems necessary. Within the framework that we have outlined, the Inter-American system also appears as a state control tool to compensate for the precarious democratic-deliberative measures taken in the context of states of emergency. As has been indicated, the Inter-American Court has affirmed that States do not enjoy an unlimited discretion; it is up to the Inter-American system's organs to exercise this control in a subsidiary and complementary manner, within the framework of their respective competences.[25]

Thus, the Inter-American system recognises that in extreme circumstances emergency measures can be utilised with validity, which implies an automatic vertical concentration of power and, at the same time, the suspension of certain rights and guarantees. This occurs, considering the framework defined in this article, in order to make quick and efficient decisions in order to protect the constitutional order. The Inter-American Court has highlighted that '… under certain circumstances the suspension of guarantees may be the only way to deal with emergency situations and, thereby, to preserve the highest values of a democratic society'.[26]

[25] *cf Zambrano Vélez v Ecuador*, para 47.
[26] Inter-Am. Ct. H.R. Advisory Opinion OC-8/87, para 20.

It also states that 'As the Court has already noted, in serious emergency situations it is lawful to temporarily suspend certain rights and freedoms whose free exercise must, under normal circumstances, be respected and guaranteed by the State.'[27] This implies that decisions can be made immediately and without respecting the previous deliberative schemes that legitimise decisions from the democratic point of view.

In return, it has been stipulated that the guarantees that control the emergency measures, especially those of a judicial nature, must be active and further strengthened in these exceptional contexts. This means that, given the precariousness of decisions that are made urgently and without due prior deliberation, there must be a series of strict control mechanisms (as a way of compensating for the democratic deficit that they entail). Thus, the Court has highlighted that:

> From Article 27(1), moreover, comes the general requirement that in any state of emergency there be appropriate means to control the measures taken, so that they are proportionate to the needs and do not exceed the strict limits imposed by the Convention or derived from it.[28]

An important issue in this regard that should be highlighted is that the Inter-American system itself assumes a state responsibility structure. This is relevant because, in moments of emergency, and as a result of the concentration of power that occurs – generally in the executive powers – the danger of authoritarian impulses and the weakening –and even manipulation – of the other state powers arises. This could create a breakdown in the balance of powers from within the states that cannot be corrected internally. For this reason, the Inter-American Court warns that there must be guarantees and control mechanisms, and that they must be truly effective. Along these lines, for example, it has indicated that:

> A remedy which proves illusory because of the general conditions prevailing in the country, or even in the particular circumstances of a given case, cannot be considered effective. That could be the case, for example, when practice has shown its ineffectiveness: when the Judicial Power lacks the necessary independence to render impartial decisions or the means to carry out its judgments; or in any other situation that constitutes a denial of justice, as when there is an unjustified delay in the decision; or when, for any reason, the alleged victim is denied access to a judicial remedy.[29]

In the same sense, that is, in establishing itself as a control body against a state that, due to the emergency situation, is experiencing a relaxation of deliberative mechanisms, the Commission recalls that in these situations it is necessary to:

> immediately, in the event of a suspension of human rights, inform the other States Party to the American Convention, through the Secretary-General of the Organization of American States, of those provisions that have been suspended, the grounds for the

[27] ibid, para 27.
[28] Inter-Am. Ct. H.R. Advisory Opinion OC-9/87, para 21.
[29] ibid, para 24.

> suspension, and the date on which the suspension is to end. The Commission recommends to those States that are not Party to the American Convention that they adopt the same practice, as a safeguard against abuse of extraordinary powers during a suspension, and as a good means of demonstrating solidarity and cooperation among member states in respect of measures that may be adopted to deal with the emergency.[30]

In other words, this mechanism also implies control by the international community over a member state that may justify excessive measures with the excuse of facing an emergency.

In summary, then, the Inter-American system stipulates that constitutional emergencies, in certain extreme situations, are legitimate and that, during these emergencies, although some deliberative mechanisms may be relaxed and certain rights suspended, the institutional control mechanisms must be strengthened, both internally and internationally.

[30] IACHR. Resolution 1/2020, 11.

EPILOGUE

A Comparative Outlook

13

The COVID-19 Emergency and Instability in Latin America

DAVID LANDAU

The standard story is that emergencies are dangerous because they centralise power in the executive, undermining checks on power, allow for abuses of rights, and potentially erode the democratic order. Scholars have long wrestled with how to design emergency powers so as to avoid these pitfalls, and Latin Americanists have a deep historical familiarity with the abuses posed under the guise of suppressing emergencies.

Yet the experience of many Latin American countries during the COVID pandemic belies the standard story. While presidents in a few countries (such as Mexico and Venezuela) did indeed seem to use the pandemic to centralise power in anti-democratic ways, in many countries presidential governance was extremely difficult, with weak, embattled presidents contending with waves of instability. Rather than accruing power, in other words, presidents in a number of countries across the region were merely trying to hold on to it. Consider, for example, that Peru saw two pandemic-era impeachments and a resignation, Ecuador narrowly-survived an impeachment attempt in the midst of mass protests, Chile a failed attempt to rewrite a constitution, and Colombia a series of escalating protests that forced the incumbent President to make a U-turn on austere economic policy.

Why has experience across the region been so discordant with theoretical expectations about political behaviour during emergencies? First, many countries in the region were facing instability *before* the pandemic occurred, so COVID added governance challenges during already-difficult periods. Challenges like political polarisation and economic inequality, which in turn worsened governance, were exacerbated rather than eased by the pandemic, making it even more difficult for political systems to function effectively. Second, as Versteeg and Ginsburg have pointed out, emergencies come in different flavours, and the last round of theorising (which was based largely on the post-9/11 context) may be less applicable to the distinct patterns of politics caused by the pandemic.[1]

[1] T Ginsburg and M Versteeg, 'The Bound Executive: Emergency Powers During the Pandemic' (2021) 19 *International Journal of Constitutional Law* 1498; D Landau, 'Rethinking the Federal Emergency Powers Regime' (2023) 83 *Ohio State Law Journal* 603.

The pandemic may have caused less of a rally-around-the-flag effect, and had less of a politically-unifying impact, than emergencies caused by war, internal armed conflict, or terrorism.

And third, as emphasised in this brief chapter, the pandemic itself, and the many restrictions imposed by governments in response to it, had devastating economic effects on already-fragile and patchy economies and social safety nets. Inflation spiked, while GDP contracted and unemployment and poverty rates increased sharply. In Europe and the US, governments responded to these challenges in unprecedented ways, creating new temporary or permanent programs and expanding new ones. But across most of Latin America, the response was much less adequate. Governments across the region were not able to figure out adequate responses to the economic side of the emergency, and this in turn fed many of the protests and other forms of instability seen throughout the region.

The rest of this brief chapter is organised as follows. Section I briefly surveys existing approaches to emergency powers, both globally and within Latin America. It develops the standard focus on the aggrandisement of executive power, and also shows how global experience during the pandemic has led to some revisionist scholarship that has challenged the earlier view and is perhaps pushing towards a differentiation between types of emergency. Section II shows how countries in Latin America pursued divergent outcomes during the pandemic, in part dependent on what their starting point was when COVID hit. Many countries across the region were facing deep social, political, and economic instability on the eve of the pandemic, and the arrival of COVID seemed to exacerbate these factors, feeding further cycles of instability.

Section III discusses the failures across much of the region to contend with the economic aspects of the COVID crisis, and particularly to develop an adequate safety net for the vulnerable. Countries pursued austerity measures, populist and shallow economic fixes such as early pension withdrawals, and even attempted to rewrite the constitution to enshrine greater socioeconomic rights, but all of these approaches seem to have failed to meet the moment. Finally, section IV concludes by emphasising how the pandemic strained constitutional governing structures to the breaking point. The most direct problem at the moment is not autocracy, but rather patterns of governance that seem too weak and fragmented to respond to social and economic problems.

I. Theorising the Impact of Emergency

There is a vast literature on emergency powers. Almost all of that literature emphasises the threat that emergencies pose to both the separation of powers and individual liberty. Emergency, for example, is almost always seen as centralising power in the hands of the executive, in ways that bend the normal functioning of the political system. In Rossiter's famous phrasing, a 'constitutional dictatorship' might need to be established in situations of great stress or challenge to a democratic polity, but the challenge is making sure that the exercise of power is appropriately controlled, lest a host of ills emerge.[2] The most dramatic is a descent into authoritarianism, and there are examples both regionally and globally of such a slide. But even short of the breakdown of democracy, theorists worry about the exceptional rules of emergency bleeding into times of normality, and distorting them, through a dynamic of never-ending emergency where rights are eroded and the separation of powers permanently disfigured.[3]

Thus, constitutional scholars working on emergency have focused in large part on ways to envision or design emergency powers so as to avoid these problems. They have debated different kinds of checks on power, including temporal limits on emergency, political constraints posed by legislative bodies, and judicially-imposed limits such as non-derogable rights and proportionality requirements.[4] There is sharp disagreement about how effective these kinds of design checks really are. An important strain of modern scholarship, led by Posner and Vermeule, has taken the neo-Schmittian view that emergencies tend to (and ought to) be legally uncontrollable.[5] This revisionist view suggests that any attempt to put legal checks on emergency power is likely to be a fool's errand. Posner and Vermuele, and others, also point out that modern emergencies tend to be characterised by extensive delegations of legislative power to the executive, such that regimes often do not need to resort to formal emergency powers at all.[6] As we will see, this was also an important feature of the Latin American (and global) response to the COVID pandemic.

The emphasis on the threats posed by emergency powers to democratic governance has also been an important strain of Latin American scholarship. Historical work has argued that the region's nineteenth century constitutions were written by drafters who distrusted popular democracy and privileged order, and who thus distorted constitutionalism by permitting excessive, unconstrained resort to emergency.[7] And formal use of emergency powers has continued to be an important problem in the constitutional systems of at least some countries. In Colombia, for example, the country was governed under a state of siege for the vast majority of time in the decades before the 1991 Constitution was drafted, leading to frequent critiques of abuse.[8] The 1991 Constitution was written under the shadow of the

[2] C Rossiter, *Constitutional Dictatorship: Crisis Government in the Modern Democracies*, 2nd edn (New York, Routledge, 2017).

[3] O Gross, 'Chaos and Rules: Should Responses to Violent Crises Always Be Constitutional?' (2003) 112 *Yale Law Journal* 1011.

[4] B Ackerman, 'The Emergency Constitution' (2004) 113 *Yale Law Journal* 1029.

[5] E Posner and A Vermeule, *Terror in the Balance: Security, Liberty, and the Courts* (New York, Oxford University Press, 2007).

[6] ibid; J Ferejohn and P Pasquino, 'The Law of the Exception: A Typology of Emergency Powers' (2004) 2 *International Journal of Constitutional Law* 210.

[7] B Loveman, *The Constitution of Tyranny: Regimes of Exception in Spanish America* (Pittsburgh, Pittsburgh University Publishing, 1994).

[8] R Uprimny, 'The Constitutional Court and Control of Presidential Extraordinary Powers in Colombia' (2003) 10 *Democratization* 46.

state of siege – it maintained emergency powers but also subjected them to greater constraints.[9] Since then, an aggressive Constitutional Court has played an important role in limiting presidential declarations of states of emergency.[10]

The COVID pandemic has led to some notable (if still nascent) shifts in the scholarly discussion of emergency. Ginsburg and Versteeg, for example, demonstrated in an early empirical study that the classic pattern of unconstrained executive power did not seem to be emerging worldwide during the pandemic.[11] Instead, they found evidence that both legislatures and courts were playing an important role in shaping responses. Ginsburg and Versteeg noted that there are different types of emergency, including wars, internal armed conflicts, terrorism, and organised criminality, financial crises, natural disasters, and public health calamities. They theorised that the degree of executive centralisation may depend in part on the nature of the emergency, and thus that the sharp consolidation of power that would tend to occur during a war or armed conflict may be less apparent during the pandemic. Of course, this is a complex empirical question that might depend on a large number of factors, including the psychological reactions of the public and of elites, the nature and location of the response, and the duration of the crisis. But the observations of Ginsburg and Versteeg seem plausible.

Indeed, some subsequent work has tended to run in the same vein. Scheppele and Pozen discuss what they consider 'executive underreach' during emergencies.[12] Their conception is that at least sometimes, chief executives will lack either the willingness or capacity to formulate a sufficiently robust response to an emergency. They use as examples Trump in the US and Bolsonaro in Brazil during the pandemic. In contrast to, say, Orban in Hungary, who capitalised on the pandemic by having the legislature delegate large unconstrained emergency power,[13] Scheppele and Pozen argue that Trump and Bolsonaro declined to take adequate measures to meet the pandemic, and in fact used underreach as part of a political strategy to disclaim responsibility for difficult or unpopular decisions. Implicit in the argument is again the idea of different kinds of emergencies, where some types of crises are more likely to lead to underreach as a possible response than others. Few leaders, for example, would last long if they responded to an invasion, an outbreak of regional violence, or a terrorist attack with a non-response.

This recent work on emergency has been very useful in suggesting that the centralisation thesis that has dominated almost all discussion of emergency is oversimplified. This is not to say that executive aggrandisement is not a concern –

[9] AB Rozo, *La generación del Estado de Sitio: El juicio a la anormalidad institucional en la Asamblea Nacional Constituyente de 1991* (Bogota, U. Los Andes, 2011).

[10] AS Katz, 'Taming the Prince: Bringing Presidential Emergency Powers under Law in Colombia' (2020) 18 *International Journal of Constitutional Law* 1201.

[11] Ginsburg and Versteeg (n 1).

[12] DE Pozen and KL Scheppele, 'Executive Underreach, in Pandemics and Otherwise' (2021) 114 *American Journal of International Law* 608.

[13] KL Scheppele, 'Orban's Emergency,' *VerfBlog*, 2020/3/29, verfassungsblog.de/orbans-emergency/, DOI: 10.17176/20200330-012828-0.

it clearly is, including (as I will discuss in more detail below) in some Latin American countries during the pandemic. But it is not the only concern, and different kinds of emergencies may bring different kinds of risks to the fore.

Where Latin America is particularly helpful in framing the debate is in showing how the pandemic itself, and political responses to it, can play a destabilising role. Rather than aggrandising power and strengthening political regimes in the manner of the standard story about emergency, the pandemic in the region has often laid bare weaknesses, helping to fuel cycles of instability and political dysfunction. In many cases, as I will show, the pandemic did not start these cycles – protests and political instability often preceded the pandemic. But COVID seems to have accelerated and sharpened these trends, leading to a number of countries that are currently facing serious political crises.

The reasons why are complex. But I will argue below (in section III) that at least one significant cause is that the pandemic itself, and policy responses to it, increased problems of economic inequality that have long plagued the region. Governments generally enacted strict containment measures that affected livelihoods, but existing and reinforced safety nets remained patchy and insufficient, often leading to sharp rises in unemployment and poverty. Administrations across the region have not developed adequate economic responses to these dynamics, and indeed often did not treat serious socioeconomic problems as within the core wheelhouse of the emergency in the same way as they did with containment measures.

The focus on emergency as a source of political instability (rather than establisher of authoritarian order) is not entirely new. It has just often been deemphasised. In Colombia, for example, it is sometimes forgotten that the critique of the widespread use of state of siege before the 1991 constitution was adopted was not just that it was abusive, but also that measures were frequently ineffective at reestablishing order.[14] The ever more frequent resort to state of siege laid bare the dwindling capacity of the state, undermining the legitimacy of the entire political regime. So, the analysis here of the destabilising impact of the pandemic in Latin America may also have implications for other regions, and other types of emergencies.

II. The Varied Impacts of the Pandemic Emergency

Some countries in Latin America, such as Colombia, responded to the pandemic by declaring a formal, constitutional state of emergency – in Colombia, the state of economic, social, and ecological emergency, one of several types of emergency included in the 1991 Constitution.[15] Others did not. In many countries, leaders

[14] Barreto Rozo (n 9).
[15] Decree 637 of 2020, 6 May 2020.

instead relied primarily on ordinary statutes, sometimes existing public health legislation, in many cases supplemented by new statutory authority delegated at the start of the pandemic. In Argentina, as Garcia-Mansilla and Ramirez-Calvo find in this volume, the President relied heavily on unilateral decree power that was not explicitly tied to an emergency.[16] In Mexico, likewise, the executive relied on legislative and constitutional powers empowering the Council of General Health and Secretary of Health, without reliance on a formal state of emergency.[17]

The variation in source of authority, sometimes even within the same country, seems typical of the global response to the pandemic. Some countries around the world relied on formal declarations of emergency, although many others did not. Some filed formal derogations under international and regional human rights instruments, while many others did not.[18] I am sceptical that these distinctions reflected deep philosophical differences regarding the nature of emergency; rather they reflected pragmatic judgments about adequate pathways for state power during the pandemic.

Another notable difference between countries lay at the level at which decisions were made. Several countries in the region (Mexico, Argentina, Brazil, and Venezuela) are federal in form, and here the states were potentially relevant actors. There seemed to be variation in how involved they were. In Brazil, where as mentioned President Bolsonaro was at times blamed for a timid, underreaching response that downplayed the severity of the pandemic, the states seem to have played more of a role in pushing and setting policies.[19] The Supreme Court also filled the gap, including by issuing decisions that affirmed state governmental power to issue public health measures after administration attempts to disable them from acting.[20] This dynamic echoed (although to a lesser degree) that in the US, where in the face of a similar 'underreaching' response by President Trump, states made most of the major policy decisions on questions like lockdowns, masking orders, and school closures.[21] In Mexico and particularly Argentina, the states seem to have played less of a role.[22]

Even in non-federal countries, local governments have become important entities across most of Latin America, and in some contexts they seem to have mattered immensely. In Colombia, for example, the mayor of the capital of Bogota

[16] MJ Garcia-Mansilla and R Ramirez-Calvo, ch 3 in this volume.

[17] JoM Serna de la Garza, ch 6 in this volume.

[18] A Zysset, 'To Derogate or to Restrict? The COVID-19 Pandemic, Proportionality and the Justificatory Gap in European Human Rights Law' (2022) 4 *Jus Cogens* 285.

[19] AL Bonifácio de Carvalho, E Rocha, RF Sampaio, and ALM Ouverney, 'State Governments in Confronting Covid-19: A New Protagonism in Brazilian Federalism?' (2022) 46 *Saude Debate* 62.

[20] J Biehl, LEA Prates, and JJ Amon, 'Supreme Court v. Necropolitics: The Chaotic Judicialization of COVID-19 in Brazil' (2021) 23 *Health and Human Rights Journal* 151.

[21] Pozen and Scheppele (n 13).

[22] Garcia-Mansilla and Ramirez-Calvo (n 16); Serna de la Garza (n 17); AM Hernandez, ch 10 in this volume.

emerged as a major figure in managing the pandemic, setting especially strict measures on questions like lockdown orders, curfews, and business closures.[23]

Yet all of this variation in the source and level of response may mask the basic point that the public health measures that were issued had some similarity throughout the region, as elsewhere around the world. The focus was on measures that imposed restrictions on the movement of individuals, closed businesses, required or encouraged vaccination and masking, closed schools, etc. The response was, of course, more or less strict in some countries than others, and more or less uniform in some countries than others. But the basic dynamics were pretty similar.

Nonetheless, the impacts of the pandemic, and measures taken in response, have been radically different across the region. Those differences are well-mapped in the other chapters of this volume. In a couple of contexts, the 'standard story' of emergency powers being abused by strong presidents for authoritarian ends seems to fit the evidence. In Venezuela, as Daniela Urosa and Jose Ignacio Hernandez argue, the pandemic response seems to have strengthened the powers of President Maduro, who has headed a deeply authoritarian, repressive regime since the death of Hugo Chavez.[24] Maduro had been facing a challenge from an opposition-held legislature, which he attempted to neutralise through various legal devices, and an alternative President, Juan Guaidó, who was recognised by the US and many other governments in the region. The Maduro administration also faced a catastrophic economic environment, which fed unrest. Yet the pandemic seemed to strengthen Maduro's hand, perhaps by showing that the regime (and not the opposition) had capacity to deal with the emergency, and to deliver economic and other forms of relief during it.[25] Maduro's awful approval ratings seemed to have improved somewhat, and the regime certainly faces less credible challengers now than it has in a long time.

In Mexico, the pandemic also may have strengthened the hand of the populist President Andres Manuel Lopez Obrador (AMLO). Before the pandemic, AMLO concerned many observers for undertaking steps that seemed to centralise power in a personalist executive, while undermining institutional capacity and checks on presidential power. The pandemic seemed to accelerate these trends. AMLO has been criticised by many domestic and international observers for his management of the pandemic, including a sluggish initial response.[26] On the eve of the pandemic, he carried out cutbacks to healthcare programs covering poorer and informal-sector workers, increasing the share of the population that was uninsured and plausibly increasing its impact. More broadly, he undertook austerity

[23] 'La alcaldesa de Bogota marca el paso de la respuesta a la pandemia en Colombia', *El País*, 30 April 2020, at elpais.com/internacional/2020-04-30/la-alcaldesa-de-bogota-marca-el-paso-de-la-respuesta-a-la-pandemia-en-colombia.html.

[24] D Urosa and JI Hernandez, ch 8 in this volume.

[25] ibid.

[26] V Felbab-Brown, 'AMLO's Feeble Response to COVID-19 in Mexico', *Brookings*, 30 March 2020, at www.brookings.edu/blog/order-from-chaos/2020/03/30/amlos-feeble-response-to-covid-19-in-mexico/.

measures during the pandemic that further weakened state capacity. Nonetheless, AMLO's approval ratings remained high, and his party and allies performed well in the 2021 midterm election. The Congress, controlled by AMLO's allies, have not played much of a role in checking his power, although the courts have occasionally stepped in.[27]

His allies also undertook a number of new actions during the pandemic that may have centralised power and weakened democracy. In 2022, his allies organised a bizarre recall referendum on his presidency, asking if his term should be ended. While recall referendums are often organised by opponents in an attempt to oust an unpopular or despised leader (see, for example, the Chavez referendum in Venezuela), in Mexico AMLO himself sought to hold the recall referendum as a way to demonstrate popular support.[28] Predictably, AMLO won the recall election overwhelmingly, with 93 per cent of voters agreeing he should remain in office, albeit with low turnout. In early 2023, the regime passed a Bill that largely defunded the National Election Institute (INE), a celebrated institution that played a major role in stabilising Mexico's democratic transition by developing a reputation for conducting free and fair elections.[29]

One possibility – which seems to fit the pattern of Latin American responses to the pandemic fairly well – is a narrative about starting points, with the pandemic accelerating and exacerbating trends in democratic governance that were already present. Venezuela was, of course, an autocratic regime before the pandemic, and Maduro was able to use the crisis to consolidate power further. In Mexico, AMLO's more ambiguous, but concerning, populist attacks on independent institutions predated the pandemic, but the COVID crisis may have given him more autonomy to pursue his agenda.

In contrast, on the eve of the pandemic many other countries in the region were facing a different kind of crisis, a crisis of instability and governance. In Chile, for instance, massive, nationwide protests in fall 2019, sparked by a planned rise in the Santiago metro fare, basically brought the political regime to a halt, and forced incumbent President Piñera's approval ratings down to unimaginable levels. The protests sounded largely in economic issues, but also more broadly in themes of inequality and dignity. The political regime reached agreement on a process to replace the 1980 Constitution, as an exit from the crisis and a way to calm the protests. The pandemic hit Chile in the midst of this instability. As I will explain in more detail below, the constitution-making process did not end up serving as an adequate response to the protests, and indeed the draft was resoundingly

[27] Serna de la Garza (n 17).

[28] M Velasco-Rivera, 'Mexico's Upcoming Presidential Recall Election has been Hijacked by the President's Party,' *International Journal of Constitutional Law Blog*, 9 February 2022, at www.iconnectblog.com/2022/02/mexicos-upcoming-presidential-recall-election-has-been-hijacked-by-the-presidents-party/.

[29] A Applebaum, 'How Do You Stop Lawmakers From Destroying the Law?' *The Atlantic*, 1 March 2023, at www.theatlantic.com/ideas/archive/2023/03/mexico-election-law-ine-amlo-new-law-lorenzo-cordova/673245/.

defeated in a September 2022 exit referendum. Nor did the pandemic act as a way to centralise or aggrandise executive power – instead, as Verdugo's chapter shows, the Congress took the lead in formulating policy.[30]

Many other countries in the region were also facing largescale instability in the runup to the pandemic. In Peru, Pedro Pablo Kuczynski (the elected President for the 2016–20 term) had already been forced to resign in 2018, after being hit with a series of corruption scandals. His successor and former vice-president Martín Vizcarra narrowly survived an impeachment attempt in 2019 (but would subsequently be removed in a second attempt in late 2020). Again, the pandemic hit in the middle of this instability, and seems to have heightened it, with cycles of largescale protests, corruption scandals (some tied to COVID), and presidential removal continuing. All of this, of course, seems to have hamstrung Peru's response to the pandemic.

In both Colombia and Ecuador, the pandemic was preceded by enormous and complex protests. In Colombia, protests in 2019 were sparked by both police brutality and broader concerns about economic and social wellbeing and equality.[31] In Ecuador in 2019, massive protests occurred against the Lenin Moreno administration's austerity measures, particularly the removal of fuel subsidies.[32] The protests paralysed the country in fall 2019 and subsided only when the administration agreed to reduce many of the austerity measures that had been undertaken. In these countries as well, to sound a now-familiar refrain, the pandemic did not serve as a moment for strong presidents to seize and centralise power. Instead, weaker presidents have faced continuing cycles of protest and instability.

So the argument about starting points seems significant: in countries throughout the region, the pandemic did not act as a critical juncture, but instead may have exacerbated tendencies already present in Latin American political systems. Still, it is worth unpacking why pandemic-era politics seem to have fed cycles of instability in many countries.

A full answer to this question goes beyond the scope of this brief chapter. There were a number of social, political, and economic effects unleashed by the pandemic. But there seems little question that economic factors played a relevant role. First, supply disruptions and other factors linked to the pandemic caused inflation across the world, and this inflation heightened problems like poverty and inequality. Second, the policy responses to the pandemic themselves may have worsened a sense of economic insecurity, and these factors seemed to be especially important in Latin America. Measures within the region, like those elsewhere

[30] S Verdugo, ch 2 in this volume.

[31] IM Franco, 'Paro Nacional de 2019, la protesta social que sacudió a Colombia,' *El Espectador*, 20 November 2020, at www.elespectador.com/bogota/paro-nacional-de-2019-la-protesta-social-que-sacudio-a-colombia-article/.

[32] 'Crisis en Ecuador: el controvertido anuncio de Lenín Moreno sobre el inicio de un diálogo que el movimiento indígena rechaza,' *BBC News Mundo*, 10 October 2019, at www.bbc.com/mundo/noticias-america-latina-49995547.

around the world, closed businesses and schools, and restricted movement. As cycles of viral spread ebbed and flowed, these cycles were often repeated several times. The economic cost to lower-income individuals tended to be severe.

While these impacts were cushioned fairly effectively across Europe and even in the US, the social welfare state in Latin America has always been problematic – patchy and unequal, with relatively privileged formal sector workers often enjoying superior benefits to the vast informal sector. As Gargarella has emphasised, the widespread inclusion of justiciable socioeconomic rights across most of the region has not been an adequate solution, although judicial enforcement of these rights has played a meaningful role in sparking positive change in a few countries.[33]

One difficult challenge posed by the pandemic, then, was whether Latin American states could develop fitting responses to the economic instability and vulnerability that it caused. They did not rise to the challenge, I will argue in the next section, instead succumbing to poorly-thought out populist policies, doubling down on the elusive promise of socioeconomic rights, or adopting (under macroeconomic constraints) austerity policies that worsened inequality. In contrast to the relatively standardised playbook of public health measures that emerged during the pandemic, there was much less clarity as to how states should respond to economic issues, and these problems would of course bite particularly deeply across the 'global south'.

III. Economic Instability During the COVID Emergencies

Chile offers one example of the kinds of economic measures that tended to be widely discussed in Latin America. As discussed in detail in Verdugo's chapter, the Chilean Congress proposed and passed a series of Bills allowing withdrawals of portions of pension funds invested in individual accounts, before retirement age.[34] These proposals were framed as giving people assistance during the restrictions and disruptions caused by the pandemic. Some leftwing groups also supported the proposals because they would put pressure to reform Chile's partially privatised pension system.

Verdugo notes how the initial plan illustrated the strength of Congress and weakness of President Piñera during the beginning of the pandemic – the President was forced to give way to congressional pressure to adopt a plan he did not support, even though under the Constitution he had exclusive power to introduce Bills altering the social security system.[35] But once initiated, the policy took

[33] R Gargarella, 'Latin American Constitutionalism: Social Rights and the 'Engine Room' of the Constitution' (2014) 4 *Notre Dame Journal of International and Comparative Law* 9.

[34] Verdugo (n 30).

[35] ibid.

on incredible life and became one of the central axes of debate during the Chilean pandemic. Three million Chileans took advantage of the first package to withdraw funds on the very first day of the program's validity.[36] Lawmakers eventually passed several Bills successively allowing early withdrawal of up to 10 per cent of invested pension funds, and debate continued even into 2022 and 2023, after Piñera had left office. While the idea of allowing additional withdrawals has continued to demonstrate popular and political support, proposals since 2022 have not prospered in Congress.

Similar policies were discussed and passed elsewhere in the region. Peru and Bolivia passed legislation allowing pension-holders to withdraw funds early.[37] Such policies were discussed as well in Colombia, although legislation was ultimately not passed.[38]

The enthusiasm for premature withdrawal of pensions has the markings of economic populism. The policies had considerable popular support, especially early in the pandemic, and were framed as ways to alleviate the burden of the pandemic itself, as well as the control measures passed during it. But they were sharply criticised by economists as responses to the pandemic. From a macroeconomic perspective, they were blamed for exacerbating already-present problems of inflation, and the rising cost of living of course increased the need that households had to tap into their pension funds.[39] And while they provided immediate relief for pension-holders, they also had questionable long-term effects. They of course drained an enormous amount of money out of the pension system and did so at the expense of the future retirement prospects of contributors.

As noted above, some of the supporters of withdrawal in Chile actually hoped or expected that the plan would galvanise reform measures that might result in a different, more fully public system. Discussions along those lines proceeded in the 2021–22 Constitutional Convention alongside other ambitious measures, but ultimately the impact of the draft's provisions on the shape of the pension system were shrouded in ambiguity, and the draft itself failed in a September 2022 referendum.

While countries across the region enacted similar policies to contain the spread of COVID, they generally did not figure out economic policies to respond to the unrest that preceded the pandemic, but was seemingly galvanised by it. Narratives from a few countries might suffice to demonstrate the point.

[36] 'Tres millones de chilenos piden 10% de pensión en primer día,' *DW*, 31 July 2020, at www.dw.com/es/tres-millones-de-chilenos-piden-10-de-pensi%C3%B3n-en-primer-d%C3%ADa/a-54387413.

[37] I Rojas, 'Consecuencias del sexto retiro de fondos de pensiones en Perú,' *LexLatin*, 6 June 2022, at lexlatin.com/reportajes/consecuencias-retiro-afp; DB Ramírez, 'El Gobierno de Bolivia promulga una ley para el retiro anticipado de aportes a pensiones,' *France24*, 10 September 2021, at www.france24.com/es/programas/econom%C3%ADa/20210910-el-gobierno-de-bolivia-promulga-una-ley-para-el-retiro-anticipado-de-aportes-a-pensiones.

[38] 'Proponen en Congreso de Colombia retiro parcial de pensiones ante pandemia de coronavirus,' *Reuters*, 30 July 2020, at www.reuters.com/article/economia-colombia-pensiones-idLTAKCN24V3SG.

[39] 'Chile ante el dilema de un nuevo retiro de pensiones que amenaza con más inflación' *France24*, 12 April 2022, at www.france24.com/es/minuto-a-minuto/20220412-chile-ante-el-dilema-de-un-nuevo-retiro-de-pensiones-que-amenaza-con-m%C3%A1s-inflaci%C3%B3n.

First, to return again to Chile. The political system's response to the massive, nationwide 2019 protests was agreement on a mechanism to rewrite the country's Constitution. The public overwhelmingly agreed in a plebiscite to an elected Constitutional Convention. The Convention elections in May 2021 were held in unusual conditions, not only because of the pandemic but also because of the anti-political atmosphere and unusual electoral rules (by Chilean standards), which allowed independent lists. All the parties performed poorly, but particularly those in the centre and right, which resulted in a Convention that was both dominated by independents, including civil society activists, and was far to the left of the Chilean Congress.[40] COVID set the backdrop over which the Convention met – access by the public was greatly restricted, for example, and the Convention used a hybrid model based on social distancing, where not all of the delegates could attend the main chamber at any given time, with many participating in Committee and plenary sessions remotely.

Economic issues played a major role underlying the protests that sparked the Convention but were, perhaps surprisingly, not the dominant issue during the Convention itself. Instead, the Convention was dominated by important identity issues, such as the rights of women and of indigenous groups, and by a marked focus on new environmental provisions. That said, the Convention included a battery of new socioeconomic rights content. The rights found in the 1980 Constitution (such as the rights to education, social security, and healthcare) were given much more detail, and made fully justiciable via individual complaint. Many new socioeconomic rights, such as the rights to housing, to food, to water, and to a vital minimum of energy, were added to the draft. The property rights regime was also altered, particularly with respect to water where a private property regime was replaced with a system of administrative permission.[41]

The overall thrust of the rights was ambiguous, but tended to favour the role of the state in providing and guaranteeing the rights, in contrast to the neoliberal and subsidiary model of the 1980 Constitution. That said, all of the major rights provisions contained a clause specifying that the right would need to be implemented by statute. Congress was given virtually exclusive power, in the draft itself and in its transitional provisions, to pass the new legislation and social programs that would be required.[42]

The new socioeconomic rights content might be seen as the most direct point of connection between the protests and the constitutional draft. But it elicited

[40] G Larrain, G Negretto and S Voight, 'How Not to Write a Constitution: Lessons from Chile' (2023) 194 *Public Choice* 233.

[41] 'Dueños de derechos de agua se agrupan y lamentan pérdida de patrimonio con propuesta de Nueva Constitución,' *El Mostrador*, 18 July 2022, at www.elmostrador.cl/destacado/2022/07/18/duenos-de-derechos-de-agua-se-agrupan-y-lamentan-perdida-de-patrimonio-con-propuesta-de-nueva-constitucion/.

[42] D Landau, 'The New Chilean Constitutional Project in Comparative Perspective', *International Journal of Constitutional Law Blog*, 16 July 2022, at www.iconnectblog.com/07/16/the-new-chilean-constitutional-project-in-comparative-perspective/.

relatively little attention in the media, again overshadowed by issues of identity. During the campaign for the exit referendum, the socioeconomic rights content did not become a major selling point in favour of the draft. Instead, it seems to have become a liability, contributing to the landslide defeat. The ambiguous content dealing with pensions, health, and education was read by opponents in ways that would eliminate existing private programs and entitlements in those areas, and thus was seen as a threat to the Chilean middle class.[43] In other words, rather than focusing on the possibilities of the new rights to improve economic conditions, opponents successfully framed the debate around the fear of loss. The destabilising effect of pandemic-era policy, such as the pension withdrawal plans examined above, interacted with these fears in complex ways.

It is true that many members of the Convention were motivated by a critique of Chile's existing, significantly privatised social safety net, and also that the rights seem aimed at enhancing the public role in social provision, moving away from the 1980 model. But it seems doubtful the fears of the opponents would have been realised. The ambiguity of the clauses, and the heavy reliance on implementing legislation, meant that much effective power would have been in the hands of the Chilean Congress, a far more conservative institution.[44] The Congress would have been unlikely to have even passed much of the implementing legislation for years, and when it did act it probably would not have made radical changes to existing programs. Nor is it likely that the judiciary, a traditionally conservative institution, would have pushed or required such changes.

This point may frame the problem with the Chilean constitution-making process in more productive terms: constitution-making as a political response to economic unrest never made much sense. In retrospect, it seems either cynical or naïve. The problem is not that the Constitution was likely to unleash radical economic changes, but rather that it was too abstract a mechanism to produce significant economic change.

Compare Colombia. There too the pandemic was preceded by major protests in Bogota and elsewhere, sparked by a range of factors, including police brutality and political violence but also socioeconomic issues such as the cost of living and failures in the education and healthcare system. The pandemic, and the emergency measures accompanying it, actually dampened these protests for a while. When major protests resumed in late 2020, the Duque administration tried to suppress them by arguing that protestors were increasing risks of the spread of the virus.[45] The pandemic nonetheless worsened economic conditions for low income and

[43] A Pena, 'Paradoja: la nueva Constitución amplía el derecho a la salud, pero aun así no convence a los chilenos,' *Ambito*, 1 September 2022, at www.ambito.com/paradoja-la-nueva-constitucion-amplia-el-derecho-la-salud-pero-aun-asi-no-convence-los-chilenos-n5523942.

[44] Landau (n 42).

[45] N Bocanegra, '"Ni la pandemia nos va a parar': Colombia enfrenta nuevas protestas en desafío a presidente Duque,' *Reuters*, 21 October 2020, at www.reuters.com/article/colombia-protestas-idESKBN276393.

vulnerable groups in Colombia, reducing economic activity, lessening opportunities to earn a livelihood, and doing so without a sufficient social safety net to cushion the blow. In addition, an August 2020 decree designed to implement a legal obligation for a 'floor of protection' for informal and low-income workers was heavily criticised by labour unions and other allies involved in the protests, who complained that the social safety net established by the decree was insufficient and also encouraged employers to rely on hourly and informal forms of work without adequate protection for workers.[46]

A major flashpoint of the protests occurred in April 2021, when massive protests broke out, triggered by the Duque administration's plans to undertake a very unpopular tax reform. The proposal would have vastly increased the range of those forced to file income taxes to anyone making over about US$660 per month, and would also have broadened the VAT tax base to include traditionally exempt or discounted necessities.[47] Protestors noted that the burden would fall heavily on the middle and lower classes, which had also been hit hard by the pandemic. A report by the government in 2021 found that poverty had increased significantly during the pandemic, while inflation was also very high during this period.[48] Other complaints were that the system of government subsidies set up during the pandemic was insufficient and beset by corruption. The government, meanwhile, argued that the tax reform was necessary to pay for the new social programs that had been introduced during the pandemic.

The initial version of the tax project was retired, but that failed to quell protests and general strikes, which resulted in significant violence and repression, continuing into 2022 and the presidential elections held that year. The protests were blamed for at least 29 deaths according to the government, although NGO estimates were considerably higher.[49] In fall 2021, the Duque administration passed a revised version of the tax reform through Congress, which had less regressive fiscal effects on the middle and lower classes.[50]

As in Chile, instability stemmed in significant part from economic insecurity and inequality, exacerbated by the effects of the pandemic. The right-wing Duque government not only failed to respond effectively to these demands, but it actually worsened the situation by introducing regressive measures in the middle of the pandemic, which it justified by reference to the pandemic itself.

[46] The decree was struck down by the Constitutional Court in 2021. See Decision 276 of 2021, 19 August 2021.

[47] 'Colombia: Gobierno presenta al Congreso polémica reforma tributaria,' *DW*, 16 April 2021, at www.dw.com/es/colombia-gobierno-presenta-al-congreso-pol%C3%A9mica-reforma-tributaria/a-57222032/.

[48] 'Pobreza e indigencia aumentaron en Colombia durante 2020 en medio de pandemia de COVID-19,' *Reuters*, 29 April 2021, at www.reuters.com/article/colombia-pobreza-idLTAKBN2CG2IW.

[49] 'ONU registra 46 muertes durante protestas en Colombia,' *Associated Press*, 15 December 2021, at apnews.com/article/noticias-f6fc6d1d2d3654adac9e821551746ad7.

[50] "La reforma está concebida para el empleo': Duque,' *El Tiempo*, 14 September 2021, at www.eltiempo.com/economia/sectores/ivan-duque-firmo-la-reforma-tributaria-este-14-de-septiembre-617969.

Similarly, consider Ecuador. There again, the political and economic environment was in crisis even before the pandemic. The prior, populist administration of Rafael Correa had relied heavily on oil revenue to fund increased social spending, but the macroeconomic situation worsened significantly towards the end of his tenure, as debt increased and oil prices fell. This left his successor, Lenin Moreno, to clean up the mess. As noted above, Moreno faced massive, nationwide protests when he sought to eliminate fuel subsidies, and to pursue other austerity measures, in 2019. A tense truce was achieved when Moreno agreed to reverse the policy changes.

Cycles of protest have continued since the pandemic hit. The COVID pandemic and its policy responses had a drastic effect on the Ecuadorian economy. Surveys showed large increases in unemployment, as well as a ten percent drop in GDP and an increase in the poverty rate from 27 to 38 per cent of the population.[51] Moreno reimposed modified economic austerity measures early in the pandemic during a growing liquidity crisis, creating a new system of reduced fuel subsidies and changes to labour contracts. In response, unions and civil society organisations again took to the streets, in May 2020.[52]

After Moreno limped to the end of his term in 2021 with a single digit approval rating, his right-wing successor Guillermo Lasso faced protests almost from the start of his term which again used fuel prices and subsidies as the focal point. Major protests occurred in October 2021 and again (on a larger scale) in June 2022.[53] During the June 2022 protests, after Lasso declared a state of emergency in order to suppress the protests, opponents in the National Assembly attempted to impeach Lasso – a majority of delegates (81 of 137) voted for impeachment, but this was short of the 92 needed to remove Lasso from office.[54]

In February 2023, Lasso sought a referendum on a package of constitutional amendments that focused on security measures, including expanding the role of the Armed Forces in fighting drug trafficking and increasing extradition against the leaders of criminal enterprises. All eight proposed amendments failed in the referendum, further destabilising the presidency and fuelling speculation that Lasso may not be able to complete his term.[55] As of February 2023, the National

[51] K King, P Altmann and RP Bonilla, 'Ecuador's mishandled COVID-19 health crisis has also had serious economic, educational, and emotional impacts,' *LSE Blog*, 18 November 2020, at blogs.lse.ac.uk/latamcaribbean/2020/11/18/ecuadors-mishandled-covid-19-health-crisis-has-also-had-serious-economic-educational-and-emotional-impacts/; 'Ecuador Country Report 2022,' *BTI* Transformation Index, at bti-project.org/en/reports/country-report/ECU.

[52] 'El gobierno de Ecuador se enfrenta a protestas ante las medidas económicas por la pandemia,' *Reuters*, 26 May 2020, at www.reuters.com/article/salud-coronaviurs-ecuador-protestas-idESKBN2320L8.

[53] MS Borja, 'Opinion: Lo que 18 días de protestas dejaron en Ecuador', *Washington Post*, 14 July 2022, at www.washingtonpost.com/es/post-opinion/2022/07/14/paro-nacional-protestas-en-ecuador-2022-guillermo-lasso/.

[54] ibid.

[55] ME Vizcaino, 'How Ecuador President's Constitutional Play Backfired,' *Bloomberg*, 8 February 2023, at www.bloomberg.com/news/articles/2023-02-08/how-ecuador-president-s-constitutional-play-backfired-quicktake?.

Assembly has again opened impeachment proceedings against Lasso, for alleged corruption, after a broad majority of the Assembly voted to proceed.[56]

Finally, take Peru, probably an even more complex case than the ones already examined. The pandemic again arrived in the middle of a period of instability, which in this case had rocked the core of the political system. Between 2016 and 2021, Peru had seen four presidents in the space of one term. The winner of the 2016 election resigned under pressure, his successor was impeached and removed by Congress after a finding of 'moral incapacity' because of alleged corruption and mismanagement of the pandemic, and his successor in turn resigned after largescale protests triggered by the removal of his predecessor.

In the 2021 election, the left-wing populist Pedro Castillo won an extremely close, and highly polarised, election with a largely rural, low-income, and indigenous support base. Castillo came into office wielding an ambitious program that included tax and agrarian reform, as well as an attempt to call a Constituent Assembly, but given the composition of Congress his proposals had no chance of being enacted. The opposition in Congress in fact made a series of efforts to remove Castillo from office, beginning even before he had been inaugurated.[57]

The pandemic had disastrous effects on both human mortality, with Peru having the highest COVID death rate in the world, and the economy, with the poverty rate soaring from about 20 per cent at the end of 2019 to about 30 per cent at the end of 2020.[58] In this context, transportation and other unions with ties to the opposition parties played a key role in destabilising the Castillo regime. In March and April 2022, these unions called a series of nationwide strikes and protests against the regime, complaining of high inflation and fuel costs exacerbated by sanctions against Russia, and seeking support and better working conditions.[59]

After several attempted impeachments against him, Castillo attempted an autogolpe in December 2022, which failed, and he was then impeached and removed by Congress. This again set off a massive series of protests, which have continued into 2023 and seem based on a mix of political, racial, and economic grounds. The protestors have called, inter alia, for the resignation of the new president and the calling of a Constituent Assembly.[60]

[56] A Valencia, 'Ecuador Assembly Backs Report Calling for Lasso Impeachment Process,' *Reuters*, 4 March 2023, at www.reuters.com/world/americas/ecuador-assembly-backs-report-calling-lasso-impeachment-process-2023-03-04/.

[57] For a more detailed recounting of these events, see T Valdivia, ch 7 in this volume.

[58] 'COVID-19 and its Impact on Poverty in Peru,' *Project Peru*, 10 January 2021, at projectperu.org.uk/2021/01/10/covid-19-and-its-impact-on-poverty-in-peru/.

[59] 'Paro de transportistas: saqueos, bloqueos y muertes en una caótica semana en Lima, Ica y Huancayo,' *El Comercio*, 10 April 2022, at elcomercio.pe/peru/protestas-en-peru-2022-paro-de-transportistas-de-carga-saqueos-bloqueos-y-muertes-en-una-caotica-y-dura-semana-en-lima-ica-y-huancayo-protestas-contra-pedro-castillo-marcha-en-lima-rmmn-noticia/.

[60] P del Carpio Ponce, 'Perú: ¿Cuánto (más) afectan las protestas a una economía ya golpeada?,' *Forbes Peru*, 10 February 2023, at forbes.pe/economia-y-finanzas/2023-02-10/peru-cuanto-mas-afectan-las-protestas-a-una-economia-ya-golpeada/.

All four of these cases – Chile, Colombia, Ecuador, and Peru – demonstrate political leaders unable to accommodate longstanding economic and social demands that were exacerbated by the pandemic, albeit in somewhat different ways. Fragmented and polarised political systems had difficulty formulating or enacting structural reforms. Systems responded instead with facile, populist solutions like pension withdrawals that actually made aspects of the problem worse (Chile and Peru). Buffeted by difficult macroeconomic environments, leaders imposed austerity measures that weakened social programs (Ecuador and Colombia). Perhaps most interestingly, Chile offered citizens a new constitutional text with expanded socioeconomic rights, but voters overwhelmingly rejected the draft, seeing a threat rather than a promise in the constitution's ambitious new provisions.

IV. Conclusion

Latin America has, in recent years, faced the spectre of democratic erosion and autocracy, both from left-wing figures like Chavez and Maduro and right-wing actors such as Bolsonaro. But interestingly, in most countries the COVID emergency did not offer the standard narrative of strong presidents centralising power and eliminate checks on it. Instead, in many countries across the region, governance was extraordinarily difficult. Presidents faced mass protests, impeachment attempts, and had extreme difficulty enacting their platforms. In many Latin American countries, then, emergency governance during the pandemic has seemed like a problem of excessive state weakness, rather than excessive executive strength.

In this sense, COVID highlighted and sharpened longstanding economic and social problems across the region. The resultant pressures on political systems have weakened political capacity in many states both inside and outside of Latin America. Nearly every country in the region has enacted justiciable socioeconomic rights, and indeed more broadly an increasingly expansive set of constitutional rights covering diverse questions. Yet these transformative constitutions have had difficulty living up to their promise, in turn helping to breed disillusionment. The dramatic failure of the 2022 Chilean constitutional draft, a text so laden with transformative content as to perhaps be called 'utopian', may offer the clearest case in point.[61] The failure of constitutions in Latin America to respond to growing economic, social, and political pressures is an urgent problem, one which must be solved in order to safeguard the future of democratic governance in the region.

[61] R Dixon and D Landau, 'Utopian Constitutionalism in Chile' (forthcoming 2023) 12 *Glob. Const*__.

14

Out of Balance? Revisiting Separation of Powers During the COVID-19 Pandemic

KONRAD LACHMAYER

I. The COVID-19 Pandemic as a Democratic Stress Test

A. Effects of the COVID-19 Responses

The COVID-19 pandemic posed a challenge to all forms of government around the world. Different strategies were applied to deal with this health emergency, ranging from ignoring the risks of the pandemic to highly restrictive measures which dramatically limited public life. The various strategies employed also had different effects on democracy. And while the strategies proved to be challenging in all countries, the effects did not necessarily correlate to the intensity of the responses to the pandemic. In some cases, weak measures were able to uphold democracy (as in Sweden)[1] and strict measures had the effect of weakening democracy (eg, Hungary).[2] In other countries, the opposite was true with weak measures by the Brazilian President weakening democracy[3] and relatively strict measures in Austria[4] not substantially affecting it.[5]

[1] See J Dahlqvist and J Reichel, 'Swedish Constitutional Response to the Coronavirus Crisis. The Odd One Out?' in MC Kettemann and K Lachmayer (eds), *Pandemocracy in Europe. Power, Parliaments and People in Times of COVID-19* (Oxford, Hart Publishing, 2022) 135–54.

[2] Z Szente and F Gárdos-Orosz, 'Using Emergency Powers in Hungary: Against the Pandemic and/or Democracy?' in MC Kettemann and K Lachmayer (eds), *Pandemocracy in Europe. Power, Parliaments and People in Times of COVID-19* (Oxford, Hart Publishing, 2022) 155–78.

[3] T Bustamante and PN Meyer, 'Brazil – COVID-19, Illiberal Politics and the Rule of Law' in J Grogan and A Donald (eds), *Routledge Handbook of Law and the COVID-19 Pandemic* (London and New York, Routledge, 2022) 225–36; D Landau, ch 13 in this volume.

[4] See, for a comprehensive overview of public health measures, K Stöger, 'Austria: Legal Response to Covid-19' in J Kind and OLM Ferraz et al. (eds), *The Oxford Compendium of National Legal Responses to Covid-19* (Oxford, OUP, 2021) 49–69, oxcon.ouplaw.com/display/10.1093/law-occ19/law-occ19-e28?rskey=Eos6sC&result=2&prd=OCC19, (accessed 27 April 2023).

[5] K Lachmayer, 'Constitutional Compliance or Governmental Mismanagement? Rights Limitations in Austria from Lockdowns to Compulsory Vaccination' in A Vedaschi (ed), *Government Policies*

Liberal democracies had to prove that the balance they struck between health, safety and personal liberty held up to democratic standards while also providing an effective public health response in their respective societies. Decisions had to be made in the face of infection rates and casualties[6] as well as under political and time pressure.

Characteristically, global pandemics tend to feature an alternation between phases of rapid spread of the disease and less dramatic phases of lower infection rates. This pattern of a recurring and changing pandemic is a key feature which requires flexibility in response measures, but also enables decision-makers to learn from mistakes and adapt to the next wave. The circulating nature of pandemic waves meant that – after the first wave – there was time to adjust the law, deliberate new measures and assess the measures taken using parliamentary scrutiny and judicial reviews.

A closer look at national responses, however, reveals a huge variety of approaches, which had to take the particularities of the countries concerned into consideration.[7] The pandemic occurred at a time of existing challenges to the state of democracy[8] and increased the pressure on democratic deliberation, public debate and social consensus.

B. Pressure on the Separation of Powers

Within the particular settings and existing challenges of specific countries, all branches of government came under pressure to fulfil their function during the pandemic. This led to different results, which could be qualified – apart from those cases where the separation of powers has functioned properly – as either underreach or overreach.[9] These malfunctions, however, did not only concern the executive branch, but involved all branches of government and led to legislative overreach and underreach as well as judicial overreach and underreach. Therefore, it is necessary to analyse more closely how the separation of powers was put off balance by the COVID-19 pandemic.

to Fight Pandemics: Defining the Boundaries of Legitimate Limitations on Fundamental Freedoms (Intersentia, forthcoming).

[6] K Lachmayer, 'Democracy, Death and Dying: The Potential and Limits of Legal Rationalisation' in MC Kettemann and K Lachmayer (eds), *Pandemocracy in Europe. Power, Parliaments and People in Times of COVID-19* (Oxford, Hart Publishing, 2022) 47.

[7] See, eg, J Grogan and A Donald (eds), *The Routledge Handbook of Law and the COVID-19 Pandemic* (Abingdon, Routledge, 2022); J King and OLM Ferraz et al. (eds), *The Oxford Compendium of National Legal Responses to Covid-19* (Oxford, OUP, 2021); E Hondius et al. (eds), *Coronavirus and the Law in Europe* (Cambridge, Intersentia, 2021); VV Ramraj (ed), *Covid-19 in Asia: Law and Policy Contexts* (Oxford, OUP, 2020); P Kahn and M Maduro (eds), *Democracy in Times of Pandemic: Different Futures Imagined* (Cambridge, Cambridge University Press, 2020).

[8] See J Couso, ch 5 in this volume.

[9] See DE Pozen and KL Scheppele, 'Executive Underreach, in Pandemics and Otherwise' (2020) 114 *American Journal of International Law* 608–17.

A separation of powers perspective cannot only evaluate the constitutional and legal frameworks, but also has to integrate the de facto interrelation between the different branches of government.[10] First of all, the role of the different branches of government already depends on the particular institutional design of checks and balances in a specific country. While within presidential systems, as is often found in Latin America,[11] the focus lies on the President (even in regular times), the emphasis in a parliamentary system is placed on the legislator to provide legal solutions via statutory law. Second, besides such a formal-institutional perspective, the political setting of a democracy is crucial to understand the COVID-19 situation. While a lot of countries (eg, the UK)[12] were already struggling with populism before COVID-19, in other countries (eg, in Chile)[13] a constitutional crisis was already challenging the government.[14] Third and finally, the role of law in the culture of a society is also an important factor in understanding the response to COVID-19, for example, with regard to compliance with legal rules, corruption or the willingness of a society to follow voluntarily government recommendations.

C. Effective Separation of Powers Instead of Declaring a State of Emergency

The common myth concerning separation of powers in emergency situations is that a strong executive will be able to resolve the situation by effective measures. In such an interim period of a public health emergency, parliament has to rely on the executive giving the government enough leeway. Rights and liberties will be restricted and courts will have to accept the prerogative of government in times of emergency. It is argued that only this approach will guarantee fast decision-making and quick adaptation to the situation. This chapter opposes this state of emergency approach concerning the COVID-19 pandemic for different reasons.

First, it was shown that the COVID-19 pandemic could be managed by applying traditional constitutional concepts within an existing constitutional and legal framework. The pandemic did not justify constitutional panic and did not require

[10] E Carolan, *The New Separation of Powers: A Theory for the Modern State* (Oxford, OUP, 2009); E Carolan, 'What Is the Core of the Separation of Powers?' (29 May 2016). Available at SSRN: ssrn.com/abstract=3855410 or dx.doi.org/10.2139/ssrn.3855410; E Carolan, 'Revitalising the Social Foundations of the Separation of Powers?' in A Baraggia, C Fasone and LP Vanoni (eds), *New Challenges to the Separation of Powers* (Cheltenham, Edward Elgar Publishing, 2020) 11–30.

[11] See, eg, for an overview of hyper-presidentialism in Argentina, Brazil and Mexico, AM Hernández, ch 10 in this volume.

[12] R Thomas, 'Virus Governance in the United Kingdom' in MC Kettemann and K Lachmayer (eds), *Pandemocracy in Europe. Power, Parliaments and People in Times of COVID-19* (Oxford, Hart Publishing, 2022) 71–90 (75).

[13] See S Verdugo, ch 2 in this volume.

[14] ibid; T Valdivia, ch 2 in this volume, stating that the state of emergency in Peru lasted 955 days.

constitutional states of emergency.[15] It did, however, remind states and societies that death and dying are an inherent part of the democratic decision-making process[16] and cannot be understood as an issue that is relevant only in times of emergency.

Second, the concept of democracies in the twenty-first century cannot be compared to that of centuries ago. In particular, the role of the different branches of government and their means of checks and balances are highly differentiated and more elaborate. Over the decades, and in some cases over the centuries, a legal culture has been established to foster separation of and constructive collaboration between powers. Therefore, a need for a state of emergency did not arise in the pandemic in that regard.

Third, technology and science provided many tools and possibilities which did not exist in previous comparable situations. These include the possibilities of virtual meetings, online collaboration tools, or predictions and models about the further developments of the pandemic. Moreover, medical science was able to swiftly create effective vaccines that limited the effects of COVID-19.

Public health emergencies demand effective performance of state powers. Responses to the pandemic do not require an accumulation of powers by the executive but rather a cooperation between all branches of government with regard to the particular constitutional design of the country in question. This may mean a stronger reliance on the executive in a presidential system or on the legislative in a parliamentary system. Nevertheless, all branches of government have to play their part.

D. Comparative Approach Europe – Latin America

This chapter primarily focuses on a comparative approach to European perspectives regarding the COVID-19 pandemic. Furthermore, developments in Latin America are contrasted to those in Europe. This enables us to identify different challenges posed by COVID-19 for different democracies.

From a European perspective, populism has been the underlying topic challenging the traditional government party system.[17] COVID-19 led to new political currents, which opposed government measures in response to COVID-19, especially lockdowns and vaccination programs. The declaration of a state of emergency was a highly contentious topic across Europe, while the lack of

[15] One might argue that from an ex-ante perspective this has not been the case. This argument, however, has to be relativised. Although a lot of people died, the government was never affected to such an extent that it was not possible to function effectively.

[16] Lachmayer (n 6) 47–67.

[17] See Jan-Werner Müller, 'Populism versus Democracy during a Pandemic: Some Preliminary Considerations' in MC Kettemann and K Lachmayer (eds), *Pandemocracy in Europe. Power, Parliaments and People in Times of COVID-19* (Oxford, Hart Publishing, 2022) 315; G Halmai, 'The Pandemic and Illiberal Constitutional Theories' in MC Kettemann and K Lachmayer (eds), *Pandemocracy in Europe. Power, Parliaments and People in Times of COVID-19* (Oxford, Hart Publishing, 2022) 299 (306) regarding the authoritarian use of emergency power.

parliamentary involvement, especially concerning parliamentary scrutiny, was even more evident.[18] The limitation of rights and restrictions of legal protection served to highlight relevant issues concerning the separation of powers.

Latin American countries had a completely different starting point. The declaration of states of emergencies was already quite common before the COVID-19 pandemic.[19] (Hyper-)presidentialism[20] was a prevailing approach to government already in place in some countries. Underlying democratic issues, however, centred on social inequalities, social unrest and corruption, though populism also played a significant role (eg, in Brazil, Ecuador),[21] as did authoritarianism (eg, Venezuela).[22] The COVID-19 pandemic was often characterised in the region by an executive underreach for populistic (eg, Brazil)[23] or more general political reasons (eg, Chile).[24] Economic scope for providing compensation for the lockdown and other consequences was much more limited than in European countries.[25]

Comparative knowledge of risk-management and the resilience of democratic countries in the context of public health emergencies must always take into account the different political, historical, societal and legal implications of a specific country, which cannot simply be transferred to another country, where other preconditions apply.[26] When it comes to a separation of powers perspective, the relevance of institutional design (eg, presidential or parliamentary system; strong or weak supreme or constitutional courts) comes into play.[27] There was more pressure on the respective stronger branches in government to engage in the fight against the pandemic. However, the increase or decrease of power of different branches was also related to their performance during the pandemic, which led to over- and underreach of the other branches.

E. Four Claims

Based on the overall assumption that COVID-19 responses could have been based on a regular constitutional framework in functioning democracies, the chapter

[18] See MC Kettemann and K Lachmayer, 'Conclusions: Pandemocracy – Governing for the People without the People?' in MC Kettemann and K Lachmayer (eds), *Pandemocracy in Europe. Power, Parliaments and People in Times of COVID-19* (Oxford, Hart Publishing 2022) 329 (330–43).

[19] See P Riberi ch 1 in this volume.

[20] M Alegre and N Maisley, 'Presidentialism and Hyper-Presidentialism in Latin America' in CH Mendes et al.(eds), *The Oxford Handbook of Constitutional Law in Latin America* (Oxford, OUP, 2022) 380; AM Hernández ch 10 in this volume.

[21] See D Landau ch 13 in this volume; Bustamante and Meyer (n 3) 226.

[22] D Urosa and JI Hernández ch 8 in this volume.

[23] D Landau ch 13 in this volume.

[24] See S Verdugo ch 2 in this volume.

[25] D Landau ch 13 in this volume.

[26] See, regarding general comparative challenges, eg, G Frankenberg, *Comparative Constitutional Studies* (Cheltenham, Edward Elgar, 2018) 67–107.

[27] See Carolan *The New Separation of Powers* (n 10); Carolan, 'What Is the Core of the Separation of Powers?' (n 10).

analyses the developments of COVID-19 responses from a separation of powers perspective regarding the following four claims: First, a health emergency does not legitimise a constitutional emergency (II). The existing constitutional framework should be able to deal with a pandemic in the twenty-first century. Second, a health emergency demands a strong involvement of parliament (III). In contrast to regular assumptions, the chapter argues in favour of amendments of statutory law and development of oversight mechanisms by parliament. Third, the performance of governments should be evaluated on the basis of effectiveness and accountability for their measures (IV). Fourth, the courts should maintain their functionality. They should, however, still be involved in a health emergency (V).

II. No Need for a Constitutional State of Emergency

A. Constitutional State of Emergency or Not? A Question Beyond the Constitutional Framework.

A pandemic is not a single event but rather an ongoing, repetitive process with different waves. While the onset of the COVID-19 pandemic was unexpected and rather dramatic, the need to react to new waves showed that it was necessary to learn from the past and adapt strategies accordingly. Three strands of development shall be traced to illustrate that there was no need to declare a constitutional emergency as a basis for taking measures to fight the pandemic:

(1) In the first weeks of the worldwide spread of the virus, it was not clear if and how the functionality of constitutional institutions such as parliament, the government or the (supreme) courts would be affected. It became clear relatively quickly that strategies of social distancing, protective masks and virtual meetings could prevent the collapse of these institutions. Precise technical and organisational measures became important to ensure the functioning of governmental institutions, but they did not require the declaration of a state of emergency.

(2) The particular situation of the pandemic repeatedly led to the partial collapse of the public health system, that is, due to the overcrowding of ICUs or hospitals in general. The public health system was no longer able to provide adequate treatment for all patients. Triage systems had to be introduced and many people died due to the lack of proper medical care. Governments had different options to counter the lack of capacity directly. These included mobilising people, setting up new hospital beds and providing financial and organisational support for the procurement of drugs, vaccines and other essential equipment. Nevertheless, all of these counter-measures could not stop the pandemic from exacting a heavy toll. COVID-19 challenged not only the capacities of the public health system but also the ability of the

governments to react adequately. Declaring a constitutional state of emergency, however, could not have improved the situation.

(3) A third strand concerned government response measures taken to prohibit the spread of the virus, which led to significant restrictions of liberties. Quarantine regulations directly affected personal freedoms. Lockdowns restricted freedom of movement as well as freedom of assembly, religious freedom or economic freedom. While severe restrictions of fundamental rights are a typical reason for calling for a state of emergency, it seems highly doubtful if a suspension of rights would have been necessary. The legal, especially statutory basis for these restrictions may have to be established first but a proportionality test and other balancing mechanisms already in place are able to take such circumstances into account. As long as the situation of a pandemic justifies the means, the interference with human rights can be legitimised. In contrast to this, a state of emergency suspending fundamental rights cannot be justified.

If one looks at the different approaches to the declaration of a state of emergency in the COVID-19 pandemic, it becomes clear that the declaration of a state of emergency did not depend on the existing constitutional design. While some countries with a constitutional concept of a state of emergency did not activate the existing possibilities, other countries lacking a general (or particular) state of emergency concept within the constitution declared a state of emergency nonetheless. Moreover, other countries with a pre-existing state of emergency concept stuck to it and declared a state of emergency, while other countries with no constitutional basis abstained from such a declaration.[28] A closer look reveals that constitutions also distinguish between different states of emergency, like state of siege, state of danger or state of catastrophe, for example, and that rules differ between these. The way different states responded to the COVID-19 pandemic illustrated that it is necessary to distinguish between emergencies and the responses to them. The focus of this legal analysis focusing on the effect of the pandemic on the separation of powers, however, must lie on the legal measures taken, regardless of whether these measures are taken under an emergency paradigm.

B. The Rise of the Emergency Paradigm and its Limits

The last 25 years have featured a host of crises which have brought back the relevance of the emergency paradigm. While Latin American countries have experienced crises and emergencies over the last decades in many different ways, the 9/11 attacks and the ensuing counter-terrorist measures led to the re-emergence of the state of emergency concept in the US and European democracies. The challenges, however, did not end with global counter-terrorist activities. Economic and

[28] See Kettemann and Lachmayer (n 18) 329 (330–35).

migration crises followed, but the emergency paradigm was not as prominently debated in that regard. This showed that not every crisis automatically led to a state of emergency. Moreover, a distinction regarding emergencies has to be made between different countries and different situations.[29]

In Latin America, presidents have been rather quick in the use of emergency powers as has been proven many times before.[30] Peru was under a state of emergency for almost three years, which nonetheless did not prevent pandemic mismanagement in the country.[31] This illustrates that a state of emergency in no way guarantees a more effective handling of the situation. In Latin America, the pandemic did not always lead to the strengthening of governments, with some being weakened too. Authoritarian presidents like in Venezuela[32] were able to misuse the pandemic to strengthen their authoritarian approach. Similar developments could be observed in Hungary, for example.[33]

The concept of emergency is based on a singular event, which has to be addressed by extraordinary measures. In contrast to this, the characteristics of global pandemics are marked more by an alternation between phases of rapid infections and rather undramatic periods of minor infection rates. This feature of a reiterating and changing pandemic shows that the concept of a state of emergency does not adequately address this kind of public health crisis. Learning processes, changing responses and the development of new tools for dealing with the pandemic are more important than an emergency paradigm. The stabilisation of societies in terms of unity, economic stability and reducing inequality while limiting freedoms remained crucial.

The emergency paradigm did usually not reach the constitutional sphere. All branches of government remained involved and crucial in fighting the pandemic in democracies. This does not ignore the fact that other developments like the Chilean constitutional crisis, which began before the pandemic, created a situation that affected the constitutional institutions during the pandemic as well.[34] Thus, the pandemic revealed cracks and shortcomings in democracies that had already been in existence prior to the pandemic. While these enabled some authoritarian governments to expand their power (eg, in Venezuela),[35] other populistic leaders could not profit from the pandemic. On the contrary, their power was questioned (eg, in Brazil).[36] Still others had to instigate wars to distract attention from their poor performance during the health crisis.

It is important to keep in mind that, even without a constitutional state of emergency, measures restricting rights with far-reaching consequences can be

[29] T Ginsburg and M Versteeg, 'The Bound Executive: Emergency Powers During the Pandemic' (2021) *International Journal of Constitutional Law* 1498–535.

[30] See P Riberi ch 1 in this volume.

[31] See T Valdivia ch 7 in this volume, stating that the state of emergency in Peru lasted 955 days.

[32] See D Urosa and JI Hernández ch 8 in this volume.

[33] Szente and F Gárdos-Orosz (n 2) 155–78.

[34] See S Verdugo ch 2 in this volume.

[35] D Urosa and JI Hernández ch 8 in this volume.

[36] Bustamante and Meyer (n 3) 225–36.

implemented. While no need to deviate from the existing system of separation of powers can be argued for, it is still necessary to analyse the impact of this health crisis on democracy, rule of law and human rights in that regard.[37]

III. Adequate Involvement of Parliament

A. Parliamentary Meetings

The COVID-19 pandemic did not prevent the involvement of parliaments. While in the first weeks the possibility of parliaments functioning normally seemed uncertain, they developed a wide variety of organisational approaches to continue their work. The measures ranged from organisational health measures, for example, increasing the individual space for the MPs or the re-location of parliamentary meetings into other buildings, to online meetings of parliamentary bodies and even the development of entire e Parliament concepts.[38] It was possible to maintain the functioning of parliaments. The involvement of technology led to an increase in digitalisation of parliaments and parliamentary processes.[39] Nevertheless, digitalisation of parliaments always carries the risks of reduced or at least altered deliberation. While it might be a proper tool to maintain the functioning of parliaments in times of health emergencies, it is problematic to substitute real parliamentary discourse with online debates for practical or pragmatic reasons when it is not necessary.

B. Supporting and Ongoing Involvement of Parliaments

The role of parliaments in the COVID-19 pandemic primarily consisted of the enactment of statutory bases necessary for the government to be able to respond appropriately to arising challenges. In many cases, existing statutory law failed to provide a fitting legal foundation for taking measures in a health emergency. On the contrary, many statutory acts were outdated or simply did not offer a differentiated toolkit for the government. It was therefore necessary to act quickly and amend existing acts as well as enact new statutory law.

The reaction times of parliaments were very different. While in some countries parliament was not involved at all in the beginning and governments acted based on pre-existing statutory law or emergency clauses,[40] in other countries

[37] Thanks to Joelle Grogan for this insight.
[38] See Inter-Parliamentary Union, *The World e-Parliament Report 2020* (2021), *2022* (2022), available at www.ipu.org/resources/publications.
[39] ibid.
[40] See Ginsburg and Versteeg, (n 29) 1498–535.

parliaments were involved from the very start.[41] In the latter cases, however, this involvement was of a formal nature only, since a proper deliberation in parliament could not take place due to time constraints.

As a result of the ongoing pandemic, the approach of parliaments was adjusted and a more substantial process of participation was often possible. The lessons learned from the first wave enabled new parliamentary responses.[42] Legislative measures were not only concerned with the legitimisation of rights restrictions, but also with setting limitations on governments or at least obliging them to stick to certain procedures.

Sunset clauses were also frequently introduced to limit the empowerment of the government[43] to a certain time period. However, the effect of such sunset clauses was limited by the ongoing willingness to extend these measures again and again.

Following a rule of law approach, the procedures limiting rights were or could have been based on a cooperation between parliament and the president or government. In regular times, parliament provides the necessary statutory basis, while the government decides upon the concrete measure taken. Upholding this concept in times of health emergencies would have been a possible strategy, yet this was not the case at all in many countries.[44] The involvement of parliament in concrete government action observed in some countries went one step further. In Austria, ordinances providing for a lockdown could not be adopted by the Minister of Health alone, and the main committee of the national council (first chamber of the Austrian Parliament) had to approve the measure by majority vote.[45] Such a formal involvement of parliaments established the cooperation between the government and parliament, which is possible under the Austrian Constitution.[46]

C. Oversight and Parliamentary Control of Governments

The role of the parliament, however, was not limited to providing the necessary statutory framework.[47] With regard to executive overreach and underreach, parliaments have important powers of oversight. In many countries these oversight

[41] See, eg, in Lachmayer (n 5).

[42] See, eg, in Switzerland, O Ammann and F Uhlmann, 'Switzerland: The (Missing) Role of Parliament in Times of Crisis' in MC Kettemann and K Lachmayer (eds), *Pandemocracy in Europe. Power, Parliaments and People in Times of COVID-19* (Oxford, Hart Publishing, 2022) 179.

[43] See S Molloy, 'Approach with Caution. Sunset Clauses as Safeguards of Democracy?' [2021] *European Journal of Law Reform* 147–66.

[44] See, eg, regarding Austria, Lachmayer (n 5).

[45] ibid.

[46] ibid.

[47] E Griglio, 'Parliamentary Oversight under the Covid-19 Emergency: Striving against Executive Dominance' (2020) 8 *The Theory and Practice of Legislation* 49; J Petrov, 'The COVID-19 Emergency in the Age of Executive Aggrandizement: What Role for Legislative and Judicial Checks?' (2020) 8 *The Theory and Practice of Legislation* 71.

powers were not activated to create accountability.[48] In France, the attempt at parliamentary oversight by the senate failed.[49] Besides, parliamentary fourth branch institutions whose role is to protect democracy[50] were involved in monitoring the government as well. The impact of the pandemic on these institutions also weakened democratic oversight.

D. Legislative Under- and Overreach

While a regular involvement of parliament could be observed in some countries, legislative underreach was the norm,[51] with the Mexican[52] and Swiss Parliaments[53] being typical examples. Both were not involved at the beginning of the emergency. While the Swiss Parliament became more engaged later on,[54] the Mexican Parliament remained quite passive.[55] The Peruvian Parliament was more occupied with struggles with the executive rather than dealing with the pandemic properly.[56] Depending on the state of democracy, an even higher level of parliamentary passivity (as in Hungary)[57] could also be observed. In such cases, parliament accepted all measures. The Venezuelan case was also an example of the pandemic being used to destroy what remained of the legislator.[58]

Although it was uncommon, the situation in Chile illustrates that legislative overreach could also happen during the pandemic.[59] While the Chilean constitutional design gives the President a dominant position, and one would assume this to be even more relevant in times of emergency, the opposite was true. Coming from

[48] Best practices refer to Australia, Canada, Finland, Germany and the Netherlands. www.europarl.europa.eu/RegData/etudes/STUD/2023/740217/EPRS_STU(2023)740217_EN.pdf.

[49] See Sylvia Brunet, 'The Hyper-Executive State of Emergency in France' in MC Kettemann and K Lachmayer (eds), *Pandemocracy in Europe: Power, Parliaments and People in Times of COVID-19* (Oxford, Hart Publishing 2022) 201 (214).

[50] Regarding the discussion on the independent institutions protecting democracy as a fourth branch, see M Tushnet, *The New Fourth Branch. Institutions for Protecting Constitutional Democracy* (Cambridge, CUP, 2021).

[51] See Kettemann and Lachmayer (n 18) 329.

[52] Serna de la Garza, ch 6 in this volume.

[53] Ammann and Uhlmann (n 42) 179.

[54] F Uhlmann, 'Switzerland and the COVID-19 Pandemic: A Look Back and a Look Into the Future', VerfBlog (1 January 2021), verfassungsblog.de/switzerland-and-the-covid-19-pandemic-a-look-back-and-a-look-into-the-future.

[55] Serna de la Garzach 6 in this volume.

[56] T Valdivia, ch 7 in this volume: 'The idea was that, at the beginning, the Executive and Legislative branches of power were collaborating to fight the pandemic. However, this proved not to be the case. As we will show in the coming sections, the two branches were locked in a series of never-ending political and legislative clashes that prevented them from putting all their efforts into combating the pandemic.' The situation ended up with the world's highest COVID death rate.

[57] Szente and Gárdos-Orosz (n 2) 177.

[58] D Urosa and JI Hernández, ch 8 in this volume.

[59] See, regarding a critical analysis of the development, S Verdugo, ch 2 in this volume, who speaks about congressional empowerment.

an already existing constitutional crisis, the political role of the President deteriorated even more. The consequence was that parliament took over and, driven by a populist agenda, created momentum to intervene in people's pensions.[60]

While overall – against the backdrop of legislative underreach – the claim for a stronger involvement of parliament seems legitimate and necessary in times of a pandemic, the Chilean example shows that it is also necessary to protect the existing system of checks and balances from legislative overreach.[61]

IV. Effective and Accountable Government

A. Providing Resources, Limiting Freedoms, Financial Support

Pandemic management as a specific form of health management under extraordinary circumstances is a governmental task. In a constitutional democracy, government actions have to stick to the rules set out by parliament; the government's compliance will be under the oversight of parliament and other democratic institutions, which evaluate the government's performance, as well as being under review by the courts, which check that the government complies with the rules in place. Even in a presidential system with more power on the President's side, parliament defines the rules and limits of presidential action within the constitutional framework.

A pandemic does require governments to accumulate more power, but only to fulfil their tasks. First of all, public health challenges had to be addressed by specific health services, for example, the provision of medication, ICUs, etc. Second, measures to limit the spread of the virus had to be taken; these often have effects on individual liberties. Such measures included personal quarantine, general lockdowns for certain areas, cities or whole regions, restrictions on businesses, etc. Moreover, restrictions affected the freedom of assembly, religious freedoms or the freedom of education, etc. Third, governments provided financial support to different groups of society to compensate for the financial damage caused by the pandemic directly or by the restrictive government measures as a response to the pandemic.

The effectiveness of these measures varied greatly and can be distinguished according to the three mentioned dimensions (public health services, limiting freedoms and providing financial support). Moreover, the circularity of the pandemic led to a situation whereby different measures proved to have varying degrees of success during different stages of the pandemic. While the availability of ICUs was crucial at the very beginning, the availability of vaccines and

[60] ibid.
[61] ibid.

increasing vaccination rates were relevant in the second phase of the pandemic. The liberal Swedish approach illustrated that governmental strategies could differ fundamentally.[62] At the other end of the spectrum of strategies, the government of New Zealand opted for restrictive measures.[63] The authoritarian Chinese approach not only revealed its own limits but also led to extremely repressive situations throughout the pandemic.[64] The ability to adapt to the permanently changing situation became crucial in the pandemic.

Financial support was essential to counter the financial damage incurred during the pandemic. While European countries as well as the US invested a lot of financial resources in this, other countries have not been able to provide the same amount of funding.[65] As David Landau points out, Latin American countries were less able to respond to the COVID-19 pandemic by providing economic programs.[66] Measures like in Chile, where the pension funds were used to generate money, will have long-lasting negative effects on society and increase inequalities, which again has huge implications for societies.[67]

B. Strong Government, Strong Rule of Law

Pandemics require decisive and clear responses by the governments. The Swedish way, however, illustrates that governments can come to the conclusion that a pandemic can also be handled by an informative approach. The Swedish decision-making had, however, taken the particularities of the culture and the country into consideration, like a specific culture of self-responsibility and voluntary compliance with non-binding recommendations.[68] Asian countries that had more recently experienced an epidemic (SARS, MERS) were able to provide responses more quickly and could rely on people being familiar with public health measures like wearing masks or social distancing.[69] While this approach proved to be

[62] See Dahlqvist and Reichel (n 1) 135–54.

[63] DR Knight, 'Accountability through Dialogue. New Zealand's Experience during the First Year of the COVID-19 Pandemic' in J Grogan and A Donald (eds), *The Routledge Handbook of Law and the COVID-19 Pandemic* (Abingdon, Routledge, 2022) 31.

[64] See ZJ Wang and J Chen, 'People's Republic of China: Legal Response to Covid 19', in J Kind and OLM Ferraz et al. (eds), *The Oxford Compendium of National Legal Responses to Covid-19* (Oxford, OUP, 2021) 49, doi: 10.1093/law-occ19/e22.013.22 (accessed 29 June 2023), who refer already to the initial Chinese public health measures as 'some of the strictest measures ever undertaken by any country in response to an epidemic'.

[65] See, for an overview of fiscal measures taken in response to the pandemic, the IMF Fiscal Affairs Department's Fiscal Monitor Database of Country Fiscal Measures in Response to the COVID-19 Pandemic, www.imf.org/en/Topics/imf-and-covid19/Fiscal-Policies-Database-in-Response-to-COVID-19.

[66] D Landau, ch 13 in this volume.

[67] See S Verdugo, ch 2 in this volume.

[68] See, however, how Sweden changed its approach in the second year of the pandemic. Moreover, the Swedish decisions were also contested in the country itself. See Dahlqvist and Reichel (n 1) 135–54.

[69] See, for a short overview of the varying measures in Asia and the relevance of factors like previous epidemics or cultural norms (especially in Japan) for effective measures and the compliance of

successful in the first part of the pandemic, this changed in later waves as COVID-19 became much more infectious. By that time, however, vaccines were already available, which made it easier to address the challenges of the pandemic.

The pandemic also illustrated that the specific combination of different approaches with varying cultural and societal dimensions affected how effectively a pandemic could be countered. While authoritarian approaches seemed to be more successful at the beginning of the pandemic, the picture changed over time[70] and more liberal approaches brought greater success for societies as a whole. Weak governments during the pandemic in Latin America also illustrated that the negative effects on society of executive underreach were significant and that society itself had to compensate for the lack of effective action on the part of the government.[71] Partially federal systems showed that decentralised state governments were also able to take over responsibility for the COVID-19 response measures.[72]

The pandemic did not prevent the establishment of a strong rule of law during the health crisis, especially as it continued for more than two years. Compliance with the rule of law was not impeded by the pandemic's challenges and made governmental strategies more predictable.

C. Separation of Powers within the Government

Separation of powers does not only concern different branches of government, but also different authorities within the government. It makes a difference if the Minister of Health is in charge or the Minister of Interior,[73] independent agencies[74] or the army.[75] In many countries, multiple institutions worked together to fight the pandemic. However, different approaches reveal different forms of governmental logic. The core question was who really decided on the relevant measures. The role of advisory boards and scientific experts also proved to be crucial. The intensity of involvement of experts varied significantly as did the selection of disciplines included. The relevance of experts could support the effectiveness and precision of the measures taken.

Moreover, the role of technology was decisive throughout the pandemic. While certain measures such as social distancing apps might not have proven successful in the European context, they were used, for example, by China[76] to expand social

the public, VV Ramraj and M Little, 'A Short History and Thematic Overview' in VV Ramraj (ed), *Covid-19 in Asia: Law and Policy Contexts* (Oxford, OUP, 2020) 3–23 (14–15).

[70] See F Xu and Q Liu, 'China: Community Policing, High-Tech Surveillance, and Authoritarian Durability' in VV Ramraj (ed), *Covid-19 in Asia: Law and Policy Contexts* (Oxford, OUP, 2020) 27–42; Wang and Chen (n 64).

[71] D Landau, ch 13 in this volume.

[72] M Figueiredo, ch 4 in this volume.

[73] See, regarding the securitisation of the Covid response, DM Ferreira Rubio, ch 9 in this volume.

[74] See, eg, regarding Sweden, Dahlqvist and Reichel (n 1) 135–54.

[75] See J Couso, ch 5 in this volume.

[76] See Xu and Liu (n 70) 27–42; Wang and Chen (n 64).

control over people. Contact tracing, prediction models and rapid development of drugs and vaccines are all part of immense (bio-)technological efforts to address the pandemic, reducing the number of casualties and limiting the potential for much greater effects of the pandemic on society. The COVID-19 pandemic illustrated that it was not governmental superpowers that overcame the challenges of the health emergency, but rather a collaborative approach between government and society.

D. Executive Overreach and Underreach

As David E Pozen and Kim Lane Scheppele have analysed, both executive overreach and underreach carry significant implications.[77] Pozen and Scheppele define executive underreach as a 'national executive branch's wilful failure to address a significant public problem that the executive is legally and functionally equipped (though not necessarily legally required) to address'.[78] By 'denying responsibility and cultivating chaos',[79] governments did not fulfil their tasks and other actors (eg, states in a federal system) had to take over responsibility for effective measures. Effects on society will be long-term instability, which then fosters authoritarianism. Government overreach could be observed, for example, in Hungary[80] or Venezuela,[81] while executive underreach played a significant role in Latin America. The response of the Brazilian President as well as the Presidents in Chile or Peru are examples of executive underreach failing to provide the necessary measures.[82]

For society, the impact of a pandemic is not over when the pandemic is over. Post-pandemic effects will last for a long time with regard to many different social and institutional issues. One example is budgetary implications. If the government invested a great amount of money in fighting the pandemic, the depleted state budget could prevent further investments after the pandemic. The Chilean example of using pension funds will also lead to long-lasting damage to the social welfare system.[83] If the government did not invest a significant amount of money (because it was unwilling or simply unable to) the economy might suffer to a much greater extent and not be able to recover as quickly. Different measures restricting rights might have led to new societal movements opposing governmental activities and could lead to a rise of populism after the pandemic. In many Latin American countries, governmental instabilities occurred during the pandemic and led to greater instabilities with more serious economic challenges after the pandemic.

[77] Pozen and Scheppele (n 9) 608–17.
[78] ibid.
[79] ibid.
[80] Szente and Gárdos-Orosz (n 2) 155–78.
[81] D Urosa and JI Hernández, ch 8 in this volume.
[82] See T Valdivia, ch 7 in this volume; S Verdugo, ch 2 in this volume.
[83] S Verdugo, ch 2 in this volume.

V. Judicial Review as a Tool of Scrutiny

A. The Necessity of Judicial Review During the Pandemic

In a pandemic situation, it seems that courts cannot contribute to overcoming legal challenges. The government must make rapid decisions while courts can review these afterwards anyway. The legal effect of the courts' judgments might come too late to intervene in government action. The plausibility of this argument is, however, more than fragile. The function of the courts is to review governmental measures, but it is not their task to prohibit them. Nevertheless, an ex-post review has important legal consequences which can lead to political or economic responsibility on the one hand and can serve as guidelines for future government action on the other hand, especially in times of a pandemic when similar challenges occur periodically. Thus, in times of a health crisis, when infringing rights is necessary, legal control of the measures taken is even more important. Judicial review becomes an important tool of legal scrutiny and supports the upholding of the rule of law.

B. Speed of Judicial Decisions

Whether courts are making fast or slow decisions depends on the constitutional framework and particular procedural rules.[84] The COVID-19 pandemic proved that courts were involved in different ways in different countries. Due to its specific role, the French Constitutional Council[85] was the first to be involved. In Germany, the Constitutional Court decided on cases related to pandemic measures relatively quickly.[86] The Austrian Constitutional Court[87] took until Summer 2020 to pass its first decision on COVID-19 measures.[88] In contrast to this, the Italian Constitutional Court lacked competence to decide in cases concerning decrees issued by the executive in 2020, but was able to intervene later on, when

[84] See K Lachmayer, 'Judging, Fast and Slow. Constitutional Adjudication in Times of COVID-19' in S Zagorc and S Bardutzky (eds), *Constitution at the Brink of a State of Emergency. Celebrating Thirty Years of the Constitution of Republic of Slovenia (1991–2021)* (University of Ljubljana, Faculty of Law, forthcoming), available at papers.ssrn.com/sol3/papers.cfm?abstract_id=3935820.

[85] See Brunet (n 49) 201 (217–18); A Golia, L Hering, C Moser and T Sparks, 'Constitutions and Contagion. European Constitutional Systems and the COVID-19 Pandemic', Max Planck Institute for Comparative Public Law & International Law (MPIL) Research Paper No 2020–42 (2021) *ZaöRV / HJIL* 147.

[86] AK Mangold, 'Germany and COVID-19: A Most Eventful Year', *VerfBlog* (7 April 2021), verfassungsblog.de/germany-and-covid-19-a-most-eventful-year/; S Jürgensen and F Orlowski, 'Critique and Crisis: The German Struggle with Pandemic Control Measures and the State of Emergency', *VerfBlog* (19 April 2020), verfassungsblog.de/critique-and-crisis-the-german-struggle-with-pandemic-control-measures-and-the-state-of-emergency/.

[87] Lachmayer (n 5).

[88] See, for the Austrian response to the pandemic, Stöger (n 4) 18.

cases related to COVID-19 legislation were brought before it.[89] Meanwhile, the Hungarian Constitutional Court refused to deal with many petitions regarding pandemic measures on procedural grounds, as they were no longer in force by the time the Court decided on the case, therefore not deciding on their constitutionality in substance.[90]

While the speed of the decision-making depends on the constitutional framework of the particular country, the temporal proximity or distance of the review procedure to the measures in question comes with varying advantages and disadvantages. Faster decision-making by the courts reduces the deliberative function of court decisions as well as their rationalising function; moreover, it carries the risk of a higher politicisation of the court.[91] Slower decision-making by the courts, however, might come too late to prohibit violations of rights or irreversible damage to people's health. The courts, however, usually decide after the event; thus, the pandemic did not change the overall concept and function of courts in that regard.[92]

C. The Judicial Perspective

The function of courts is not to take over decision-making, but to assess whether the measures taken conform with the existing legal framework. Although the courts are deciding ex post, the benchmark for the evaluation is an ex-ante perspective. This is especially important in a pandemic as decisions have to be made on the basis of uncertainty and predictions. The assessment by the courts also contributes to the transparency of governmental processes as the government agencies have to justify their decisions.

Most of the decision-making processes within a pandemic are a balancing act. The leeway afforded for balancing must be greater when the need to restrict freedoms is higher. The infringement of freedoms is justified in light of the immediate danger to the life and health of people. Nevertheless, it is possible to review the balancing and criticise disproportionate measures. Most of the measures were upheld by courts. Thus, courts usually did not interfere with the measures taken by governments.

However, as the pandemic is not a singular event, but an ongoing process of circular but also changing challenges, the role of the courts is crucial. As the

[89] See, for the Italian response to the pandemic, C Fasone, 'Coping with Disloyal Cooperation in the Midst of a Pandemic: The Italian Response', *VerfBlog* (8 March 2021), verfassungsblog.de/coping-with-disloyal-cooperation-in-the-midst-of-a-pandemic-the-italian-response/.

[90] K Kovács, 'The COVID-19 Pandemic – A Pretext for Expanding Power in Hungary' in J Grogan and A Donald (eds), *Routledge Handbook of Law and the COVID-19 Pandemic* (Abington, Routledge, 2022) 259 (264); Gárdos-Orosz and Szente (n 2) 155, 165.

[91] See Lachmayer (n 84).

[92] ibid.

pandemic progresses, the courts can clarify constitutional and legal limits at the outset. In a later stage of the pandemic, they are then able to fine-tune the arguments. The role of the courts thus becomes crucial in guaranteeing the legality and proportionality of the overall pandemic responses.

While European countries were focusing on balancing freedom rights with health-related restrictions, Latin American countries also had to consider social rights as a relevant dimension. The proportionality test applied when interfering with liberties created a greater leeway for governments to act as the pandemic justified more restrictive measures. The courts, however, accepted these necessities.

D. Upholding Checks and Balancing

While courts have the potential to stop executive overreach, their possibilities to limit the effects of executive underreach are much more limited.[93] As courts cannot enact laws or take measures on their own, they can only point out occurring problems, but not resolve them. In the case of a federalist country, the states might compensate the executive underreach of the federation. In that regard, courts can support a measure taken and protect it against federal attacks like in Brazil.[94] When it comes to legislative overreach as in Chile, the courts were countering these developments at the beginning, but in the longer run fell into line with parliament.[95]

E. Judicial Overreach and Underreach

During a pandemic the involvement and role of the courts might be different from during regular times due to judicial over- or underreach. The courts are able to maintain or even improve the rule of law during the pandemic. However, there is also risk of politicising the court if there is judicial overreach during the pandemic, yet this was typically not the case. Judicial underreach, however, could be observed more often. In Latin America, Brazil, for example, was deciding very fast but denied the existence a violation of the Federal Constitution.[96] Captured courts like the Hungarian Constitutional Court did not react to constitutional complaints brought before them but on the contrary supported the executive overreach with judicial underreach.

[93] See S Verdugo, ch 2 in this volume.
[94] M Figueiredo, ch 4 in this volume.
[95] See S Verdugo, ch 2 in this volume; in contrast to the Chilean situation, the Constitutional Tribunal in Peru declared the withdrawal of public pensionary funds as unconstitutional; see T Valdivia, ch 7 in this volume.
[96] M Figueiredo, ch 4 in this volume.

VI. Conclusions

The COVID-19 pandemic has shown that the concept of separation of powers can be upheld in a public health crisis. Accountability of the government, however, should be strengthened as governments are primarily tasked with responding to health challenges. Governments have to take responsibility for an active response towards a pandemic, as a pandemic does not necessarily lead to the weakening of either democracy standards or the rule of law. In a lot of countries, however, the opposite occurred. The pandemic has proven to be an endurance test for the quality of democracy and the rule of law in each country. Countries already featured their own particular challenges to democracy. Thus, the pandemic put extra pressure on structures which were – at least partly – already fragile and it revealed existing deficits. This created the necessity for extra effort to maintain accountability and guarantee responsibility, though this often did not happen.

From a separation of powers perspective, maintaining the collaboration of the three branches seems crucial. Over- and underreach is an issue for all branches of government in times of a health emergency. It is necessary for the states to prepare collaboration under pressure. Maintaining separation of powers requires different modes of collaboration, for example, guaranteeing effective measures and strengthening control. The circularity as a specific feature of a pandemic has to be taken into account as both health and social challenges appear in waves.

In a post-pandemic phase, it is not possible to simply declare a pandemic as over and carry on as before. While the public seems to be quick to dismiss the pandemic and its consequences – almost as it never happened – pandemics have long-lasting impacts on societies. These need to be addressed in order to stabilise democracy after the core period of the pandemic is over. This includes, for example, evaluating which statutory law shall remain in force and which has already expired, for example, through sunset clauses. The post-pandemic situation also provides a chance to update concepts of organisational and social resilience against future health emergencies.

Moreover, it is time to assess the state of democracy (before, during and after the pandemic). The pandemic revealed pre-existing social challenges to constitutional democracy in the very particular setting of each country. This includes social inequalities,[97] corruption,[98] populism[99] or authoritarianism.[100] The necessity to respond to these challenges to democracies became even more evident when the pandemic put even greater pressure on democracies around the world.

Finally, climate change, the huge pressure on biodiversity and the further spread of mankind into the last untouched parts of nature will increase the potential for

[97] D Landau, ch 13 in this volume.
[98] See DM Ferreira Rubio, ch 9 in this volume.
[99] See Müller (n 17) 315–27.
[100] Halmai (n 17) 299 (306).

future pandemics and other forms of health emergencies. While the pandemic certainly claimed a high death toll and the effects of long COVID on societies cannot yet be accurately determined, the need to prepare for future emergencies with even greater effects on societies is urgent. From a constitutional perspective, it is necessary to rethink the application of the state of emergency paradigm and to create procedures and statutory frameworks that allow flexible responses and can be adapted quickly while upholding the constitutional standards of democracy and the rule of law.

INDEX

www.ingramcontent.com/pod-product-compliance
Ingram Content Group UK Ltd.
Pitfield, Milton Keynes, MK11 3LW, UK
UKHW022012240925
463269UK00001B/15